Elena Ferrante as World Literature

Literatures as World Literature

Can the literature of a specific country, author, or genre be used to approach the elusive concept of "world literature"? Literatures as World Literature takes a novel approach to world literature by analyzing specific constellations—according to language, nation, form, or theme—of literary texts and authors in their own world-literary dimensions. World literature is obviously so vast that any view of it cannot help but be partial; the question then becomes how to reduce the complex task of understanding and describing world literature. Most treatments of world literature so far either have been theoretical and thus abstract, or else have made broad use of exemplary texts from a variety of languages and epochs. The majority of critical work, the filling in of what has been traced, lies ahead of us. Literatures as World Literature fills in the devilish details by allowing scholars to move outward from their own areas of specialization, fostering scholarly writing that approaches more closely the polyphonic, multiperspectival nature of world literature.

Series Editor:
Thomas O. Beebee

Editorial Board:
Eduardo Coutinho, Federal University of Rio de Janeiro, Brazil
Hsinya Huang, National Sun-yat Sen University, Taiwan
Meg Samuelson, University of Cape Town, South Africa
Ken Seigneurie, Simon Fraser University, Canada
Mads Rosendahl Thomsen, Aarhus University, Denmark

Volumes in the Series
German Literature as World Literature, edited by Thomas O. Beebee
Roberto Bolaño as World Literature, edited by Nicholas Birns and Juan E. De Castro
Crime Fiction as World Literature, edited by David Damrosch, Theo D'haen, and Louise Nilsson
Danish Literature as World Literature, edited by Dan Ringgaard and Mads Rosendahl Thomsen
From Paris to Tlön: Surrealism as World Literature, by Delia Ungureanu
American Literature as World Literature, edited by Jeffrey R. Di Leo
Romanian Literature as World Literature, edited by Mircea Martin, Christian Moraru, and Andrei Terian
Brazilian Literature as World Literature, edited by Eduardo F. Coutinho
Dutch and Flemish Literature as World Literature, edited by Theo D'haen
Afropolitan Literature as World Literature, edited by James Hodapp
Francophone Literature as World Literature, edited by Christian Moraru, Nicole Simek, and Bertrand Westphal
Bulgarian Literature as World Literature, edited by Mihaela P. Harper and Dimitar Kambourov
Philosophy as World Literature, edited by Jeffrey R. Di Leo
Turkish Literature as World Literature, edited by Burcu Alkan and Çimen Günay-Erkol
Elena Ferrante as World Literature, by Stiliana Milkova Rousseva

Elena Ferrante as World Literature

Stiliana Milkova Rousseva

BLOOMSBURY ACADEMIC
NEW YORK • LONDON • OXFORD • NEW DELHI • SYDNEY

BLOOMSBURY ACADEMIC
Bloomsbury Publishing Inc
1385 Broadway, New York, NY 10018, USA
50 Bedford Square, London, WC1B 3DP, UK
29 Earlsfort Terrace, Dublin 2, Ireland

BLOOMSBURY, BLOOMSBURY ACADEMIC and the Diana logo are trademarks of
Bloomsbury Publishing Plc

First published in the United States of America 2021
This paperback edition published 2022

© Stiliana Milkova Rousseva, 2021

Cover design by Simon Levy / Levy Associates

For legal purposes the Acknowledgments on p. ix constitute an
extension of this copyright page.

All rights reserved. No part of this publication may be reproduced or
transmitted in any form or by any means, electronic or mechanical, including
photocopying, recording, or any information storage or retrieval system,
without prior permission in writing from the publishers.

Bloomsbury Publishing Inc does not have any control over, or responsibility for, any
third-party websites referred to or in this book. All internet addresses given in this
book were correct at the time of going to press. The author and publisher regret
any inconvenience caused if addresses have changed or sites have ceased
to exist, but can accept no responsibility for any such changes.

Library of Congress Cataloging-in-Publication Data
Names: Milkova, Stiliana, author.
Title: Elena Ferrante as world literature / by Stiliana Milkova.
Description: New York: Bloomsbury Academic, 2021. | Series: Literatures as world literature |
Includes bibliographical references and index. | Summary: "Examines the global impact and
relevance of Elena Ferrante's narratives of feminine identity"– Provided by publisher.
Identifiers: LCCN 2020036726 (print) | LCCN 2020036727 (ebook) |
ISBN 9781501357527 (hardback) | ISBN 9781501357534 (epub) | ISBN 9781501357541 (pdf)
Subjects: LCSH: Ferrante, Elena–Criticism and interpretation. | Women in literature. |
Femininity in literature. | Identity (Philosophical concept) in literature.
Classification: LCC PQ4866.E6345 Z77 2021 (print) | LCC PQ4866.E6345 (ebook) |
DDC 853/.914–dc23
LC record available at https://lccn.loc.gov/2020036726
LC ebook record available at https://lccn.loc.gov/2020036727

ISBN: HB: 978-1-5013-5752-7
PB: 978-1-5013-7191-2
ePDF: 978-1-5013-5754-1
eBook: 978-1-5013-5753-4

Series: Literatures as World Literature

Typeset by Deanta Global Publishing Services, Chennai, India

To find out more about our authors and books visit www.bloomsbury.com
and sign up for our newsletters.

In Memory of Jed Deppman

Contents

Acknowledgments		ix
Chronology of Elena Ferrante's Works and Abbreviations Used		x
1	Introduction: Elena Ferrante, World Literature, and the Work of Literary Translation	1
	World Literature and the Creation of Elena Ferrante	1
	Ferrante's Feminine Imaginary	10
	Ferrante's Female Genealogies	13
	The Translator as Seamstress: Figures of Translation from the Periphery to the Center	16
	Elena Ferrante as World Literature: An Overview	21
2	*Frantumaglia* and *Smarginatura*: The Borders of a Universal Feminine Imaginary	27
	Incisions and Inscriptions of the Body	30
	The Parameters of *Frantumaglia*	34
	Smarginatura in the Neapolitan Novels	38
	The "Mothers" of *Smarginatura*	43
	Women Who Write	54
3	Binding and Unbinding the Maternal Body and Voice	61
	Desire and Disgust for the Mother	63
	Conflations and Inversions: Mothers, Daughters, Dolls	74
	Enclosing the Maternal Body: Cellars, Locked Apartments, Clothes	86
	Laughing Bodies and Grotesque Gestures	95
	Dead Mothers and Corporeal Flows	101
4	Outside the Frame: The Aesthetics of Female Creativity and Authorship	105
	Inside the Frame: The (Nude) Female Body-as-Parts	109
	Inside the Frame: Mirrors, Collages, Still Lifes	114
	Outside the Frame: Creating a Female Artistic Legacy	119
	The Neapolitan Novels and Female Friendship, Writing, Authorship	125

5	Mapping Urban Feminine Topographies	131
	Walking the Streets of Topographic Memory in *Troubling Love*	135
	Symbolic and Literal Labyrinth in the Neapolitan Novels	144
	From Naples to Turin: Urban Itineraries of Abandonment	153

Epilogue: Reverse Maps, Familial Objects, and Open Frames in
   The Lying Life of Adults   165

Notes   173
Works Cited   187
Index   201

Acknowledgments

I wouldn't be writing this sentence had not Jed Deppman rushed into my office one day and exclaimed, "You should write a book on Elena Ferrante!" Jed, my mentor and the director of our two-person Comparative Literature program at Oberlin College, inspired me to embark on this adventure. This book is dedicated to his memory.

Along the way I have been accompanied by many great friends, colleagues, and scholars. Tiziana de Rogatis, Serena Todesco, and Katrin Wehling-Giorgi, whose work and friendship mean the world to me. John Hobbs, who patiently read my drafts and pushed me to improve my writing. The generous community of Ferrante scholars and enthusiasts: Barbara Alfano, Laura Benedetti, Daniela Brogi, Richard Carvalho, Leslie Elwell, Rebecca Falkoff, Enrica Ferrara, Elisa Gambaro, Adalgisa Giorgio, Claudia Karagoz, Janaya Lasker-Ferretti, Stefania Lucamante, Maria Muscariello, Kate Noson, Isabella Pinto, Olivia Santovetti, Paolo Scartoni, Gianni Turchetta. And the outstanding interlocutors who gave me food for thought: Karoline Amaury and Dominique Haenecour, Chiara Belluzzi, Adam Brin, Roberto Carretta, Kristin Cully, Ann Goldstein, Carlo Grande, Alex Hurd and Sandhya Iyer, Michele Monserrati, Silvio Perrella, Beatrice Priest, Andrea Raos, Kathryn Schild, Jonathan Stone, Sarah Vassos, Antonia Virone, Maurizio Vito, and Dario Voltolini. My remarkable colleagues and friends at Oberlin: Taylor Allen, Corey Barnes and Doris Jankovits, David Breitman and Kathryn Stuart, Cindy Chapman, Hsiu-Chuang Deppman, Ana Maria Diaz Burgos and Sergio Gutiérrez Negrón, Wendy Hyman, Libby Murphy, Kirk Ormand, Matt Senior, Claire Solomon, and Ellen Wurtzel. My brilliant student research assistants: Leah Barber and Sophia Zandi. And all my students and everyone in the Spring 2019 Elena Ferrante course.

I am grateful to Oberlin College for supporting my research through a Grant-in-Aid and a Powers Travel Grant. I also thank Durham University, Università degli Studi di Napoli Federico II, Rutgers University, New York University, Università per Stranieri di Siena, and Oberlin College for welcoming and accommodating many productive discussions of Elena Ferrante. Short modified sections from an early draft of Chapter 4 were published as essays in *California Italian Studies* 6:1 (2016) and *The Works of Elena Ferrante*, edited by Grace Russo Bullaro and Stephanie Love (2016). A section of an early draft of Chapter 5 was published in Italian in *Contemporanea* 15 (2017). I thank the editors of these publications as well. Many of my ideas were presented at international conferences, seminars, and symposia. I am especially grateful to all the participants in what was possibly the first scholarly event dedicated entirely to Elena Ferrante—the two panels I organized at the American Association of Italian Studies conference in March 2015. Many thanks to the "Literatures as World Literature" Editor Thomas Beebee who believed in this book.

My deepest gratitude is to my family for giving me the time and space to write. My intellectual debt is to Valentina, Malvina, and Liliana—three generations of creative, independent, and resilient thinkers who have forged my identity.

Chronology of Elena Ferrante's Works and Abbreviations Used

In Italian

Am	L'amore molesto (1992)
Iga	I giorni dell'abbandono (2002)
La fr	La frantumaglia (2003, 2007, 2015)
Lfo	La figlia oscura (2006)
Lsn	La spiaggia di notte (2007)
Ag	L'amica geniale (2011)
Snc	Storia del nuovo cognome (2012)
Sfr	Storia di chi fugge e di chi resta (2013)
Sbp	Storia della bambina perduta (2014)
Lio	L'invenzione occasionale (2019)
Lvb	La vita bugiarda degli adulti (2019)

In English

DA	The Days of Abandonment (2005)
TL	Troubling Love (2006)
LD	The Lost Daughter (2007)
MBF	My Brilliant Friend (2012)
SNN	The Story of a New Name (2013)
TLTS	Those Who Leave and Those Who Stay (2014)
SLC	The Story of the Lost Child (2015)
BN	The Beach at Night (2016)
Fr	Frantumaglia: A Writer's Journey (2016)

Column for *The Guardian* (January 2018–January 2019)

II	Incidental Inventions (2019)
LLA	The Lying Life of Adults (2020)

1

Introduction

Elena Ferrante, World Literature, and the Work of Literary Translation

When several years ago I began teaching *My Brilliant Friend*, the first of Elena Ferrante's four best-selling Neapolitan Novels (2011-14), it would often come out that both my students and their mothers were reading the tetralogy. When in March 2019 I gave a talk on *My Brilliant Friend* in New York, half a dozen of my current and former female students arrived accompanied by their mothers (it was our spring break so they were back home for the week). My mother, spurred by my scholarly interest in Ferrante, read everything Ferrante has written—from the first three novels to the Neapolitan Novels and her volume of essays *Frantumaglia*. Not only did my mother read them in both English and Bulgarian, but she also underlined and annotated the books before she handed them back to me. A productive dialogue ensued, pushing me to think creatively and challenging some of my own interpretations. This exchange of books between mothers and daughters based not on kinship but on shared intellectual interest, this collective reading of a female author who delves into the mother-daughter relationship, illustrates the central concerns of Ferrante's poetics and the cultural phenomena the Neapolitan Novels have engendered. *Elena Ferrante as World Literature* illuminates the workings of Ferrante's literary imagination and her construction of an embodied female subjectivity, a maternal body and voice grounded in psychical, corporeal, and spatial realities. And it is the product of the creative and intellectual exchange with my own mother.

World Literature and the Creation of Elena Ferrante

In an editorial for *The Guardian*, the pseudonymous writer Elena Ferrante reflects on her national identity and what it means to her to be Italian. She claims that "national characteristics are simplifications that should be contested," especially when they lead to "imposing language through economic power" (*II*, 23-4). To counter the perils of such uniformity and impoverishment she envisions linguistic nationality "as a point of departure for dialogue, an effort to cross over the limit, to look beyond the border—

beyond all borders, especially those of gender" (*II*, 24). As this book will show, borders and boundaries are central to Ferrante's literary, conceptual, and feminine lexicon—from her maternal word *frantumaglia* which connotes a psychical fragmentation or collapse to the harrowing experience of *smarginatura*, a semantic neologism that Ann Goldstein translates as "dissolving margins" or "dissolving boundaries." But in her editorial Ferrante pays tribute to translators as the real border-crossing artists capable of dissolving boundaries and enabling the circulation of ideas:

> Thanks to them, Italianness travels through the world, enriching it, and the world, with its many languages, passes through Italianness and modifies it. Translators transport nations into other nations; they are the first to reckon with distant modes of feeling. Even their mistakes are evidence of a positive force. Translation is our salvation: it draws us out of the well in which, entirely by chance, we are born. (*II*, 24)

In this passage Ferrante articulates a theory of world literature—the circulation of literary texts, ideas, or forms in translation, beyond their culture of origin and outside their national linguistic boundaries, creating a mobile and composite map of the local and the global, the distant and the familiar. This definition, along with Ferrante's emphasis on translation, applies to the status of her own works as world literature.[1] This introductory chapter examines the gender politics underpinning the Ferrante phenomenon or what I call "the creation of Elena Ferrante" and then maps the principal coordinates of Ferrante's literary imaginary. It explores the critical role of literary translation in the circulation of her novels, focusing on Ferrante's metaphorics of translation. This introduction concludes by delineating the scope and interpretive trajectories of *Elena Ferrante as World Literature*.

Elena Ferrante's resounding success in the Anglophone world, the appeal of her literary imaginary to a wide range of readers, and the pronounced visibility of her works in both mainstream media and academic publications attest to her active role in today's cultural landscape. To be considered works of world literature, texts must circulate in translation and be actively present within a literary system outside their original culture (Damrosch 2003, 4).[2] Damrosch defines world literature not as a canon of texts or established classics, but as a mode of reading and engaging with other texts, ideas, or forms: "the great conversation of world literature takes place on two very different levels: among authors who know and react to one another's work, and in the mind of the reader, where works meet and interact in ways that have little to do with cultural and historical proximity" (2003, 298). With more than sixteen million copies sold worldwide, and with translation rights purchased by more than fifty countries, Elena Ferrante's novels have reached far beyond their Italian culture of origin and become a global sensation, actively present on the world literary scene. Ferrante's cycle of four novels known in Italy as *My Brilliant Friend* (*L'amica geniale*, 2011-14), and in English translation as the Neapolitan Novels (2012-15), garnered significant critical and popular attention. The literary success of the Neapolitan Novels inspired other cultural phenomena and texts. The phrase "Ferrante Fever" was coined to capture American readers' insatiable thirst for each new installment in the tetralogy. The documentary film *Ferrante Fever* (directed by Giacomo Durzi, 2017) explored the literary-cultural significance of Elena Ferrante's popularity especially in the Anglophone world. The Neapolitan Novels were adapted into a five-hour play that premiered at the Rose Theater in London in 2017. They were recreated for television as an immensely popular and critically acclaimed TV series whose first (2018–19) and second (2020) seasons aired on Italian national television and on HBO.[3]

Ferrante's new novel *The Lying Life of Adults* (*La vita bugiarda degli adulti*, 2019) triggered another bout of Ferrante Fever in Italy with readers lining up for hours to await the book's release at midnight on November 7, 2019. In America, the publication of its translation was hailed as one of the most anticipated book events in 2020, while the Neapolitan Novels were ranked among the best books of the past decade and one of its cultural milestones. Elena Ferrante herself has become a prominent cultural figure consecrated by *Foreign Policy* as a leading global thinker and by *Time* magazine as one of the most influential people in the world. The Neapolitan Novels were included in a canon of masterpieces of world literature so that Elena Ferrante joined the circle of famous male writers such as Fitzgerald, Faulkner, Tolstoy, and Flaubert as a new powerful *female* voice chronicling the exigencies and transformations of our contemporary world. In 2018–19 she wrote a weekly editorial for *The Guardian* and she regularly contributes essays to major American newspapers and magazines.

There are many reasons for the global success of the Neapolitan Novels at this particular cultural-historical moment. The tetralogy belongs to the emerging genre of the global novel heralded as a new form of narrating the political, sociocultural, and environmental crises plaguing our contemporary world (Kirsch 2017; de Rogatis 2018, 2019a).[4] As Ganguly (2016) proposes, world literature "opens up the category *world* to emergent literary sensibilities not overdetermined by spatial and regional configurations of capital accumulation but informed rather by a constellation of aesthetic, affective, and ethical forces generated by the conflicts of a post-1989 world" (2016, 24, italics in the original). Triggered by the inequalities of its Italian culture and literary landscape, Ferrante's literary works respond also to our era of global violence and gender inequality. This conjunction of national and transnational, local and translocal facilitates its circulation in translation far beyond its culture of origins.

The Neapolitan Novels recount the story of two girls growing up in a sub-proletarian neighborhood, the *rione*, which bears the markers of any poverty-stricken, crime-ridden peripheral urban community of illiterate or semiliterate population. Life in the neighborhood likewise revolves around recognizable local structures of capital—the school, the bar, the grocery shop, and the church. Ferrante's novels inscribe the rites and structures of what Appadurai terms "locality" (1996), situating their protagonists within socially and spatially defined communities. Ferrante's locality is Naples with its own stratified social and spatial geography. At the same time, Naples exceeds its boundaries and transforms into a microcosm of the world, with its crises and triumphs. Ferrante envisions Naples as a synchronous vertical landscape encompassing ancient and contemporary worlds, from the Mediterranean to Europe and the United States (*Fr*, 252).

In terms of plot, the tetralogy strikes a balance between local and translocal, story and history. It narrates context-specific yet universally relatable stories about class, education, and social mobility; about family dramas and domestic abuse; about practices of labor; and about different forms of violence against women—from symbolic subjugation to rape. Spanning the period from 1950 to 2010, it presents the history of postwar Italy and Europe through the stories of the many characters' ordinary lives, through the intimate cycles of birth and death, marriage and childbirth viewed through the lens of its female narrator.[5] These stories combine gritty realism, profound psychological perspicacity, and a rich repertoire of literary devices borrowed from popular genres. This unique combination is what makes her novels both aesthetically sophisticated and readable page-turners (Turchetta 2016).

The English translations of the Neapolitan Novels and their glocal appeal contribute to their popularity as well.[6] While Ferrante's writing is gripping and imaginative, grounded in a Neapolitan reality, it avoids using the Neapolitan dialect that its characters speak and employs instead a neutral, standard Italian with subtle echoes of dialect and regional speech—it is writing that, to quote David Damrosch, "gains in translation" (2003, 281). Her novels resort to metalinguistic glosses that allow readers to imagine the dialect while not reproducing it, leaving an empty verbal space for readers to inhabit (Librandi 2019). Ferrante utilizes both standard Italian and Neapolitan dialect as an indexical tool—that is, to align spaces, ideas, emotions, and experiences with a character's choice of language (Cavanaugh 2016). The consistent and repeated metalinguistic attention to the language a character speaks or in which an interaction occurs allows readers to gain an understanding of the sociocultural-spatial meaning of those choices (Cavanaugh 2016). Ferrante teaches her readers how to understand the nuances and implications of a character's speech so that this linguistic-pedagogic aspect of the Neapolitan Novels can be seen as working in favor of their translatability (Cavanaugh 2016).

Even if Ferrante's tetralogy gains in translation, it does not fit the model of "translatability" that Emily Apter (2013) critiques or what Tim Parks (2010) defines as "the dull global novel."[7] Apter argues against the translatability of world literature as a potentially dangerous means of endorsing cultural equivalence or commercializing ethnically branded differences. Parks laments the erasure of literary style from the contemporary novel to comply with the international market, while Rebecca Walkowitz contends that some contemporary novels are "born translated"—that is, they are written for translation (2017, 3–4). Ferrante's novels may offer an empty verbal space for readers to insert their own lived experience, but they do not efface their linguistic, literary, or cultural singularity for the sake of an international readership. Ferrante, for example, coins two words intimately entwined with the poetics of her novels—*frantumaglia* and *smarginatura*—that are practically untranslatable. Translating those concepts which contain an entire feminine *psychical-corporeal-spatial* landscape requires inventiveness and respect for the text's "underlying network of signification" (Berman 2012).

The circulation of Ferrante's novels in Anglophone cultures situates them within world literature. Her status as a translated author who has chosen a female pseudonym and whose writing addresses both feminine and feminist issues merits consideration within this framework as well. Elena Ferrante's literary capital, the recognition of her literary value and authorial position by the world literary market, stems from her uncompromising representation of the mechanisms of gender inequality, oppression, and violence in our contemporary reality. Ferrante's adamant stance as a woman novelist writing from the semi-periphery (Moretti 1998) of the politicized "world literary space" (Casanova 2004) interrogates the very structures of power that define the ontological and expressive forms of female identity and authorship.[8]

"Elena Ferrante" is the pen name, gendered female, of an Italian writer whose biographical identity remains unknown. She is the author of three short novels—*Troubling Love* (*L'amore molesto*, 1992), *The Days of Abandonment* (*I giorni dell'abbandono*, 2002), and *The Lost Daughter* (*La figlia oscura*, 2006); of the four books comprising the Neapolitan Novels (2011–2014); of a children's book, *The Beach at Night* (*La spiaggia di notte*, 2007); and of two volumes of collected nonfictional writings—*Frantumaglia* (*La frantumaglia*, 2003, 2007, 2015) and *Incidental Inventions* (*L'invenzione occasionale*, 2019). All of these works have been translated in English by Ann Goldstein whose name has become synonymous with Ferrante's. In 1991, shortly before the publication of her first novel, Ferrante wrote a letter to her publishers Sandra Ozzola and Sandro Ferri announcing her decision to divorce herself from the afterlife of her novel: "I do not intend to do anything for *Troubling Love*, anything that might involve the public engagement of me personally. I've already done enough for this long story: I wrote it. If the book is worth anything, that should be sufficient" (*Fr*, 14). And then she expounded on her theory of the author's irrelevance: "I believe that books, once they are written, have no need of their authors. If they have something to say, they will sooner or later find readers; if not, they won't" (*Fr*, 15). Ever since, Ferrante has kept her resolution and conceded interviews only remotely, staying entirely away from the prying eyes of the media.[9] The disappearance of the biographical author as the necessary condition for the appearance of the text liberates literary critics and readers from "the shackles of authorial intent" (Falkoff 2015) and opens a space for close readings and interpretation. This removal of authorial biography de-contextualizes the writer, freeing her from the limitations of the local, the ethnic, and the national, and re-situating her within a broad literary realm where the foundational principles of literary narrative—plot and character, ideas and images, setting and structure—hold universal currency.

A work of world literature, Damrosch stipulates, is both locally inflected and translocally mobile (2003). It carries and displays its ethnic identity or cultural difference while also embodying universal themes and values. Ferrante's erasure of her biographical identity was—and still is—an act of resistance to the exclusivity of the Italian literary establishment, to the status- and image-obsessed Italian media, and to a culture where the value of a literary text is judged not by its quality but by the author's existing reputation or "aura" (*Fr*, 270–1). To promote and sell literature, Ferrante proclaims, the Italian media "*invent* the author, engaging a mechanism by which the writer sells not only his work but himself, his image" (*Fr*, 271, italics in the original). To resist the vicious cycle of selling her image along with her texts, Ferrante does not merely remove herself from it, remaining distant and uninvolved. By insisting on her absence and taking on a pseudonym, she *invents* the author "Elena Ferrante" and constructs an entire biography to suit her literary imaginary. This act of self-invention exposes the mechanisms of commodification and consumerism underlying Italian culture. Ferrante invents the author "Elena Ferrante" on her own terms, constructing an image of her own choice and design—that is, a representation not contingent on the criteria defined by the media and the publishing industry.

Although the creation of "Elena Ferrante" originated as a local response to national dynamics, it has taken on a translocal resonance, particularly through the lens of her gender. Until Ferrante's Neapolitan Novels became bestsellers in English translation and began to attract significant popular and critical attention, the question of her identity was mostly considered a creative eccentricity. Nonetheless, what she had begun as a refusal to play the game of publicity became a long-term project of curating her pseudonymous image. In 2003, after Ferrante's second novel had come out the previous year, her publisher convinced her to compile a collection of her unpublished letters and interviews. This volume, titled *La frantumaglia* (translated in English as *Frantumaglia*) after a Neapolitan word Ferrante attributes to her mother, was the first installment of what I call "the creation of Elena Ferrante" and was the first step toward the construction of her authorial identity.

La frantumaglia is a hybrid text, mixing correspondence, interviews, and long narrative passages excised from her two published novels and reflective essays explicating key themes, influences, and references in her books. It functioned as an exegesis of sorts, as an exploration of her narrative mechanisms, literary imaginary, and creative process. In fact, *La frantumaglia* was the first scholarly monograph on Elena Ferrante, a detailed (self-)study of her poetics drawing on Western literary and philosophical texts while also constructing its own theoretical framework. The 2003 original edition was followed by two expanded versions, in 2007 and in 2015. The 2015 volume, almost 400 pages long, included interviews Ferrante had given after the global success of the Neapolitan Novels. This last edition was the first one to be published in English in 2016, owing to the success of the tetralogy in America.[10] The latest installment in the narrative of Elena Ferrante's life is a collection of short essays, *Incidental Inventions* (*L'invenzione occasionale*, 2019), that she wrote for *The Guardian* over the course of a year.

These volumes of nonfictional writing contribute to the piecemeal composition of the author's biography. Scattered throughout the individual essays are Elena Ferrante's biographical details or "fragmented snapshots" (Buonanno 2008)— childhood memories, family incidents, mundane and formative experiences alike. This accumulation of life material assembles a coherent and plausible, albeit partial portrait of the author while foregrounding the theme of shattered or fragmented female identity that recurs throughout Ferrante's novels. She consolidates the literary persona of the author "Elena Ferrante" by mapping her narrative poetics—images, tropes, settings, thematics—onto her biography and vice versa, inventing her biography as a map of her narrative poetics. Elena Ferrante can be said to perform what the Russian symbolists conceived of as "life creation," life as an object of artistic creation or as a creative act.[11]

When asked in an interview about the identity of "Elena Ferrante," she endorses the correlation between creating a literary world and the author created by that world:

> Elena Ferrante is the author of several novels. There is nothing mysterious about her, given how she manifests herself—perhaps even too much—in her own writing, the place where her creative life transpires in absolute fullness. What I mean is that the author is the sum of the expressive strategies that shape an invented world, a concrete world that is populated by people and events. (*Fr*, 355)

In other words, *La frantumaglia* marshals the author's expressive strategies and transforms them into the invented biography of the author who deploys those strategies. She corroborates this procedure by including sections excised from her novels as well as passages which read like—and could easily be—unpublished sections from *Troubling Love* and *The Days of Abandonment*. These passages, masked as biographical details, employ many of the novels' imagery and characters—the seamstress-mother, the storeroom, the mother's pierced finger, the sisters-rivals, the jealous father, the daughter lost in the labyrinth of Naples, abandoned or suffering women, to name a few.

Ferrante's artistic project is both an aesthetic-philosophical performance of female authorship and a practical rebellion against a global patriarchal system which dictates notions and representations of femininity, motherhood, authorship, and creativity. It is significant that Ferrante, whatever her real gender, adopts the pen name of a woman, electing a female identity despite all the obstacles this choice implies. Italian scholar Tiziana de Rogatis summarizes the meaning of such a choice in the Italian context:

> This is no easy choice in a country like Italy, where male-dominated journalism, publishing, and academia den[y] visibility—and I should add respect—to women writers, despite a long stream of extraordinary women of letters. Nonetheless, Ferrante has chosen to identify as a woman. In essence, this means that, for a long time, the author chose to count for less: she's had fewer opportunities for publication; she's been labelled as a writer of sentimental novels aimed at a female readership; and she's been ignored by cultural reviews. (de Rogatis 2016d)

Ferrante's choice of gender identity situates her at once in an Italian and a global context. Her worldwide success in the era of #MeToo brought her international visibility and criticism at home. She was attacked by the Italian press primarily by male literary critics who attributed her popularity in the Anglophone world to her novels' plain style, exotic settings, and banal plots.[12] The Neapolitan quartet both exemplifies and challenges the circumscribed place assigned to women's writing in the male-dominated Italian literary sphere. Italian critics, academics, and journalists reacted against her transgression of traditional literary hierarchies (de Rogatis 2018, 19–20). Her pseudonym was construed as a marketing and publicity mechanism.[13] Because she eschews stylistic and formal experimentation, privileging storytelling and plot over abstruse literary structures, her writing was deemed melodramatic, simplistic, second-rate, and even the result of what Antoine Berman terms "ennoblement and popularization" (2012) in translation.[14]

Despite this harsh scrutiny, Ferrante garnered acclaim from academics both at home and abroad. Ferrante scholarship exploded on the international scene around 2013, after the success of the first volume of the tetralogy, *My Brilliant Friend*, and its translation into English. Established Italian and American scholars, literary critics, and journalists celebrated Ferrante's unprecedented, visceral explorations of women's identities and of motherhood in particular.[15] The universal resonance of her thematic concerns, coupled with the local but easily recognizable and relatable settings, provides familiar frames or *topoi* which Ferrante employs only to implode them from within. Likewise, her female pseudonym licenses her representation of uniquely feminine experiences and bodily functions in a brutally honest way. Her avowed female identity and her narrative brand of individuality and universality amplify the global echoes of her ferocious representation of misogyny, patriarchal oppression, and gender violence.

In October 2016 she was controversially unmasked by the investigative journalist Claudio Gatti who examined the revenues of Ferrante's publisher Edizioni e/o and looked into its employees' earnings and real estate records (2016a, 2016b). His investigation pointed a finger at Anita Raja, a literary translator from German who had worked at Edizioni e/o and whose income had suddenly increased after the global success of the Neapolitan Novels. Gatti published his article online simultaneously in four languages and in four international venues—the Italian *Il Sole 24 Ore*, the American *New York Review of Books*, the German *Frankfurter Allgemeine Zeitung*, and the French website *Mediapart*. The sheer international scope of this unmasking already speaks to Ferrante's status as a name in world literature. In addition to citing financial and real estate records that pry into Anita Raja's private property (and describe it in detail, in the Italian and English versions at least), Gatti makes an interpretive leap: he reads Ferrante's novels for factual clues, and then looks for their corroboration in Anita Raja's and her husband's lives. Gatti's second methodological leap is that he cites *La frantumaglia* as if it provided factual evidence of Elena Ferrante's biographical life. Comparing the narratives presented in *La frantumaglia* with Anita Raja's curriculum vitae he concludes that the two do not coincide and hence Anita Raja is guilty not only of posing as Elena Ferrante but also of inventing Ferrante's life story. In other words, Gatti misses altogether the metafictional complexity and programmatic resistance to the image-obsessed media culture that inform *La frantumaglia*.

Besides subjecting Ferrante to the kind of media attention that she condemns through her absence, Gatti's endeavor can be situated within the patriarchal culture Ferrante denounces. He insinuates that since Anita Raja is married to the well-known and prolific Neapolitan writer Domenico Starnone, the possibility of her collaboration with him remains likely (Gatti 2016a). Gatti implicitly attributes Ferrante's success not to Raja's individual talent but to her collaboration with a talented male writer thereby reinforcing a traditional gendering of creative genius as male. This insinuation made in the *New York Review of Books* illuminates the workings of gender inequality on a transnational scale, bridging the gap between local and translocal, culturally specific and globally relevant. The theme of female genius underlies Ferrante's narratives—her characters are seamstresses, writers, or artists animated by an innate talent that is often suppressed or exploited by men. The Neapolitan quartet questions the construct of male genius by positing at the center of the plot not one, but two, genius women—the "brilliant friends" from the first volume's title which in Italian is *L'amica geniale* or, literally, *The Genius Girlfriend*. In dramatizing the trials of feminine creativity, Elena Ferrante's novels portray the workings of misogyny, patriarchal oppression, and violence in their local manifestations—Naples, Elena and Lila's *rione*, Turin—but they also reference a much wider world. As Elena Greco realizes in the third volume of the tetralogy, "the neighborhood was connected to the city, the city to Italy, Italy to Europe, Europe to the whole planet. And this is how I see it today: it's not the neighborhood that's sick, it's not Naples, it's the entire earth, it's the universe" (*TLTS*, 28).

Ferrante's novels, like her pseudonym and her self-creation in *La frantumaglia*, dramatize a resistance to the visible and invisible mechanisms of female subalternity. Her female protagonists struggle through an androcentric, misogynist reality to cobble together their identities and achieve agency and autonomy. They are all "falling women" who must break apart and collapse in a male-dominated social order before they can recompose their identities (Alsop 2014). They lose their grip on reality, but they survive and transform their traumas into creative acts.[16] We see this cycle of disintegration and reconstruction in all of her novels as an exploration of the dark sides of female subjectivity and lived experience. Her narrative capacity to portray the fragmentation of the feminine psyche while reproducing her characters' various forms of psychic disequilibrium in the formal structures of her novels characterizes Ferrante's underground mimetic realism.[17]

Elena Ferrante is perhaps the most widely read and reviewed author in translation in the United States today. Her writing has engendered a boom in literary scholarship both in Italy and abroad. And her vast and diverse readership has prompted the English translation (or re-translation) and publication of other Italian women writers—Anna Maria Ortese, Elsa Morante, and Natalia Ginzburg so that an expansion of the Italian literary canon abroad is in progress (Caserta 2019). This growing visibility of female voices today has invigorated the literary scene in Italy as well, encouraging a new wave of women writers and disrupting the male-dominated literary establishment, producing what Anna Momigliano defines as the "Ferrante Effect" (2019). When viewed within the framework of world literature, the "Ferrante Effect" complicates Moretti's (2000) metaphor for the development of the modern novel as a tree or a wave. While growing out of a local context (tree), Ferrante's literary imaginary has spread (wave) throughout the world, but it has also returned to its original culture revitalizing and innovating it, importing its literary capital accumulated through translation. The ontology of the Elena Ferrante phenomenon recalls Damrosch's conception of world literature as mobile and contingent. It changes shape as it crosses borders, becoming "a fundamentally different work abroad" and eliciting new ways of reading at home (Damrosch 2003, 140).

This positive model, however, must be qualified and amended in the context of a mainstream and entrenched Italian literary criticism which is suspicious, if not fearful, of world literature and hence resistant to Ferrante's potential to innovate (Caserta

2019). Although many Italian (female) scholars have celebrated Ferrante's narrative originality and written insightful analyses of her works, she remains systematically either excluded from Italian-language studies of contemporary Italian literature or else dismissed by patronizing and deliberately denigrating appraisals by male critics (Schwartz 2020).[18] Ferrante's exclusion from her culture of origins attributes a new urgency to the study of her poetics while highlighting the currency of the theme of pervasive patriarchal power explored in her novels.

Ferrante's Feminine Imaginary

Reading Elena Ferrante as world literature requires an examination of her poetics—how and why her texts construct a reality so immersive that it captures readers around the globe. She violates cultural or literary taboos in a gut-wrenching, realistic manner so that reading her novels blurs the borders between literature and reality. Her novels explore both overwrought moments of ordinary life and overwhelming crises of identity. The painful realities of menstruation, pregnancy, and motherhood, and the brutal experiences of domestic abuse, rape, and abandonment haunt her female protagonists. "Are Elena Ferrante's four Neapolitan Novels even books?" asks Joanna Biggs, implying that they are the raw material of women's lives (2015). Ferrante's narratives capture the breadth and depth of life while also framing it through their local, Italian and Neapolitan, lens. She resorts to all the literary devices at her disposal to grab the reader (*Fr*, 269), mixing elements from various genres and literary traditions—myth and epic narrative, the *Bildungsroman*, the crime thriller, the melodrama, the romance novel, the historical novel, the metafictional postmodernist text, and even the modern epic (de Rogatis 2018). But when reworking each of these genres or texts, she filters it through a feminine perspective and locates a female subject at the center of the narration.

Read together Ferrante's novels compose a narrative intended to recuperate the female body and voice from their subordinate position within a male-dominated culture. As she has stated, her goal is to create a feminine "I" which reflects the complex and contradictory drives that form the feminine psyche (*Fr*, 285). At stake in her novels is the articulation of female subjectivity and identity grounded in the corporeal, psychical, and spatial ontology of women. Ferrante's writing constructs and sustains a new female embodied subjectivity emerging from the structures of patriarchal oppression and producing new expressive forms that bypass or eliminate altogether these structures. The modes of patriarchal oppression her novels dramatize—physical and symbolic violence; objectification and commodification of the female body; imprisonment within traditional constructs of femininity; linguistic and intellectual subordination; and topographic and spatial configurations of power—are both uniquely situated and easily relatable. They evoke a long-standing cultural tradition of marginalizing, vilifying, silencing, or subjugating women who challenge existing hierarchies. Political theorist Mihaela Mihai proposes the notion of "prosthetic knowledge" to read the Neapolitan Novels and account for their unique seductive power (2018). Ferrante,

Mihai argues, invites readers to become acute perceivers of epistemic injustice and prosthetically incorporate the perspective of the silenced or marginalized into their repertoire of knowledge and meanings (2018). This prosthetic experience can help explain the empathy—the self-identification and self-recognition—that informs the responses of Ferrante's female readers worldwide.

Ferrante's foundational layer in constructing a feminine imaginary is the reworking of classical mythology and the epic. Each of her novels enacts several myths presenting an eclectic, dialogic mosaic of myth and reality, modern sensibilities and ancient mores.[19] In *Troubling Love* (1992), her first published novel, Delia returns to Naples for the funeral of her mother, the seamstress Amalia, and embarks on a quest to reconstruct her mother's last days. In the process, she descends literally and figuratively into the underworld in order to reclaim her mother's story, following the clues that her mother has left her. This novel intertwines the mythological figures of Demeter and Persephone with the image of Ariadne's thread. The underworld of violence Delia recollects when she descends into an underground shop becomes the Minotaur's labyrinth. But Ferrante alters the myth—the thread that leads Delia-Ariadne out of the labyrinth is constituted by the traces of her seamstress-mother. This maternal thread helps Delia recover and narrate the memory of her molestation, so that her silence is undone in the novel's final image. Delia creates a double portrait of herself as her mother, acknowledging their shared history of violence and transforming, like Philomela or Arachne, trauma into art.

Ferrante's second novel, *The Days of Abandonment* (2002), dramatizes updated versions of Medea and Dido, exploring the psychic undoing of a "modern Medea in downtown Turin" (Lucamante 2008, 81). Olga, whose husband has left her and her two children for a younger woman, goes through stages of denial, rage, violence, and self-degradation while pondering suicide and revenge. Trapped within a doubly masculinist space Olga negotiates the patriarchal labyrinth of a hostile home and a hostile city, following the thread of her symbolic mothers Medea and Dido. But unlike the mythological characters, she replaces wrath and despair with writing as a means of healing, so that *The Days of Abandonment* constitutes Olga's narrative of survival and creative expression. Ferrante's subsequent novel, *The Lost Daughter* (2006), features another configuration of classical myths reinvented. The main character, Leda, is a university professor whose grown-up daughters have left the house. When she goes on vacation, Leda steals the doll of a little girl called Elena and thus evokes the myth of Leda, the mother of the beautiful Helen. Ferrante revives and updates a lesser known version of the myth in which Helen is not Leda's biological daughter but the daughter of another rape victim—Nemesis. The non-mother Leda raises her non-daughter and, as Ferrante puts it, finds herself "in the middle of a complicated, modern question of maternity" (*Fr*, 206). The plot of *The Lost Daughter* revolves around this question of surrogate or symbolic mothers and daughters, complicating traditional notions of maternity and proposing nonbiological configurations of the mother-daughter bond.

Ferrante's first three novels therefore narrate modern versions of classical myths as the cultural foundation for their own revised, female-centered structures. Her children's book *The Beach at Night* (2007) revisits plot elements of *The Lost Daughter* but narrates from the point of view of the doll, abandoned like Ariadne on the beach. The doll, Celina, goes courageously through trials by fire and water, but is undone when an ominous male figure steals her words by extracting them from her chest with a Hook. This rape-like scene metaphorically cuts off her tongue in an iteration of the Philomela myth. The only word Celina manages to protect is "mamma." Dolls return in the Neapolitan Novels as the framing device of the tetralogy. The narrator, Elena Greco—another mythological reference to Helen and Greek mythology—is a writer who lives in Turin and whose childhood friend Lila Cerullo has disappeared from their native Naples. Elena sets out to write about Lila's life and ends up recounting their collective biography. The first volume, *My Brilliant Friend*, narrates Elena and Lila's childhood and adolescence. The story of their friendship begins when they throw their dolls into the underworld of a dark cellar, and it unfolds as the girls negotiate the labyrinth at the end of which awaits the monstrous Minotaur Don Achille. In the tetralogy the labyrinth becomes an architectonic symbol of patriarchal urban space, but we can see it already at work in both *Troubling Love* and *The Days of Abandonment*.[20] And yet Ferrante reconfigures the gendered space of the labyrinth by positioning Lila and Elena—a double Ariadne—at its center and as its triumphant conquerors. This restructuring of the labyrinth as feminine is reproduced on the level of plot when Lila expounds to Elena an architectonic reading of Carthage in the *Aeneid* as a feminine city devoid of love and Elena writes an essay elaborating on her friend's ideas.

The myths Ferrante integrates in her novels are stories about violence, scenarios "already staged by patriarchy" (Muraro 1994). Ancient narratives of abandonment, rage, muteness, and rape underlie her modern plot lines and lurk behind her characters' composed exteriors. Ferrante's female protagonists confront the different forms of violence in their own lives by descending into the underworld of their repressed memories, excavating a stratum of raging, vengeful, or suicidal women as archetypes of feminine suffering. But Ferrante's characters are contemporary women even if they are haunted by female archetypes. They enter and exit the labyrinth of patriarchal oppression, inhabiting and appropriating it for their own psychical, physical, or expressive needs. Ferrante's poetics is then lined with a mythological realism, animating a host of characters, and envoicing the silenced women of Greek mythology. She admits she borrows from ancient and modern narratives—Homer, Apollodorus, Virgil, Robert Graves. In fact, in *La frantumaglia* Ferrante constructs "Elena Ferrante" as a scholar and translator of classical texts who has learned how to write by reading and translating them (*Fr*, 145, 252, 347). As she states, "I have to say that I've never seen the classical world as an ancient world. Instead I feel its closeness, and I think I've learned many things from the Greek and Latin classics about how to put words together" (*Fr*, 252).

The interweaving of modern and ancient worlds in Ferrante's narratives grounds them in a Mediterranean and universal matrix of feminine marginalization.[21] In co-opting classical myth and epic narratives for her plots Ferrante recuperates women from their liminal position within masculinist texts and translations and dramatizes their subjectivity in its complexity and ambiguity. The Neapolitan Novels rewrite Virgil's *Aeneid* as a female-centric epic doubly authored by Lila and Elena (McCarter

2016). The project of creating the author "Elena Ferrante" can be understood in relation to the myth of the lives of Homer and Virgil who have survived only in their writing (Geue 2016). When asked about her identity, Ferrante refers to Homer: "We continue to love the Homeric poems even though we know nothing about Homer" (*Fr*, 199). In insisting on her absence and her textual presence, she creates the myth of her own authorship—the life of the writer takes place in and as writing (Geue 2016).[22] Elena Ferrante's life in/as writing unleashes her creative imagination and licenses a truthful narrative—what she calls "literary truth"—of the subject matter closest to her heart: female identity and subjectivity.[23] She constructs a modern feminine mythology, a contemporary classical text authored by a woman. Her books acquire the status of the classical texts she evokes to explain her authorial absence, "those mysterious volumes, both ancient and modern, that have no definite author but have had and continue to have an intense life of their own" (*Fr*, 15).

Ferrante's Female Genealogies

Beyond mythology and the classics, Ferrante taps into the vast repository of Western thought, integrating a wide array of ideas while filtering them through the narrative demands of her plots and adapting them to serve her storytelling. Three prominent strands of intertextual influences are interwoven in her texts—Freudian psychoanalysis, feminist philosophy, and modern literature. In *La frantumaglia*, Ferrante identifies these intertexts supplying the interpretive lens through which her novels can be read. She engages extensively with Freudian psychoanalysis and states that she reads "passionately" Melanie Klein (*Fr*, 122-3). Freud's essay on female sexuality, for example, inspired the title of *Troubling Love* (*Fr*, 123). Permutations of the Oedipus complex, castration anxiety, and fetishism often underlie the fraught interactions between mothers and daughters in her novels without, however, reducing them to static narrative formulas. On the contrary, Ferrante translates or better, literalizes, the mechanisms of the unconscious into lively images and evocative encounters focalized by a female subject who at once sanctions and interrogates them.

Compiling a catalogue of her intellectual "mothers," Ferrante lists many French, Italian, and Anglophone feminist psychoanalysts and philosophers. She explains that their writing "helps me look critically at the world, at us, our bodies, our subjectivity. But it also fires my imagination, it pushes me to reflect on the use of literature" (*Fr*, 332). Her debt to feminist theories is threefold: they provide narratives of embodied female subjectivity, they spur her literary imagination, and they situate her within a tradition of women philosophers. She is wary, however, of the hegemony of any single theory or prescribed formula, advocating for a literary syncretism which better serves the narration—and reality—of feminine experience: "I fear the linearity of militant causes; in literature they have a terrible effect. I describe points of incoherence" (*Fr*, 309). To exemplify her reluctance to subscribe to a single approach, Ferrante names the women philosophers who have shaped her literary imagination: "I'll name some women to whom I owe a great deal: Firestone, Lonzi, Irigaray, Muraro, Cavarero,

Gagliasso, Haraway, Butler, Braidotti. In short, I am a passionate reader of feminist thought and I also combine distant positions" (*Fr*, 332).[24]

As she does with Freudian psychoanalysis, she animates a variety of feminist ideas into vivid plot events, dramatizing, without ever naming them, concepts such as female fetishism, abjection, *jouissance*, *affidamento* or symbolic entrustment, and the narratable self. Ferrante's novels provide the discursive space where these ideas can meet and intersect. She weaves a tapestry of theories, images, and scenarios reified in plot and character. Instead of rehashing the principles of psychoanalysis and feminist theory, she uses them as narrative building blocks, as points of departure and exploration of the female body and psyche, but especially of the mother's body and the mother-daughter relationship central to Irigaray's thought.[25] This project of "feminist storytelling" brings to life feminist theories and reconfigures them into a universally shared logic (de Rogatis 2019a). The result is a comprehensive, relatable, and addictive "practical *écriture féminine*" (Wood 2013).

Ferrante's *écriture féminine* includes her literary "mothers" as well. Although she admits that her formation as a writer is indebted to the male narrative tradition,[26] she acknowledges the influence of Virginia Woolf, Elsa Morante, Anna Maria Ortese, Alba de Cespedes, Clarice Lispector, and Alice Munro. Women writers, she contends, continue to emulate the male canon and are still considered inferior to male writers (*Fr*, 307). In the expanded edition of *La frantumaglia* she calls for the creation of a female literary genealogy which appropriates and surpasses the male tradition to establish its own female-centered theories and practices:

> I wouldn't recognize myself without women's struggles, women's nonfiction writing, women's literature: they made me adult. My experience as a novelist, both published and unpublished, culminated, after twenty years, in the attempt to relate, with writing that was appropriate, my sex and its difference. But for a long time I've thought that if we have to cultivate *our* narrative tradition, we should never renounce the entire stock of techniques that we have behind us. We have to demonstrate, precisely because we are women, that we can construct worlds as wide and powerful and rich as those designed by male writers, if not more. So we have to be well equipped, we have to dig deep into our difference, using advanced tools. (*Fr*, 266, italics in the original)

Ferrante's concept of a female genealogy can also be understood in terms of Luisa Muraro's (1994) reading of Irigaray: "I am not referring to the feminism of rights and equality, but to the movement that has led us to choose to stay among women, to choose to act in accordance with the judgment of our fellow women, to accept the authority of women, and to seek the nourishment of female thought for our minds" (1994, 331). The narrative fabric of her novels is interwoven with this kind of feminism, with implicit or explicit references to a female literary tradition which she theorizes and in which she participates.[27] Her novels put into conversation female philosophers, psychoanalysts, and writers, enabling the discursive creation of a genealogy of creative women, building a textual space for their judgment and authority, recognition and acknowledgment. Conversely, writers Elizabeth Strout, Rachel Cusk, and Jhumpa Lahiri, and feminist philosophers Adriana Cavarero and Luisa Muraro have responded to Ferrante's texts, thus continuing the conversation.[28]

One of the distinctive ways in which she builds a female genealogy is by crafting a new lexicon which links mothers to daughters. She introduces two neologisms, *frantumaglia* and *smarginatura*, and deploys them as a framework for representing and interpreting her female protagonists. Ferrante inherits the word *frantumaglia* from her mother's dialect but develops it into a theory of female subjectivity in general, and of the maternal subject in particular. *Frantumaglia* encompasses a host of symptoms and sensations, but it broadly signifies a feminine corporeal and psychical fragmentation, a psychic disequilibrium as a reaction to the mechanisms of patriarchal violence that connect mothers to daughters through their shared marginalization. *Smarginatura* is a concrete manifestation of *frantumaglia* as a terrifying experience of losing boundaries and corporeal dissolution. Ferrante's female subjects suffer from both *smarginatura* and *frantumaglia* and many of the key moments in her novels portray the ravaging effects of fragmentation and dissolving boundaries.

Ferrante's theory/practice of creating a female genealogy goes beyond its textual and discursive boundaries and infiltrates our contemporary reality. The formula "my brilliant friend," borrowed from the title of the first of the Neapolitan Novels, has become a sign of women's mutual recognition and acknowledgment. Nancy Miller's *My Brilliant Friends. Our Lives in Feminism* (2019) is a collective biography of her late feminist scholar friends Carolyn Heilbrun, Diane Middlebrook, and Naomi Schor. The book's approach also stems from Ferrante's exploration of female friendship, death, memory, and narrative. She envisions her project of narrating her friends' biographies as similar to Elena's textual resurrection of Lila through the writing of the Neapolitan Novels. Miller prefaces her book by affirming the connection between writing, discursive life, and creative exchange: "As long as I'm writing about my friends, I'm keeping them alive, and in keeping them alive, I'm staying alive with them. We are still in conversation, even if I'm doing most of the talking" (2019, 5). Muraro's definition of feminism as choosing to stay among women comes to mind.

Another feminist project has emerged from Ferrante's pages. Written by four female scholar friends, Sarah Chihaya, Merve Emre, Katherine Hill, and Jill Richards, *The Ferrante Letters. An Experiment in Collective Criticism* (2020) was incited by Elena's dream of creative collaboration with Lila in the Neapolitan Novels. It enacts the kinds of intellectual exchanges between women that Elena envisions for herself and Lila. The book and its first iteration as online epistolary criticism situate both their ontology and methodology within the framework of feminine creativity, authorship, and friendship that Ferrante outlines in the Neapolitan Novels. Its authors proclaim Ferrante's appeal to contemporary feminist collaborations and see themselves as the protagonists in a cultural moment of burgeoning feminist collectivity (2020, 1–13). Since none of its authors specializes in Italian literature, this project corroborates Elena Ferrante's relevance to a broader academic and nonacademic Anglophone audience, confirming the status of her works as world literature. Before I outline the scope and goals of *Elena Ferrante as World Literature*, I turn to one of Elena Ferrante's productive genealogies engendered through the metaphorics of translation and the status of her texts as literature in translation.

The Translator as Seamstress: Figures of Translation from the Periphery to the Center

Elena Ferrante's works have been circulating outside their culture of origin thanks to the creative and intellectual labor of translators worldwide. The success of the Neapolitan Novels in America can be attributed to some extent to their translator Ann Goldstein, a former director of copyediting at *The New Yorker* who, in addition to translating all of Ferrante's works, has translated an impressive number of other Italian writers as well. She has become Ferrante's spokesperson (Benedetti 2016) on the book market. Translated literature has less currency in America's cultural economy. Conditioned by demand, presses in America focus primarily on literature written in English. Only about 3 percent of books published in the United States are works in translation (Post 2011). In this cultural landscape the translator's presence, together with the arduous intellectual, linguistic, and creative work entailed in translation, is barely visible. The translator's labor is effaced twice: once metaphorically as it submits to the reigning demands for fluency and readability in the target language, and then again, literally, in the typographic deemphasis of the translator's name on the book cover or title page. As Lawrence Venuti (1992, 2008) argues, translation continues to be an invisible practice.

In the case of Elena Ferrante's Neapolitan Novels, her pronounced absence has shifted readers' attention from the author's identity to that of her translator so that Goldstein has become a substitute for the pseudonymous author. She has gained visibility as the voice—and face—of Elena Ferrante, and thus has underscored the significance of the translator's work as well (Milkova 2016b). Because Ferrante is not accessible, her absence has been filled by Goldstein as the replacement for the actual author. Numerous interviews have granted Goldstein authority over the exegesis of the Neapolitan Novels, attributed insight into the Ferrante mystery, and even asked if *she* was Elena Ferrante. A sought-after speaker, she has discussed publicly the Neapolitan Novels with literary scholars and famous writers alike. Or to put it more directly, Elena Ferrante's invisibility has enabled the translator's visibility. The translator's invisibility, the extent to which the translator must submit to requirements (on behalf of the market and the reader) for readability and accessibility, for fluency and transparency of style have been much discussed by scholars of translation studies in the past twenty-five years. Ferrante's novels have, if not reversed, then at least unsettled the paradigm of invisibility. In America Ferrante's absence has generated not only the translator's visibility but also the readers' close engagement with her texts, an evaluation of their merits as literary works and not as a product of their author's cultural capital—a phenomenon which did not occur in Italy (Benedetti 2016). This unprecedented attention to the translator of a literary text alongside the literary text itself has had a beneficial effect on other translated Italian literature in the United States (Benedetti 2016).

Ferrante constructs her authorial persona as a translator as well. She states several times in *La frantumaglia* that she translates from Greek and Latin and that translating helps her write (*Fr*, 177, 252, 347). The process of translation and the figure of the translator recur in her novels as well. Translation in the Neapolitan Novels takes the form of the cultural-linguistic mediation which her characters perform when moving between the Neapolitan dialect and standard Italian. Dialect in Ferrante's novels occupies a double space of visibility and invisibility—it is at once absent and present. All of Ferrante's novels are written in standard Italian using metalinguistic glosses (Librandi 2019; Cavanaugh 2016) to alert the reader to when a character speaks in dialect but without reproducing the dialectal form itself. These metalinguistic glosses signal the narrator's implicit process of translating, by writing, from dialect into standard speech and make the reader complicit in that process as well. The omission of dialect has made the literary translator's task easier and the texts themselves more accessible.[29] Nonetheless, Ferrante's narrative art immerses readers into the sounds and sights of the Neapolitan *rione* so that dialect becomes almost audible. As Vera Petrova, the Bulgarian translator of *My Brilliant Friend* and *The Story of a New Name*, comments, "The most exquisite aspect of the Neapolitan Novels is the absence of dialect—you are *already* submerged up to your ears in Naples and the *rione*" (2019). Because Ferrante emphasizes dialect as the language of strong feelings and verbal abuse by frequently glossing the emotive inflection of dialectal phrases (for example, "yelled in dialect, angrily," *MBF*, 283), dialect takes on a concrete narrative presence through the violent emotions it expresses.

Dialect has another important connotation in Ferrante's novels and especially in the tetralogy, as a marker of education and class and therefore as a constitutive element of identity. Elena Greco's and Lila Cerullo's semiliterate parents speak almost entirely in dialect, rarely resorting to a stilted Italian. Both Lila and Elena learn a standard, literary Italian. Although Lila's linguistic abilities are superior to Elena's, she oscillates between dialect and Italian, eventually expressing herself only in dialect. Elena, conversely, erases dialect from her speech as a means of erasing her sub-proletarian origins. She perceives language as a form of emancipation and a symbol of social mobility. In shifting between standard Italian and the implicit Neapolitan dialect, the tetralogy itself performs a translation. Elena, the narrator, struggles to communicate with Lila, and their interactions occur through translation: "It occurred to me that now it was a linguistic question. She resorted to Italian as if to a barrier. I tried to push her toward dialect, our language of candor. But while her Italian was translated from dialect, my dialect was increasingly translated from Italian, and we both spoke a false language" (*SLC*, 362). Elena's goal in writing the Neapolitan Novels is to narrate Lila's life, forcing her friend to send her a sign, thus nullifying her self-erasure. But Elena employs a standard literary idiom to narrate or better, to translate Lila's life, dialect, and "false" Italian. In other words, the narrator is a translator as well (Pinto 2020).[30] Elena displays her identity, along with her adoptive class and social status through the intralingual translation the result of which is the text of the Neapolitan Novels. This novelistic blurring of writer and translator, already suggested in *La frantumaglia* as part of Ferrante's constructed identity, is another reason why Ann Goldstein has occupied in our collective imagination the position of author-translator.

The blurring of boundaries is the thematic and structural core of Ferrante's works. In the early novels it takes shape as *frantumaglia*, and in the Neapolitan Novels as *smarginatura*. Chapter 2 discusses at length these two concepts and their deployment in Ferrante's texts, but it is important to note here that both words are unusual in Italian as well. While Ferrante and her character Leda attribute "frantumaglia" to the maternal Neapolitan dialect, "smarginatura" is based on a typographic term invested by Ferrante with a new and complex network of signification. Capturing the capacious meanings of these two words in Ferrante's literary imaginary poses a challenge for the English translator. In her 2007 translation of *The Lost Daughter*, Goldstein translates "frantumaglia" as "shattering" (*LD*, 106) to render Leda's definition of psychic fragmentation, opting for a word that conveys the violent breaking into pieces of the maternal subject but does not sound dialectal or odd as it does in Italian. In 2016, Goldstein changes her approach when she undertakes the translation of Ferrante's 400-page volume titled *La frantumaglia*. In this volume, beginning with the title, *Frantumaglia*, the translator preserves the original word, italicizing it throughout to signal its foreignness. But to mitigate some of the word's foreignness, Goldstein inserts the stealth gloss "a jumble of fragments" to explicate Ferrante's concept: "She said that inside her she had a *frantumaglia*, a jumble of fragments" (*Fr*, 99).[31] Viewed through Antoine Berman's analytic of translation (2012), the translator's intervention clarifies the word, but obscures the original's own mode of clarity. The insertion of "a jumble of fragments" expands Ferrante's compact sentence "Diceva che aveva dentro una frantumaglia" (*La fr*, 94), slackening its dense semantic and syntactic structure. Nonetheless, the fact that Goldstein does not domesticate the word and includes it as it is, as *frantumaglia*, attests to the cultural and literary capital Ferrante has accrued since the translation of *The Lost Daughter* in 2007 when the same word was rendered as "shattering."

Smarginatura is an obscure technical term from typography which denotes the cutting of the page's edges or margins. Ferrante invests this term with new semantics, recontextualizing it within the psyche as Lila's horrifying experience of "dissolving margins." During those panic attack-like moments, Lila sees the insides of bodies spilling out and solid surfaces melting. These episodes dramatize her painful awareness of women's fragility and marginalization in the archaic patriarchal world of the *rione*. *Smarginatura* thus functions as a symptom of *frantumaglia*, a feminine expression of internalized violence, of fragmentation and mutilation. In the first volume of the tetralogy, Goldstein translates *smarginatura* as "dissolving margins," and in the other three books as "dissolving boundaries." The translation of *smarginatura* oscillates as if it too were affected by the unfixed landscape it depicts. This lexical instability in English grants further rhetorical and semantic capaciousness to Lila's discourse of *smarginatura*. It expands the range and scope of that term so readers can grasp its foundational role in the creation and narration of Lila and Elena's story. But unlike *frantumaglia* which is imported into English untranslated, *smarginatura* never appears in the text of the Neapolitan Novels. In this case, Goldstein prefers to find a descriptive definition in English instead of inserting the word itself accompanied by a gloss. Instead, it infiltrates the extradiegetic world by becoming a mandatory interview question for

Ann Goldstein and a centerpiece in many reviews of the tetralogy. *Smarginatura* has inhabited English-language discourse implicitly, by inviting explication and unfurling of the Italian word for "dissolving margins."

In *Incidental Inventions* Ferrante envisions translators as agents of world literature, dissolving cultural and linguistic boundaries, and enabling the circulation of ideas and texts beyond national borders (*II*, 24). Her own language—*frantumaglia, smarginatura,* "dissolving margins," "my brilliant friend"—has crossed the borders of Anglophone cultures proposing new ways of conceptualizing feminine experience. In her narratives she articulates a metaphorics of translation that too crosses literary borders, migrating from her Italian semi-peripheral place in the "World Republic of Letters" (Casanova 2004) to the Anglophone center of literary capital and thereby reversing the traditional trajectory of literary influence (Damrosch 2014) from the center to the periphery. We see this migration of Ferrante's tropes in the work of one of her passionate readers, the American Pulitzer Prize-winning writer Jhumpa Lahiri. Lahiri's story "The Exchange" ("Lo scambio," 2015), written in Italian and translated in English by Ann Goldstein, shares many of Ferrante's prominent tropes.[32] The story, like Lahiri's language memoir in which it appears, thematizes the negotiation of female identity, authorship, and translating the self in a new language. Figures of disappearance, anonymity, and erasure are employed in conjunction with imagery drawn from the seamstress's art—cutting, sewing, and dressing—to depict the process of translation. And these figures seem to emerge directly from Ferrante's pages.[33]

In "The Exchange" a woman translator wishes to reinvent herself and become someone else, "to produce another version of herself, in the same way she could transform a text from one language into another" (2016, 66-7). This analogy establishes a parallel between the self and the (re)creation of the self as translation. Transforming the translator's identity entails self-erasure: "she had the impulse to remove her presence from the earth as if it were a thread on the hem of a nice dress, to be cut off [*da tagliare via*] with a pair of scissors" (66-7). The desire to eliminate her identity through translation acquires sartorial dimensions and is eventually fulfilled: "she decided one day to eliminate the signs of her existence" ("eliminare i segni della sua esistenza," 68-9). This project of self-erasure recalls Lila's project in the Neapolitan Novels of "eliminating all the traces," of "disappearing without leaving a trace" (*MBF*, 21-2). In the prologue to the tetralogy, Lila even cuts her image out of all family photographs, and the narrative uses the same verb as Lahiri (*tagliare via*; *MBF*, 22; *Ag*, 18). Lahiri's sartorial image moreover evokes Ferrante's seamstresses who cut, sew, and clothe the female body as a way to undo some of the symbolic or physical damage done to it.

The sartorial motif as a metaphor for the translator's self-erasure structures the rest of "The Exchange." The translator moves to a foreign city where she doesn't speak the language and begins to feel "anonymous" (70-1), blending with the urban landscape and emptying out her mind, her identity a *tabula rasa*. In this new city she happens to enter an apartment where women are trying on black dresses, designed by the apartment's owner who welcomes them with open arms. The translator tries on several dresses, but she doesn't like any of them. Observing the other women, she sees a collage of fragmented body parts: "they were a collection of arms, legs, hips, waists" (72–3; "erano una collezione di braccia, gambe, anche, vite"). This image reads like an intertextual reference to Ferrante's construction of the female body as violated, mutilated, and fragmented. In *Troubling Love*, for example, the Vossi painting depicts two women with severed arms as an image of patriarchal violence—"a mutilated movement or hands, feet, part of the head" (*TL*, 117; "un movimento mutilato do mani, di piedi, di parte delle teste," *Am*, 149). As Chapter 3 argues, the Vossi painting stands as a visual analogy for the protagonists, Delia and her seamstress-mother Amalia who too cuts, sews, and wields the scissors to create new dresses and new identities for her clients. In *Frantumaglia*, Elena Ferrante uses the same image of the battered and fragmented female body explicitly relating it to her seamstress-mother: "the dress was [. . .] scarred, pricked by the pins, because of the words of suffering, because of their malevolent touch—the body of a woman worn out by her troubles, without a head, without legs, without arms and hands" (*Fr*, 156). And in the Neapolitan Novels, we see a similar process of self-destruction, cutting, and fragmentation when Lila defaces her image in her wedding photo as a statement of autonomy and creative authority.[34] Lahiri's "collection" of female body parts seems to be in conversation with Ferrante's feminine imaginary.

In Lahiri's story, the connection between translation and sewing is made explicit when the translator examines her reflection in a large mirror and sees another woman behind it: "She was working at a table, with an iron, a needle in her mouth" (74–5). The seamstress appears as the specular image or alter ego of the translator who has already conceived of herself in sartorial terms. "The Exchange" establishes a clear textual genealogy with Ferrante's works through the shared imagery of self-erasure, corporeal fragmentation, cutting, and sewing. Translation as the negotiation of identity in "The Exchange" echoes Elena's translation of her own and Lila's identities between standard Italian and dialect, the figure of the narrator as translator. Moreover, Elena's narration of Lila is contingent on Lila's absence, on her disappearing and eliminating the signs of her existence. These thematic and conceptual overlaps can be inscribed within a larger framework of metaphors of translation as anonymity (Weinberger 2013), as invisible and self-effacing labor (Venuti 1992, 2008), as deformation (Berman 2012), and as gendered female (Chamberlain 1988).

The nexus between sewing and translation can also be found in an essay by Anita Raja, another possible influence on Lahiri. In her essay "Translation as a Practice of Acceptance" ("La traduzione come pratica dell'accoglienza," 2016), Raja uses a sartorial metaphor to describe the relationship between the original text and its translation: "clothes cut from another language are always too tight" ("ogni veste in un'altra lingua va stretta"). In Lahiri's story when the translator moves to the foreign city, she brings a black dress and a black sweater as her only clothes. These clothes become emblematic of her new, anonymous, *tabula rasa* self. At the designer's apartment she takes off her sweater to try on the dresses. Later, she thinks her black sweater has been exchanged for another because she doesn't recognize it anymore. This image central to "The Exchange" can be approached through Raja's metaphor: Lahiri's translator has worn the designer-author's "clothes cut from another language" and her own black sweater, her own identity, no longer fits her as the new language has transformed her. On the following day the translator accepts her old-new sweater and her own difference: "Now, when she put it on, she, too, was another [un'altra]" (80–1). Notably, Lahiri's story presents a feminine model of translation consisting of the author-designer of the dresses, the translator whose mirror image is the seamstress-maker of the dresses, and the apartment as a place frequented only by women.

Raja also conceives of translation as an act of disappearance or self-effacement: "the translator must retreat so as to accept [accogliere] the language of the other, to allow herself to be invaded by it so as to accommodate it" (2016). She uses the verb *accogliere*—to welcome, to accommodate, to accept—to describe the translator as submitting to the authority of the other language. Submission does not equal surrender, however. On the contrary, for Raja it means to accommodate and celebrate difference, acknowledging the potential of translation to transform the translator's worldview and language, opening new signifying possibilities. The title of her essay describes translation as an act of *accoglienza* or welcoming acceptance. The same verb *accogliere* appears in Ferrante's answer to a question about Ann Goldstein's translations: "I trust her completely. I believe she has done everything possible to accommodate [accogliere] my Italian into her English with the best intentions" (*Fr*, 352; *La fr*, 342). Like Raja and Lahiri, Ferrante conceives of translation as an act of acceptance or accommodation, a co-habitation and negotiation of languages and identities.

The image of the translator as a seamstress who accepts and molds the other's body/language establishes a literary genealogy between Ferrante, Raja, Lahiri, and Ann Goldstein as the translator of both Ferrante and Lahiri. This genealogy reverses the direction of literary influence from the center to the periphery. It also enables the circulation of metaphors and imaginaries as a practice of exchange between women. The feminist scholar of translation Luise von Flotow (2009) re-conceptualizes the gendered discourse on translation as *metramorphic*, positing the feminine and the maternal as a positive paradigm and therefore productive, generative, and transformative. The *metramorphic* paradigm creates a feminine symbolic not contingent on patriarchal familial relations but rather on acceptance and exchange between women (von Flotow 2009). The literary genealogy inaugurated by Ferrante through the shared metaphorics of translation, sewing, and acceptance can be situated within this paradigm, as its product and as its result.

Elena Ferrante as World Literature: An Overview

Despite her increasingly more visible presence in scholarly debates, currently there is only one monograph on Elena Ferrante in the Anglophone world—Tiziana de Rogatis's richly informative *Elena Ferrante: Parole Chiave* (2018), published in English translation by Ferrante's American publisher Europa Editions. De Rogatis's investigation and other Italian and Anglophone scholarship, however, tend to focus on the Neapolitan Novels—understandably so. The sheer size of the tetralogy—the four novels together amount to more than 1,700 pages in English translation—offers an embarrassment of riches for the literary critic, inviting a plethora of approaches and readings. If we add the 400-page translation of her nonfictional writing *Frantumaglia* (2016), then readers and scholars alike face more than 2,000 pages of Ferrante's textual corpus. This abundant accretion of literary material has mostly obscured her first three novels, the compact but more experimental *Troubling Love* (1992), *The Days of Abandonment* (2002), and *The Lost Daughter* (2006).

My book recuperates these three short novels for the study of Ferrante's poetics and charts a literary genealogy within her writing. Ferrante's feminine imaginary is already fully shaped in these slim volumes which serve as points of departure for her children's book *The Beach at Night* (published in 2007 and mostly ignored by literary scholars) and for the tetralogy. The reasons for the global success of the Neapolitan Novels are already encoded on a more intimate scale in her first three novels. In putting all of Ferrante's novels in conversation, this book provides a panoramic view of the plots, figures, and narratives that together construct a universal feminine imaginary. *Elena Ferrante as World Literature* argues that Ferrante forges a theory of feminine experience, subjectivity, and identity, building a compound scaffolding for her own literary practice. She conceptualizes and then narrates the linguistic, psychical, and corporeal-spatial realities that constitute the female subjects she has theorized. To keep pace with Ferrante's multifaceted theory-practice, this book approaches her novels through the interdisciplinary lens of intra- and intertextual juxtapositions within her narrative corpus and vis à vis a larger philosophical, literary, and artistic tradition. Each of these juxtapositions requires its own set of analytical tools while staying close to the text and its modes of signification. I use her expanded volume *La frantumaglia* as a composite master narrative or map of her theory and practice.

While maintaining an active dialogue with existing Ferrante scholarship, this book proposes its own readings, summoning her entire textual production—from her first three short novels and her children's book to the four Neapolitan Novels and the expanded edition of *La frantumaglia* to the volume of editorials collected in *Incidental Inventions* and to her most recent novel, *The Lying Life of Adults*.[35] My inquiry addresses Ferrante's theory of an embodied and spatialized subjectivity reified as *frantumaglia* and *smarginatura*—words that denote the shattering of the female body and psyche. Ferrante's feminine imaginary is paradoxically constituted by fragmentation, disintegration, or mutilation as the necessary conditions for the reconstitution of female identity and subjectivity. *Frantumaglia* and *smarginatura* are always triggered by what Ferrante calls "the male cage" (*II*, 86; "la gabbia maschile," *Lio*, 82) of a patriarchal society and an androcentric literary tradition. Trapped within traditional discourses of motherhood and femininity, Delia, Olga, Leda, Lila, and Elena transform the maternal body and mind into a site of contestation. When they exit the male cage—or the literal and symbolic labyrinth of patriarchal space—they reconfigure the topographic, cultural, and corporeal signs of their subalternity into symbols of agency. Although initially destructive and disruptive, the experiences of *frantumaglia* and *smarginatura* unleash productive forces that Ferrante's female subjects use to articulate their own identities and claim for themselves traditionally male ideas of genius, authorship, and creativity.

Ferrante's deployment of *frantumaglia* and *smarginatura* creates a *psycho-corporeal-spatial* female subject who negotiates and exceeds the restrictive frame of the male imaginary by claiming her own discourses and spaces. The book's chapters likewise trace the textual unfolding of this subjectivity from *Troubling Love* to the Neapolitan Novels. More broadly, the chapters chart an interpretive trajectory that moves from the innermost workings of the body and psyche to mechanisms for controlling and containing the female body and mind to forms of female authorship and creativity to corporeal negotiations of urban topography and patriarchal space. The book is structured to expand outward, from the study of psychical landscapes to the exploration of cityscapes and urban geographies. Although the chapters are held together and propelled forward by the thrust of my overarching argument, each can be read on its own, as a window into Ferrante's poetics.

The present chapter, which also serves as an introduction to the book, situates Ferrante within broader discourses of world literature, gender politics, and literary influence. Chapter 2, "*Frantumaglia* and *Smarginatura*: The Borders of a Universal Feminine Imaginary," examines the terrain of Ferrante's two neologisms, first in relation to her sustained imagery of incision instruments and tools for penetrating the female body as the inscriptions of a phallocratic and phallocentric system. In Ferrante's revision of this system patriarchal incision becomes feminine introspection which ruptures the reigning order and imposes a new one. This chapter then reads the words constitutive of her theory of female subjectivity as the symptoms of an internalized sexist geography. Although the word "frantumaglia" appears only in Ferrante's third novel, *The Lost Daughter,* its causes and effects permeate her two preceding novels, *Troubling Love* and *The Days of Abandonment.* Likewise, the concept of "smarginatura" originates in Ferrante's early texts and gains visibility in the Neapolitan Novels. Chapter 2 then proposes a genealogy and typology of these two neologisms as the lexical, psychic, and spatial coordinates of Ferrante's novels.

As a word inherited from her mother, *frantumaglia* describes a female ontology, verbalizing a specifically maternal psycho-corporeal reality. Ferrante's texts interrogate and undo a powerful maternal imaginary in which womanhood and creativity have been obliterated by motherhood. Chapter 3, "Binding and Unbinding the Maternal Body and Voice," argues for Ferrante's construction of a maternal discourse by questioning normative notions of mute, self-sacrificing mothers and by envoicing a host of problematic maternal narrators. To counter the literary and cultural alignment of self-erasure and motherhood, her novels focus on devious mothers who resist restrictive norms and boundaries. Chapter 3 locates the articulation of maternal discourse in five textual mechanisms spanning all of her works—the poetics of desire and disgust underlying the mother-daughter relationship; the conflation-inversion of mothers, daughters, and dolls; the mother's containment within spatial or symbolic boundaries; the trope of the transgressive, laughing mother who lifts her skirt and exposes her flesh; and the topos of the dead mother which paradoxically animates her novels as a generative force.

The image of the contained female body recurs in different visual permutations in Ferrante's novels—as mutilated figures on a truncated canvas, as the eroticized and commodified spectacle of a painted seminude gypsy, in official photographs, or framed by mirrors. Framed literally and symbolically by an androcentric creative tradition, Ferrante's women artists struggle against a canon which not only excludes them but also defines and represents them as objects or sights. Chapter 4, "Outside the Frame: The Aesthetics of Female Creativity and Authorship," explores Ferrante's female protagonists who carve out a creative practice of their own by resisting and subverting the male cage (and male gaze), dismantling what Ferrante describes as "the great warehouse of the arts, set up mainly by men" (*II*, 86). Chapter 4 argues for Ferrante's elaboration of a theory of feminine creativity and maps its parameters and manifestations in her literary iconography. I contend that Delia and Amalia, Olga and Leda, Lila and Elena dismantle the cage of patriarchal aesthetics by exposing the operations of its frame and inaugurating their own artistic legacy. This legacy originates in the arts of writing, sewing, painting or drawing, and in the deployment of framed objects such as paintings, photographs, and mirrors. By focusing on tropes of pictorial objectification, commodification, and fragmentation, this chapter shows how Ferrante's female subjects appropriate the visual strategies of an androcentric artistic tradition to claim an authorial position or creative autonomy. Their artistic practice inaugurates a female genealogy based on shared artistic skills, collaboration, and mutual representation.

Elena Greco's writing of the Neapolitan Novels occurs within a concrete topographic frame—the northern Italian city of Turin where she has settled after leaving Naples definitively. This setting acquires cartographic specificity as Elena's apartment overlooks the Valentino Park and the Princess Isabella bridge. This is the location of Olga's apartment in *The Days of Abandonment* as well. Chapter 5, "Mapping Urban Feminine Topographies," explores the recurring mapping of urban space by tracing the walking itineraries of Ferrante's female subjects in *Troubling Love*, *The Days of Abandonment*, and the Neapolitan Novels. The chapter shows that Delia, Olga, and Lila and Elena traverse a cityscape where structures of patriarchal power are embedded in the urban fabric so that negotiating city streets and public spaces exposes them to the oppressive effects of gendered geography. By focusing on three representations of urban space—Naples in *Troubling Love*, the *rione* in the Neapolitan Novels, and Turin in *The Days of Abandonment*, the chapter shows how Ferrante's ambulatory female subjects erase the violent inscriptions of masculinist cartography by appropriating and remapping the city.

Each of these chapters relies on a combination of analytical tools, a practice warranted by Ferrante's own creative approach detailed in *La frantumaglia*. Each chapter draws on Greek mythology, Freudian psychoanalysis, and French, Italian, and Anglophone feminist thought to show how Ferrante translates abstract concepts into concrete plot events. The analyses are augmented through the lenses of feminist geography, visual studies, and art history as well. Methodologically, the book pays attention to how Ferrante's texts convey meaning, unpacking her repertoire of tropes through close reading and textual interpretation, never losing sight of form and content. Although the book quotes the English translations of Ferrante's texts, the Italian originals are discussed where they can shed light on her poetics. Each chapter revisits scenes I deem critical to her construction of a feminine imaginary to show how Ferrante's writing lends itself to a multilayered and multidisciplinary approach beyond its culture of origins.

For example, in *The Days of Abandonment* Olga's urinating and defecating in the Valentino park in Turin is an effect of *frantumaglia* manifested as *smarginatura* or as a breach of boundaries but it also enacts a double abjection of the female body *and* of the oppressive urban space, liberating Olga from the cityscape which weighs on her as if painted on her nightgown. The image of the city map painted on her also evokes Olga's symbolic subjugation by her husband in a hostile city which encodes male power in its every monument, street, and public urinal. Painting then visualizes the inscriptions of gendered space on the maternal body and subjectivity. Viewed through the perspectives of Kristevan abjection, Elizabeth Grosz's concept of "bodies-cities," feminist geography, and feminist art history, this scene illuminates Ferrante's deft wielding, and welding, of both theory and narrative practice.

I conclude with an epilogue that situates her latest novel, *The Lying Life of Adults*, within the framework proposed by the book and delineates directions for further investigation.[36] *Elena Ferrante as World Literature* is the first English-language monograph on Ferrante and as such it aims to engage with current scholarship and highlight Ferrante's key narrative strategies while also proposing its own interdisciplinary readings. I approach Ferrante's works as a comparatist and not as an Italianist—that is, I do not make claims for Ferrante's place in an Italian tradition of women's writing, for it has already been done convincingly and compellingly. Rather, I situate her at the intersection of texts, theories, and methodologies to show the relevance and appeal of her imaginary to different disciplines and lines of inquiry. Ultimately, *Elena Ferrante as a World Literature* aims to introduce Ferrante's writing to a broader academic audience and to provide a scholarly apparatus for studying it.

2

Frantumaglia and *Smarginatura*

The Borders of a Universal Feminine Imaginary

> *I suggest mothers create opportunities to use the feminine plural with their daughter(s). They could also invent words and expressions to designate realities they feel and share but for which they lack language.*
>
> (Irigaray 1993a, 48)

Ferrante's novels narrate the vicissitudes of women's biological, emotional, and intellectual lives in a contemporary society ordered by inequality and difference. Her protagonists belong to an ostensibly modern world in which emancipated, educated women can aspire to have careers and thrive as autonomous agents. Nonetheless, as they pass through the stages and rites of childhood and adulthood, they confront a violent, oppressive, and exploitative patriarchal system which forces them to surrender their corporeal and intellectual agency, coercing them to define their identities within its gender, class, and sociocultural confines. Misogyny and sexualized violence are the shared concerns of the twenty-first-century global novel which Adam Kirsch sees as representative of a rising world consciousness of the cardinal sins of our time (2017). Ferrante's novels capture the construction and deconstruction of female subjectivity grounded in a psychical and corporeal reality always at odds with a dominant, hegemonic, heteronormative conception of acceptable margins. Her female protagonists grapple with the universally recognizable tensions and challenges of femininity in a global patriarchal society. In an interview with Italian feminist philosopher Luisa Muraro, Elena Ferrante declares:

> The patriarchy, in short—I say this in anger—seems to me more alive than ever. It holds the planet firmly in its hands and whenever it can, insists even more than before on making women cannon fodder. [. . .] It seems to me we are in the midst of a very hard battle and every day we are at risk of losing everything, even the syntax of truth. (*Fr*, 222–3)

This is precisely the battle fought in her novels: to expose, condemn, and begin to unravel the structures of patriarchal power which suffocate women within prescribed sociocultural and spatial boundaries.

Ferrante's texts portray through the local lens of a circumscribed place such as the Neapolitan *rione* of the tetralogy (Fusillo 2016) a crisis of female identity or a crucial step in the constitution of female subjectivity, critical moments comprehensible within a transnational context. These crises of identity are often spurred by the brutal and pervasive forms of violence (physical, ideological, psychological, even spatial) against women that break their bodies literally or fracture their subjectivities already construed as troubled and discontinuous (Wehling-Giorgi 2017, 1). Women's corporeal and psychical fragmentation is perhaps the most prominent feature of Ferrante's plots. Her protagonists succumb to systematic assaults which leave them bleeding or broken. Jealous or enraged husbands, fathers, and brothers are the agents of this abuse. Battered, bleeding, disfigured, mutilated, or penetrated female bodies frame the representation of women's corporeality (Wehling-Giorgi 2016a, 2017). In turn, this corporeal fracturing informs women's subjectivity as shaped by, and lived as, fragmentation, liminality, and slippage. Ferrante's heroines fall apart physically, they suffer from breakdowns, disorientation, multiple falls and descents—into basements and tunnels; into delirium or into the painful territories of the past; into verbal or corporeal incontinence; or into irrationality and excess.

Ferrante invents a name for this psychical and corporeal phenomenon—*frantumaglia*. To be afflicted with *frantumaglia* is to acknowledge—and submit to—the protocols of a universal patriarchy. The concept of *frantumaglia* encompasses a universal feminine imaginary spanning the various ages, stages, and aspects of female ontology such as menstruation, pregnancy, and parturition, linking mothers to daughters and establishing ineradicable connections between female friends. The notions of fragmentation, rupture, slippage, and breakdown are contained within her definition and narrative embodiment of *frantumaglia*. Paradoxically, the female body and psyche must first disintegrate, breach all boundaries and bleed outside the margins, experiencing the full force of patriarchal violence and bearing the traces of its social inscriptions and transformations, before they can be reconstituted as autonomous entities. Only by completing the process of disintegration—by falling into the depths of trauma, depression, and abjection—can Ferrante's protagonists resurface from the chasm of their suffering.

Frantumaglia can be read as Ferrante's own word for the mechanisms and manifestations of the woman's unconscious, the repressed traumas of femininity, and the irrepressible "vigor" (*Fr*, 104) of the female body. Her new word wrests the female psyche away from the entrenched phallocentric discourses that have shaped its understanding and representation, and supplies a new conceptual and literary map for approaching it. Despite its seemingly geographic and local specificity, her theory of *frantumaglia* is profoundly intertextual and interdisciplinary, drawing on literary, mythological, linguistic, psychological, and visual vocabularies to illuminate and narrate a range of universal feminine experiences within a global patriarchal order. Ferrante captures the female gaze in its manifold forms and envoices accounts of female subjectivity, motherhood, and authorship (Wehling-Giorgi 2016a). By doing so she also portrays the struggle of her female protagonists to emancipate themselves from the power structures that govern their lives, resist their ingrained sense of enforced marginalization, and elide the colonizing force of the male gaze and the male pen.

Ferrante's universal feminine imaginary is rooted in the corporeality and psychical interiority of her characters who struggle with violence, objectification, and subjugation, regardless of whether they are in their poverty-stricken and crime-ridden neighborhood or in cosmopolitan, civilized society (Mandolini 2016). In the third volume of the Neapolitan Novels, *Those Who Leave and Those Who Stay*, Elena Greco summarizes the universal scope of what she witnesses at home in the *rione* by connecting the plights of her neighborhood to those of the whole world (*TLTS*, 28). Her statement recalls Ferrante's own declaration about the prolonged and robust life of patriarchy, whose forms and institutions leave permanent traces on the female body conceived as "cannon fodder." The concept of *frantumaglia* defines female corporeality and psychical interiority as permeable and fragile, marked by external pressures, marred by regulatory discursive systems. Ferrante's theory and literary practice of *frantumaglia* as embodied subjectivity seeks to dislodge these discourses.

Her novels, along with *frantumaglia* as a theory of feminine experience, excavate with brutal, visceral, and often graphic honesty the realities of being a woman today. Ferrante's narratives recover women excluded from history's political, cultural, social, and economical discourses, granting them voice and a feminine "I" capable of maintaining its force because of, and in spite of, inner turmoil, fragmentation, or collapse (*Fr*, 283). Ferrante's characters are notably women who write, authors of their own textual representations, who reposition themselves as autonomous subjects and purveyors of knowledge about feminine psychical corporeality. By producing knowledge about the nexus between the feminine psyche and the female body they elide male-centered narratives and claim ontological, epistemological, and literary/creative power.

This chapter traces the parameters of Ferrante's universal feminine imaginary by analyzing her theory of *frantumaglia* and its literary manifestations in her first three novels, *Troubling Love*, *The Days of Abandonment*, and *The Lost Daughter*. It also examines the corollary concept of *smarginatura*, the experience of dissolving margins, which Ferrante deploys throughout the Neapolitan tetralogy as its overarching trope (de Rogatis 2018). The chapter locates *smarginatura* as a symptom of *frantumaglia* already surreptitiously at work in Ferrante's first three novels.

The workings of *frantumaglia* and *smarginatura* along with their apposite tropes and narrative strategies map the terrain of a feminine imaginary mobilized by the embedded sense of alienation, marginalization, and subalternity lived by Ferrante's protagonists. In this endeavor Ferrante joins a lineage of feminist thinkers such as Julia Kristeva, Luce Irigaray, Hélène Cixous, and Elizabeth Grosz, who have questioned the cultural constructions of femininity and have sought to reclaim and articulate forms of feminine corporeality, subjectivity, creativity, and authorship. At the same time, she also dialogues with an Italian tradition of women's writing by invoking some of its prominent voices—Sibilla Aleramo, Anna Maria Ortese, and Natalia Ginzburg, among others. Ferrante's unique contribution lies in her captivating storytelling that delves into the deepest recesses of the feminine psyche and, undaunted, revels in the flows and flaws of feminine corporeality. And, as Barbara Alfano (2015) has shown with respect to the Neapolitan Novels, Ferrante's narratives rely on a shared ground of moral certitudes, constructing an ethical framework of motherhood, friendship, and gratuitous violence that transcends cultural and national specificities.

Incisions and Inscriptions of the Body

Scissors, paper cutters, rusted safety pins, needles, burins, knives, hatpins, glass shards—instruments that sever or pierce the surface of objects and people—pervade Ferrante's writing, constituting a substantial category of vivid, brutal, disturbing, and even disgusting images. These instruments become tools for the literal and symbolic disfigurement and fragmentation of the female body or mind, for their inscription and hence appropriation by external forces. Metaphorically, these tools for penetration align with the phallus which in Ferrante's novels penetrates the female body and subjugates it with its painful lacerations.[1] In *Troubling Love* Delia imagines men and women as living organisms erased into anonymity through violent incision: "I imagined the work of the burin polishing us like ivory, reducing us until we were without holes and without excrescences, all identical and without identity" (63). The burin is a scalpel-like tool used for engraving metal plates. Delia, who is an artist, uses the vocabulary of her profession to describe her visionary fear of sameness and uniformity. She dreads being reduced to a blank face or a mute image, the kind of women her father paints—commodified objects to be exchanged between men. Delia's vision also posits women's bodies as the opposite of perfectly polished and smooth surfaces that have no ridges or gaping, oozing openings. She seems revolted at the prospect of the burin erasing women's bodily specificity.

Delia again uses her professional lexicon to describe another image of mutilation and disfigurement—the painting in the Vossi lingerie shop which illustrates Ferrante's iconography of male physical and symbolic violence against women.[2] Her description emphasizes the truncating of both painted bodies and canvas: "The image seemed to have been cut away from a much larger scene, and so only the legs of the women were visible and their extended arms were severed at the wrists" (*TL*, 67). Delia encounters the painting again in her father's studio. She depicts it as a "mutilated movement of hands, feet, part of the head" (*TL*, 117) which hints generally at the objectification, commodification, and fragmentation of the collective female body within a patriarchal culture, and particularly at the brutal abuse inflicted on Amalia herself, whose battered body Delia often recalls as a jumble of bleeding body parts (*TL*, 100). Moreover, this canvas whose margins have been cut off is the only example in Ferrante's novel of actual, typographic *smarginatura*—a printer's term meaning to trim or crop the page's margins. This literal cutting off of the female bodies in the painting, their violent reduction to a mutilated movement of body parts, foregrounds Lila's psychical state that she names *smarginatura*, a sensation that the borders of people dissolve and living matter oozes out, that surfaces are unstable, violable. On the other hand, the women whose limbs have been cut off can be seen as exceeding the boundaries of representational and corporeal space, their bodies reaching beyond the restrictive picture frame. Ferrante thus codes the female body as both trapped and uncontainable.

Like the burin, needles penetrate the surface of the skin and leave their mark. Delia recalls the needle of the sewing machine piercing her mother's finger, perforating and sewing it (*TL*, 63). This perforation of Amalia's finger and its disfigurement attest to the exploitation of her body for labor, for production, and reproduction: Amalia never stops working at her sewing machine, whether she is pregnant or nursing her children. She is branded by the needle-burin as the property of her husband in an economy that valorizes women either as sexual objects or as laborers. In fact, after picturing the burin, Delia recalls the needle puncturing her mother's finger. The two images are linked in her memory and in her narrative as instruments of violence and corporeal breakdown. The scars and perforations on the female body are the discursive engravings of a phallocratic and phallocentric system.

The breaking of the skin and the subcutaneous insertion of a substance can be traced further in *Troubling Love* in the way Delia figures the biological and psychic bond with her mother: "I had Amalia under my skin, like a hot liquid that had been injected into me at some unknown time" (*TL*, 86). In a novel that brims with images of male bodily fluids—for example, Delia masturbates Antonio in a scene suffused with her own corporeal discharge—Ferrante depicts Amalia's presence inside Delia's body through the inverted and gender-defiant logic of feminine insemination through penetration. The mother injects a hot liquid inside the daughter's body which impregnates the daughter with her mother's physical legacy—Delia looks like Amalia—and her psychical makeup. *Troubling Love* is a novel that grapples precisely with this problem: the mother inhabiting the daughter and the daughter's journey to accepting in herself her mother's traces. At the end of the novel, Delia embraces her mother's heritage inside her: "Amalia had been. I was Amalia," she claims in the novel's last sentence (*TL*, 139). The same inverted logic of feminine insemination occurs in *The Lost Daughter* as a bodily transaction between symbolic mothers and daughters. The little girl Elena "impregnates" her daughter-doll Nani with a worm she inserts in her belly. Leda's "adoptive" daughter, Nina, stabs her "mother-mentor" with a hat pin at the end of the novel.

We witness a similar act of bonding through bodily insertion in the opening page of the narrative proper of *My Brilliant Friend*. The narrator Elena Greco describes her friend Lila using a rusty safety pin to break the surface of her skin as a way to test her courage and prove her strength: "I watched the metal point as it dug a whitish tunnel into her palm, and then, when she pulled it out and handed it to me, I did the same" (*MBF*, 27). The safety pin attaches them to each other, going in and out of their skin like the needle in Amalia's finger. This act of penetration is a ritual that consolidates their friendship. The safety pin (*spilla francese*) belongs to the same category of "incision" images as the hat pin (*spillone*) with which Nina stabs Leda at the end of the *The Lost Daughter* and Leda watches the blade go in and out of her skin (*LD*, 124–5). The paper cutter Olga hands to her daughter in *The Days of Abandonment* keeps Olga alert, literally engraving self-awareness onto her body: Olga rouses herself from her delirium when Ilaria makes a deep gash in her leg (*DA*, 142). The paper cutter, shared between Olga and Ilaria, stands as the emblem of what Ferrante defines as women's "conscious surveillance" (*Fr*, 103–5) or vigilance and self-analysis. Ferrante literalizes the inscription/incision of the female body so that women act as its conscious agents. The phallus as the symbolic and physical instrument of penetration in Ferrante's literary universe begins to lose its firmness. Throughout the tetralogy Lila continues to wield sharp, lethal objects—the knife with which she threatens Marcello Solara, the knives with which she dismembers frozen meat at Soccavo's factory, and the scissors she uses to fragment and disfigure her wedding portrait, and ultimately to cut herself out of all photographs.

Scissors break the surface of things, they cut and puncture, but they also sew and reconstruct. Like the two women in the Vossi painting, they reach outside the frame of a male-dominated world. As a seamstress Amalia uses scissors to cut the outlines of female bodies from paper and fabric (*TL*, 103), therefore restoring to them a surrogate wholeness. In *The Days of Abandonment*, Olga's mother is a seamstress who transforms sewing into storytelling. Olga recalls sitting under the table while her mother and her workers "cut, sewed, and talked, talked, sewed, and cut" (*DA*, 15). The word "rhapsode" (*il rapsodo*) or the bard of Homeric epic, the storyteller par excellence, derives from the Greek verb ῥάπτω, to sew (Conti 2015, 107). And it is this connection between cutting and talking, between "stories and gossip and sewing" (*DA*, 44) that engenders in Olga the impulse to write and hence is at the origin of the novel we are reading as her written record of the ordeals of abandonment. In women's hands, cutting turns into narrative, and sewing words with the thread of storytelling is passed down from mother to daughter. Weaving and sewing are two of the major metaphors Ferrante employs both in her novels and in *Frantumaglia* to refer to the creative act of writing.[3] Ferrante's female characters sew and weave a new feminine way of storytelling—a narrative truth not perfectly structured and organized, a narrative truth that is disorderly, messy, and fluid, and thus more real, more honest (*Fr*, 233; 261; 330). Narrating the female body must embrace its liquidities and corporeal specificity, so that the scars and cuts show, and flows seep through. Writing, by way of the needle's penetrating thrust, incarnates the women's phallus, women's right to autonomous authorship in a tradition which endorses the myth of literary paternity and enshrines the pen as the instrument of male generative power (Gilbert and Gubar 1979, 6–7).

Olga too uses scissors in a creative manner: she cuts, fragments, and puts together images of her own and her children's bodies as a way of separating herself from her husband's identity: "I took a pair of scissors and, for a whole long silent evening, cut out eyes, ears, legs, noses, hands of mine, of the children, of Mario. I pasted them onto a piece of paper" (*DA*, 164). This artistic collage exorcises Mario's presence from her life, severing her dependence on him and restoring her agency to create, to connect and disconnect. It evokes the Vossi painting with its "mutilated movement of hands, feet, part of the head" (*TL*, 117), but here Olga appropriates pictorial agency to represent herself and her children, to cut, to sew or paste. As the story unfolds, she gains control of her own body and mind, and thus of her story as well. Ferrante's claim that "the process of fragmentation in a woman's body interests me very much from the narrative point of view" (*Fr*, 223) points in that direction.

Olga's collage anticipates another crucial image in Ferrante's visual poetics—Lila's wedding photo project in *The Story of a New Name*, in which Lila uses scissors and black tape to disfigure her own portrait as the sign of her domestic subjugation as wife. She mutilates her photographed body, transforming the image into a surrealist advertisement for the shoes she has designed so that the resulting collage conceals Lila's body and foregrounds her eye. This self-disfigurement is a visual metaphor for Lila's rebellion against the colonization of the female body (Wehling-Giorgi 2017, 10), her way of asserting her subjectivity and autonomy (Santovetti 2018, 544).[4] Lila takes charge of her own bodily transformation at a moment when she seems out of control—pregnant with Stefano's child, which she will soon lose, she wishes to control at least her visual representation. Moreover, the creation of this collage is described as a euphorically fulfilling experience Lila shares with her friend Elena—two seamstresses sewing together (Wehling-Giorgi 2019a). It is an act of joint feminine creation which for Lila supplants Stefano's role as the male creator/inseminator, and for both Lila and Elena circumvents, albeit momentarily, the rigid male-centered order (Milkova 2016c). Scissors become a tool for feminine appropriation of the instruments and practices of representing the female body.

The instruments that break the surface and penetrate the body at first glance uphold a fixed archaic order—the male symbolic and keep women contained within its social, cultural, and gender boundaries. But in their subversive and unsettling effects, they can also be empowering and affirmative. In Ferrante's literary imagination these tools can be repurposed to serve women rather than men. Women's bodies, traditionally conceived as porous, leaking, and ontologically unstable (Grosz 1994; Hanson 2015), in Ferrante's novels emblematize women's subjection to male violence and patriarchal control. But when Ferrante's female protagonists appropriate the tools for penetration, mundane tools associated with women's labor such as scissors and pins, and perform the physical or symbolic thrust of the scissors or the paper cutter, embracing the reversibility and porousness of the female body, they inscribe their protest and carve out spaces to enact and express their subjectivities. Incision doubles as introspection. As this chapter argues, writing their experience, weaving or sewing its fragments into a narrative, becomes an introspective feminine practice.

The scenes analyzed here form a typology of "incisive" images underlying Ferrante's theory of feminine experience developed in her novels and in her volume *Frantumaglia*. The rupture of borders and fixed boundaries, physical and metaphorical implosions, eruptions, shatterings, and earthquakes at once destabilize the surface and appearance of things in Ferrante's literary universe and impose a new order. These moments of breakdown work to erect a stable frame of reference, an entire poetics of incision or rupture that Ferrante encloses within two words: *frantumaglia*—a dialectal neologism implying fragmentation, shattering, or a jumble of fragments, and *smarginatura*—an obscure technical term Ferrante employs in an innovative way to signify the dissolving or cutting off of margins, the collapse of physical outlines or the blurring of edges. Delia and Amalia, Olga and her double, the *poverella*, Leda and her young friend Nina, Leda's mother, all suffer from *frantumaglia*. They are rent by overwhelming emotions, often in relation to the normative forms of womanhood foisted on them. These emotions bring to the surface memories that complicate their daily negotiations of femininity. In short, *frantumaglia* is the feminine unconscious made visible as the effect of intense emotional experiences, as the eruption of the repressed past into the present. *Smarginatura*, on the other hand, has to do with the permeability and fragility of the body. It constitutes a way of perceiving reality as corporeally fluid, lacking fixed borders. Lila, the character who most prominently suffers from *smarginatura*, experiences the permeability and reversibility of all solid things. Her sense of *smarginatura* results from the systematic physical and symbolic violence—the engravings or inscriptions of the body—she has endured and witnessed since childhood. It is a condition at once caused by phallocratic penetration and exposing, condemning it.

In other words, if *frantumaglia* is a woman's internal suffering within the symbolic order, *smarginatura* is its symptom, the external manifestation of women's subjugation, objectification, and exploitation within a patriarchal economy. Together *frantumaglia* and *smarginatura* outline a theory of feminine ontology along with a textual phenomenology that maps a universal status quo within still predominantly patriarchal cultures and opens ways for resisting and countermanding it. Both *frantumaglia* and *smarginatura* chart psychic landscapes that slide into physical, topographic spaces and vice versa. Significantly, both words and their descriptions rely on the vocabulary of space (including spatialized abstractions) to trace the coordinates of a larger territory—that of the universal alterity of women's experience in an unjust and "sick" universe, as Elena Greco puts it in her spatial metaphor for interconnected violence and suffering (*TLTS*, 28).

The Parameters of *Frantumaglia*

Elena Ferrante readily admits her indebtedness to Freud's works, especially in her first three novels which stage various pre-Oedipal and Oedipal scenarios (*Fr*, 122–3). The tools of bodily penetration discussed before lend themselves to a psychoanalytical reading as fetishized objects or as manifestations of penis envy and castration anxiety, key elements of Freud's theories of infantile sexuality.[5] Whereas Freud notoriously conceptualized the female body entirely through the eyes of a male, Ferrante conceptualizes the female body from a woman's perspective, focusing the female gaze inward as an incisive tool for self-analysis. Her theory of feminine psychic and bodily experience corrects and counteracts Freud's phallocratic scheme and proffers its own psychological and narrative parameters: *frantumaglia* and *smarginatura*.[6]

In her essay "La frantumaglia," written after the publication of *The Days of Abandonment*, Ferrante supplies an exegesis of her poetics. The essay is her response to a question from two women journalists about women's suffering in her first two novels. Ferrante replies circuitously, with a word she inherited from her mother to describe a singularly feminine affliction. It is worth quoting the entire passage:

> My mother left me a word in her dialect that she used to describe how she felt when she was racked by contradictory sensations that were tearing her apart. She said that inside her she had a *frantumaglia*, a jumble of fragments. The *frantumaglia* (she pronounced it *frantummàglia*) depressed her. Sometimes it

made her dizzy, sometimes it made her mouth taste like iron. It was the word for a disquiet not otherwise definable, it referred to a miscellaneous crowd of things in her head, debris in a muddy water of the brain. The *frantumaglia* was mysterious, it provoked mysterious actions, it was the source of all suffering not traceable to a single obvious cause. When she was no longer young, the *frantumaglia* woke her in the middle of the night, led her to talk to herself and then feel ashamed, suggested some indecipherable tune to sing under her breath that soon faded into a sigh, drove her suddenly out of the house, leaving the stove on, the sauce burning in the pot. Often it made her weep, and since childhood the word has stayed in my mind to describe, in particular, a sudden fit of weeping for no evident reason: frantumaglia tears. (*Fr*, 99)

The word "frantumaglia" itself seems to derive from the Italian verb *frantumare* which means to shatter or to fragment, to break into shards or splinters. The concept Ferrante attributes to her mother expresses an inner fragmentation, a splitting of the self, but also the self's irrational and chaotic sensations breaking through the surface of logic and reason and metaphorically spilling out.

The symptoms of *frantumaglia* bear uncanny similarities to the widespread nineteenth-century medical discourses about female hysteria and puerperal insanity, conditions that betrayed the instability of the maternal body and aimed to stabilize it through marriage and childbirth (Hanson 2015). Freud's study *Dora: Fragment of an Analysis of a Case of Hysteria* codified the narrative and interpretation of hysteria in relation to female sexuality by documenting his treatment of his young patient (1997 [1905]). In the text, Freud's authoritative and paternalistic voice (he was a friend of Dora's father) drowns Dora's feeble attempts to tell her story of sexual abuse (1997 [1905]). In fact, he reads her "No" as a clear "Yes," thereby denying her even the right to consent (1997 [1905], 50–1). The hysterical body was not only a voiceless one but also a highly theatricalized spectacle to be examined, displayed, and documented (Didi-Huberman 2004). Charlotte Perkins Gilman in her story "The Yellow Wallpaper" (1892) and Rachilde in her novel *The Juggler* (1900) have left us literary representations of unwieldy, hysterical women under the supervision or surveillance of male doctors, women who find outlets for their sensual or creative impulses in madness or self-destruction. Ferrante's mother's word thus encompasses a history of feminine experience and its medicalization beyond the word's origins in Neapolitan dialect. It also conceptualizes women's suffering as the sensation of being torn and fragmented, a sensation which manifests outwardly through irrational behavior. *Frantumaglia* elides the logic of causality; it is both the cause and the effect of suffering. The maternal word gives the feminine unconscious a name, and it provides the author with material for her own interpretation.

Ferrante collects and displays her own catalogue of images associated with *frantumaglia* and transforms the maternal word into her own feminine imaginary:

> The *frantumaglia* is an unstable landscape, an infinite aerial or aquatic mass of debris that appears to the I, brutally, as its true and unique inner self. The *frantumaglia* is the storehouse of time without the orderliness of a history, a story.

> The *frantumaglia* is an effect of the sense of loss, when we're sure that everything that seems to us stable, lasting, an anchor for our life, will soon join that landscape of debris that we seem to see. [. . .] I, who sometimes suffer from the illness of Olga, the protagonist of *The Days of Abandonment*, represent it to myself mainly as a hum growing louder and a vortex-like fracturing [sfaldamento a vortice] of material living and dead: a swarm of bees approaching above the motionless treetops; the sudden eddy in a slow body of water. But it's also the right word for what I'm convinced I saw as a child—or, anyway, during that time invented by adults that we call childhood—shortly before language entered me and instilled speech: a bright-colored explosion of sounds, thousands and thousands of butterflies with sonorous wings. Or it's only my way of describing the anguish of death, the fear that the capacity to express myself would get stuck—as if the organs of speech had been paralyzed—and everything I'd learned to control, from the first year of life until now, would start fluctuating on its own [fluttui per conto suo], dripping or hissing out of a body becoming a thing, a leather sack leaking air and liquids. (*Fr*, 100)

Even in the author's own reimagining, *frantumaglia* resists precise definition and remains slippery and permeable, like the "leaky" female body. On the one hand, it is described as an external force, a whirlwind of detritus and wreckage that appears to the self as that very self's interiority. The self is splintered, fragmented and, at the same time, externalized and spatialized, which is why her characters often examine their reflection in a mirror, perceiving specters of themselves or else seeking confirmation of their physical integrity. *Frantumaglia* also undoes all chronological order so that the self is no longer narratable within linear, historical time and requires a different mode of representing chronology. It appears as the imposition of primeval chaos on the ordered world of the (feminine) psyche, a return to a timeless, borderless existence.

On the other hand, *frantumaglia* entails a synesthetic regression to a prelinguistic state where the senses overlap in an explosion of colors and sounds. It recalls the time before the child's participation in a system of language that differentiates and acculturates the self within the symbolic order. Thus, *frantumaglia* has the potential to grant voice to what lies outside the symbolic order—a feminine experience not yet initiated within a gender and power hierarchy. Lastly, it seems to suggest a certain fear of the undifferentiated self, that is, of losing control over one's language and body, of the dissolution of corporeal contours. The fear of death as the ultimate form of non-differentiation and liquefaction of the flesh underlies *frantumaglia* as well. Then *frantumaglia* is the loss of boundaries, the porousness or reversibility of inside and outside, self and other, past and present, life and death. It is the female body out of control, incontinent and leaking, like the conceptualization of women as "leaky vessels" which held sway in Europe beginning in the Early Modern period (Paster 1993, 23–5).

We see precisely this framework underlying Ferrante's novels, which break down narrative chronology, enacting the fragmentation of time, sliding between past and present, archaic and modern (de Rogatis 2018, 108). The cause of this rupture, as Ferrante declares, is suffering. Suffering appears equivalent to a spatiotemporal disorder, a retreat into a Jungian (1981) collective feminine unconscious with its characteristic archetypes:

> The eruption of suffering cancels out linear time, breaks it, makes it into whirling squiggles. [...] Suffering casts us down among our single-celled ancestors, among the quarrelsome or terrorized muttering in the caves, among the female divinities expelled into the darkness of the earth, even as we keep ourselves anchored— let's say—to the computer we're writing on. Strong feelings are like that: they explode chronology. An emotion is a somersault, a tumble, a dizzying pirouette. (*Fr*, 108)

Suffering women plummet into the caves of the mothers where they succumb to a long-standing archaic violence and find death or destruction as the only possible outcomes.[7] But the women of today, Ferrante's protagonists, bring their computers with them to write about the experience that annihilates them, and this is what allows them to work through their suffering. This anachronism or the cancellation of linear time is reflected on the level of narrative and also entails a set of mythological references to which I turn later in the chapter. Ferrante's first two novels are rife with references to disorder, collapse, and physical breakdown—of communication, of families, of bodies—which augur the female protagonist's loss of her grip on reality (Alsop 2014, 475). These moments of "weakness" are reproduced in the formal structures of the texts—temporal lacunae, "wrinkles in time," flashbacks, and interruptions create rifts or gaps in the texts' ostensibly seamless realism (Alsop 2014, 476). This fractured narrative is intended as mimetic realism, as the narrativization of psychic disequilibrium (Alsop 2014, 476). In other words, Ferrante's texts narrate and perform the experience of *frantumaglia*.

On the level of plot, the female protagonists fall inside the "vortexes" of their complex, intense emotions and see their "unique inner selves" as fractured. Delia, Olga, Leda, Lila, and Elena descend into dark abysses, literal and metaphorical: the "void" in *The Days of Abandonment*, the "black well" in *The Lost Daughter*, the cellar in *Troubling Love* and in the Neapolitan tetralogy. There they encounter their biological or symbolic mothers, their female ancestors, along with a host of mythological (or literary) figures and female archetypes as alternative models of femininity.[8] These encounters suspend narrative and chronological time as her characters negotiate their identities:

> Delia and Olga [...] are women who tell their story from the middle of a dizzy spell. So they don't suffer because of the conflict between what they would like to be and what their mothers were, they are not the painful end result of a female genealogy that moves, in chronological order, from the ancient world, from the great myths of the Mediterranean, to end up at them as a visible peak of progress. Suffering derives, instead, from the fact that crowding around them, simultaneously, in a sort of achrony, is the past of their ancestors and the future of what they seek to be, the shades, the ghosts: up to the point, for example, where Delia, after taking off her clothes of the present, can put on her mother's old dress as the definitive garment; and Olga can recognize in the mirror, in her own face, as a constituent part of her, the figure of the poverella-mother who has killed herself. (*Fr*, 108–9)

Narrating from "the middle of a dizzy spell," from inside the whirlwind of suffering, is also narrating the movements of the unconscious populated by ghosts. Ferrante insists on the role of "strong feelings" or extreme affectivity as the cause of this dizzying descent into the collective unconscious. Under strong emotive pressure we experience, irrationally, opposing or incompatible entities as reversible, equivalent, and exchangeable (Carvalho 2018).[9] Accordingly, the reversibility of the unconscious can be seen in the abrogation of linear time and contiguous space, the confusion of past and present, inside and outside, sound and color as the distinguishing features of *frantumaglia* and its literary narratives.

Smarginatura in the Neapolitan Novels

The breakdown of reality and linear chronology entails the slippage between borders, the permeable boundaries of people and objects. Death and the image of the body as "a leaking leather sack" haunt Ferrante's poetics as causes and symptoms of *frantumaglia*. The most developed and sustained symptom of *frantumaglia* is *smarginatura*—Lila's perception of reality as permeable and porous, bodies turned inside out, stable surfaces unable to contain what lurks underneath. Lila first experiences "dissolving margins" during the New Year's celebration on December 31, 1958, but she does not recount it to Elena until the earthquake in Naples on November 23, 1980, when both she and Elena are pregnant. The narration of *smarginatura* thus stretches for the duration of the four volumes, from its first mention in *My Brilliant Friend* to its culmination in *The Story of the Lost Child*. Its definition remains slippery, like the landscape of *frantumaglia* or the leaky, ontologically unstable, pregnant female body. Its etymology points to an obscure technical term from typography which denotes the cutting of the page's edges or margins. Ferrante invests this term with new semantics, recontextualizing it within the psyche.

From its first textual appearance the term seems to break open established meanings. Elena begins the section "Adolescence" in *My Brilliant Friend* by recounting Lila's first episode of dissolving margins. The word "smarginatura" appears in the Italian through Lila's forceful appropriation and revision of its common usage. Elena, in telling about her friend's neologism, admits that "The term isn't mine, she always used it" (*MBF*, 89), but the Italian explicitly references Lila's forcing a new meaning from an old usage: "Il temine non è mio, lo ha sempre utilizzato lei *forzando il significato comune della parola*" (*Ag*, 85). My italics indicate the phrase omitted in English—*forcing the common meaning of the word*. Lila's utterance, the word she reinvents, points to her forcing the limits of language and signification, just like the concept itself describes the forcing of boundaries. Moreover, she hijacks the term's typographic usage—to cut off the edges of a page—and employs it to describe a state of female suffering, hinting perhaps at women's complete erasure as (writing) subjects—their banishment outside the marginalized status and marginalized spaces they already occupy. In Lila's recontextualization in the feminine psyche *smarginatura* acquires an entirely new network of significations. Lila experiences it primarily within gender and power-inflected situations, when male arrogance and brutal force threaten the boundaries of the female body and female subjectivity. Elena's description of Lila's first episode of *smarginatura* is worth quoting:

> It was—she told me—as if, on the night of a full moon over the sea, the intense black mass of a storm advanced across the sky, swallowing every light, eroding the circumference of the moon's circle, and disfiguring the shining disk, reducing it to its true nature of rough insensate material. Lila imagined, she saw, she felt—as if it were true—her brother break [. . .] something violated the organic structure of her brother, exercising over him a pressure so strong that it broke down his outlines, and the matter expanded like a magma, showing her what he was truly made of. Every second of that night of celebration horrified her, she had the impression that, as Rino moved, as he expanded around himself, every margin collapsed and her own margins, too, became softer and more yielding. [. . .] I was struck, I think, by her expression, which seemed increasingly fearful. I also realized that she was staring at the shadow of her brother—the most active, the most arrogant, shouting the loudest, bloodiest insults in the direction of the Solaras' terrace—with repulsion. It seemed that she, she who in general feared nothing, was afraid. (*MBF*, 176–7)

The opening images—"black mass" and "its true nature of insensate material"—situate the experience of *smarginatura* within the landscape of *frantumaglia*. Lila's horrifying perception of her brother's disintegration is triggered by Rino's excessive arrogance, by the fireworks and the men shooting their guns, by the male bodies capable of inflicting pain and suffering. Her gaze penetrates her brother's skin to reveal the "magma" underneath, the body bared of its defenses, eviscerated, turned inside out. This is one of the visionary moments of breakdown that Alsop (2014) examines but taken to an all-encompassing extreme. In *The Story of the Lost Child*, Lila recounts to Elena her inner turmoil during that New Year's eve celebration, turmoil even more explicitly linked to violence:

> First, even before they started shooting, I was afraid that the colors of the fireworks were sharp—the green and the purple especially were razor-like—that they could butcher us, that the trails of the rockets were scraping my brother Rino like files, like rasps, and broke his flesh, caused another, disgusting brother to drip out of him, whom I had to put back inside right away—inside his usual form—or he would turn against me and hurt me. All my life I've done nothing, Lenù, but hold back moments like those. (*SLC*, 176–7)

Lila's vision of colors as razor-sharp recalls the synesthesia underlying the sensations associated with *frantumaglia*. But the cutting, penetrating blades Lila pictures align with Ferrante's catalogue of incisions on the female body as inscriptions of male/patriarchal appropriation. Lila sees herself as the one who has to put her brother's oozing viscera inside his body, as if he were one of the sausages she stuffs in Soccavo's salami factory in *Those Who Leave and Those Who Stay* and whose smell reminds her of Stefano beating her during their marriage (*TLTS*, 112). This gesture not only signals the pervasive violence in the *rione* but also positions Lila as the agent to contain it.

The primary engine of *smarginatura* is the struggle between men and women in a patriarchal culture—gender inequality, domestic violence, sexual abuse, psychological torture, and various forms of control and subjugation (de Rogatis 2018, 91). Lila watches as women in the *rione* are erased, physically or psychologically, by a system in which they are objectified and reduced to "an absolute zero" as she puts it (*SNN*, 115). Her episodes of *smarginatura* intensify after she gets married and is raped and beaten by Stefano on their wedding night. After Rino, Stefano becomes the second "disgusting" male body that precipitates Lila's perception of dissolving boundaries:

> [T]he disintegration of Stefano in the passage from fiancé to husband terrified her. I learned only from her notebooks how much her wedding night had scarred her and how she feared the potential distortion of her husband's body, his disfigurement by the internal impulses of desire and rage or, on the contrary, of subtle plans, base acts. Especially at night she was afraid of waking up and finding him formless in the bed, transformed into excrescences that burst out because of too much fluid, the flesh melted and dripping, and with it everything around, the furniture, the entire apartment and she herself, his wife, broken, sucked into that stream polluted by living matter. (*SNN*, 355–6)

This passage charts the parameters of Lila's *smarginatura* and attributes its recurrence to Stefano's transformation from an attentive fiancé to a monster like his father Don Achille, the moneylender and black-market dealer who had terrorized the whole neighborhood in Lila and Elena's childhood. When Stefano rapes her on their wedding night, Lila sees Don Achille emerge from inside her husband's body: "Don Achille was rising from the muck of the neighborhood, feeding on the living matter of his son. The father was cracking his skin, changing his gaze, exploding out of his body" (*SNN*, 41). Notably, Don Achille's cannibalistic and demonic possession of his son's flesh shares the vocabulary of *smarginatura*—cracking the skin, exploding out of the body. The sons become the fathers in a vicious cycle of violence and abuse.[10] As this passage suggests, *smarginatura* has an ethical dimension as well. It designates a lacking moral core, the dominance of evil, "base acts," the prevalence of destructive emotions.

One final example to illustrate the psychic and narrative mechanisms of *smarginatura* as related to a literal, seismic cracking of the earth: during the destructive earthquake of November 23, 1980, Lila is immobilized with horror as the *rione* is literally "crashing and shattering," and the room where Lila and Elena, both pregnant, are sitting, is swaying (*SLC*, 170–1). Elena drags Lila outside, and the two of them take refuge in Enzo's car and watch people and cars go by. There Lila finally reveals to her friend that she has been suffering from *smarginatura* for years and employs the term "dissolving boundaries" to name her condition:

> [S]he wanted me to understand what the dissolution of boundaries meant and how much it frightened her. She was still holding my hand tight, breathing hard.

She said that the outlines of things and people were delicate, that they broke like cotton thread. She whispered that for her it had always been that way, an object lost its edges and poured into another, into a solution of heterogeneous materials, a merging and mixing. She exclaimed that she had always had to struggle to believe that life had firm boundaries, for she had known since she was a child that it was not like that. [. . .] She muttered that she mustn't ever be distracted. (SLC, 175–6)

Lila holds tight Elena's hand as if to draw from it stability and courage to recount the horror of *smarginatura*. This corporeal connection enables the mechanism of Lila's narration in a moment of crisis. It also repeats the childhood gesture that initiated their friendship in another critical situation—holding hands on their way to Don Achille's apartment to claim their dolls. As Elena writes decades later in the opening chapter of *My Brilliant Friend*, "this gesture changed everything between us forever" (*MBF*, 29). This gesture mobilizes both their friendship and Elena's four-volume narrative of it. Their holding hands originates and holds the narrative together, granting it a fixed narrative frame, solid textual boundaries.

Ferrante uses the earthquake as a literalized metaphor for *smarginatura*—the cracking open of the earth that reveals what lies underneath.[11] Elena describes the earthquake as an infinite shattering, "un frantumare infinito" (*Sbp*, 158), so that the verb "frantumare" immediately evokes the word *frantumaglia* as well. Carvalho uses the earthquake as a metaphor to illustrate the universality of Lila's feeling of "dissolving boundaries" to suggest that we all experience and narrate strong emotions through the vocabulary of fragmentation, shattering, or falling apart (Carvalho 2018, 104–5).[12] Lila's *smarginatura* warrants constant vigilance and the suppression of her affectivity. Her refusal to write, her repudiation of her imaginative capacity and hence her capacity to feel intense emotions are informed by reversibility (2018, 103). To keep her sense of reality, to not succumb to the reversibility of boundaries, to not drown in the corporeal "magma" or the neighborhood's "muck," and to evade the mass of "heterogeneous materials" of *frantumaglia*, she must keep a close watch on herself and on others. "Dissolving margins" entails self-control and self-policing—an internal surveillance. Holding Elena's hand grants Lila a stable, solid surface to keep her grounded in reality.

Although *smarginatura* is associated with Lila who articulates its effects, in fact it is Elena who first experiences its symptoms in childhood (Wehling-Giorgi 2017, 8; de Rogatis 2018, 89–90). After the loss of their dolls, Tina and Nu, which they throw into a cellar, Lila tells Elena that Don Achille took them. Elena is affected by Lila's vivid description of the monster Don Achille and recounts what in retrospect can be construed precisely as "dissolving margins": "I was overcome by a kind of tactile dysfunction; sometimes I had the impression that [. . .] solid surfaces turned soft under my fingers or swelled up, leaving empty spaces between their internal mass and the surface skin" (*MBF*, 57). This *smarginatura* expands and modifies the space around Elena who feels "crushed" and "chained" inside the spatial coordinates of her neighborhood: "I felt that the space, too, had changed. It seemed to be chained between two dark poles [. . .] which in my imagination obliquely crossed the apartments, the streets, the countryside, the tunnel, the railroad tracks, and compressed them. I felt squeezed in that vise" (*MBF*, 57). The traumas of inhabiting the violent and oppressive patriarchal *rione* are experienced as spatial and corporeal constrictions. *Smarginatura* is itself a spatial metaphor—the removal of edges, the cutting off of margins. In Elena's narration, topography itself becomes deformed through violence and horror and hence the source of traumatic encounters. The *rione* is figured as a literal and symbolic labyrinth, the site of punishment and entrapment (Milkova 2017). Elena's *smarginatura* is both tactile and spatial, morphing the surface and layout of her environment.

The experience of "dissolving margins" can be approached not only through the logic of reversibility and affectivity but also in terms of its traumatic spatiality and corporeality. The experience lived by Lila and Elena aligns with the symptoms of agoraphobia as a reaction to the physical and symbolic restrictions imposed on women in a traditional patriarchal spatial hierarchy and within a geographical imagination which privileges the male subject. That is, Lila and Elena are subjected to the socio-spatial traumas of a violent and restrictive patriarchal space. As feminist geographers have shown, women's constricted sense of spatiality originates in their heightened awareness of embodiment, associated with an awareness of being the object of the male gaze that creates and strengthens the notion that space is not their own (Bondi and Davidson 2004). That is why, women "rarely claim or control space but instead are caught and confined by it" (Bondi and Davidson 2004). Feminist analyses of agoraphobia and the gendered experience of urban space can illuminate Lila and Elena's visceral response to the masculinist spatial power structure of the *rione* within the logic of Ferrante's text. As a spatial experience lived by Ferrante's female characters, *smarginatura* can be understood in relation to the traumas inflicted by their negotiations of hostile, violent urban spaces.[13]

A fear of open and/or social spaces, agoraphobia is characterized by panic attacks—overwhelming horror, trembling or shaking, nausea, dizziness, feelings of unreality or depersonalization (being detached from oneself), and terror of losing control or dying. It can be seen as an extreme example of the restricted, excluded spatiality underlying women's lives in the masculinist cityscapes and public spaces of Ferrante's Naples and Turin that Chapter 5 examines. The panic attacks constitute "boundary crises" in which subjects cease to sense themselves as separately and securely bounded from the external world and which therefore fundamentally unsettle their sense of self and ontological security (Davidson 2003, 14; Bondi and Davidson 2004, 21–2). As Davidson writes, this panic "entails a horrendous sense of dissolution of self into one's environs and a simultaneous feeling of invasion by one's surrounds" (2003, 14). Davidson's description of the etiology of agoraphobia strikingly resembles that of Lila's and Elena's *smarginatura*: the two share the overwhelming horror, the dissolution of boundaries, the sense of unreality and depersonalization, the fear of losing control. They are reactions generated by the traumas inflicted by negotiating gendered space and place in a patriarchal society. Bondi and Davidson (2004) propose that the "boundary crisis" and "disorderly spatiality" of agoraphobia relate to what Gillian Rose (1993, 151) conceptualizes as women's "paradoxical space"—that is, their position as both trapped and excluded, the paradox of occupying simultaneously the center and the margin.

Lila's and Elena's visceral response to male domination within the social and spatial landscape of their neighborhood arises from their traumatic situatedness inside a paradoxical space of exclusion and imprisonment. Women in Ferrante's Neapolitan periphery are restricted to the home as housewives (where they are often beaten or otherwise mistreated) or to the husband's shop where they become unpaid laborers (and are often abused or insulted). *Smarginatura* can be understood as a kind of agoraphobia—a terror of a traumatic masculinist urban topography that colonizes and fractures female identity. At the same time, agoraphobia with its incitement of strong emotions and disorientation, can be a productive, transformative, and liberating experience (Bondi and Davidson 2004, 22). We see this constructive effect on both Lila and Elena. In her mature age, Lila conducts extensive research on the history of Naples's topography, with its public squares, streets, and monuments, digging up ancient knowledge and unearthing the city's stratigraphy of recurring violence. Elena embarks on her four-volume narrative in order to counteract her own sense of disorientation and loss, and to give shape to Lila who has disappeared without a trace, engulfed by the "magma" underneath the surface of things. Writing the Neapolitan Novels is the creative result of women's suffering, of the paradoxical space of *frantumaglia* and *smarginatura*. They fight against the disorderly and traumatic spatiality of agoraphobia by ordering and structuring it into narratives of the masculinist space that triggered it in the first place. As Emanuela Caffè has shown, trauma and creativity in the Neapolitan Novels fuel each other so that fear and pain give rise to writing (2021).

When in the aftermath of the earthquake Lila struggles to depict the terror of *smarginatura*, she emphasizes its effects through a spatial image: "the terror remains, it's always in the crack [*nello spiraglio*] between one normal thing and the other" (*SLC*, 178). *Spiraglio* is a fissure or crack; in the context of the earthquake Lila and Elena have just witnessed it refers also to the earth's shattering. This scene is Lila's only verbal eruption in which she seeks to describe to her friend the experience and meaning of *smarginatura* and reveal its lasting traces even in the spaces between things. If "dissolving margins" is the destabilizing explosion of the irrational unconscious as the effect of overwhelming emotional states (Carvalho 2018), it can also be located in the interstices or "cracks" of reality, in what Monica Seger calls "interstitial landscape" or "the unaccounted for in-between" (2015, 4). In other words, it is an internal and external phenomenon that captures women's marginalized corporeal and psychical lives.

The "Mothers" of *Smarginatura*

Before Elena and Lila grapple with *smarginatura* in the tetralogy, the protagonists of Elena Ferrante's first three novels experience its causes and effects as the ineluctable, inextricable components of *frantumaglia*, as moments of breakdown, incision, fracturing, and penetration. Another semantic layer of "smarginatura" derives from the scientific vocabulary of botany where it names a light incision made into the organ of a plant. *Smarginatura* as breaking into the surface of solid objects belongs to

Ferrante's category of "incision" images explored in this chapter. Before she develops fully her notion of *smarginatura* in the Neapolitan Novels, Ferrante unfolds a textual map of *frantumaglia* interspersed with symptoms of *smarginatura* in her first three novels. And she provides a framework for combating, if not eliminating, the vortex or whirlpool that sucks women in. She constructs a system to counteract "the anguish of death" and contain "the jumble of fragments," to stabilize the effects of *smarginatura* and rechannel them into a creative outlet. The rise of *smarginatura* from the depths of *frantumaglia* can be traced to its literary "mothers" Delia, Olga, and Leda, the protagonists of Ferrante's first three novels.

In Ferrante's description *frantumaglia* stems from a woman's suffering. It produces irrational behavior and manifests itself in spatial and chronological disorder, blurring the line between inside and outside, past and present, self and other. It accompanies the female protagonists' liminal states—pregnancy and parturition, for example—or emerges in times of crisis such as death, loss, or abandonment. It triggers strong feelings of disgust toward the female body, especially when the body's integrity is compromised through pregnancy or motherhood. In Western thought, the affect of disgust establishes and regulates normative social, ethical, emotional, and physical behaviors by imposing boundaries and enforcing what the German sociologist Norbert Elias has called "the threshold of repugnance" (2000, 51). Disgust entrenches taboos, limits contamination, and contributes to a culture's cohesiveness, thus ensuring and regulating socializing and civilizing processes (Walton 2004, 91) and representing the dominant, prescriptive voice of society (Wilson 2002, 56). Disgust, then, is the psychosomatic reaction most closely related to *frantumaglia* and *smarginatura*, for it signals the dissolution of established bodily habits or social norms in relation to feminine experience.

In the crucial scene of Lila's narrating her *smarginatura* to Elena immediately after the earthquake, struggling to explain it and express what it means to her, both she and her friend are pregnant. In her first three novels Ferrante explores the pregnant woman's or the mother's identity, scrutinizing its origins and probing its limits, anatomizing its mechanisms at times of crisis. When reduced to mere reproduction, pregnancy relegates the female body to a primitive state, converting it into a formless mass of humors nourishing a formless creature that threatens to rupture the mother's body. Ferrante exposes the ravaged maternal body and its animal nature, to rid it of its luminous "Mother of God" aura: "it is essential to describe the dark side of the pregnant body" (*Fr*, 221). During her first pregnancy, Lila fears that she would spill out: "Her stomach seemed a bubble of flesh that was expanding because of the baby's breathing. She was afraid of that expansion, she feared that the thing she was most afraid of would happen: she would break apart, overflow" (*SNN*, 372). And after the earthquake she tells Elena "this thing in my belly is a responsibility that cuts me, scratches me" (*SNN*, 178). In *The Lost Daughter* Leda's pregnancy is figured as an injection into her flesh, "repellent, like an insect's poison injected into a vein" (*LD*, 33). And in *The Days of Abandonment* Olga experiences her maternal, lactating body as cannibalized: "I was like a lump of food that my children chewed without stopping; a cud made of living material that continually amalgamated and softened its living substance to allow two greedy bloodsuckers to nourish themselves" (*DA*, 91–2).

The corporeal demands on the maternal body approximate the language of both *frantumaglia* and *smarginatura*, rendering the female body liminal and porous, slippery and ambiguous. It is devoured by the patriarchal exigencies of procreation, and hence disgusting in its inability to withstand physical invasion and symbolic consumption by its offspring. Ferrante debunks the narrative of pregnancy and motherhood as "always good and grandiose" (Alfano 2015, 26). She turns inside out the mother's body and shows it as cannibalized by the life form it creates. She refuses to give the maternal experience a morally and aesthetically gratifying register. By embracing the formless female body, Ferrante not only appropriates male discourses of female corporeality as seeping or disgusting but also constructs a new cultural vocabulary for representing the challenging aspects of pregnancy, parturition, and lactation.

Ferrante conceives of *frantumaglia* as the anguish of the mother who in giving birth must relinquish a part of her body, and as the anguish of the daughter who must reconcile herself to always being a fragment, a severed part, of the maternal body:

> [F]eeling literally in pieces could be traced back to that sort of original fragmentation that is bringing into the world–coming into the world. I mean feeling oneself a mother at the price of getting rid of a living fragment of one's own body; I mean feeling oneself a daughter as a fragment of a whole and incomparable body. (*Fr*, 224)

Ferrante's rewriting of motherhood as physical and psychical fragmentation, as *frantumaglia*, encompasses the mothers, the daughters, and the daughters' daughters, its span is generational and cyclical. The literal or symbolic death of the mother, or of a mother figure, then can be experienced by the daughter as her own annihilation. The psychosomatic state of *frantumaglia* invades Ferrante's characters through "the anguish of death" produced by the encounter with the mother's corpse, with the suicide of an abandoned woman, or with forms of social, cultural, or intellectual death. In *Troubling Love*, Delia returns to her native Naples after her mother Amalia has drowned. Faced with her mother's corpse, Delia loses her grip on reality but paradoxically regains it by holding onto Amalia's body: "I saw the body, and, faced with that livid object, felt that I had better grab onto it in order not to end up in some unknown place" (*TL*, 14). This "unknown place" (*chissà dove* in Italian) is precisely the space of *frantumaglia*, the unstable psychical-topographic landscape Delia explores throughout the novel. Delia crosses this landscape to reconstruct her mother's last days, excavate her own repressed traumas, and come to terms with her own and her mother's past. This "unknown place" also evokes the cracks of interstices (*spiragli*) where Lila locates her own *smarginatura*. Not to fall inside, Delia must anchor herself in the (fleeting) solidity of her mother's corpse. The mother's body is both the source of *frantumaglia* for Delia *and* its antidote. Only by telling herself her mother's story can she accept her mother's role in her life and affirm her own identity.

Like the slippery terrain of *frantumaglia*, the narrative itself oscillates between past and present. Painful memories and harsh realities coincide so that the text becomes, like Ferrante's image, "a storehouse of time without the orderliness of a history, a story"

(*Fr*, 100). As Delia recollects her mother's life and walks through her mother's city, scenes from forty years prior begin to emerge and populate her field of vision. She walks tirelessly for two days within a spatiotemporal limbo whereby the Naples of her childhood explodes the restrictions she has imposed on her body and memories in order to differentiate herself from her mother. And yet in order for Delia to recall the violence she both endured and witnessed as a child, she must dissolve those restrictions. When she visits her mother's apartment after Amalia's death, Delia is already on the brink of *smarginatura*: "I had trouble keeping myself on the margins" (*TL*, 29). Her affliction manifests itself in her obsessive conjuring up of her mother's ghost as a sketch she keeps drawing and coloring, the past infiltrating the present always at key liminal junctures—underground subway stations, tunnels, and basements, as Chapter 5 shows. Her reconciliation with her mother occurs when Delia, revisiting the site of her mother's death, uses her pen to transform her own photograph into a portrait of Amalia. The novel ends with this image of Amalia-Delia as the incarnation of the mother-daughter's suffering but also as its conquest.

The *frantumaglia*-like fragmentation of Ferrante's narratives and their problematization of linear chronology in the Neapolitan Novels has been analyzed by Tiziana de Rogatis (2018, 109). This fragmentation of time characterizes *all* of her other novels as a key mode of narration which alternates between analepsis and prolepsis, a mode consistent with Ferrante's conceptualization of the achronic landscape of *frantumaglia* (*Fr*, 108–9). The past always seeps into the present in manifold and often visual ways, destabilizing the female subject's spatial coordinates and her ability to orient herself. *The Days of Abandonment*, Ferrante's second novel, likewise dramatizes the failure of linear chronology to capture Olga's psychic disequilibrium after her husband leaves her unexpectedly and her world falls apart. Faced with this loss, Olga, like Delia, loses her grip on reality, but hers is a tactile breakdown: "I had to hold on to something but I could no longer remember what. Nothing was solid, everything was slipping away" (*DA*, 107). Like Delia faced with her mother's corpse, and like Lila's experience of *smarginatura* in the Neapolitan tetralogy, Olga perceives reality as permeable and malleable: "At times the solidity of things is entrusted to irritating elements that appear to disrupt their cohesion" (*DA*, 126).

Olga becomes disoriented inside her own apartment, the site of her maternal and conjugal life dominated by the male imaginary, and the very locus of her suffering: "How inconclusive it was to traverse this known house. All its spaces had been transformed into separate platforms, far away from one another. [. . .] I was pulled here and there, as if in a game, I had a sense of vertigo" (*DA*, 125). Unstable landscapes, irrational actions, vertigo, and loss of control belong to the imaginary of *frantumaglia* and *smarginatura*. Olga's spatial disorientation is an existential one as well. As a dutiful housewife, she has dedicated her life to her husband and children, sacrificing her own time to them, losing herself inside Mario's aspirations and crises (*DA*, 63). When Mario leaves, her carefully constructed identity as mother and wife disintegrates, depleted of meaning and purpose—a social and cultural death of sorts. The more Olga delves into the vicissitudes of her relationship with Mario, the more her marital life appears an intellectual or professional death for her as well—she has sacrificed her own literary career to stay at home. When she stops taking care of the apartment and performing her maternal duties, she gradually erases Mario's stamp on the objects that constitute her domestic life and re-appropriates her own space. To do that she first dismantles the familiar hearth, allows it to be invaded by the outside (ants and a lizard penetrate her fifth-floor apartment), and seduces her downstairs neighbor Carrano. In that way Olga eliminates her home's known dimensions and boundaries, dissolving the solid walls between her apartment and Carrano's, finding a new spatial and psychical equilibrium.[14]

Olga's domestic space is invaded by her past as well, through a ghost who haunts her thoughts and offers an alternative solution to her suffering—suicide. The *poverella* from Piazza Mazzini emerges from Olga's Neapolitan childhood as the abandoned woman who in losing her husband had lost her vitality and had drowned herself in the sea by Capo Miseno. Olga imagines the slippage of past and present in spatial terms:

> I felt, then, that day and the very space of the apartment would be open to so many different times, to a crowd of environments and persons and things and selves who, simultaneously present, would offer real events, dreams, nightmares, to the point of creating a labyrinth so dense that I would never get out of it. (*DA*, 113)

Figured as a labyrinth, *frantumaglia* becomes a spatiotemporal prison and a cacophonous public square where Olga is at once exposed and enclosed, simultaneously "trapped and excluded" (Rose 1993, 150). Moreover, this crowding of interior space threatens Olga's sense of self and ontological security. She is open, invaded, and colonized, no longer in control of her surroundings. Like Lila, Olga realizes her own porousness and combats it by seeking to reestablish her awareness of an objective, material reality. She attempts to exorcise the *poverella*: "I had to anchor myself to things, accept their solidity, believe in their permanence. The woman was present only in my childhood memories" (*DA*, 115). But she nonetheless sinks deeper inside the void of her emptied-out identity, in the abyss of *frantumaglia*.

The *poverella* inhabits Olga's body and mind so that Olga sees her ghost in the mirror: "She was keeping herself alive with my veins, I saw them red, uncovered, wet, pulsing" (*DA*, 126). Olga's porous identity allowing for the *poverella*'s invasion, even possession, of her body, grants her the ability to penetrate the corporeal surface and expose the flesh underneath. This moment of somatic breakdown anticipates Lila's *smarginatura* when she sees people's corporeal borders shatter, revealing their insides. Olga exercises similar vision when faced with Mario's lover and blinded by anger. In her murderous rage she attacks Mario and leaves him bleeding, but what she really wants to do is to strip Carla, his lover, of her "garment of flesh" and expose her real appearance: "an ugly skull stained with living blood, a skeleton that had just been skinned. Because what is the face, what, finally, is the skin over the flesh, a cover, a disguise, rouge for the insupportable horror of our living nature" (*DA*, 72). Olga's gaze performs an act of *smarginatura* triggered by her husband's symbolic violence which she has channeled into physical violence against him. Although her rage is directed at Carla, she sees not Mario, but the other woman as "skinned," both dead and alive, like the image of the *poverella* in the mirror. Olga's intense suffering, her feeling of loss, her "anguish of death," her constant fluctuation between awareness and disorientation, her irrational actions, and her conversations with the *poverella*'s ghost, give bodily and narrative form to *frantumaglia* and *smarginatura*.

The specter of *frantumaglia* haunts Elena Ferrante's first two novels. It surges from the cracks and interstices of her characters' painstakingly soldered lives and often elicits a sense of *smarginatura* without yet articulating its mechanisms. The word "frantumaglia" itself, however, appears only in her third novel, *The Lost Daughter*, named by the protagonist Leda as a diagnosis, recognized and acknowledged by her young friend Nina, the mother of the little girl Elena. *Frantumaglia* emerges to label the shared experience of two women, both of them mothers, and both of them struggling with their maternal roles. It is the fracturing of a woman's identity when she questions her assigned roles, the shattering that breaks her apart when she dares to desire something for herself outside of the normative patriarchal cage. It is a shared fatigue from performing according to accepted standards. Like for Olga who exclaims "I was tired, tired, tired" (*DA*, 98) before she urinates and defecates in the park at the culmination of her identity crisis, both Leda and Nina, at different times, confess their gut-wrenching, devastating exhaustion from sacrificing themselves to their children (*LD*, 62, 102). This exhaustion expresses the "anguish of death" that persecutes Ferrante's protagonists with its attendant disgust. It appears as the relinquishing of bodily fluids as the body transforms into "a leather sack leaking air and liquids." Leda's mother from whom Leda has inherited the word and malaise of *frantumaglia* had died from it. Leda recalls the farewell words of her mother: "The last thing she said to me, some time before she died, in a fractured dialect, I feel a little cold, Leda, and I'm shitting my pants" (*LD*, 79). This scatological moment links, textually and corporeally, Olga to Leda's mother, as Chapter 3 discusses in more depth.

Leda is herself afflicted by this dissolution of bodily boundaries during the time of crisis the novel narrates. Like Ferrante's two preceding novels, *The Lost Daughter* unfolds as a narrative of the past that transpires in bursts and flashbacks that perforate the present. But this third novel features a more complex narrative frame. It opens in the present as Leda, afflicted with a mysterious wound has a minor car accident and ends up in the hospital.[15] The novel narrates the events leading up to the accident—the story that Leda must tell herself in order to understand an enigmatic and disturbing gesture that caused her to interrupt her vacation. But that narration of the recent past is interspersed with recollections, vivid memories, and long digressions that recount Leda's more distant past—her life as a young wife and mother who desperately tries to juggle motherhood and graduate studies.

The narrative proper begins when Leda, a professor of English literature in Florence, reflects on a recent change in her life. Her now adult daughters, Bianca and Marta, have left their mother's home and moved to Canada to live with their father. Absolved of her maternal responsibilities, Leda decides to celebrate her independence by taking a vacation in a beach town in Southern Italy. But she unravels at the compelling sight of a Neapolitan mother and her daughter on the beach, a model of parenting perfection. And she begins to recollect her own problematic motherhood, recounting to herself her failures, shifting between the present of narration and her painful past. These maternal breakdowns turn out to be moments of resistance to her enslavement within the house as a mother and wife, moments of physical and psychological exhaustion. Leda's maternal fiascos, we learn over the course of the novel, result from her inability to accept an oppressive patriarchal culture which excludes her from the world of her career-minded and often absent husband and obstructs her from pursuing her own professional ambitions.

Her summer vacation begins with an experience of *smarginatura*. In her rented apartment she finds a tray of appetizing fruit. On second glance, the fruit turns out to be rotten. Leda takes a knife and cuts out large black areas trying to salvage the edible parts, but disgusted, she throws it in the garbage (*LD*, 12–13). The rotting fruit recalls the body's mortality, its own violable boundaries, and hence disgust toward the ultimate violation of boundaries—death. Soon after, Leda observes that in this unknown place "everything is undefined, every object is easily exaggerated" (*LD*, 13), noticing a blurring of lines. The Italian "ogni cosa passa facilmente il segno" (*Lfo*, 11) in fact suggests that every single thing easily crosses a sign or line of demarcation. This blurring of borders is confirmed two sentences later when Leda tries to fall asleep in her rented apartment and feels her body lacks firm outlines: "I had no contours" (*LD* 13). Leda's *smarginatura*, her ability to see the permeable nature of objects and people, and feel her own porousness, presages Lila's life-long struggle to stabilize the contours of things.

Leda's fear of dissolving boundaries finds its incarnation in a scene which blurs the lines between Nina, the perfect mother, her daughter Elena (called Lenù by her relatives), and the doll Nani. Mother and daughter are playing with the doll: "Now they gave her words in turn, now together, superimposing the adult's fake-child voice and the child's fake-adult voice" (*LD*, 21). This envoicing of the doll with a double feminine speech, the instability of the mother's and the daughter's own voices, roles, and functions, causes Leda both repulsion and "unbearable pain" (*LD*, 21). Faced with these indeterminate boundaries and with her own excruciating experience as a mother, Leda steals the doll, pulverizing the mother-and-daughter equilibrium as well as her own: "I felt very unhappy. I had a sense of dissolving (dissolvimento), as if I, an orderly pile of dust, had been blown about by the wind all day and now was suspended in the air without a shape" (*LD*, 76).[16] She employs the vocabulary of *frantumaglia* here and elsewhere when she depicts a "sensation of flaking layers" (*LD*, 32) or "racing thoughts and whirling images" (*LD*, 41) sucking her into the vortex of her memories.[17] The doll clearly informs the role Lila and Elena's dolls play in the Neapolitan Novels. And the doll becomes the protagonist, literally envoiced and endowed with multiple words, of *The Beach at Night* which recounts the doll's story after being abandoned on the beach.

Just like the *poverella* emerges from Olga's childhood as the embodiment of an archaic femininity and a symptom of *frantumagllia*, Nina and Elena remind Leda of her own resented Neapolitan origins. Nina, an uneducated young woman who married at nineteen and speaks in dialect, stands in sharp contrast to Leda, a sophisticated university professor who teaches literature and speaks standard

Italian and English. Nina and Elena have materialized from inside the "black well" (*pozzo nero*) of Leda's ancestors' past: "I felt them as my time, my own swampy (acquitrinosa) life, which occasionally I still slipped into" (*LD*, 78; *Lfo*, 92). Leda's word choice almost reiterates the lexical features of *frantumaglia* as "aquatic mass of debris that appears to the I, brutally, as its true and unique self" (*Fr*, 100) and signals Leda's own slippage inside its unstable landscape. This unstable landscape finds yet another visual and material expression in *The Lost Daughter*. During the town fair Leda catalogues the inanimate objects, disparate and unrelated, held together only by the congested city-labyrinth:

> The square [. . .] the streets [. . .] were a labyrinth [labirinto] of stalls, while the traffic on the edge of town was choked as if it were a city [metropoli]. I mingled with a crowd of mainly women who were rummaging through a huge variety of goods—dresses, jackets, coats, raincoats, hats, scarves, trinkets, household objects of every kind, real or fake antiques, plants, cheeses and salumis, vegetables, fruit, crude marine paintings, miraculous bottles from herbalists. I like fairs, especially the stalls that sell old clothes and the ones with modern antiques. I buy everything, old dresses, shirts, pants, earrings, pins, knickknacks. I stopped to dig among the jumble, a crystal paperweight, an old iron, opera glasses, a metal sea horse, a Neapolitan coffee pot. I was examining a hatpin with a shiny point, dangerously long and sharp, and a beautiful handle of black amber, when my cell phone rang. (*LD*, 100; *Lfo*, 120)

The square, bustling with activity and people, can be read as the ἀγορά, the *agora*—the ancient Greek public square, the center of political assemblies and the marketplace. In fact, the verb "ἀγοράζω" derives from *agora* and means to be in the market, to wander around the market, and to buy goods from the marketplace (Liddell and Scott 1999). This is precisely what Leda does: she wanders around the market, she contemplates the merchandise, confesses her consumer compulsions, and she eventually buys as well. The *agora* is of course the open public space which causes anxiety and panic attacks, which occasions a "border crisis" akin to Lila's and Elena's *smarginatura*. The *agora* then can be approached as the spatial embodiment of *frantumaglia* and *smarginatura*. In fact, Leda's extensive description (ekphrastic in its vivid details) of the fair and its stalls resembles the landscape of *frantumaglia* with its mass of debris and "jumble of fragments" (*Fr*, 99), with its assemblage of dead and living material, with its disorderliness which betokens the lack of history, the lack of narrative.

When Leda's cell phone rings at the end of the long description of the fair, it is Nina calling her. The two of them meet and, standing among the stalls, Leda buys and gives Nina the hatpin with a dangerously sharp point. Leda, a compromised wife and mother, arms Nina, another compromised wife and mother, with an instrument to pierce or penetrate. This is a transaction between women who are both tired of being mothers and desire to reclaim their autonomy. It is here too that Leda tells Nina about her cultural crime as a mother. When her daughters were little, she left them for three years while she pursued a successful academic career abroad. This confession occasions the explicit naming of *frantumaglia* as what has plagued generations of women:

> [Nina] made a gesture to indicate a vertigo but also a feeling of nausea.
> "The turmoil [lo scombussolamento]"
> I remembered my mother and said:
> "My mother used another word, she called it a shattering [frantumaglia]"
> She recognized the feeling in the word, and her expression was that of a frightened girl. "It's true, your heart shatters [ti si frantuma il cuore]: you can't bear staying together with yourself and you have certain thoughts you can't say"
> [...]
> "With my mother it became a sort of sickness. But that was another time. Today you can live perfectly well even if it doesn't pass" (*LD*, 106; *Lfo*, 127)

It is here that Ferrante identifies the slippery, dreadful landscape of maternal turmoil and shattering as both the narrative core of her novel and the shared experience of all her female characters. The hatpin that Leda gives to Nina as a sign of this shared rupturing becomes an instrument of literal rupture when Leda admits she had taken the doll and unwittingly caused the unraveling of Nina's ostensibly perfect motherhood. In an outburst of rage, Nina stabs Leda with the hatpin just above her stomach in a gesture that recalls Ilaria stabbing Olga in *The Days of Abandonment* and anticipates Lila's thrusting a rusted safety pin under her skin in *My Brilliant Friend*. After Nina stabs Leda, the young mother grabs her daughter's doll and leaves Leda the hatpin. This exchange simultaneously forms a corporeal bond between them and severs it, reinstating the cultural rift between the educated, refined university professor and the semiliterate young mother. Nina restitutes the hatpin to Leda along with the mentorship she desired of Leda. In resorting to violence, the young woman falls back inside the "black well" of the mothers, inside the world of the raging or suicidal women of the past.

In diagnosing both Leda and Leda's mother with *frantumaglia*, Ferrante differentiates between the mothers who were overpowered and perhaps died from it and the daughters, modern women of today, who can learn to live with it. As Leda puts it, "I seemed to be falling backward toward my mother, my grandmother, the chain of angry or mute women I came from" (*LD*, 64). But in effect it is Nina who descends into the caves of her ancestors by stabbing Leda in revenge, like a furious Medea. This is precisely the distinction between the "old" mothers immersed within a patriarchal society or an archaic culture and the "modern," emancipated daughters in Ferrante's two preceding novels—between Delia and Amalia, Olga and the *poverella*. Nina, in other words, has not broken the chain of mute, submissive mothers ("la catena di donne mute," *Lfo*, 70) that Leda perceives as her own maternal inheritance.

Ferrante's particular word choice, "the chain of mute women," is a reference to her own matrilineal literary heritage, Sibilla Aleramo's 1906 feminist novel and fictionalized autobiography *Una donna* (*A Woman*).[18] *Una donna* recounts the formation and self-realization of a woman writer as an act of emancipation from the patriarchal chains of motherhood. The narrator, a mother and an aspiring writer, commits what Barbara Spackman has called "the cultural crime of having refused to sacrifice her ambition to her child" (2009, 222). Aleramo defines the problem as that of a "monstrous chain" which traps mothers and daughters in a vicious cycle of self-sacrifice and self-immolation (2011 [1906], 144–5). Ferrante's text evokes Aleramo's once more when Leda states that she must break the chain ("interrompere la catena"; *Lfo*, 138) of events she has activated by stealing the doll and which chains her to her own past as a problematic mother. *The Lost Daughter* thus joins an Italian literary tradition initiated by Aleramo that opposes motherhood to female creativity.[19]

Like Aleramo's unnamed protagonist whose marriage is an imprisonment within the home and a time of "regression, subjugation, and abjection" (Caesar 2014, 11), as a mother and wife Olga endures the loss of selfhood and of her ambitions as a writer. Suicide is the solution the *poverella* suggests to Olga, who also contemplates the fate of the abandoned and destroyed women she knows from literature: Tolstoy's *Anna Karenina* and Simone de Beauvoir's *Woman Destroyed* (*DA*, 20, 106, 183). As Ferrante herself explains in *Frantumaglia*, the *poverella* is also the resurrection of an archaic femininity, that of Dido who kills herself after Aeneas's departure (*Fr*, 105). Even Aleramo's emancipated woman attempts suicide. When equilibrium is finally restored to Olga, she can distance herself from these literary and archaic models of women's suffering and overcome the vortex of *frantumaglia*: "I was no longer like those women, they no longer seemed a whirlpool sucking me in. I realized that I had even buried somewhere the abandoned wife of my Neapolitan childhood, my heart no longer beat in her chest, the veins had broken" (*DA*, 184). Olga manages to appease the raging woman inside her, to open herself to productive affectivity and to exhume her buried creativity. This rejection of destruction as a way out can be seen as Ferrante's discursive expropriation of the trope of "the fallen and falling woman" which haunts her texts, an exorcism of this plot from the field of fiction (Alsop 2014). Ferrante adopts and then subverts this trope, not to reiterate or romanticize this archetype but to resist its influence, to suggest that her characters deserve other and better options.[20] Concurrently Ferrante rewrites the literary model of Aleramo's woman writer by allowing Olga to remain a mother and to resume her career as a writer. Women today, Ferrante suggests, have the tools and capacities to reconcile motherhood and creativity.

Nonetheless, the archaic, mythological model of women betrayed who turn to rage, violence, or suicide resides inside Ferrante's female protagonists. It is an ancient form of *frantumaglia* as a reaction against the male-dominated violent world of myth in which the rape, abduction, and mutilation of women is a divine order. In her essay "La frantumaglia," Ferrante explores this chronological, sociocultural model of femininity as another bond between mothers and daughters—what the daughters inherit from their mothers. That Ferrante ascribes the very *frantumaglia* to her mother's lexicon establishes a linguistic tie to her mother's body and mind, but also to the archaic mothers who inhabit the modern ones (de Rogatis 2018, 103). The archaic mothers in Ferrante's imaginary are the traditional submissive mothers of the past accustomed to a patriarchal culture that silences and oppresses them; they are the archetype of the abandoned and furious woman in Mediterranean mythology—Ariadne, Medea, Dido, and they are also the genealogy of suffering and abandoned "madwomen" traced within Ferrante's own texts—Olga and her symbolic mother, the *poverella* from Piazza Mazzini in *The Days of Abandonment*; Lila and her relative, the crazy widow, Melina in the Neapolitan Novels (de Rogatis 2018). Two other symbolic mother-daughters can be added to this lineage: Elena's lost doll Nani in *The Lost Daughter* and her symbolic mothers Nina, Elena, and Leda; the forgotten doll Celina in *The Beach at Night* and Mati, the girl who plays mother to Celina. This is the origin of Ferrante's mother's word "frantumaglia." And although Ferrante is at first reluctant to acknowledge it, by the end of the essay she reveals the synchronic genealogy of women's suffering she intends to represent through her characters (*Fr*, 107–8).

In the temporal logic of Ferrante's *frantumaglia*, suffering threatens to transform the daughters into replicas of the maternal body or behavior, to hurl them into the dark prison-caves of patriarchal culture. This threat undoes linear chronology so that mythological time overflows into historical time: Olga, Delia, Lila, and Elena oscillate between the past and the present, between the passive and unexamined roles of their mothers and their own modern, active stance of emancipated daughters.[21] *Frantumaglia* and the fragmentation of time in the narrative transpire through the symbolic container of Naples, the liminal city that encloses in itself both the archaic and the modern, the local and the world. It is not just Naples, it is the global metropolis, the cosmopolitan cityscape at large—such as Turin in *The Days of Abandonment* and in the narrative frame of the Neapolitan Novels, or the stifling *agora* of the marketplace in *The Lost Daughter*—that accommodates this layering of female identities and mythological frames of suffering within urban topography.

Throughout her volume *Frantumaglia* Ferrante explains the Greco-Roman mythological and literary origins of her plots and her feminine imaginary, with a focus on abandoned women such as Ariadne, Medea, and Dido. Like Ariadne, Delia walks through the labyrinth of Naples to find traces of her drowned mother (*Fr*, 66). Olga, the *poverella*, and Melina reenact Medea's wrath and Dido's despair when Aeneas abandons her in Virgil's *Aeneid* (*Fr*, 105). Leda in Greek mythology is the mother of Helen of Troy and hence the symbolic mother of Elena, the little girl in *The Lost Daughter* (*Fr*, 218). Ferrante complicates Leda's character by linking it to a variant of the myth found in Book III of Apollodorus's *Library of Greek Mythology* (*Fr*, 206). Apollodorus first recounts the story of Zeus who in the shape of a swan raped Leda and Helen was born as a result (2008, 120). Then he gives another version: Nemesis, transformed into a swan, was raped by Zeus in the guise of a goose. Nemesis laid an egg, which then Leda cared for, and when Helen was hatched, Leda raised the girl as her own daughter (Apollodorus 2008, 120–1). In Ferrante's words, Leda finds herself embroiled in "a complicated, modern question of maternity," so that "this Leda and this Elena, her daughter-non-daughter, gave me the names for the two characters in *The Lost Daughter*" (*Fr*, 205–6). Leda functions as a surrogate mother to Elena and to her doll, but also as the mentor and symbolic mother to Nina who struggles with the demands of motherhood.

Women Who Write

If Leda is the modern, surrogate, symbolic mother of Elena, she is also the progenitor of Elena Greco, the narrator of the Neapolitan Novels. Leda can also be seen as their author, for she writes her characters into existence by recording in her notebook all the names Elena and Nina's relatives use to refer to the mother and daughter: "For a while I didn't know if it was the mother or the daughter who was called Nina, Ninù, Ninè [. . .] The child in reality was called Elena, Lenù; the mother always called her Elena, the relatives Lenù. I don't know why, I wrote those names in my notebook, Elena, Nani, Nena, Leni." (*LD*, 19; see also 89). Elena Greco, called Lenù by all her friends and relatives, is the narrator of the Neapolitan Novels and hence also their creator. Variants or parts of the names Leda writes in her notebooks appear in the tetralogy as well. Lila is in fact Lina to the whole neighborhood; Lila's doll is called Nu, Elena's Tina. Tina is also the name of Lila's daughter who disappears in the fourth volume. The entire narrative is framed through the disappearance and return of the two lost dolls, Tina and Nu. Leda in a sense engenders the characters of the Neapolitan Novels by writing their names down and by telling a story about a child, her doll, and her mother, and about the friendships that spring from her encounter with them. In a chapter in *Frantumaglia* called "Women Who Write," Ferrante underscores the connection between Leda, *The Lost Daughter*, and the genesis of the Neapolitan Novels:

> Those two elements—the dark background of the mother-daughter relationship and a budding friendship that's equally dark—carried me farther and farther into the complicated relationship that forms between women. [. . .] It's no coincidence that when I came to the Neapolitan Quartet I started off again with two dolls and an intense female friendship captured at its beginning. (*Fr*, 275)

The emotional turmoil that plagues Leda and Nina in *The Lost Daughter* then becomes the textual origin of the friendship between Lila and Elena. One novel generates another as the productive, creative result of *frantumaglia*. The dolls in *The Lost Daughter*—Nani, Elena's doll, and Leda's own doll, Mina—travel to the *rione* in the Neapolitan Novels and become the symbolic or literary "mothers" of Tina and Nu. Lila and Elena's quest for the two lost dolls in *My Brilliant Friend* generates the friendship between the two girls and with that, the story of Lila and Elena's friendship beginning with the loss of the dolls in their childhood.

All of Ferrante's protagonists are women who produce narratives in order to dissect their own psyches. They use writing as a form of introspection in times of crisis. Written language provides them with an epistemological grid to harness chaos and the drifting of female subject identity (Ferrara 2016, 130). It counteracts the threat of dissolving boundaries and contains the irrational. Ferrante conceives of her characters as women who need the order of narrative, the grammatical syntax of a sentence, to organize their emotional and psychic flow:

> Delia, Olga, Leda, Elena write, they have written or they are writing. On this I would insist: the four protagonists are imagined not as first but as third persons

who have either left or are leaving a written testimony about their experience. It very often happens that women, in moments of crisis, try to calm ourselves by writing. It's private writing intended to control unease—we write letters, diaries. I always started from this assumption—women who write about themselves in order to understand themselves. (*Fr*, 285)

Leda's writing is a gesture of autonomy against the reign of *frantumaglia* as the imposition of the order of narrative on an otherwise formless and unstable psychic landscape: "Reading, writing have always been my way of soothing myself" (*LD*, 45). Writing is the modern woman's instrument for controlled and conscious self-surveillance which allows her to retain her agency in the face of *frantumaglia* and *smarginatura*. Delia, Olga, and Leda, along with Elena Greco, are all women who write, using the page as a mirror in which they scrutinize their lives and see reflected the anguish of *frantumaglia*. It is not a coincidence that mirrors play an important part in Ferrante's visual poetics.

But before Ferrante's female protagonists reach the stage of what Elizabeth Alsop calls "expressive surveillance" or productive, creative self-analysis, they must undergo "repressive" or disciplinary surveillance (2014, 467–75). The concept of "surveillance" (*sorveglianza*) belongs to Ferrante's critical-theoretical apparatus. In *Frantumaglia*, she elaborates on two kinds of surveillance that women such as Delia and Olga practice:

They are women who practice a conscious surveillance on themselves. Women of the preceding generations were closely watched over by parents, by brothers, by husbands, by the community, but they did not watch over themselves, or, if they did, they did so in imitation of their watchers, like jailers of themselves. Delia and Olga are, rather, the product of a new, yet very ancient sort of surveillance, a surveillance that has to do with the need to expand their lives. (*Fr*, 103)

The mothers of the past practiced a repressive surveillance, imitating the way men watched and controlled them, subjecting themselves to the disciplinary power of the male gaze. Women such as Amalia, the *poverella*, and Leda's mother were defined by the male gaze, their identities constituted in their awareness of being observed. In his seminal analysis of Western art and modes of looking, John Berger summarizes women's internalization of the male gaze: "Women watch themselves being looked at. This determines not only most relations between men and women, but also the relation of women to themselves. The surveyor of woman in herself is male, the surveyed—female. Thus she turns herself into an object—and most particularly, an object of vision, a sight" (1972, 47). This model of "woman as surveyor and surveyed" informs the mothers' self-observation within patriarchal optics.

This model of self-observation is literalized in Charlotte Perkins Gilman's story "The Yellow Wallpaper" (1892) which, as I argue in Chapter 3, is an intertext to Ferrante's figurations of maternal embodied subjectivity. The story's narrator is confined to bedrest at the orders of her physician-husband who treats her for postpartum depression. The narrator, disobeying the imperative to abstain from any intellectual activity, performs productive self-surveillance through writing. By writing, she bypasses the physician-husband's clinical gaze and gives free rein to her creative imagination outside the "surveyor and surveyed" model. Sibilla Aleramo's protagonist in *A Woman* is forced to obey the patriarchal modes of conduct demanded by her husband who is both her rapist and her jailer, and who subjects her to immobilizing "surveillance and containment" (Caesar 2014, 8). After a failed suicide attempt, she eventually turns to writing and the reacquisition of public language to escape the confines of marriage and motherhood and to avoid her mother's fate—silenced and oppressed, her mother is incarcerated in a mental asylum. Tolstoy's Anna Karenina, a woman at once exposed to public scrutiny and shunned by everyone, trapped and excluded, is a writer as well. She has written a novel for children, as her brother Stiva tells Levin shortly before Levin sees Anna's astonishingly life-like portrait and meets Anna herself. Thus, the themes of women's writing and women as objects of the male gaze are interlaced in Tolstoy's novel as well. Anna declines to have her novel published claiming it is unfinished. Instead, Tolstoy finishes the novel of her life with suicide, disallowing her even the prospect of a career as a writer.

Ferrante's narrators are aware of the self-disciplinary mode of surveillance, but they seek to unsettle it. Both *frantumaglia* and *smarginatura* are the effects of internalized repressive surveillance, violence, and objectification. In *Troubling Love*, as a child Delia imitates her father's possessive attitude toward Amalia and occupies the male subject position with its disciplinary gaze. Amalia lives as the perennial object of men's lascivious gazes for which she is brutally punished by her jealous husband-owner. She is also exploited as the model for the father's crude, erotic paintings of a seminude dancing gypsy, her painted body literally circulating in the streets and fairs of Naples. In *The Days of Abandonment,* Olga willingly curates her body to please her husband visually and sexually. She disciplines her language and regulates her mind to fit her role as mother and wife, sacrificing her writing and her ambitions. And in the Neapolitan Novels, Lila's *smarginatura* echoes the men's physical and symbolic violations of the female body, its constant objectification, subjugation, and penetration. *Smarginatura* requires alertness and awareness, a constant watch over oneself, an autonomous female vigilance that eschews the patriarchal gaze.

Both *frantumaglia* and *smarginatura* therefore serve as instruments for effective, affirmative surveillance which allows women to deploy their own gaze. Olga's controlled existence implodes when she remains locked inside her apartment, unable to open the door. She is the embodiment of women's internalized mechanism of disciplinary surveillance, of women as "jailers of themselves," to quote Ferrante's words. It is then that Olga delegates the act of watchfulness to her daughter Ilaria and arms her with the paper cutter as an instrument to keep the mother alert. Ferrante depicts a gaze shared between women, transforming the repressive effects of *frantumaglia* into creative, even if painful—Ilaria does stab Olga—surveillance. Ferrante defines this new kind of feminine watchfulness:

> The female body has learned the need to watch over itself, to take care of its own expansion, its own vigor. [...] I'm very attached to forceful women [donne vigenti]

who practice surveillance on themselves and others in precisely the sense that I'm trying to explain. I like writing about them. I feel that they are heroines of our time. That's how I invented Delia and Olga. (*Fr*, 104–5; *La fr*, 99)

Her revision of the "surveyor and surveyed" model of feminine self-observation mobilizes shared vision and complicity between women, and specifically, between mothers and daughters. She continues with her theory of feminine surveillance:

> Olga, for example, who has exercised over herself a "masculine" surveillance, who has learned self-control, and has trained herself to the prescribed reactions, emerges from the crisis of abandonment only by virtue of the close surveillance of herself that she manages to achieve: to remain vigilant, that is, to recover the desire for wakefulness, to mobilize for this purpose little Ilaria, entrust to her the paper cutter, tell her, if you see me distracted, if you see that I don't hear you, if I don't answer you, prick me—as if to say, hurt me, use your hostile feelings, but remind me of the need to live. (*Fr*, 105)

Even hostility between women, even a violent act such as Ilaria pricking her mother or Nina stabbing Leda with the hatpin, can be a productive form of surveillance inasmuch as it breaks the hegemony of the male gaze and releases women from its colonizing hold, establishing an outlet for expressing feminine suffering.

In Ferrante's novels, women who write are women who practice self-conscious surveillance, transforming their pain, their "frantumaglia tears" (*Fr*, 99) into their own feminine "white ink" (Cixous 1976, 881). Her novels articulate a mode of writing rooted in the experience of *frantumaglia* as a means of combating this very experience. Delia's narrative is chronologically disjointed, slipping between past and present, gushing with bodily fluids (menstrual blood, vaginal discharge), and corporeally unstable. Delia's identity is slippery: it shifts between her own and her mother's. In the final pages of *Troubling Love*, she literally puts on her mother's body by wearing her mother's old suit and by modifying the features on her passport photograph to resemble those of her mother's. In *The Days of Abandonment*, Olga's identify drifts as she loses Mario. Her narrative also drifts, as her calm and lucid tone gives way to obscenities, to lurid descriptions of copulation, to violence imagined and enacted. Her writing too shifts between past and present, while her reality is invaded by the specter of the *poverella*. Female bodily fluids too overflow in this text: Olga's menstrual blood, her visualizations of the bodily fluids of Carla, her husband's lover, and Olga's urine and feces in the park. *The Lost Daughter* brims with "women's corporeal flow," as Elizabeth Grosz calls it (1994, 202), with moments in which women's bodies spill out or are eviscerated in a narrative that like the previous two novels deals as much with the repressed past as with the oppressive present.

The "frantumaglia tears" transformed into writing undo the censoring of both women's voices and bodies. They restore women's corporeal presence, their leakiness, but in a text produced and owned by women. Ferrante's writing protagonists echo Cixous's imperative for women to write so as to "realize the decensored relation of woman to her sexuality," to gain access to "her goods, her pleasures, her organs, her immense bodily territories which have been kept under seal" (1976, 880). Ferrante who is "a passionate reader" of American, French, and Italian feminist thought (*Fr*, 332), seems to assert, along with Cixous, that "it is by writing, from and toward women, and by taking up the challenge of speech which has been governed by the phallus, that women will confirm women in a place other than that which is reserved in and by the symbolic, that is, in a place other than silence" (Cixous 1976, 881). In Ferrante's own statement about women who write, "we know how to think, we know how to tell stories, we know how to write them as well as, if not better than, men" (*Fr*, 334).

By writing, Delia, Olga, Leda, and Elena avail themselves of the power to tell their own story, to appropriate the pen-phallus associated with the myth of literary paternity (Gilbert and Gubar 1979) and to describe—and then perform themselves—the incisions, penetrations, and ruptures symptomatic of male violence against the female body. When Delia returns to the sites of her childhood abuse, she has a vision of herself as a figure from Neapolitan cards—the eight of spades (*l'otto di spade*) or the woman brandishing a sword who advances calmly on foot (*TL*, 107; *Am*, 135). When she decides to regain her autonomous selfhood, Olga has an identical vision: "I am the queen of spades [l'otto di spada], the bee that stings [che punge]," she says (*DA*, 76; *Iga*, 83), referring to the same Neapolitan card depicting a woman with a sword, but also to an insect that punctures the skin (*che punge*). This image recurs on the most excruciating day of her ordeal when Olga envisions Ilaria brandishing the paper cutter as precisely the "lady of the sword [la donna di spade]" (*DA*, 136; *Iga*, 153). Both mother and daughter wrest the pen/sword/paper cutter away from its male proprietors and advance as agents of their own stories.

Unlike Aleramo's woman writer who severs herself from her maternal obligations, Ferrante's women writers wield the pen fully aware of their alleged psychical fragility and moral fallibility, recounting truthfully and brutally their reprehensible actions or their compromised motherhood. In narrating their own foibles, they also take responsibility for their actions, asserting their autonomy outside a male-imposed order. They achieve what Ferrante calls a feminine "I" (*Fr*, 285), a new female subjectivity paradoxically founded upon the archaic models of surveillance yet adapted to fit the corporeal and creative exigencies of modern women. The agent in this process of liberation through writing is *frantumaglia*, which mobilizes women's suffering as storytelling. This process informs Ferrante's own writing: "for me the story truly functions when you have in your head the steady sound of the *frantumaglia* that has prevailed over everything and now is pressing steadily to become a story" (*Fr*, 287). The act of writing is the translation of *frantumaglia* into words and sentences. When *frantumaglia* takes over and spills out onto the page, the pressure is relieved and the story comes to life. The intertwining of writing, *frantumaglia*, and storytelling informs not only Ferrante's creative process but also that of her heroines.

In *Troubling Love*, the daughter narrates the mother's story from inside the vortex of converging past and present and through the traversal of psychical and topographic landscapes. As an artist, Delia recognizes Amalia's art of sewing clothes and creating female bodies out of fabric. In the novel's final scene, the daughter acknowledges her mother's artistic legacy by taking a pen and drawing over her own photograph to turn it into a double portrait of Amalia-Delia, doubly authored by women. She literally wields the pen, thereby undoing a long-standing androcentric monopoly of art and creative work and occupying a subject position outside the optics of the male gaze. Delia's new subjectivity as both surveyor and surveyed allows her to overcome the whirlpool of contradictory emotions and slippery chronology, and inaugurate a female legacy, a shared female gaze between creative women (Milkova 2016a).

In the Neapolitan Novels it is this reciprocal gaze, this shared surveillance, that Lila perceives as the antidote to *smarginatura*, as her anchor in a crumbling reality. After one of Lila's most crushing episodes of dissolving margins, when she is working at the Soccavo salami factory and enduring abuse, molestation, and atrocious work conditions, she tells Elena: "Watch me until I fall asleep. Watch me always, even when you leave Naples. That way I'll know that you see me and I'm at peace" (*TLTS*, 178). In Lila's brutal world where women are reduced to objects of male desire and violence (or "cannon fodder," *Fr*, 222), Elena's observation has the power to stabilize her friend's body and psyche, to give her form and keep her whole. And since in Lila's experience of *smarginatura* the distinction between subject and object is mixed up or reversed (Ferrara 2017, 53–5), Elena's perception of Lila's corporeal form as impermeable in fact gives it the status of a solid object. The gaze shared between the two friends is the optical equivalent to the tight grip of their hands.

Elena's bespectacled gaze, her feminine surveillance of herself and of Lila, can be traced back to their childhood when Lila holds the power of seeing. As an adolescent, Elena invents a metaphor that attributes the power of seeing to her friend: "The need for glasses intensified my mania for finding a pattern that, in good as in evil, would bind my fate and hers: I was blind, she a falcon" (*MBF*, 257). In Elena's imagination—and certainly in her narrative—Lila is the visionary, the seer, the one who in *The Story of a New Name* portrays herself as an all-seeing eye. This reciprocal attribution of vision expands Ferrante's notion of surveillance and renders it collaborative, creative, and mutually constitutive. Lila needs Elena to anchor her in a stable, solid world, whereas Elena needs Lila as inspiration to experience and narrate that world.

Elena writes the text we are reading, the Neapolitan Novels, to give her friend stable margins and fix her existence in a narrative form: "I who have written for months and months and months to give her a form whose boundaries won't dissolve, and defeat her, and calm her, and so in turn calm myself" (*SLC*, 466). Elena's writing materializes the gaze Lila attributes to her and enacts a prolonged literary surveillance of her friend's life, a decades-long holding of hands. At the same time Elena's narrative is also four volumes of self-observation and self-analysis. Thus, the tetralogy employs affirmative, creative feminine surveillance as an instrument to harness the destructive potential of *smarginatura* and construct a doubly powerful, authorial feminine "I" founded on a double and mutually constitutive female gaze.

Ferrante's emphasis on vision recalls another image of eyesight as (feminine) knowledge—the spectacles Eugenia puts on in Anna Maria Ortese's short story "A pair of eyeglasses" ("Un paio di occhiali"). For the myopic Eugenia, the ability to see clearly her surroundings arrives at the cost of perceiving the squalor and degradation of her Neapolitan neighborhood. Ferrante admits (*Fr*, 64, 370) the formative influence of Ortese's *Neapolitan Chronicles* (*Il mare non bagna Napoli*, 1953) where "A Pair of Eyeglasses" was first published, and hence the shared optical metaphor is likely not a coincidence. Ortese's story concludes with Eugenia's disorientation and collapse—doubled up, she vomits—in a scene that aligns vision, knowledge, and the female body. Interestingly, Mario Martone's film adaptation of *Troubling Love* (*L'amore molesto*, 1995) elaborates on this visual metaphor but in reverse. The bespectacled Delia is able to acknowledge her past only once her glasses have been broken and she approaches the *rione* without their delimiting and falsifying frame. Ferrante develops the trope of Eugenia's eyeglasses so that Elena's glasses lead to the articulation of a shared female gaze. Lila and Elena become each other's "eyeglasses" and together they train a more penetrating eye on their grim and violent Neapolitan reality. What is more, Lila's episodes of *smarginatura* are visual experiences—she sees the boundaries of people and things dissolve. *Smarginatura* then implies and entails a female view of reality.

In tracing the history of her mother's word "frantumaglia" and then Lila's episodes of *smarginatura*, Ferrante creates a lexicon for expressing the anxieties and plights of lived feminine experience. In *The Lost Daughter*, Leda comments on a quote she and her daughters used ("una nostra frase complice," *Lfo* 106; "our private phrase," *LD*, 89) as a code word to express discomfort or dislike. This phrase, Leda explains, was part of their "family lexicon" (*LD*, 89; "lessico familiare," *Lfo*, 106). *Lessico famigliare* is the title of Natalia Ginzburg's perhaps most famous work—her autobiographical novel *Family Lexicon* (1963), which chronicles the life of her family in the first half of the twentieth century through their private lore of idiosyncratic sayings, references, and code words. Ginzburg's family lexicon constitutes a form of resistance to the horrors of fascism and anti-Semitism in Italy, a creative and humorous approach to a bleak reality. The father's authoritative voice frames the novel, as his words open and close the text, but the narrative ends with the father quoting his wife's stories—the words of Natalia's mother. In *The Lost Daughter*, Ferrante invokes Ginzburg's book to propose a specifically feminine vocabulary passed on from mother to daughter(s) while also paying homage to her own matrilineal literary heritage. Or, as Irigaray postulates, mothers and daughters should "invent words and expressions to designate realities they feel and share but for which they lack language" (1993a, 48).

3

Binding and Unbinding the Maternal Body and Voice

It's also important for mothers and daughters to find or make objects they can exchange between themselves so that they can be defined as female I/you.
(Irigaray 1993a, 48)

In a 2015 interview with Elena Ferrante, the Belgian journalist Ruth Joos asks, "Do you know that some readers feel an aversion to what you write about women, about mothers and daughters, and about their relationships, while others have the sensation that you know them profoundly?" Elena Ferrante's response is unapologetic: "A book should push the reader to confront himself and the world. Then it can end up on a shelf or in the trash" (*Fr*, 325). Both the question and the response relate to Ferrante's feminine imaginary that hinges on the nexus between aversion, mothers, and daughters. The question pries open Ferrante's literary concerns with the psychic and corporeal reality of women across geographic boundaries as they struggle with their biological and sociocultural roles. She does that by dissecting the maternal body and granting it a mind and a voice, restoring to the mother her nuanced, un-simplified, non-idealized identity. Or, as she puts it, "The roles of daughters and mothers are central to my books; sometimes I think I haven't written about anything else" (*Fr*, 251).

The mother's voice has long been marginalized if not erased altogether in Western cultural discourses and artistic representations. The maternal figure has occupied the restrictive Madonna/whore dichotomy underwritten by the tenets of Christian ideology, reduced to a reproductive function and enclosed within the domestic space of the house. The maternal body has been conceived as constitutively unstable, troubling, and disruptive. Its copious bodily fluids and its mutability have provoked fear and fascination, thereby engendering the disciplinary discourse of its threatening formlessness and its unclean, uncontainable leakages. The maternal discourse—the articulation of the mother's subjectivity—has likewise been lacking in the Western literary tradition. The mother's story has been submerged in traditional conceptions of family, femininity, and the maternal (Hirsch 1989). When a novel's plot centers around unconventional motherhood, the daughter's perspective takes over and frames it as a negative model (Hirsch 1989). Even in recent novels structured by the mother/daughter plot, the daughter still focalizes and controls the mother's story.[1] On the other hand, recent memoirs by established women writers address openly the challenges of motherhood and authorship, reflecting on the tangled history of feminine creativity and intellectual work. Theirs is the perspective of female authors who seek to maintain their already successful careers despite the cage of pregnancy and motherhood.

In *Black Milk*, her 2011 memoir about postpartum depression, the Turkish writer Elif Shafak explores the incompatibility of writing and motherhood.[2] Shafak's book title modifies Hélène Cixous's feminist directive that women "write in white ink" (1976, 881), that they draw on their bodily fluids and physiological processes to recount their uniquely feminine experience. Shafak employs the metaphorics of women's bodily fluids to juxtapose motherhood and intellectual, creative work. She uses her own writing as evidence of the commensurability of authorship and motherhood, stating that "this book was written with black milk and white ink—a cocktail of storytelling, motherhood, wanderlust, and depression, distilled for several months at room temperature" (2011, xii). She appropriates the discourse of female liquidity in the service of writing. Her memoir of postpartum depression gives voice to a new maternal subjectivity grounded in female corporeality—a maternal subjectivity already at work in Elena Ferrante's novels.

In her memoir *A Life's Work: On Becoming a Mother* (2001), the British novelist Rachel Cusk defines motherhood as "a compound fenced off from the rest of the world" (2). In a review of Elena Ferrante's Neapolitan Novels in *The New York Times*, Cusk summarizes the protagonists' predicaments as "the struggles of the female artist or intellectual with her biological and social destiny as a woman; and, perhaps most strikingly, with motherhood as it is lived by that woman" (2015). Ferrante's novels help fill in a gaping abyss in the Western maternal imaginary, wresting the narrative of motherhood away from dominant patriarchal discourses. They reclaim women's primacy over the narrative of the maternal as literary truth: "Motherhood seems to me precisely one of those experiences which are ours alone and whose literary truth has yet to be explored" (*Fr*, 347). And unlike Shafak's and Cusk's accounts of successful women writers struggling with their new role, it is precisely the unspeakable ordeals of motherhood that temper Ferrante's characters as writers who write "from the depths of the maternal womb" (*DA*, 127), articulating a veritable maternal discourse.

Ferrante's novels are grounded in an embodied female subjectivity, in the reality of female anatomy with its natural processes and functions as the locus of enunciation, of saying "I." They depict the challenges and mechanisms of control women confront in their daily lives. Ferrante's feminine imaginary maps maternal subjectivity and identity by exploring the coordinates that define the mother's being in the world—desire and disgust, entrapment and containment, laughter and grotesque gestures. This foundation confers to Ferrante's maternal subjects a universally resonant relevance, exposing and battling what Cusk calls "the slide into deeper patriarchy," a sociocultural corrective activated when women aspire to be both mothers and writers (2001, 5). Ferrante's texts work against a powerful maternal imaginary in which womanhood and creativity have been obliterated by motherhood.[3] In the Italian literary context, representations of motherhood were almost invariably focalized through the son's perspective even in narratives by women or else conveyed almost exclusively the daughter's point of view (Benedetti 2007, 4; Sambuco 2012, 6). Until the feminist movements of the 1970s and 1980s there was very little literary and cultural space devoted in Italy to mothers as subjects (Benedetti 2007, 4–6). What has distinguished Ferrante's novels since her first novel came out in 1992 is their doubly inflected female embodied psyche—that of mother and daughter. Although *Troubling Love* recounts the mother's story through the daughter's reconstruction of it, all of Ferrante's subsequent novels prioritize the dual perspective of mothers and daughters. Ferrante's texts envoice a complex maternal subjectivity filtered through the double, cyclical and generational, perspective of a daughter who is the mother of daughters. In other words, the mother of daughters negotiates her maternal identity in relation to her own mother, that is, as the daughter of the mother of daughters. Ferrante's novels problematize an Italian literary and cultural paradigm which has traditionally presented the mother-child relationship either as one of maternal self-sacrifice for the son or as one of renouncing maternal duties in the name of self-fulfillment. Ferrante therefore enters in a conversation with some of the Italian women writers whose works center around the question of maternal identity—Sibilla Aleramo, Elsa Morante, Natalia Ginzburg, and Alba de Cespedes.[4]

Reviews of Ferrante's novels in Anglophone mainstream publications along with now dozens of academic articles in both English and Italian focus on variations of the theme of motherhood.[5] Her texts provide a literary model of unconventional maternity, a model that constitutes the mother as subject. Her female protagonists are often bad mothers, and sometimes dead mothers, they are at once desirable and disgusting. In her figurations of the maternal body and mind Ferrante draws on a range of philosophical approaches without fully subscribing to any of them. She mixes Freud, Melanie Klein, Irigaray, Cixous, Kristeva, Bakhtin, and other literary or theoretical texts to create a layered picture of the experience of motherhood. This chapter examines Ferrante's representations of maternal embodied subjectivity by focusing on five recurring mechanisms crucial to her construction of a universal maternal imaginary. First, the poetics of desire and disgust underlying the mother-daughter relationship. Second, the conflation-inversion of mothers, daughters, and dolls. Third, the mother's containment within physical or symbolic boundaries. Fourth, the trope of the laughing mother whose obscene language and grotesque gestures enact a subversive, liberating performance. And fifth, the image of the dead or moribund mother whose body animates the plots of Ferrante's narratives.

Desire and Disgust for the Mother

The mother's body as the site of simultaneous attachment and detachment already occupies a prominent place in Ferrante's first novel, *Troubling Love*, whose dedication reads "For my mother." The mother as paratext frames this novel which narrates the daughter's gradual reconstitution of the mother's body and story. The novel's opening line—"My mother drowned on the night of May 23rd, my birthday" (*TL*, 11)—transitions seamlessly from the dedication to the mother's death and to the daughter's birthday. As Delia sets out to reconstruct her mother's last days, the maternal corpse animates and drives the plot forward. Her ontological detachment from the mother's body in effect enacts a permanent narrative attachment to it. Toward the end of the book, Delia articulates the significance of re-establishing the corporeal connection between mother and daughter as both the outcome of her search for answers and the rationale for the narrative itself: "Maybe in the end, all that mattered of these two days without respite was the transplanting of the story from one head to the other, like a healthy organ that my mother had given up to me out of affection" (*TL*, 109).

The story Delia refers to is a series of events from the past, a tangle of repressed abuse involving her and her mother Amalia. Returning to Naples after her mother's death, she begins to confront the past and to tell herself the truth about those events. At the funeral, Delia feels relief at her final separation from her mother, but this relief is immediately compensated by the onset of her menstruation, a copious flow that makes her nauseous (*TL*, 15–17). Delia's bodily fluids evoke the leakages of the maternal body, and she recalls scenes of her mother's menstruation: "The flow of blood was heavy. I felt nauseous and slightly dizzy. In the shadows I saw my mother, her legs spread, as she unhooked a safety pin and, as if they were pasted on, removed some bloody linen rags from her sex" (*TL*, 19). The daughter watching her mother change her sanitary napkin not only shocks and disturbs but the shared experience of menstruation also establishes a physical bond between Delia and Amalia that anchors the narrative in the maternal body.[6]

The bleeding maternal body in *Troubling Love* is also a topos of domestic violence. Delia recollects her father beating Amalia for attracting attention on the tram or accepting flowers from Caserta: "I was telling myself about the blood. In the bathroom sink. It dripped from Amalia's nose, thick, without stopping, and first it was red, then, when it touched the water from the tap, faded. It was also on her arm, up to the elbow" (*TL*, 100). Blood becomes a signifier of the mother's subjugation within a patriarchal social order. The farther Delia ventures into her memories, the more Amalia's corporeality emerges as a succession of battered and bleeding body parts. Delia remembers her father striking Amalia and hurling her against the armoire in the bedroom, then pounding her head against the armoire's mirror (*TL*, 113). Blood signals the abuse of the mother's body, her corporeal shattering—a literalization of Ferrante's concept of *frantumaglia* as women's psychic fragmentation as a response to male-inflicted violence. The mutilated, shattered female body recurs in Ferrante's feminine imaginary to problematize traditional notions of femininity and maternity. The Vossi shop painting in *Troubling Love*, Olga's photo collage in *The Days of Abandonment*, the doll disfigured with a pen in *The Lost Daughter*, and Lila's artistic fragmentation of her wedding portrait in *The Story of a New Name*, all attest to the symbolic and physical violation of the female body as "cannon fodder," in Ferrante's words (*Fr*, 222).

Delia recalls details of her mother's body, in turns attractive and repulsive. The mother's finger, pierced by the needle of her sewing machine, constitutes a locus of longing for the child: "For a long time I'd wanted to lick it and suck it, more than her nipples" (*TL*, 64). Delia desires to inflict the same wound on her own finger so as to erase any difference between her body and Amalia's: "Anything in her that had not been conceded to me I wanted to eliminate from her body" (*TL*, 64). The child's fantasy of being identical to Amalia is a desire to return to the pre-symbolic, prelinguistic realm where the maternal body supplies nourishment and sense of completeness and where the subject is still undifferentiated as a physically bounded self. We find this desire in *Frantumaglia* as well where it informs Ferrante's memories of her mother's body. In a passage that reads like a section from *Troubling Love*, the author and her sister watch their mother breastfeed the youngest daughter Gina, and then are allowed a taste: "our mother smiled at us with her dark eyes and let white drops from her breasts drip into our mouths, a warm, sweet taste that stunned us. She had a miraculous and cruel body, our mother, she did wonderful things but granted us only a small taste" (*Fr*, 116).[7] Nursing—the transfer of fluids from the mother's to the daughter's body—constructs the mother's body as an object of desire and consumption. Lactation also literalizes Cixous's "white ink" metaphor by serving as the focus of Delia's and Ferrante's narratives about their mothers.

Delia laments her inability to become one with Amalia, to return to the maternal womb. The separation from the desired maternal body coincides with initiation into language: "Already at that point her voice could say to me only: do this, do that. But I could no longer be part of the cavity that conceived those sounds and decided which ones should sound in the external world and which should remain sounds without sound. This pained me" (*TL*, 74). The awareness of the child's separateness occurs through the awareness of language as the product of the mother's discrete subjectivity. Ferrante narrativizes language as a necessary step in subject formation: to enter the social-patriarchal order (the symbolic order of paternal law), to become a speaking subject, the child must submit to the laws of language. Ferrante seems to align Delia's longing for the mother with Jeanne Lampl de Groot's analysis of the girl's pre-Oedipal desire to possess the mother and eliminate the father (2015 [1928]). Freud developed his essay "Female Sexuality" based on Lampl de Groot's case studies and proposed that for the little girl the father is a "troublesome rival" for the mother's love (Freud 2000 [1931], 22). This "troublesome rival" (*rivale molesto*), as Ferrante explains, inspired the title of her novel (*Fr*, 122). But Ferrante complicates Freud's paradigm by depicting the mother's body as "molesto" as well, for it remains for Delia an unwieldy locus of disgust and desire.[8]

The daughter's attachment to her mother generates a strong identification with Amalia—a psychical process crucial for the events of her childhood and for her identity formation, and hence for the novel's plot and structure. As a child, she plays games with her friend Antonio in which she believes she is Amalia and enacts the games she imagines Amalia plays outside the house with Antonio's father, Caserta: "I played with him only to see if I knew how to play as I imagined Amalia secretly did" (*TL*, 84). Fantasy and reality merge when Delia is sexually abused by Antonio's grandfather. Since Delia believes she is identical to Amalia, she reports the sexual act to her father as if it were her mother who was involved with Caserta. In Delia's attempt to possess her mother, she becomes Amalia and displaces what happens to her onto her mother: "I was I and I was her [. . .] I loved Caserta with the intensity with which I imagined my mother loved him. [. . .] I was identical to her and yet I suffered because of the incompleteness of that identity" (*TL*, 131). This game of superimposition and convergence of identities is what Delia has repressed and what comes to the surface during her two days in Naples.

The impossible desire to reattach herself to her mother ultimately results in Delia's rejection of her mother and the maternal body. Having reported to her father that Amalia had engaged in the illicit sexual act of which Delia herself was the victim, Delia cannot remain both Delia and Amalia. Amalia's compromised identity is seen as a threat to Delia's emerging subjectivity. In Kristeva's logic of abjection, the daughter must sever her relationship with the maternal body, rejecting it as unclean, as something that threatens the subject's own boundaries (1982). This psychic procedure constitutes the primary repression of the maternal body, which is relegated to the realm of the abject and the disgusting (1982). Delia's desire transforms into disgust for her mother and she tries to erase all the traces of her mother in herself: "I had wanted to eliminate every root I had in her, even the deepest: her gestures, the inflections of her voice [. . .] All of it remade, so that I could become me and detach myself from her" (*TL*, 64). Delia's subjectivity is contingent on repressing and renouncing Amalia's. But it amounts to a disavowal. Of Amalia's three daughters Delia most resembles Amalia, so in order to remove her mother from herself she needs to suppress her own identity—that is, disavow her language and sexuality.

The abjection of the mother operates through disgust for the maternal body and for the mother's language—the intimate Neapolitan dialect she associates with Amalia. When after the funeral Delia visits Amalia's apartment, she finds there her mother's threadbare, shapeless undergarments and feels disgust toward the body they evoke (*TL*, 28). The recurring vision of a "red tongue" (*TL*, 31, 35, 77, 78, 83, 132) Delia associates with the abuse she-as-Amalia endured as a child also elicits Delia's strong repugnance for the mother's and her own sexed bodies. Delia's mother tongue, doubled in the phallic red tongue as the sexual organ of abuse (Lombardi 1999, 289), gives to the Neapolitan dialect a register of violence and obscenity. Dialect, for Delia, is tantamount to verbal abuse; but it is also the language of domestic and sexual abuse, of beaten and bleeding female bodies.[9] The Neapolitan dialect speaks and enacts the breaking or the disfigurement of the body, be it the maternal body or Delia's own. This confluence of dialect, aggression, and leaking, shattered bodies is what Delia calls the disgusting, "sticky realism" of the Neapolitan dialect (*TL*, 107).

Delia's attraction/repulsion for the mother's corporeality, her repressed identification with Amalia, and her adoption of the male subject position with respect to Amalia's deviant sexed body, thwart the development of her own sexuality. This oscillation between love and hate for the mother, or to put it in psychoanalytic terms, between the little's girl's negative and positive Oedipus attitude, defines Delia's frigidity. As Lampl de Groot has shown, this unresolved tension can lead to the inability to feel sexual pleasure (2015 [1928]). Delia is unable to experience orgasm because of her body's excessive fluids, "the copious liquids spilling out of me" (*TL*, 91). In a passage overflowing with descriptions of bodily fluids (sweat, saliva, vaginal discharge), Delia describes the "well-known rite" (*TL*, 90) of her blocked sexuality which is a response to Amalia's imagined overabundant sexuality, to her excessively female body. As Zarour Zarzar has argued, discharge in Ferrante's first three novels is related to the "metabolism of grief" (2020, 332), a corporeal processing of trauma and mourning. Because it has to do with her mother's body and language, Delia's blocked sexuality also relates to the "sticky realism" of the Neapolitan dialect. Early on in the novel, Amalia's friend Caserta attacks Delia with a verbal deluge: "I was hit by a stream of obscenities in dialect, a soft river of sound that involved me, my sisters, my mother in a concoction of semen, saliva, feces, urine, in every possible orifice" (*TL*, 19). This is the kind of corporeal and verbal leakiness that Delia associates with Naples by way of its dialect and then displaces onto her own body as an excess of fluids.

In eliminating in herself all traces of her mother, Delia renounces both her sexuality and femininity. She cultivates a masculine appearance, cutting her hair short to distance herself from Amalia's long, thick hair. She adopts masculine behavior as well—she is "strong, lean, quick, and decisive" (*TL*, 37) and during the funeral procession carries her mother's coffin with three men. Despite Delia's elective masculinity, the rust-colored dress her mother had intended to give her for her birthday suddenly confers a more feminine look on her body: "it slid over my tense and muscular thinness and softened it" (*TL*, 59). Incidentally, the color of rust approximates the color of coagulated blood, further underscoring menstruation as the nexus between Delia's birthday and her mother's death, the physiological bond between mothers and daughters. This bond is made visible in Natalia Ginzburg's memoir *Family Lexicon* (1963) where the mother, Lydia, wears a red dress to her mother's funeral (2017, 151). But it turns out it is impossible for Delia to eliminate her mother's traces from her body. Mothers leave material and immaterial vestiges in their daughters: they impregnate them with their legacy. The rhetoric of maternal bodily presence and procreation through the daughter recurs in *Troubling Love* as the substance that binds mothers to daughters—it is Amalia's breast milk, Cixous's "white ink," or Shafak's "black milk."

Over the course of her reconstruction of her mother's last two days, Delia recognizes that Amalia is part of her own body: "I realized with unexpected tenderness that in fact I had Amalia under my skin, like a hot liquid that had been injected into me at some unknown time" (*TL*, 86). This acceptance precipitates a physical transformation in Delia: for the first time in her life she feels beautiful. It is the maternal beauty that emerges in the daughter's face, which she herself admits "had been adapted from Amalia's" (*TL*, 61). The theme of the two identical faces—Delia's and Amalia's—runs throughout the novel as the solution to the daughter's desire and disgust for her mother. At the end of the novel Delia takes out her photo id card, and with a pen draws over her photograph to create an image of Amalia, so that the two look identical. This final convergence of mother and daughter inscribes the daughter's re-attachment to the mother's body. Delia performs this visual reappropriation of the maternal legacy as a conscious choice:

> I drew around my own features my mother's hair. I lengthened the short hair, moving from the ears and making two broad bands that met in a black wave, over the forehead. I sketched a rebel curl over the right eye, barely contained between the hairline and the eyebrow. I looked at myself, smiled at myself. That old-fashioned

hairstyle, popular in the forties but already rare at the end of the fifties, suited me. Amalia had been. I was Amalia. (*TL*, 139)

The mother's death rendered in the past perfect tense ("Amalia had been") allows Delia to reconstitute Amalia's face as her own in the present, to acknowledge her resemblance to her mother while also establishing her own separateness. The daughter looks at herself and smiles at the completeness of her image. Her act establishes the mother as the creative source for Delia's artistic claim of authority over her identity, inaugurating Ferrante's female creative legacy outside the androcentric tradition dominating the representation of the maternal body and subjectivity. It also undoes the violent disfigurement of the maternal body by claiming and employing the phallic tool of male authorship and oppression—the pen.

The pen is Elena Greco's tool for narrating her mother's body in the Neapolitan quartet as well. The daughter's disgust for the maternal body is the overarching motif of the mother-daughter plot line in Ferrante's tetralogy. Elena, the narrator of the tetralogy and an established writer, feels intense repugnance toward her mother's body: "Her body repulsed me, something she probably intuited. [. . .] But you never knew where her right eye was looking. Nor did her right leg work properly—she called it her damaged leg. She limped, and her step agitated me" (*MBF*, 45). Elena's mother appears proleptically in *Troubling Love*, as a fragment of Delia's childhood memories: "I could only recall details from my childhood: a crossed eye, a lame leg" (*TL*, 18). (After all, both Delia and Elena Greco belong to the same sub-proletarian, poverty-stricken and crime-ridden Neapolitan *rione*.) We can trace Ferrante's preoccupation with the disfigured maternal body from *Troubling Love* to the Neapolitan quartet. An illiterate and vulgar housewife, Immacolata represents for Elena everything that imprisons her within her sub-proletarian class (which Maestra Oliviero calls "the plebs") and impedes her social mobility. The daughter aspires to erase from herself the bodily and cultural signs of her lowly origins inherited from her mother. Elena aligns herself with her father and with the phallic signifier in general and rejects her mother. Education, reading and writing, and marrying into an elite Northern Italian family become the means for Elena's emancipation from her mother and from her mother's Neapolitan dialect. Elena's renunciation of the maternal legacy is the renunciation of the maternal word, embodied as dialect, and performed as abjection. To enter the symbolic, to be initiated into the structures of language and patriarchal power, Elena, like Delia, must sever herself from the mother's body and disavow the mother tongue.[10]

Always fearful that her mother's disability will affect her healthy body as well, Elena invents mechanisms to counteract the maternal legacy. And since the maternal body is conceived as lacking both physical and mental vigor, the daughter substitutes it with Lila's prodigious intellectual and linguistic capacities.[11] Lila's body functions as a fetish with which Elena at once conceals the maternal disability and compensates for it. As she states early in the first volume, "I became focused on Lila, who had slender, agile legs [. . .] Something convinced me, then, that if I kept up with her, at her pace, my mother's limp, which entered into my brain and wouldn't come out, would stop threatening me" (*MBF*, 46). While in childhood this fetish takes the form of imitating Lila's games, the adult Elena fetishizes Lila's writing and models her own style on her friend's. The game that initiates the children's friendship—Lila throwing Elena's doll in the basement and Elena throwing Lila's—provides a model for the girls' relationship. Elena imitates Lila and uses Lila's actions, words, and ideas as both a measure of her own abilities and sources for her creative or journalistic work. This collaborative and competitive relationship defines their lives, and in the narrative frame of the Neapolitan Novels it motivates Elena Greco to begin writing Lila's story despite her friend's prohibition.

The first volume, *My Brilliant Friend*, establishes the narrative frame of the tetralogy and inserts Elena and Lila's story within it. Elena Greco, sixty-six years old and a successful writer living in Turin, finds out that her childhood friend Lila has disappeared without a trace from her home in Naples. She has even cut her own image from photographs and erased every sign of her existence. Her mysterious disappearance propels the narrative when Elena decides to write Lila back into existence, to substitute her physical body with a textual one. The mechanism of fetish formation (Freud 1927)—disavowal and substitution, replacing something lacking to conceal and compensate for its absence—activates the storytelling of Lila and Elena's friendship. As in *Troubling Love*, the narrative springs to life through the animating force of a disappearance, in this case Lila's corporeal erasure. Elena appropriates the power of Lila's words to reconstitute Lila's body and thus to fill the lack left by Lila's self-erasure. Lila's agile body and astute mind—this time as textual corporeality, as discursive life—structure the quartet.

Narrating in chronological order the vicissitudes of their lives, Elena tells the story of her relationship with her mother and her becoming a mother of daughters herself. Reconstructing Lila's role in her life, Elena also discovers the significance of her mother's body and mind. As in *Troubling Love*, Elena's hatred for her mother defines her childhood and adolescence as efforts to escape the maternal flaws. Elena watches with horror her developing adolescent body: "I no longer knew who I was. I began to suspect that I would keep changing, until from me my mother would emerge, lame, with a crossed eye, and no one would love me anymore" (*MBF*, 96). The terrifying maternal image haunts Elena when she is pregnant with her first child and begins to limp like her mother (*TLTS*, 236). This maternal inheritance appears to her as punishment for the original abjection of the maternal body. Unable to breastfeed her daughter, Elena rejects her own body as abject: "What poison had polluted my milk? And the leg? Was it imagination or was the pain returning? My mother's fault? Did she want to punish me because I had been trying all my life not to be like her?" (*TLTS*, 239). Elena's own unwieldy body chains her to a maternal lineage of women chained to motherhood, to use Sibilla Aleramo's phrase. Lila tells Elena that motherhood is a prison: "This life of another [...] when it finally comes out, it takes you prisoner, keeps you on a leash, you're no longer your own master" (*TLTS*, 233). Women like Elena and her mother already trapped within traditional domesticity are therefore doubly contained.

Like Delia in *Troubling Love*, Elena cannot erase the maternal legacy from her body. When she menstruates for the first time, she thinks immediately of her mother punishing her for staining her underpants. She implicitly associates bleeding with motherhood and the disciplining of leaking female bodies (*MBF*, 93). When she finds out she is pregnant, Elena calls her mother as a tacit acknowledgment of their shared maternal role. And although she refines her language and mind, she cannot delete her biological origins. When Elena's social status is elevated to that of her fiancé Pietro Airota, her mother reminds her of the indelible physiological fact of her birth from the repugnant maternal womb: "the young lady thinks she's somebody because she has an education, because she writes books, because she's marrying a professor, but my dear, you came out of this belly and you are made of this substance" (*TLTS*, 47). This corporeal bond as the origins of Elena's identity is made explicit when years later Elena announces to her mother that she is leaving Pietro for Nino Sarratore (*SLC*, 64). A violent scene between the Neapolitan mother and the daughter unfolding in a mixture of Italian and vulgar dialect demonstrates the two women's distance from Pietro's rarefied world and relegates them to what Ferrante calls "the caves" of their archaic, raging female ancestors (*Fr*, 108).[12]

Elena's third pregnancy reestablishes the bond between mother and daughter through the cycle of birth and death inaugurated in *Troubling Love*. Diagnosed with cancer, Immacolata regresses to a child-like state, and Elena takes care of her. In a reversal of mother-daughter roles, Elena keeps her ailing mother alive:

> While my stomach began to swell happily and in it grew a heart different from the one in my breast, I daily observed, with sorrow, my mother's decline. I was moved by her clinging to me in order not to get lost, the way I, a small child, had clung to her hand. The frailer and more frightened she became, the prouder I was of keeping her alive. (*SLC*, 149)

The mother's suffering brings the two closer (*SLC*, 150). The mother begins narrating her life to Elena, sharing stories from her childhood and adolescence, not unlike Elena's own novelistic account of her life in the volumes we are reading (*SLC*, 208). Immacolata tells her daughter about the childhood illness which left her lame and her storytelling transforms her disability into a different ability or what scholar of disability studies Kate Noson has theorized as "superabilità," a play on words that combines the Italian definition of "surmounting" or "overcoming" (superare) with the notion of a superhuman power, or "super-ability" (2014, 2015). Immacolata's "superabilità" is enabled precisely by her lame leg—her disability carries a generative potential for it suggests that Elena's talent for narrative stems from her mother. Then, in a gesture that recurs in Ferrante's novels, the mother displays her leg: "As she spoke she pulled up her dress and showed me the injured leg like the relic of an old battle" (*SLC*, 151). The maternal body is a battleground in a violent and oppressive world. Amalia's beaten, shattered body too belongs to this Neapolitan world. At the same time, Ferrante presents the mother's lame leg as the creative source of storytelling, her moribund body as the narrative thread suturing the mother's and the daughter's lives. In *Troubling Love* Delia observes her dead mother's "extraordinarily youthful" legs (*TL*, 14) and discovers Amalia's female identity concealed by her worn-out underwear and old, remodeled blue suit. These encounters with the dead or dying mother's nudity restore to the maternal body its sexed corporeality and confer to it a new centrality as the *source* of the narrative.

Elena's newborn daughter is named Immacolata after her grandmother. In a reiteration of the birth/death cycle, when the grandmother holds her namesake for the first time, blood starts dripping from under her dress announcing the grandmother's approaching demise (*SLC*, 199). Elena stands vigil over her dying mother whose every gesture carries meaning for the daughter: "When she embraced me before I left, it was as if she meant to slip inside me and stay there, as once I had been inside her. That contact with her body, which had irritated me when she was healthy, I now liked" (*SLC*, 208). The slippage or seepage between mother's and daughter's bodies emerges from the pages of *Troubling Love* when Delia, carrying her mother's casket, feels like the corpse "might slide" inside her body, "between the collarbone and the neck" (*TL*, 17) or when she feels Amalia has been injected under her skin (*TL*, 86). In the Neapolitan Novels, the two maternal bodies, Elena's postpartum and Immacolata's moribund, converge in their shared experience of motherhood. When Immacolata dies with Elena and the baby in the room, Ferrante asserts the twofold survival of the maternal body incarnated in the daughter and in the granddaughter: "the two of us—I and the infant [. . .] were the only living and healthy part of my mother that remained" (*SLC*, 221). After her mother's death, the pain in her hip and the limp return, but Elena decides not to treat them and to preserve these traces of her mother's body and legacy.

Although daughters in Ferrante's world initially reject their mothers with repulsion, they learn to accept them and to value the maternal legacy in the various forms it takes. For Delia the obsession with Amalia begins as a game of identity whereby Amalia is the daughter's double. It culminates in Delia's inability to possess her mother and is sublimated in disgust for the maternal body and its manifestations in the daughter's. This process of repelling or abjecting the mother is the psychic process enabling Delia's subject formation and entrance in the symbolic, the realm of structured language and patriarchal order. Delia, however, in Ferrante's twist on psychoanalysis, recovers and reassembles the maternal body after Amalia's death as an indelible part of her own psyche and physiology. Moreover, she inscribes her image onto the mother's photograph as a metaphorical re-attachment to the maternal body. Delia succeeds in articulating a posthumous maternal discourse by reconstructing and narrating her mother's story. The Neapolitan Novels trace another pattern of subject formation in relation to the mother. Elena rejects her mother's disgusting body along with her vulgar, uncultured Neapolitan dialect. To repel the mother's body is to abject its language and to substitute it with Lila's agile body and mind. The mother's body, however, slowly gestates inside the daughter's. Disgust succumbs to intimate acceptance and appreciation of her mother's crude vitality. But the question remains: If Delia is at first passionately attached to the mother, does Elena harbor a similar initial desire? To answer, we must revisit *My Brilliant Friend* and the dynamics of playing with dolls that frame the entire tetralogy.

Elena's childhood attachment to her mother's body is rerouted through her love for the doll whose clothes her mother had sewn. (The act of sewing links Immacolata to Amalia who is a seamstress.) The two girls, Lila and Elena, are playing with their dolls Tina and Nu. Liminal objects, dolls occupy the border zones between maternal and filial, animate and inanimate, "treasure and trash" (Mazzoni 2012). The dolls, in Ferrante's words, are "stand-ins for women, in all the roles that patriarchy has assigned us" (*Fr*, 125). That is, they are Lila's and Elena's daughters *and* mothers. The unifying element in these roles is the shared unhappiness, the violence women endure in the male-dominated world of the Neapolitan *rione*: "Nu and Tina were not happy. The terrors that we tasted every day were theirs" (*MBF*, 31). Elena's doll Tina is pretty, made of plastic, and wears a blue dress that Immacolata "had made for her in a rare moment of happiness, and she was beautiful" (*MBF*, 30). The doll thus stands for Elena's mother and for a fleeting moment of maternal fulfillment. Moreover, in *The Story of the Lost Child*, Lila names her daughter Tina after her mother. The two dolls then garner symbolic associations as both mothers and daughters. When Lila and Elena exchange their dolls in the opening chapters of *My Brilliant Friend*, Lila throws Tina in the basement and Elena reciprocates by throwing Nu, reciting the formula that determines her dependence not on the mother's body but first on the doll's and then on its substitute, Lila's: "What you do, I do" (*MBF*, 55). The dolls are demoted from treasured possessions to trash.[13]

The relegation of the dolls-mothers to the basement, a locus of desuetude and waste, and Lila and Elena's ensuing quest for the lost dolls invoke Elsa Morante's children's story *Le straordinarie avventure di Caterina* (*Caterina's Extraordinary Adventures*, 1959). Morante's narrative is structured as Caterina's quest for her lost doll Bellissima, a rag doll with eyes, nose, and mouth made of red thread, which Caterina has herself thrown in the garbage bin. The doll is eventually found and reunited with Caterina in "a moving scene" (Morante 2016, 65). Set in a bleak, poverty-stricken postwar reality where the doll stands for the absent and abject mother (Mazzoni 2012, 256), Morante's story comes close to Lila and Elena's childhood world. And the Neapolitan Novels are structured as Lila and Elena's search for their lost dolls: the dolls open and close the tetralogy providing some of its core images and symbolic associations. But unlike Morante's children's book which reflects obliquely on its sociocultural moment, Ferrante tackles head-on the violence, the destitution, and the complex psychological games children play in the *rione*. Dolls, as I argue in the next section of this chapter, constitute a central element in Ferrante's literary and visual imagination.

Elena is devastated at the separation from her discarded doll-mother: "I felt an unbearable sorrow. I was attached to my plastic doll; it was the most precious possession I had" (*MBF*, 54). This detachment from the maternal body is Elena's entrance in the symbolic order through the loss of the doll. To compensate for the lost doll/mother, Elena replaces her with Lila whom she does not want to lose: "I was as if strangled by two agonies, one already happening, the loss of the doll, and one possible, the loss of Lila" (*MBF*, 54).[14] In Ferrante's cultural and literary imaginary the dolls stand for both mothers and daughters, so Lila and Elena are disavowing their double positions as their mothers' daughters and as the pretend mothers to their dolls. Elena substitutes her lost mother with Lila. Ferrante therefore suggests a new model of female identity not contingent on the maternal body but rather on dolls and mimetic desire between women, that is, in relation to another woman. This is what Italian philosopher Adriana

Cavarero calls "relating narratives" (2000; Cavarero and Pinto 2016) and what she identifies as the underlying narrative mechanism of the Neapolitan Novels:

> I underline the fact that *the other woman* is necessary for my story to be told. The meaning of the story consists also in the material operation of narrating the story that comes from *the other woman*. [...] in the four Neapolitan Novels, the narrator is a woman who narrates the life of another woman, narrating at the same time the lives of others and other people's narrations of the other woman. (Cavarero 2020; italics in the original)

The episode with the dolls and the subsequent search for them are crucial for the entire tetralogy. The girls first descend into the dark and terrifying basement—a Ferrantian spatial figure concomitant with the unconscious—and then ascend to the top floor of the building to claim their dolls from the monster-moneylender Don Achille. The expedition to Don Achille does not recover the dolls but it does get them the money to buy a book, Louisa May Alcott's *Little Women*. This book fuels their ambitions to become successful writers and provide for their destitute families. Lila, who is allowed to go only to primary school, abandons her dream to become a writer. Instead, at sixteen she marries Don Achille's son, the grocery owner Stefano, and uses his wealth to support her parents and siblings. Elena perseveres with her ambition. Through enormous self-discipline and sacrifice she graduates from the most prestigious university in Italy, marries into an elite family, and becomes a successful writer. The rejection of the dolls as surrogate, neighborhood-bound mothers enables these very different means of the daughters' emancipation from poverty. Dolls are then also enmeshed in an economy of upward mobility.

Before their pivotal role in the Neapolitan Novels, dolls partake in Ferrante's maternal imaginary in *The Days of Abandonment*, *The Lost Daughter*, and *The Beach at Night*. In these texts mothers and daughters transform into dolls, and conversely, dolls act as both daughters and mothers. These reversible roles are intimately entwined with the slippery, desirable and disgusting maternal body. Dolls occupy a liminal position in our cultural and psychic landscapes as transitional objects facilitating the child's initiation into adulthood and modeling proper gender roles and identities.[15] Animated dolls, puppets, and automatons can open surreptitious paths into the unconscious, bringing to the surface repressed memories. Freud formulated his theory of the uncanny by analyzing a beguiling automaton, Olympia, and the reawakening of repressed impulses the animated doll unleashes in Hoffmann's short story "The Sandman" (Freud 1971 [1919]). All of Ferrante's dolls are in this sense uncanny; they not only bring to the surface forgotten traumas or cultural crimes but also participate in their resolution. The doll links *The Lost Daughter* to *The Beach at Night* and to the four Neapolitan Novels as the trope which reveals the repressed repulsive aspects of motherhood and daughterhood. The doll with its ambiguous maternal and filial status is also the object most closely related to the identity formation and self-expression of Ferrante's female protagonists, and therefore also to the concepts of *frantumaglia* and *smarginatura*.

Conflations and Inversions: Mothers, Daughters, Dolls

As *Troubling Love* demonstrates through Delia's desire-disgust for the mother, to develop a subjectivity and enter the symbolic order of language, which is also the symbolic law of the father, the daughter must sever herself from the mother's body. This act of repulsion (abjection) of the maternal body as disgusting is the primal repression through which a speaking subject first emerges. Like everything repressed, the maternal body continues to return through the incursions of disgust, thereby destabilizing the foundation of the daughter's subjectivity. The mother's corporeality returns and overflows in Ferrante's narratives with its copious bodily discharges. Her texts fixate on the bleeding, defecating, oozing maternal flesh or else on the mother's doll-like corpse as the image of abjection or disgust. In representing, and speaking for/from their own bodies, mothers in Ferrante's novels reclaim their agency and their voices. They undo the ventriloquism performed on the maternal body through centuries of matrophobic and misogynist discursive practices.[16]

It is not only the daughters who are filled with disgust for the maternal body. Mothers too experience their bodies as compromised through pregnancy, parturition, and the physical and cultural demands of motherhood. They struggle with their assigned roles as wives and mothers—roles they experience as restrictive at best and imprisoning at worst. The maternal voice emerges in *The Days of Abandonment* and *The Lost Daughter* through the mother's practice of writing as the "labor of self-analysis" (*DA*, 31), the productive surveillance of her own body, as Chapter 2 has argued. Mothers use writing to pry open and eviscerate their own bodies as constructs of a normative, oppressive social order. Maternal discourse, therefore, hinges on the (self-)dissection of the maternal body, on writing about the "dark side of the pregnant body" which has been erased in favor of "the luminous side, the Mother of God" (*Fr*, 221).

At first, the mothers embrace their "luminous" identity as "the angel in the house." They resort to self-objectification or what Gilbert and Gubar call "killing themselves into art" (1979), as sights displayed for the male proprietary gaze. Their female identity is constituted through a notion of beauty that entails the elimination of any corporeal traces, a practice inherited from their mothers. Olga, the protagonist and narrator of *The Days of Abandonment*, grooms her body obsessively so as not to repel her husband: "I began to feel that [Mario] would be repelled by me. Wash the body, scent it, eliminate all unpleasant traces of physiology [. . .] I thought of beauty as of a constant effort to eliminate corporeality" (*DA*, 97). She evokes the legacy of her own mother who has initiated the daughter into the patriarchal, androcentric logic of the male gaze: "My mother's fault, she had trained me in the obsessive bodily attentions of women" (*DA*, 97). The maternal body with its corporeal leakages must be concealed and neutralized. Its threatening metamorphic ability must be contained within the inanimate perfection of a pretty, mute doll.

Olga's narrative of motherhood emphasizes the shapeless and pliable form of the maternal body. She depicts lactation and breastfeeding as her children's incursions on her flesh: "I was like a lump of food that my children chewed without stopping; a cud made of a living material that continually amalgamated and softened its living substance to allow two greedy bloodsuckers to nourish themselves, leaving on me the odor and taste of their gastric juices" (*DA*, 92). What Olga describes is her own abjection as an unclean, disgusting body that reeks of the maternal: "No matter how much I washed, that stink of motherhood remained" (*DA*, 92). The surrender to the maternal function deprives Olga of voice. She gives up her career as a writer to allow her husband to succeed in his as an engineer and dedicates herself to maintaining a perfectly ordered house and a perfectly groomed body—like a doll's. When Olga's daughter, Ilaria, imitates her mother and puts on heavy makeup, Olga recognizes her daughter's grotesque image as her own (*DA*, 120), as the face of a doll (*DA*, 122).

The mothers are reduced to dolls through a double oppressive mechanism. Trapped within traditional roles as child-bearing wives and child caregivers, they must renounce their intellectual or creative capacities. Imprisoned within objectifying and sexist conceptions of feminine beauty they must censor and clean their abject, disgusting maternal bodies. What Ferrante maps is women enclosed within a psychic and sociocultural patriarchal structure, an archaic labyrinth which contains and punishes them for any transgression (Milkova 2017). Elena's and Lila's dolls too inhabit this labyrinth in their symbolic association with the unhappy mothers. But before Tina and Nu, Ferrante's novels give birth to several other dolls that propel the plot of *The Lost Daughter* and *The Beach at Night* and stand for the mother's and the daughter's bodies.

The narrative of *The Lost Daughter* centers around a pregnant doll which oozes putrid liquids and nurtures a dead worm in its womb. The doll in its permutations as daughter and expectant mother informs the novel's constructions of embodied femininity and maternal corporeality as disgusting. Dolls as projections of women's varied and complex roles in a patriarchal society function also in reverse, as women behaving like mute playthings. At first, dolls in *The Lost Daughter* appear to model proper mother-daughter behavior as objects of delight, play, and gratification. Then the doll's identity becomes slippery, as it shifts between that of mother and daughter. Like Lila's experiences of *smarginatura*, stable veneers slip away and the internal, terrifying and repulsive nature of matter is revealed. Leda, the narrator, is a middle-aged professor of English literature in Florence. Her grown-up daughters have moved to Canada. Liberated from her maternal responsibilities, she rents a small apartment in a beach town in Southern Italy. At the beach Leda becomes fascinated with a young and beautiful Neapolitan mother, Nina, her daughter, Elena, and the daughter's doll. At first, Leda admires the young mother and her effortless and selfless devotion to her daughter. Leda recognizes herself in Nina, but she also recognizes herself in the daughter who plays mother to her doll in a recursive cycle of identifications and superimpositions (Turchetta 2009). Leda observes the mother and daughter obsessively as they both play with the doll, treating her "as if she were alive, a second daughter" (*LD*, 19). The rhetorical structure "as if" animates the doll and bestows to it the status of a second daughter. Leda's voyeurism is motivated by what she perceives as Nina's complete self-effacement for the sake of the daughter and the doll: "On one occasion I saw them playing with the doll. They did it with such pleasure, dressing her, undressing her [. . .] they hugged her to their breast as if to nurse her or fed her baby food of sand" (*LD*, 18). This image revisits the mother breastfeeding her desirous daughters in *Troubling Love*,

The Days of Abandonment, and *Frantumaglia*, but with a difference—both mother and daughter are nursing an inanimate object.

The veneer of perfect motherhood falls apart when Leda hears the mother and daughter attributing a voice to the mute doll: "Now they gave her words in turn, now together superimposing the adult's fake-child voice and the child's fake-adult voice" (*LD*, 21). Motherhood—or its performance as motherliness, to cite Spackman on Aleramo (2009)—seems compromised because it is enacted by both mother and daughter on a mute object animated only by their performance of motherly behavior and ventriloquism. The conflation of mothers, daughters, and dolls undermines the women's identities reducing them to the single body of a mute, inanimate object. This de-animation is confirmed when Elena gets lost on the beach and Leda finds her: "she didn't say she had lost her mother, she said she had lost her doll" (*LD*, 38). De-animation as muteness, dolls as surrogate, voiceless mothers, is one of the central themes in this text, and it appears in diverse permutations. The narrative twist in this mother-daughter-doll scenario is that Leda has quietly taken the doll and carried it away in her bag.

This act comprises the central dramatic event in the novel which unravels Leda's composure and brings to the surface repressed memories of bad mothering. It also provokes the undoing of the Neapolitan mother and daughter. Desperate at the doll's disappearance, Elena cries violently for days, then regresses into silence and pines away after her lost doll. Exasperated by Elena's crying, Nina begins an affair with the lifeguard. Despite the chaos she causes in the Neapolitan family, Leda justifies her stealing of the doll as an act of both motherliness and daughterliness: "I saw her abandoned in the sand, limbs askew, her face half buried, as if she were about to suffocate, and I picked her up. An infantile reaction, nothing special, we never grow up" (*LD*, 41). Leda herself now inhabits at once the mother's position (taking care of the doll) *and* the daughter's—she conflates and reverses the roles of mother and daughter.

The stolen doll triggers memories of Leda's traumatic experiences of motherhood: her mother's threats to leave her daughters like abandoned dolls, and Leda's own fulfillment of her mother's threat. The doll thus brings to light all the abandoned daughters populating Leda's unconscious. We discover that she had left her daughters for three years to pursue an affair with an English professor and thus recuperate both her intellectual life and her femininity. It is the cultural crime of abandoning her children that continues to haunt Leda in the present and to surface by way of the doll. Taking the doll becomes an opportunity for her to repair the painful past. She becomes the doll's surrogate mother, washing it and buying it new clothes, then lovingly placing the doll on her bed.

Soon Leda discovers that her daughter-doll is about to become a mother too: "The doll, impassive, continued to vomit. You've emptied all your slime into the sink, good girl. I parted her lips, with one finger helped her mouth open, ran some water inside her and then shook her hard to wash out the murky cavity of her trunk, her belly, to finally get the baby out that Elena had put inside her" (*LD*, 110). Leda extracts with tweezers the contents of the doll's interior to find a worm that the girl has put inside to imitate a fetus. The scenes in which she eviscerates the pregnant doll comprise the most disturbing moments in the novel. Leda mothers a pregnant doll who is itself a baby impregnated by a girl while attempting to liberate the doll by washing it inside out. This scene posits the pregnant body as porous, slimy, and oozing. The image of the vomiting doll captures perfectly the discourse of maternal corporeality with its permeable boundaries and overflowing bodily fluids. And the doll, the animate-inanimate, living-dead object invokes the image of the dead mother animating Ferrante's plots.[17]

The inanimate body, the corpse, is the locus of abjection and disgust where the body's boundaries dissolve. When asked about the disgusting images in *The Lost Daughter*, Ferrante relates them to the pregnant body: "For Leda everything that refers to our animal nature is repellent. [. . .] Animals frighten us, repulse us, remind us—like pregnancy when suddenly it changes us, bringing us much closer to our animal nature—of the instability of the forms assumed by life" (*Fr*, 221–2). The maternal body as the threshold of nature and culture (Kristeva 1980) motivates the disgusting in the novel. Leda's act of evisceration brings about the figurative evisceration of her disgust toward her procreative and motherly role. To describe her pregnancy, she adopts the vocabulary of infestation, contamination, and putrefaction that she uses to describe the pregnant doll: "My body became a bloody liquid; suspended in it was a mushy sediment inside which grew a violent polyp, so far from anything human that it reduced me, even though it fed and grew, to rotting matter without life" (110). As Luce Irigaray suggests, the mother is the daughter's "feeder" and "food" at the same time (1981, 62). In Leda's vision of pregnancy, the formation of the daughter's being is the loss of the mother's agency. The daughter's identity seeks to find autonomy and subjectivity through a kind of maternal cannibalism. In *The Days of Abandonment* Olga's vision of breastfeeding as "two bloodsuckers" feeding on her flesh, of the maternal body devoured by its offspring, anticipates another of Leda's figurations of her pregnant body as "repellent, like an insect's poison injected into a vein" (*LD*, 33). Olga's maternal body is likewise contagious—she "secretes a poison" (*DA*, 118) and "dispenses spores of illness" (*DA*, 105). In other words, Ferrante's mothers narrate pregnancy and parturition as a threat to their autonomy and identity, a threat that stems from the construction of the maternal body as that of a powerless doll.

Elena Ferrante continues to explore the symbolic functions of dolls by endowing them with an interiority and representing them as speaking subjects. A doll narrates Ferrante's illustrated children's book *The Beach at Night*, published in 2007, the year after *The Lost Daughter* came out in Italy. In an interview from 2005, when asked whether she is working on a new novel, Ferrante responds in her laconic yet meaningful way, "No. I'm only putting in order an old story about children, dolls, beach, and sea" (*Fr*, 187). Ferrante uses the word "bambine"—little girls—to make explicit she is writing about girls and dolls. Her reply encompasses the key plot coordinates of both *The Lost Daughter* and *The Beach at Night*. Both books are set on the beach, they revolve around a lost doll, mother-daughter relationships, and various forms of disgust, bodily fluids, and violence.

The Beach at Night is the story of the doll Celina, abandoned on the beach by the little girl Mati who is also her mother: "Mati and I are also mother and daughter" (*BN*, 12). It's getting dark, Celina is alone and "half buried under the sand" (*BN*,

8). The phrase "half buried under the sand" reiterates Leda's justification for taking the doll Nani in *The Lost Daughter* as an act of motherliness (*LD*, 41). Thus, like the earlier novel, this is a story about a lost doll-daughter and a daughter-mother, about the child's separation from the maternal body and eventual reunion with it. The book is narrated by the doll who takes the reader through her horrifying nocturnal adventures on the beach. The beach is a recurring topos in Ferrante's novels as a site of transformation and identity formation. *Troubling Love* is framed by two beach scenes: it opens with the beach where Amalia drowned and closes with the same beach where Delia's final metamorphosis takes place. *The Lost Daughter* employs the beach to precipitate the undoing of Leda's social, cultural, and psychic landscape. And in the Neapolitan Novels, summers spent at the beach are transformative: Elena loses her virginity on the beach on the night that Lila and Nino Sarratore spend together. The beach, or the beach resort, is one of Foucault's "heterotopias" or counter-sites where all the sites found in a culture are simultaneously "represented, contested, and inverted" (1997). Heterotopias are liminal spaces of otherness that suspend, neutralize, and unsettle the social hierarchies and relationships outside of them. Ferrante's beaches operate through a gendered mechanism of visual, verbal, and physical violence against the female body and identity. On the other hand, they are sites where the unsettling of identities can lead to productive self-recognition and reconstruction.

Children's picture books likewise guide their young readers into culturally acceptable ideas about who they are by privileging the point of view from which they represent the events they describe (Nodelman 2005). That is, picture books place children in subject positions from where they can understand their own individuality or selfhood within the ideological grid prescribed by adults (Nodelman 2005). But pictures, as Moebius has argued, portray the intangible and the unspeakable through iconographic codes and intertextual signs borrowed from different semiotic systems (1986). *The Beach at Night*, illustrated by Mara Cerri who also illustrated the Italian translation of Alcott's *Little Women* (2007), can be examined through the lens of picture book theory as a window into Ferrante's literary and visual imagination. Moreover, Ferrante herself acknowledges the role of Cerri's illustrations in her creative process. In an interview in the art magazine *Frieze* she refers to a print by Cerri that she keeps in the space where she works (*Fr*, 318).

At the same time, a more nuanced reading of Ferrante's children's book ought to consider its literary contexts. *The Beach at Night* can be situated within the genre of doll's autobiography popular in Italy in the late nineteenth century as a response to the political and sociocultural exigencies of the post-Unification state (Myers 2011). Narrated by dolls, these stories had a moral or didactic purpose as they inducted children into accepted values and roles while also responding to pressing contemporary issues such as child abuse, gender equality, and animal rights (Myers 2011, Mazzoni 2012). An exemplary narrative is Contessa Lara's *Il romanzo della bambola* (*The Doll's Story*, 1895) in which the doll Giulia recounts her morbid and violent adventures as she moves between households, children, and social classes. She is abandoned in a dark wardrobe, her foot is chewed by a mouse, her voice box is mutilated so she is deprived of the word she can say— "mamma," and she is abused in ways "akin to rape" at the hands of her multiple "owners" (Myers 2011, 32–3). Myers' reading (2011) of Giulia's memoir as a narrative about child prostitution, domestic abuse, and violence against women lends a useful framework for analyzing Ferrante's children's book, narrated by the doll Celina.

Another intertext of *The Beach at Night* can likely be found in Dare Wright's extremely popular 1957 picture book *The Lonely Doll*. A gifted Canadian-American photographer who never separated from her painter mother Edie, Dare Wright pursued the themes of maternal and filial bonds in her illustrated books, transforming the traumas of her childhood into visual tableaux (Nathan 2004). *The Lonely Doll* uses Dare's carefully staged photographs to tell the story of the doll Edith, named after Dare's mother, who lives alone in a house. Although the house is furnished and equipped for adults, the absence of parents or children is never explained by the book's minimal text. One day two teddy bears arrive and the three become friends and playmates. This scenario is disrupted when Mr. Bear, the older and bigger of the two, goes out and Edith and Little Bear explore the house, dressing up, putting on makeup and jewelry, and writing with lipstick on a sumptuous dressing table mirror. As punishment Mr. Bear spanks Edith while Little Bear is watching in horror, covering his eyes with his paws and peeking at the same time. The corresponding photograph depicts Edith lying on Mr. Bear's lap, her underwear exposed, while he is staring at her buttocks, his arm lifted to hit her.

This spectacle of male violence bespeaks a desire for the authoritative male figures lacking from Dare's life. As Wright's biographer Jean Nathan suggests, the two bears stand for Dare's brother and father whom Edie had abandoned to pursue her career as a painter in Cleveland (2004, 195).[18] At the same time, the doll Edith, who is a double for Dare's mother Edie, is punished for transgressing the unwritten rules of the house. The ambitious Edie was not a particularly affectionate or concerned mother and thus the doll Edith stands also for the lonely daughter Dare who was sent off to boarding school at the age of nine. Edie took interest in her daughter mainly as her model and plaything—to paint her and to try out costumes and dress up (Nathan 2004, 43–54). She gave Dare a very expensive toy—the famous Italian-made Lenci doll—as a substitute for her maternal affection and presence. The Lenci doll became the protagonist of Dare's *The Lonely Doll* and its several sequels. This mid-twentieth-century narrative of male violence and maternal disaffection, of mother-daughter-doll inversions and conflations, rehearses many of the themes and images central to Ferrante's children's book. *The Beach at Night* mobilizes the tools of visual representation and pictorial meaning-making to explore maternal and filial roles from a twenty-first-century perspective.

The cover of *The Beach at Night* already signals a heterotopic space of female otherness—a doll sitting on the sand, positioned in the bottom left corner of the picture. The doll's big blue eyes framed by long black eyelashes stare at the reader while her body faces away, frozen in an awkward pose. The doll is one of several discarded objects—a watering can, a metal cap, a red plastic cap, a yellow star, and several other items cut off by the cover's edges or buried by sand. The book cover unfolds so that the sand literally wraps around the text. The visual weight placed on the doll's body emphasizes her centrality to the text while also signaling her status as a dispensable object, immobile and abandoned in a landscape of debris. Like Lila's and Elena's jettisoned dolls, like Morante's Bellissima, and Contessa Lara's Giulia, Celina participates in an economy of valorization and devaluation.

On the first page Celina introduces Mati, a five-year-old girl "who talks a lot, especially to me. I'm her doll" (*BN*, 7). Celina establishes a natural cause-and-effect logic to Mati's speech and her own status as Mati's doll. Mati's father, who comes to the beach on weekends, like Nina's husband and Elena's father in *The Lost Daughter*, has brought Mati a cat. Mati names the cat Minù. Distracted by playing with her new friend, the little girl forgets her doll on the beach. The accompanying illustration (*BN*, 9) depicts the doll half-submerged in the sand, her arms extended, and one of her blue eyes gazing directly at the reader from the bottom of the page. The doll is as if buried alive, lying by the legs of a truncated male figure that almost tramples her. This image foregrounds, by placing the doll in the foreground, the abuse she will endure in the book. Left on the beach, Celina finds herself surrounded by many other discarded objects. Two of the illustrations that portray the abandoned Celina focus on the landscape of debris in which she is drowning (*BN*, 13, 15). Turned upside down, her legs in the air, the doll lies helpless in the sand amid the beach waste (*BN*, 13). This image with its desolate and haphazard juxtaposition of disparate objects approximates Ferrante's verbal description of *frantumaglia* as "an unstable landscape," an infinite mass of "debris that appears to the I, brutally, as its true and unique self" (*Fr*, 100). The picture captures the doll's symbolic maternal and filial associations, its liminality and instability (as oscillating between dead and alive, animate and inanimate), and its permeability and vulnerability.

The book's magical world where inanimate objects speak and act is ordered by the same gender and power hierarchies that underwrite the world of Ferrante's novels. During the night Celina is hunted by the Mean Beach Attendant and the Big Rake who want to steal the words she knows and sell them at the doll market. Celina resists but finally succumbs to their violence, losing her name and all her words except for one. She is set on fire and then drowns, but she is finally saved by the cat Minù. In this children's book, the daughters-dolls are commodities exchanged between men, their bodies violated, their voices silenced. The scenes in which the Big Rake and the Mean Beach Attendant pry open Celina's mouth and shake her recall Leda's eviscerating the pregnant doll Nani in *The Lost Daughter*:

> "She still has words in her," he says to the Big Rake. Then he asks me: "How many words did your mom put inside you, eh?"
>
> I hide at the back of my throat all the words Mati taught me, the ones we use for our games, and I stay very quiet. (*BN*, 14)

The mother's words are internalized—Celina's language is the mother's tongue. The maternal discourse constitutes both her voice and her body's interior. As in Ferrante's other novels, language is inherited from the mother and forms the daughter's subjectivity. Here the maternal discourse is ventriloquized through the daughter—that is, the daughter literally speaks the mother's words. But the daughter's body is subjected to a physical dissection and symbolic mutilation through the deprivation of language. The Mean Beach Attendant assaults Celina's body with a Hook coming out of his mouth: "The Hook, hanging on a disgusting thread of saliva, drops down until it enters my mouth. I collect all Mati's words and hide them in my chest. Only the Name she gave me stays behind. The Name is very frightened, it calls itself 'Celina'! The Hook hears it and, wham, grabs it and rips if out of me—it really hurts" (BN, 16).

Bodily fluids and sharp, piercing tools figure in Ferrante's imaginary as instruments of male aggression. As in Contessa Lara's *Il romanzo della bambola*, the doll is subjected to various forms of abuse. Celina is raped by the phallic Hook, penetrated by his semen-saliva. Her most valuable possession—her name—is ripped out of her in an image that recurs throughout Ferrante's novels: the objectified, violated female body. The doll's narrative adumbrates many of Ferrante's central themes: the mother tongue and its relation to the daughter's subjectivity and identity; the maternal discourse which inhabits the daughter's body and the daughter speaking with the mother's words; the dolls-daughters and the girls-mothers; gender violence and corporeal mutilation; disgusting bodily fluids and penetrating phallic tools; and the abandoned woman (or doll) left on the beach like the Ariadne Ferrante describes in *Frantumaglia*, as I discuss in Chapter 5. These morbid and nightmarish aspects of the story are highlighted by the illustrations' surrealist aesthetic blending dream-like images, figures and objects out of proportion, and incongruent juxtapositions. The reader/viewer adopts Celina's point of view which is also the point of view of an abused child. The pictures take the reader beyond the power of words—Celina is silenced, after all—and show the intangible ideologies that shape the child's understanding of selfhood.

The disgusting and its parameters permeate *The Beach at Night* as well. Bodily fluids appear as means for violating and subjugating the female body. Not only does the Mean Beach Attendant insert his hook-sharp saliva in Celina's mouth, he also threatens her with a verbal mixture of bodily fluids like the obscenities Caserta hurls at Delia in *Troubling Love*, a "concoction of semen, saliva, feces, urine, in every possible orifice" (TL, 19). The Mean Beach Attendant sings a song to Celina that repeats Caserta's disgusting imagery: "Open your maw / I've shit for your craw / Drink up the pee / Drink it for me / Sh-h-h! Not a word" (BN, 10). This threat is enacted almost immediately when the Beach Attendant's saliva enters Celina's body and inflicts the verbal and physical violence women endure in Ferrante's texts. It is not only the nightmarish male-governed world of the nocturnal beach that violates Celina's body. The beach during the day also assaults Celina and Mati. Celina recollects how she and Mati together would fight against "boys [who] wanted to hit us, kiss us, see our underpants, pee on our feet with their little dickies" (BN, 22). The female body—the daughter-doll's and the girl-mother's—is not spared the onslaught of men's bodily fluids. A silenced and overpowered victim, Celina lies on the sand "as mute as a fish" (BN, 28). The mute doll evokes a scene from *The Lost Daughter* which is perhaps the origins of Celina's story about words—the mother and daughter playing with the mute doll, endowing her with their own voices and in turn, speaking like a doll.

Attacked by the two male figures, Celina is saved first by a fire and then by a wave, only to sink and drown in the sea. Her drowned body is depicted in three consecutive illustrations (*BN*, 27) that stretch out the visual narration of her death. In the first picture, Celina's floating head, surrounded by an "aquatic mass" (*Fr*, 100), stares directly at the reader (*BN*, 27). In the second, her body is floating, her underwear is exposed, and her head is framed by debris and fish (*BN*, 29). In both, Celina is viewed from above, from a perspective that implies both superiority and power. In the third illustration, the doll is depicted from the side, her head unnaturally illuminated and dragged upward by words coming out of her mouth (*BN*, 31). This picture recalls the violence and complicit spectatorship of Dare Wright's staged photographic realism: Mr. Bear spanking the doll Edith propped on his lap, the reader/viewer placed in the position of Little Bear who is watching and not watching. What the text of Ferrante's book tells us is that the Hook has caught Celina again, entered her mouth and extracted the last words left inside her. Cerri's illustrations then display Celina through the Hook's perspective as his penetrating male gaze explores his victim's body, implicating the viewer/reader in this act of violence. Robbing her of her speech, the Hook appropriates Celina's language as her maternal legacy:

> The Hook grabs one and tugs. The other words, terrorized, cling to one another, forming a chain. [. . .] I'm furious. I've lost my Name, but I don't want to lose anything else. With these words Mati and I were happy. With these words she talked and had me talk [. . .] If the Hook attached to the disgusting thread of saliva takes them away from me, I won't remember anything, not even the dear name of Mati. (*BN*, 30)

The chain of words Celina is clinging to becomes an umbilical cord that ties her to the maternal body: "I've barely got time to clamp my mouth around the last remaining word: mamma. With my teeth clenched tight around mamma I go up, up, up" (*BN*, 32). Word and mother coincide as Celina fights to remain attached to the maternal word while the Hook is pulling her up: "I fly through the orange air of Dawn, my teeth clenched around the "MA" of mamma" (*BN*, 34). The "MA" of mamma is also the first syllable of Mati's name. Celina's last word functions as her neonatal cry of (re)birth when the cat Minù saves her from the Hook's grip and pulls her out of the water. The mother's death and the daughter's birth linked by water is another recurring pattern in Ferrante's novels. Amalia drowns on Delia's birthday, Elena gives birth to her daughter shortly before her mother dies, and Celina's explicit drowning ("Affogo," *Lsn*, 26; *BN*, 26) coincides with her rebirth. Her identity is reconstituted through separation from and then recovery of the mother within the space of the beach as heterotopia.

The final illustration depicts a close-up of Mati's face, her features identical to her doll's. Mati is holding the tiny doll in her hands and the cat Minù is reflected in her large blue eyes. The reflection in Mati's eyes staring directly at the reader positions the reader in the place of the cat as Celina's savior. Read through Ferrante's maternal imaginary and alongside *The Lost Daughter*, *The Beach at Night* exposes the sites and sights of ideological indoctrination into the verbo-visual and sociocultural structures of patriarchal power. The reader is invited to join the cat Minù in saving Celina from the Hook's saliva-chain and restoring her bond with her mother. Moreover, when the doll is reunited with Mati, the little girl already knows about her doll's terrifying adventures and her near death: Mati "always knows everything, like a perfect mamma" (*BN*, 38; "è una mamma perfetta," *Lsn*, 38). *The Beach at Night* aligns knowledge, and not self-sacrifice, with perfect motherhood.

The maternal imaginary in Ferrante's subsequent works, her four Neapolitan Novels, revolves around dolls as well—dolls that cross over from *The Lost Daughter* and *The Beach at Night* to the tetralogy. Nani, the little girl's doll in *The Lost Daughter* and Celina, the doll lost on the beach at night, are Tina and Nu's literary mothers. Ferrante underscores the intentionality of the doll's intertextual journey: "It's no coincidence that when I came to the Neapolitan Quartet I started off again with two dolls and an intense female friendship captured at its beginning. It seemed to me that there was something that needed to be articulated again" (*Fr*, 275). Dolls as embodiments of the roles women play in a patriarchal world emblematize the mechanisms of animation and de-animation that women must succumb to as they negotiate those roles. In *The Lost Daughter* Leda recollects how her daughters had treated her as their doll: "So when Bianca was a small child I patiently became her doll [...] I played without joy, my body felt inanimate, without desires" (*LD*, 42-3). Then she recounts that she offered Bianca her own childhood doll as a substitute for herself, a doll she called "Mina" from the diminutive "mammina" (*LD*, 42). On the same page Leda recalls a childish word for doll, "mammuccia," another derivation from "mamma." Bianca disfigures the doll's body by drawing on it with a marker, expressing her frustration with both her mother and the doll (*LD*, 42-4). Leda's daughter likes to play with another toy, "an ugly [brutta] rag doll with stringy yellow yarn hair [di pezza coi capelli che erano fili di lana gialla] her father had brought as a present" (*LD* 43; *Lfo*, 48). Like Mati in *The Beach at Night*, the daughter prefers the father's gift to the mother's establishing in this way an alliance with the paternal/patriarchal position and rejecting the mother. More importantly, Bianca's rag doll is identical to Lila's doll, Tina: "Lila's doll, on the other hand, had a cloth body of a yellowish color [corpo di pezza gialliccia], filled with sawdust, and she seemed to me ugly [brutta] and grimy" (*MBF*, 30; *Ag*, 26), whereas Leda's old doll Mina resembles Elena's doll, Nu (*LD*, 42; *MBF*, 30).

This conflation-inversion of mothers, daughters, and dolls links *The Lost Daughter* to the opening of *My Brilliant Friend* and to Lila's and Elena's dolls. In throwing their dolls in the basement, Lila and Elena disown the maternal doll and along with her, the traditional notions of motherhood and the maternal body. But this gesture originates in *The Lost Daughter*. Leda, the literary mother (precursor) of Elena Greco, throws her own doll Mina from the balcony in order to punish Bianca for marring the doll's body with a pen and preferring the father's gift of the rag doll to the mother's. Then Leda watches with "cruel joy" the cars running over the doll, "mutilating her" (*LD*, 44; "macellandola," *Lfo*, 49). This mutilated doll belongs to Ferrante's vision of women's bodies disfigured by male violence. This is precisely how Lila perceives reality through her experiences of *smarginatura* or dissolving boundaries. Lila who has endured domestic abuse since childhood and is raped and beaten by her husband Stefano associates femininity with violated corporeality. In Lila's psychic world, bodily borders fall apart, inside and outside conflate, and everything is reversible. Her *smarginatura* relates to the reversibility of mothers, daughters, and dolls, to the conflation-inversion of feminine roles outlined in Ferrante's earlier novels.

In the Neapolitan Novels, the two dolls open and close the quartet. When each girl throws the other's doll in the basement in the opening section of *My Brilliant Friend*, each loses an object associated with the maternal and substitutes that object with her friend. Lila becomes Elena's symbolic mother—a mentor and teacher who instructs her in Latin and Greek and molds her writing. At the same time, Elena is intensely jealous of Lila who not only excels in everything she does but also steals Nino Sarratore, the boy Elena has loved since primary school. On the other hand, in the first volume's climactic moment, it is Lila who calls Elena "my brilliant friend" (*MBF*, 312) and tells her she must continue to study— an imperative Elena follows and becomes, over the years, an established feminist writer. Thus, for Lila, Elena is her symbolic mother and mentor.[19] Their roles are reversible within their relationship as each in turn serves as a model for the other.

Tina and Nu, the two dolls lost in the basement, reappear at the end of the last book, *The Story of the Lost Child*, to close the narrative frame. But lest the reader forget the dolls' foundational role, Elena inserts throughout the four volumes reminders of her childhood games with Lila and the girls' expedition to Don Achille's apartment to claim Tina and Nu. Notably, the fourth volume in which Elena and Lila are both pregnant teems with references to the dolls. But Elena remembers their childhood dolls and Lila does not. Memory and the story of the dolls are thus aligned with Elena's recollections and her ability to narrate. When the two women are waiting to see their gynecologist, Elena tells Lila the story of their childhood games in the courtyard where they played "at being mothers" to their dolls (*SLC*, 157) and threw them in the basement. Lila, however, struggles to "recapture the memory" (*SLC*, 157). The reference to the dolls in the context of pregnancy shows that in Elena's mind mothers are linked to dolls. The two friends name their daughters after their mothers—Imma and Tina. Elena is the first to remark that Lila's daughter has the name of Elena's doll, but Lila again struggles to remember (*SLC*, 218–19).

When she is almost four, Lila's daughter disappears without a trace.[20] A decade later, Lila suggests to Elena that Tina had been mistaken for Elena's daughter after the two had appeared together in a magazine photo. Lila supposes that Tina was kidnapped because of Elena's anti-mafia writings (*SLC*, 449–50). Elena then considers the coincidence of naming the lost doll and the lost daughter with the same name: "Lila had given her daughter the name of my beloved doll, the one that, as a child, she herself had thrown into a cellar. It was the first time, I recall, that I fantasized about it, but I couldn't stand it for long, I looked into a dark well with a few glimmers of light and drew back" (*SLC*, 451). Elena refuses to peer into the "dark well" of her childhood and acknowledge the formative influence of the dolls. This "dark well" is the same as the "black well" of Leda's past (*pozzo nero*) that the stolen doll brings to the surface and forces Leda to admit, narrate, and accept her failures as a mother (*LD*, 78). This "dark well" is of course the cellar where Lila throws Tina and where the two girls descend to look for their dolls.

Binding and Unbinding the Maternal Body and Voice

Painful memories are productive experiences for Ferrante's characters who use writing as an incisive tool for self-analysis and affirmative surveillance. Elena transforms the darkness of the cellar into a creative space and writes her most successful work, *A Friendship*, as the story of her and Lila's life-long relationship. She uses the conflation of identities, the lost daughter Tina and the lost doll, to hold the narrative together. Yet she fears she has gone too far in connecting the past to the present:

> I had deliberately [ad arte] exaggerated the moment they disappeared into the darkness of the cellar, I had accentuated the trauma of the loss, and to intensify the emotional effects I had used the fact that one of the dolls and the lost child had the same name. The whole led the reader, step by step [programmaticamente], to connect the childhood loss of the pretend daughters to the adult loss of the real daughter. (*SLC*, 465; *Sbp*, 443-4)

This short book itself works programmatically as a metatextual mise en abyme of the tetralogy, a story within the story that reflects the volume's title, *The Story of the Lost Child*. But the book is also Elena's imposition of logic and order on her friend's life story which defies easy classification and comprehension. Lila had always repeated to Elena that life is messier than literature, and when one day she vanishes altogether, she undoes the orderly narrative of Elena's book and erases the possibility of a logical ending. Nonetheless, Elena uses Lila's disappearance as the creative impetus to reconstitute her missing body as the text of the four Neapolitan Novels: "I loved Lila. I wanted her to last, But I wanted it to be me to make her last. I thought it was my task. I was convinced that she herself, as a girl, had assigned it to me" (*SLC*, 463). The dolls lost in childhood, the lost daughter, and now the lost friend, strengthen the textual ties between Lila and Elena as they motivate and drive the narrative of the Neapolitan Novels.

The narrative frame of the Neapolitan Novels closes with the appearance of the childhood dolls in Elena's mailbox in Turin. In this way the entire tetralogy can be seen as the story of the quest for the dolls—from their disappearance to their return. Tina and Nu have crossed time and space and travelled from the dark cellar in Naples to Elena's apartment in Turin. Elena, however, fails to find a rational explanation of that sudden irruption of the past into the present. She is certain of one thing—that Lila has sent her the dolls and that it is a valediction of sorts: "Unlike stories, real life, when it had passed, inclines towards obscurity [oscurità], not clarity. I thought: now that Lila has let herself be seen so plainly, I must resign myself to not seeing her anymore" (*SLC*, 473). As in her other novels, Ferrante abstains from a neat and orderly conclusion, and her characters do the same.[21] The return of the dolls can be read as Lila's renouncing her role in Elena's creative prowess—she gives back the objects that initiated their friendship. Conversely, it can be read as the final manifestation of Lila's power and control over Elena's narrative, as Lila's cruel genius at "'birthing' the dolls out of the cellar after so many years," as Emma Van Ness suggests (2016, 310). Along the same lines, this final gesture is perhaps meant to remind Elena that she has never really left Naples, that the *rione* is her proper place and she can never escape from her origins. Or it can be read as Lila's conciliatory gesture, a call for forgiveness and a gesture of love (*SLC*, 472), as Elena herself surmises at first. Or even as Lila's way of letting Elena know that she has found Tina, that mother and daughter/doll are reunited. And since the two dolls are associated with the maternal image, the arrival of Tina and Nu in Turin could imply a reclaiming of motherhood, a return of the maternal body. In any case, the exhumation of the dolls from the past completes the cycle of interchangeable mothers-daughters-dolls.

The emergence of the dolls, long dead but suddenly come to life, recalls the final line of *The Lost Daughter* in which Leda exclaims "I'm dead, but I'm fine" (*LD*, 125). The dolls authorize and validate Elena's narrative of the ordeals of the past. As mothers/daughters they have not only survived but also made it from Naples to Turin (something Lila is never able to accomplish), and they stand as the animating force behind all of Elena's writing. The emergence of the dolls also revisits the plot of *The Beach at Night* where the lost doll-daughter literally drowns and is then reanimated to re-establish the corporeal-lexical bond between mothers and daughters. The dynamics of appearance and disappearance, desire and disgust, attachment and detachment, are reinvigorated through a new conceptual paradigm. Mothers must be violated (lost, thrown in the cellar, rejected, repelled, abjected) before they can return and be reincorporated in the daughters' bodies and narratives. And this empowering return necessitates the creative exchange of objects—the dolls. Luce Irigaray, one of the philosophers Ferrante reads, asks how women can get out of the vicious circle of the patriarchal, phallocentric order which privileges the male gender and the mother and son relationship (1993a, 47). Irigaray proposes strategies for the development of positive, productive mother-daughter relationships. One is that mothers and daughters create, share, and exchange objects as a way to acknowledge their femininity and maintain unity (1993a, 48). Dolls in Elena Ferrante's imaginary fulfil precisely that function. If *frantumaglia* supplies both the lexical and psychical bond between mothers and daughters, the doll becomes the material manifestation of that bond.

Enclosing the Maternal Body: Cellars, Locked Apartments, Clothes

The dark cellar of Elena and Lila's childhood is not merely an element of urban architecture and domestic space. Ferrante's novels invest it with multiple meanings and forms. It is the storeroom and the pastry shop cellar in *Troubling Love*, and the locked apartment in *The Days of Abandonment*. It denotes the mother's confinement within the home, and it gestures toward other means of physical or symbolic enclosure. The dark cellar is also the cave of the mothers, the repressive and oppressive collective feminine unconscious Ferrante discusses in her essay "La frantumaglia" (*Fr*, 107–8)—a maternal time-space regulated by traditional, patriarchal notions of motherhood and femininity. Her characters, torn apart by *frantumaglia*, regress to the realm of their raging, murderous, or suicidal female ancestors. Eventually, they emerge by redefining their own identities and reasserting their creative power. In Ferrante's novels, the mother's identity is constructed through the prison-caves of domesticity—storerooms and locked apartments. Inside those prison-caves her body is trapped in shapeless, nondescript clothing. Thus she is doubly caged—by the restrictive norms of domesticity and by clothes that erase her femininity.

The opening chapter of *Troubling Love* introduces the relation between restricted spaces and the mother's body. When Amalia fails to arrive at Delia's apartment, Delia remembers how as a child, unable to bear her mother's absence, she hid in a storeroom (*ripostiglio*) to await Amaila's return: "I closed the door and sat in the silent dark, crying. The little room was an effective antidote. [...] 'When you get back, I'll kill you,' I thought, as if it were she who had left me shut up in there" (*TL*, 12; *Am*, 9). Delia exorcises the pain of the mother's absence by punishing her own body and psyche. Terrified, she cries in the dark while also fantasizing about punishing her mother for venturing outside the house. The storeroom gives narrative space to her fantasy of matricide. This fantasy is at once Delia's abjection of the maternal body as an act of self-differentiation, and a misogynist assertion of the mother's indelible guilt. Like her father, Delia is convinced that Amalia "bore inscribed in her body a natural guilt, independent of her will and of what she really did" (*TL*, 17). In asserting Amalia's guilt, Delia adopts the father's proprietary and disciplinary function: "At home she was modest and reserved, hiding her hair, her colored scarves, her dresses. But, just like my father, I suspected that outside the house she laughed differently, breathed differently, orchestrated the movements of her body in such a way as to make people stare" (*TL*, 84). In an essay called "The Beast in the Storeroom" (*Fr*, 109–21), Ferrante reiterates the fear of the mother's transformation outside the house: "I feared that whenever my mother went out she would betray us, abandon our just path for that of others, and that crime of hers made me detest her" (*Fr*, 120).

Ferrante's essay revisits the storeroom as the site of the daughter's fraught relationship with the mother. She recounts incidents from her childhood in Naples that read like omitted passages from *Troubling Love*. The "little room" of her childhood was "the secret location of a long conflict with my mother," where Ferrante "had a desire to kill and to punish myself for that desire" (*Fr*, 110). The topos of the storeroom is this time imagined as the lair of a terrifying, disgusting beast ready to devour her. Ferrante narrates her first experience of guilt: to punish her youngest sister Gina, she sends her to fetch a rope from the storeroom where the beast is lying in wait. This incident transforms the storeroom into a spatial metaphor for Ferrante's guilt for wishing to kill her sister. But it is also a projection of the guilt the daughter ascribes to her mother and to women in general:

> My mother had the naked guilt of being a source of possible pleasures for others. I believed in that guilt, it was a secret conviction I'd always had; even today it returns in dreams at dawn. As a child I hoped that my father would lock her in the house and not let her go out. (*Fr*, 117)

Like Delia, Ferrante feels a possessive desire for her mother, finding unbearable the mother's absence from the home, and imagining the mother "guilty of confused but repulsive crimes" (*Fr*, 119). And like Delia, Ferrante waits for her mother's return inside the storeroom, crying in the dark, terrified of the beast (*Fr*, 119–20). In Ferrante's imaginary, it is women who frequent the "shadowy storerooms" (*Fr*, 121), enclosed within the prison of their presumed crimes and haunted by the beast-guilt. The dynamics of appearance and disappearance, attachment and detachment, desire and disgust associated with the storeroom delineate the history of women's natural and internalized guilt. As Ferrante concludes, women's innocence derives from their ability to understand feminine guilt as a gender construct and interrogate it: "Today I believe that the degree of our innocence derives not from the absence of guilt but from the capacity to feel true loathing for our daily, recurring, private guilt" (*Fr*, 121).

If the storeroom in *Troubling Love* and "The Beast in the Storeroom" is a figure for women's imprisonment, in *The Days of Abandonment* Olga is literally locked inside her apartment. Her new identity as an abandoned woman and a single mother to her two children unravels both her psyche and the space around her. After Olga's husband Mario leaves her, she struggles to maintain her sense of self founded on Mario's and the children's needs and routines. Olga's voluntary conscription within a patriarchal order with its material tokens and symbolic signs has been invalidated. The apartment in Turin that she has tastefully furnished emblematizes her life and identity as a mother and wife. Or as Elizabeth Grosz reflects on Irigaray's critique of the male construction of women as guardians of their bodies and spaces, of "women as house":

> The containment of women within a dwelling that they did not build, nor was even built *for* them, can only amount to a homelessness within the home itself: it becomes the space of duty, of endless and infinitely repeatable chores that have no social value or recognition, the space of the affirmation and replenishment of others at the expense and erasure of the self, the space of domestic violence and abuse, the space that harms as much as it isolates women. (1995, 122)

Without Mario's domineering presence, the apartment loses its solid shape and becomes disorienting (*DA*, 125). Olga's compromised identity is projected onto the spatial coordinates of her house so that house and self become contiguous in a process typical of Ferrante's spatial poetics: the psyche is spatialized while space or topography is interiorized, as Chapter 5 shows.

When she has a reinforced door installed to protect both her home and her unraveling identity, she again encounters a masculinist conception of space. The two male locksmiths tell her, "Locks become habituated. They have to recognize the hand of their master" (*DA*, 61). And lest the reader miss this assertion of male power over Olga's space and psyche, the novel literalizes the question of mastery as a plot element. A few days later Olga is literally unable to turn the key in the lock, remaining trapped in her apartment for a day, with her son Gianni sick, her daughter Ilaria pricking her with a paper cutter to keep her alert, and the dog Otto dying. Imprisoned within her old identity, Olga must find a way to unlock and articulate her own desires: "The channels of my senses were blocked [I canali dei sensi si erano chiusi] [. . .] What a mistake it had been to entrust the sense of myself to his [Mario's] gratifications, his enthusiasms, to the ever more productive course of his life" (*DA*, 141; *Iga* 156). Olga uses the verb "to close" (*chiudere*) to describe her obstructed agency and the sacrifice of her needs to Mario's professional success.

The locked door stands for Olga's conception of herself as trapped and disempowered within the patriarchal economy of her domestic space. Ferrante literalizes into a plot event Anne Carson's claim that "Putting a door on the female mouth has been an important project of patriarchal culture from antiquity to present day" (1995, 121). When in desperation Olga puts the key in her mouth and tries to turn it (*DA*, 142), the locked door becomes synonymous with her "locked" mouth, her symbolic muteness as a writer who has given up her creative voice. Her attempt to unlock the door with her mouth fails, producing a sensation of facial fragmentation and mutilation. The key is tearing her face "like a can opener," her teeth are falling out, "taking with them the nasal septum, an eyebrow, an eye, and revealing the viscid interior of head and throat" (*DA*, 142). The female body and the face as the locus of identity are ruptured and dismantled as a necessary step in reassembling Olga's new autonomous self from the fragments of her old shattered identity. Relearning to turn the key in the lock is for her "to relearn life" (*DA*, 141) without Mario, to reconstruct her identity and her desires outside the norms established by him.

Ferrante's recurring trope of the female body contained within the cage of patriarchal domesticity is indebted to nineteenth-century ideas of the female body as unstable and prone to hysteria. In particular it evokes late nineteenth-century feminist texts such as Charlotte Perkins Gilman's "The Yellow Wallpaper" (1892), which can be read as an intertext to *The Days of Abandonment*. In "The Yellow Wallpaper," the unnamed narrator is confined to bedrest in an isolated attic room, a former nursery with barred windows, as a cure prescribed by her physician husband for her postpartum depression. As one of the traditional cures for hysteria required (Hanson 2015, 91–2), she is forced to abandon her writing, along with any intellectual or imaginative activity that could stimulate her mind. Trapped within a double construction of creativity and motherhood as debilitating, the narrator projects onto her room a spatialized image of her psyche. Fixated on the room's ornate yellow wallpaper, which seems to be surveying her with "bulbous eyes" (Perkins Gilman 1980, 7, 18), she begins to see a woman imprisoned behind it. Eventually, she steals the key for her room, locks herself in, and rips off the wallpaper, releasing the prisoner.

Ferrante's and Gilman's texts share a number of elements: the first-person "psycho-narration" (Cohn 1978), the imagery of locked spaces and keys, spectral feminine figures, the ordeals and sacrifices of motherhood, the prohibition of writing as an outlet of intellectual and creative thought, and the spatial metaphorics of women's entrapment within the home and within patriarchal discourses and practices. Olga and Gilman's unnamed narrator both lose their grip on reality as they give in to confounded thoughts and irrational behavior. They are both haunted by feminine ghosts—Gilman's narrator by the woman interred behind the wallpaper, and Olga by the long-dead *poverella*. Likewise, their narration conforms to their psychic instability and reflects their inner turmoil through language. Olga's polite lexicon yields to obscenities and vulgar imagery. Gilman's unnamed narrator employs short sentences and paragraphs that escalate in emotional intensity signaled by excessive punctuation (exclamation marks, dashes, italics). Olga sees reflected in the mirror her own yellow face (*DA*, 37), which is also the face of the *poverella* (*DA*, 124). But Olga, the modern woman of today, escapes from "the caves of the mothers," resorting to the means available to her—self-analysis, working, writing, separation, and a new relationship. The narrator of "The Yellow Wallpaper," however, remains caged inside her psyche. She descends into the "caves" of the mad or suicidal mothers of the past, she succumbs to the heritage of the female ancestors that all Ferrante's heroines struggle to defeat.

"The Yellow Wallpaper" concludes with the narrator creeping on the floor, ripping off the wallpaper around the room's perimeter. She is now both the woman behind the wallpaper and the narrator, and she sees many other women inhabiting this enclosed space. When he finally unlocks the door, her husband faints and she creeps over his body (Perkins Gilman 1980, 19). The verb "creep" is repeated seven times on the story's last page to describe the moving female body—confined and restricted to an isolated former nursery, its act of rebellion is to "keep on creeping" (Perkins Gilman 1980, 19). And inasmuch as all of Ferrante's novels address the spatial containment and physical entrapment of the aberrant maternal body, textual traces of "The Yellow Wallpaper" appear in *Troubling Love* as well. Delia remembers Amalia in images that recall the devious, uncontainable maternal body in Gilman's story. When Delia is taken to a hotel room by her childhood friend Antonio, she recalls her mother and Caserta, Antonio's father, creeping inside a dark cellar behind an iron door: "Then they both lay down on the floor on their stomachs and crawled along [strisciavano], laughing [. . .] Caserta and my mother crept along [strisciavano]" (*TL*, 84; *Am*, 105). The verb "strisciare" (to crawl, to creep) is the same verb used in the Italian translation of "The Yellow Wallpaper" to describe the narrator's liberating movement around the room (Perkins Gilman 2011, 62).[22] In Ferrante's novel, the topos of the creeping female body connotes a rebellion against the restrictive norms of the domestic space: Delia imagines Amalia's sexual exploits outside the house as the act of "creeping." The rebellious, uncontainable Amalia, however, crawls in a dark cellar with barred vents, another topos of feminine entrapment. And Delia's memory of Amalia's imagined adultery occurs in a hotel room where she endures Antonio's sexual attentions.[23]

The topos of the storeroom, cellar, or locked domestic space as the cage of the maternal body extends beyond the physical borders of the house and to the mother's clothing as another delimiting frame. Clothes bind the maternal body, concealing and controlling its threatening leakages, and its potentially uncontainable feminine forms. The mothers in Ferrante's novels are seamstresses who dress, undress, and shape the female body. In crafting its outward appearance, they can claim authorial power over the presentation of maternal corporeality. Ferrante's feminine imaginary juxtaposes writing, narrating, and sewing. In *The Days of Abandonment*, Olga discovers the correlation between writing and sewing by listening to the conversations between her seamstress-mother and her workers: "Stories and gossip and sewing: I listened. There, under the table, while I played, I discovered the need to write" (*DA*, 44). And when Olga confronts her own ordeal of compromised identity, she uses writing to cut herself to pieces and assemble her new self (*DA*, 163). To sew clothes and to speak are ways of creating and narrating a woman's identity. In *Frantumaglia*, Ferrante dwells on her mother-seamstress as well, making explicit the link between sewing and narrating. The mother's sewing hand approximates the writing hand: "It was the sewing that cast a spell, much more than cutting. The mobile skill of that hand put together the pieces of material" (*Fr*, 157). All of Ferrante's narrators except the doll in *The Beach of Night* deploy a distinctive rhetorical technique: they put together their fragmentary memories to suture their narratives.[24]

In an essay titled "Mothers' Dressmakers," Ferrante draws on Elsa Morante's novella "The Andalusian Shawl" ("Lo scialle andaluso," 1963) to propose her own theory of maternal clothing in a culture which deems incompatible femininity and motherhood. In this essay, which contains her speech on the occasion of being awarded the 1992 Procida Elsa Morante Prize for *Troubling Love*, Ferrante interprets Morante's text in a way that sheds light on Ferrante's own sartorial poetics. The mother's clothes, dark and shapeless, conceal and hence cancel her femininity, dissolving the contours of her body:

> [S]hapelessness [l'informe] is so powerful in conditioning the word "mother" that sons and daughters, when they think of the body to which the word should refer, cannot give it its proper shapes without revulsion [repulsione]. Not even the mother's dressmaker, who is also a woman, daughter, mother, can do so. She, in fact, out of habit, heedlessly, cuts out clothes for the mother [tagliano addosso alla madre panni] that eliminate the woman, as if the latter were a leprosy of the former. [. . .] Perhaps when Elsa Morante spoke of mothers and their dressmakers she was also speaking about the need to find the mother's true clothes and tear up the habits that weigh on the word "mother." (*Fr*, 18–19; *La fr*, 15)

The formless maternal body is in effect *smarginato*—its unstable boundaries require regulation. The woman under the mother's clothes is construed as both disgusting and disfigured by sickness. The discursive construction of the maternal body as deviant and in need of enclosure echoes Gilman's representation of the caged hysterical mother in "The Yellow Wallpaper." But Ferrante's primary reference is to Morante's "The Andalusian Shawl" in which the mother's exotic theatrical costumes indicate not only her career as a dancer at the Opera but also her lack of a properly shapeless maternal body. The mother, Giuditta, abandons her son to pursue her career and years later, when she fails as a dancer, she finally becomes a traditional self-sacrificing mother trapped in the house and dressed in dark-colored rags (Morante 2015, 184). In Morante's novel *Arturo's Island,* even Arturo's young stepmother is "bundled up" (*infagottata*) in "shapeless clothes" (*abiti informi*; Morante 2014, 75). In evoking Morante and the mothers' formless clothing, Ferrante clearly situates her own writing in a tradition of Italian literary representations of motherhood and the maternal body. In fact, she sets out to reconceive the role of the "mothers' dressmakers" in redressing the "error of the Shapeless" (*Fr*, 19).

Ferrante exposes the complicity of the seamstress—another victim of the reign of shapelessness—in perpetuating the double containment of the maternal body. To do so, she analyzes the meaning of the idiomatic expression "to cut out clothes on" (*tagliare i panni addosso*), which in Italian means to gossip or to bad-mouth. This phrase captures the twofold role of seamstresses to eliminate *and* recover the maternal body:

> If the mother's dressmaker learned to cut out her clothes and expose her, or if she cut the clothes in such a way as to recover the woman's body that the mother has, that she had, in clothing her the dressmaker would undress her, and her body, her age, would no longer be a mystery with no importance. (*Fr*, 19)

Ferrante exculpates the seamstress by envisioning for her a role in revealing the mother's corporeality, in exposing her real age and physiology. For Ferrante, cutting shapes with fabric and creating stories are modes of narrating the female body, of restoring its form and granting it both visibility and agency. The stories that the mothers' dressmakers tell are often about violated, abused women, or about women imprisoned within their clothing. In casting seamstresses as her female characters and as her own mother, Ferrante sets out to both represent and remedy this erasure of the mother's body. In the first place, maternal bodies are regulated by a patriarchal imaginary which delimits and deforms them.

In *Frantumaglia*, Ferrante recounts the rituals of her mother's work as a seamstress—from the moment of choosing fabric to measuring and cutting, and then to sewing and displaying the garment for her mother's client (*Fr*, 154). Mother and daughter have the potential to create objects together through a set of shared practices. But this ritual also reveals to the daughter the symbolic mutilation of the female body under the dress: "I [. . .] looked under the dress. There was the naked body of a woman, with the legs cut off, the hands cut off, the head cut off" (*Fr*, 154–5). This image captures the violence women endure, the psychic and physical fragmentation they experience and express creatively through the words *frantumaglia* (fragmentation) and *smarginatura* (dissolving boundaries).[25] Ferrante repeats this image to correlate women's suffering, clothing, and male violence. When her mother's client Signora Caldaro leaves, Ferrante describes her dress: "I stroked it—scarred, pricked by the pins, because of the words of suffering, because of their malevolent touch—the body of a woman worn out by her troubles, without a head, without legs, without arms and hands" (*Fr*, 156). Clothes take on the shape and meaning of the woman's deformed, oppressed body, and conversely, women's words of suffering transform the clothes into tortured, violated bodies. An awareness of this correlation is passed on from the mother-seamstress to her daughter.

Ferrante's theory of maternal clothing is elaborated through the character of Amalia, Delia's seamstress-mother in *Troubling Love*. In the novel's first chapter, Amalia is found drowned, naked save for a luxurious lace bra exposing her nipples (*TL*, 15). Thus, from the start the novel poses the question of dressing the (dead) maternal body. Like the young suicidal mother in Natalia Ginzburg's story "The Mother" ("La madre," 1948) who is buried wearing a red dress and looking like a "tiny dead doll" (*piccola bambola morta*; 1993, 405), Amalia's corpse emerges as unsettling and improper but singularly feminine. Ferrante unpacks, as it were, the opaque maternal subjectivity of Ginzburg's character by narrating Amalia's story. Delia remembers that as an attractive woman, Amalia was subjected to the disciplinary male imaginary all her life, forced to wear shabby clothes and hide her body (*TL*, 28).[26] Even the fabric of her dress amplified her innate guilt: her husband would slap Amalia on the crowded tram or funicular to punish her "for having felt in the fabric of her dress, on her skin, the warmth of that other body" (*TL*, 54). The mother's clothes not only erase her corporeality but also stifle and imprison her vitality. In fact, borrowing an image from Alba de Cespedes' novel *The Best of Husbands* (*Dalla parte di lei*, 1949) in which another unhappy mother commits suicide, Ferrante envisions the mother's neutral-colored dresses as dead women (*Fr*, 164–5). In *Troubling Love*, she uses this image but endows it with a new significance—clothes animate the mother's and the daughter's bodies. Ferrante enlists the skills of the mother and daughter who both shape bodies, Amalia as a seamstress, Delia as a comic strip artist. Like the seamstress from "Mothers' Dressmakers," Amalia restores to female bodies their proper form and measure: "For all the days of her life she had reduced the uneasiness of bodies to paper and fabric, and perhaps it had become a habit, and so, out of habit, she tacitly rethought what was out of proportion, giving it proper measure" (*TL*, 103). Delia, on the other hand, can evoke and color artfully and at will the figures from her past and thus tell their stories—her narrative strategy in *Troubling Love*. Ferrante corroborates the nexus between sewing and storytelling in an interview in the magazine *Frieze*. When she is asked, "What could you imagine doing if you didn't do what you do?" she responds "Being a dressmaker [La sarta]" (*Fr*, 319, *La fr*, 309).

Sewing, like writing, can be liberating for Ferrante's mothers. It reinvents a woman's story by recreating her body. In *Frantumaglia*, Ferrante describes her own seamstress-mother and her momentary respite from the "unbearable anguish" of domesticity: "she dreamed of salvific clothes, and drawing needle and thread straight she sewed together again and again the pieces of her fabrics. That was the time of her true beauty" (*Fr*, 168). In *Troubling Love*, Amalia possesses the same ability to imagine and invent "salvific clothes," and she passes it on to Delia. The blue suit she has worn all her life, molding it to suit the changing fashion, is emblematic of her capacity to resist the male imaginary and to reinvent the maternal body. As Delia reconstructs her mother's story, she also collects the clothing her mother has left for her as the symbolic and material maternal legacy. First, she puts on a piece of her mother's shabby, shapeless underwear (*TL*, 28). Next, she wears the expensive clothes her mother had procured for her as birthday gifts—a rust-colored dress, a white satin robe that Amalia had herself worn before she drowned, and, finally, a blue dress (*TL*, 59; 87; 127–8).[27] This exchange of clothes can be read through Irigaray's paradigm of mothers and daughters creating and exchanging objects to articulate their shared femininity. Wearing her mother's gifts Delia gives a new form to the maternal body and gains a new understanding of her mother's creativity: "I liked that woman who in some way had completely invented her story, playing on her own with empty fabrics" (*TL*, 103). Clothes are, as Sambuco argues, "a means of communication" between mother and daughter (2012, 146).

To recuperate Amalia's body and identity and make them last, Delia must inhabit the mother's old blue suit, the garment that most fully embodies her "art of making clothes last forever" (*TL*, 76). When Delia descends into the dark cellar of the pastry shop and thus into the recesses of her memory, she not only uncovers the truth about her sexual abuse by the old Caserta but also finds the blue suit synonymous with the abused maternal body (*TL*, 125). In a kind of imaginary reverse engineering, Delia undoes the blue suit, stitch by stitch, until it becomes "uncut fabric, smelling like new" *TL*, 125), and then she envisions the sewing of the blue suit, again stitch by stitch. Delia, in other words, resets the novel's chronology and tells the story backward. In dismantling the suit and then re-sewing it, she undoes the violence associated with the mother's clothes. She also positions herself in the mother's place, becoming seamstress and narrator. In fact, she finally understands Amalia's art as the art of storytelling:

> Oh, I was fascinated by her art of constructing a double. I saw the dress growing like another body, a more accessible body. [. . .] I was enthralled by her ability to extract a person from the woof and warp of the fabric, a mask that was nourished on warmth and scent, which seemed character, theater, story. (*TL*, 126)

This is the visionary moment enabling a new maternal subjectivity. By uncutting the fabric and making the suit anew, Delia retells her mother's story and reinvents Amalia as an authorial figure who can give a new narrative to a body.[28] In picturing her mother as a storyteller, Delia realizes that Amalia had orchestrated, as much as she could, the ending of her own life story. She had planned "as she did with clothes, the turn she would give to the last events of her existence" (*TL*, 127). In reconstructing her mother's death, Delia sees Amalia step out of her blue suit and put on the lingerie and dresses intended for Delia (*TL*, 128). In Delia's recreation of Amalia's last hours, the maternal body reclaims its femininity and desires. And when Amalia drowns, Delia is certain that "violence could be ruled out" (*TL*, 128). In other words, the only time Amalia finds respite from the violence of the male gaze or slap is when she puts on seductive clothing and fashions for herself an ending of her own design.

This art of reinventing herself is passed on from mother to daughter through the ritual of sewing and unsewing the blue suit. Delia puts on the blue suit and using a safety pin reshapes it to fit her body (*TL*, 134). The blue suit becomes legible to Delia as her mother's story: "I felt that the old garment was the final narrative that my mother had left me, and that now, with all the necessary adjustments, it fit me like a glove" (*TL*, 134). Amalia asserts her creative and authorial power through Delia's artful readjusting of the blue suit. The art of the seamstress, shared by mother and daughter, reverses the "error of the Shapeless" (*Fr*, 19) and liberates the mother's body from the cage of formlessness. In this way, Ferrante animates de Cespedes's "dead women" and reveals the real bodies underneath Morante's "bundled up" mothers. Ferrante's mother-seamstress as the fulcrum of the daughter's negotiation of identity is a paradigm taken up by more recent Italian writers such as Michela Murgia. Murgia's 2009 novel *Accabadora* develops the plot of the seamstress as a symbolic mother. Bonaria Urrai bequeaths to her adoptive daughter Maria both her art of sewing and her role as the archaic *accabadora*, the midwife of death who administers euthanasia. At the end of the novel Maria comes to understand and accept Bonaria's gift of death as she embraces her nonbiological mother's legacy and herself becomes both a seamstress and an *accabadora*.

Laughing Bodies and Grotesque Gestures

When Delia describes Amalia and Caserta crawling inside the tunnel-like pastry shop cellar, she imagines them laughing and shouting obscenities. At the opening of *Troubling Love*, Amalia phones her daughter and reels off obscenities in dialect, "uttering each one with enjoyment" (*TL*, 13). Likewise, only a few pages later Delia listens as Caserta attacks her with "a stream of obscenities in dialect," immersing her, as it were, in "a concoction of semen, saliva, feces, urine, in every possible orifice" (*TL*, 19). This verbal abuse inverts the flow of corporeal fluids so that they are ingested and absorbed back into the body. This grotesque image joins other disruptive scenes in Ferrante's novels where laughter and obscenities become vehicles for a subversive ideology of feminine sound. The maternal body acquires vocal presence, unmuted and uncensored, by way of laughter and irreverent language. As Ferrante puts it in *Frantumaglia*, "I reined in my tongue, I was polite and compliant. Yet secretly I was bad" (*Fr*, 113). It is this "bad tongue" that her heroines unleash in critical moments as an alternative to the language within the symbolic which structures their lives and their speech.

In Ferrante's sonic poetics women's obscenities, laughter, and other vocal emissions are symptomatic of a gendered ideology of sound spanning classical, biblical, mythological, and literary-historical contexts—from classical antiquity to Bakhtin's conceptualization of carnival laughter.[29] A woman's identity, channeled through the verbal and nonverbal sounds she produces in public, has long been the object of patriarchal regulation and legislation (Carson 1995; Beard 2018, 3–45). Women's disorderly and uncontrolled outflow of sound—shrieking, wailing, sobbing, loud laughing, and emotional eruptions—are threatening because they connote madness, hysteria, uncontainability. Woman, as Carson writes, "is that creature who puts the inside on the outside. By projections and leakages of all kinds—somatic, vocal, emotional, sexual—females expose or expend what should be kept in" (1995, 129). In classical antiquity women were expected to exercise *sophrosyne*, the masculine virtue of self-control, by submitting to male direction and remaining quiet. Ferrante's heroines are positioned between their female outpourings—verbal leakages and corporeal flows—and the self-censorship of their language, the "reining in" of their tongues as a form of internalized discipline. In Ferrante's novels, the mothers endure—and then subtly undermine—this patriarchal ideology of gendered sound. When faced with the collapse of an imposed internal or external equilibrium, they uncensor their mouths: they become laughing subjects, reveling in their verbal incontinence and corporeal flows, shouting obscenities and exposing in grotesque gestures their uncontainable female corporeality. Laughter, like the ritual of sewing and unsewing Amalia's blue suit, constitutes another form of feminine self-invention and emancipation.

Ferrante's laughing mothers echo the protocols of Bakhtin's literary-historical conceptualization of Renaissance carnival. Like disgust, laughter shatters established norms, subverting hierarchies and reversing boundaries (Bakhtin 1965; Davis 2000). Laughter in Ferrante's novels disrupts the patriarchal frame of women's muteness and enacts a liberation through unbinding the maternal body, tongue, and mind. Laughter breaks up the silencing of women's writing too and becomes what Hélène Cixous conceptualizes as "the laugh of the Medusa," which is intended to "break up the truth with laughter" (1976, 888).[30] The laughter elaborated and performed by Ferrante's maternal subjects "proposes its own language," to borrow a phrase from Catherine Conybeare (2013, 49), subverting at once the symbolic order of language and its patriarchal sociocultural counterpart. Laughter in Ferrante's novels is productive and creative—it is a new form of articulating female subjectivity through the laughing body.

Words in Ferrante's novels, whether vulgar Neapolitan dialect or refined language, are binding, violent mechanisms that subjugate and silence women within the symbolic order. In *Troubling Love*, Delia's emancipation from her past occurs through language. She abandons the Neapolitan dialect she associates with the brutal violence she witnessed as a child and with the desirable, disgusting maternal body (*TL*, 21).[31] But her proper Italian proves another cage she needs to dismantle in order to reconstruct her mother's final days and recollect the events of her childhood. The novel which opens with Amalia laughing and yelling obscenities on the phone concludes with Delia recalling—and repeating—those obscenities as the words of her abuser, the old Caserta. Obscene language, when passed from mother to daughter, has a cathartic effect allowing Delia to process the trauma of the past and transform it into narrative.[32] The last glimpse of Amalia on the novel's penultimate page is Delia's memory of her mother looking around freely and laughing (*TL*, 138). Thus, it is Amalia's laughter that frames the novel.

Amalia's most distinctive characteristic is her irrepressible vitality, her ability to resist her husband's domestic violence and Caserta's psychological abuse. This resilience, embodied in her indestructible blue suit, also resounds in Amalia's laughter, sometimes obscene and sometimes simply incongruous.[33] Her husband cannot bear her laugh, perceiving it as Amalia's rebellion against his male authority, and so he imposes on her a code of mute obedience. Nonetheless, Amalia chooses to laugh, clinging to her free will and enjoying, for example, the gifts she receives from Caserta—flowers, pastries, a dress (*TL*, 99). Her husband punishes her for the double crime of laughing and looking: "Amalia's tone of voice, according to him, was too easily engaging; the gestures of her hands were too soft and slow; her gaze was eager to the point of shamelessness" (*TL*, 100).[34] Her voice and gestures tacitly disobey the patriarchal demand for feminine silence and self-restraint. As Delia sums up her mother's life, she posits language as a prison: "Amalia had the unpredictability of a splinter, I couldn't impose on her the prison of a single adjective" (*TL*, 124).

In *Troubling Love*, Amalia cannot be narrated through the logical, rational system of patriarchal *sophrosyne*. Even in her old age, besieged by Caserta's gifts, she retains her ability to laugh in the face of established norms and hierarchies. Her last days are characterized by incessant laughter in Caserta's company. Her neighbor Signora de Riso complains about Amalia's uncontrolled hilarity which spills out and spreads beyond the prison walls of her apartment: "When he came, I heard them talking and laughing continuously. She, especially, laughed—her laugh was so loud you could hear it from the landing" (*TL*, 39). Amalia's laughter is disruptive or what Conybeare calls "subversive laughter"—"a welling up of joy even in the most unpromising circumstances—the constraints of the world are shown for an instant to be absurd"

(2013, 49). Confronted with another controlling male presence, Amalia reacts by laughing in the face of oppression. And what is more, she speaks the unspeakable, uncensoring her tongue, as Signora de Riso reports to Delia: "She had developed a mania for saying the worst words, out loud, even when she was alone. And then she would start laughing. I heard her from here, in my kitchen" (*TL*, 40). Laughter and obscenities are Amalia's mechanisms for reversing a restrictive social and discursive order which casts her out as a verbally and corporeally unstable, leaky subject. Women's projections and leakages—somatic, vocal, emotional, sexual—are what must be contained as they permit a direct continuity between inside and outside, a continuity abhorrent to the male nature (Carson 1995). Amalia's laugher and the obscenities she repeats to herself and to Delia constitute precisely those kinds of leakages threatening to undo the frames that imprison them. This crossing of boundaries—overflowing speech, erupting sounds, excessive corporeality—locates Amalia within the realm of the grotesque body, one of the elements of Bakhtinian carnival.

In *The Days of Abandonment*, Ferrante elaborates a similar opposition between obscene or vulgar speech and woman's proper place within language. Olga at first exemplifies female *sophrosyne* as self-control and self-censorship: "I had, finally, taught myself to wait patiently until every emotion imploded and could come out in a tone of calm, my voice held back in my throat so that I would not make a spectacle of myself" (*DA*, 12). But her psychical unraveling is also a linguistic one. She swings rapidly from her "self-discipline" (*DA*, 12) to uncensored verbal leakages: "I went from using a refined language, attentive to the feelings of others, to a sarcastic way of expressing myself, punctuating by coarse laughter. Slowly, in spite of my resistance, I also gave in to obscenity. Obscenity came to my lips naturally" (*DA*, 26). Proper language as a form of self-fashioning aligns with Olga's subaltern identity as a housewife trapped inside her apartment and inside a life of self-sacrifice.[35] Her liberation from the shackles of domestic subservience and polite discourse transpires by way of laughter. When she runs into Mario and his lover Carla, Olga gives in to her pent-up anger and attacks her husband. In a gory sequence, she beats him until his nose is bleeding and his shirt is ripped (*DA*, 70–1). At the end of the scene, Olga's aggression is replaced by laughter— not Amalia's laughter of delight, but the laughter of a woman freed from the bonds of proper language and behavior (*DA*, 72). The carnivalesque register of this scene with its inverted dynamics of domestic violence echoes in Olga's word choice. She describes the face of Mario's lover as a grotesque "carnival mask" (*DA*, 72) concealing the horror of corruptible human flesh.

Mikhail Bakhtin theorizes Renaissance carnival as a time of reversals enacting a temporary liberation from prevailing truth and order: "it marked the suspension of all hierarchical rank, privileges, norms, and prohibitions" (1965, 10). Bakhtin's conceptualization approximates Walter Benjamin's vision of Naples as a theatrical stage, a spectacle which blurs the line between past and present, inside and outside, public and private, performance and real life (Benjamin and Lacis, 1986). Benjamin's term for this continuous overflow is "porousness," a permeability that allows for temporal and spatial conflations and reversals. It is this porous, carnivalesque Neapolitan world that Ferrante's female characters inhabit, their own bodies rendered permeable and violable, open to physical and discursive manipulations and appropriations. Even Olga who lives in Turin is possessed by the memory of the abandoned Neapolitan woman from her childhood, the poor mad woman, the *poverella*, whom Olga keeps seeing in the streets of Turin and in her apartment. The Neapolitan carnivalesque permeates Ferrante's settings.

In Bakhtin's theory, carnival as subversion works through laughter, celebrations of the grotesque body, and the life-and-death cycle of degrading and regenerating forces. Amalia's carnivalesque resistance to established order can be located not only in her unbridled laugh and obscenities-spewing mouth but also in her self-degrading actions as tributes to the abject maternal body. Grotesque gestures, as Bakhtin contends, put on display the "life of the belly and the reproductive organs" and relate the maternal body to "acts of defecation and copulation, conception, pregnancy, and birth" (1965, 21). When Delia asks Amalia if she's had a lover since she left her husband, Amalia responds by pulling up her dress, exposing her "baggy waist-high underpants" and laughing: "Giggling, she had said something confused about her soft flesh, her sagging belly, repeating, 'Touch here,' and tried to take one of my hands to place it on her flabby white stomach" (*TL*, 24). Amalia's laughter and her abject maternal flesh situate her within the domain of the Bakhtinian grotesque.

Laughter and grotesque self-exposure belong to Amalia's expressive repertoire. When she boards the train to visit Delia, she begins laughing: "In the compartment she started laughing for no reason and began to fan herself with a hem of her skirt" (*TL*, 101). It is this "laughing for no reason" (*senza motivo*, *Am*, 28) that constitutes Amalia's subversive deployment of laughter. In her *Guardian* column from March 3, 2018, Elena Ferrante proposes her own theory of laughter which provides a useful lens for understanding her laughing heroines. In *Incidental Inventions*, her collected columns for *The Guardian*, she conceives of laughter as a moment of respite from the "injustices of the world" (*II*, 26; *angherie del potere*, *Lio*, 22):

> Yet for the moment we're laughing, we feel their grip on our life relax a little. Laughter is a short, very short, sigh of relief. That must be why the laughter that interests me most, in the context of a story, is incongruous laughter, the laughter that explodes in situations where laughing is inconceivable, in fact seems an enormity [malvagità]. (*II*, 26; *Lio*, 22)

Amalia's incongruous laughter on the train, her irrepressible giggling when responding to Delia's question, when pulling up her dress or fanning herself with her skirt, are what Conybeare calls "a coping mechanism" (2013, 49), rebellious gestures that allow a moment of relief in an otherwise unbearable situation.

In *My Brilliant Friend*, Melina, the widow seduced and abandoned by Donato Sarratore, repeats Amalia's grotesque gesture. When she receives a book of poetry written by her former lover and dedicated to her, she has "a sort of crazy outburst of joy"—an emotive overflow, and begins "laughing, jumping on the bed, and pulling up her skirt, displaying her fleshless thighs and her underpants to her frightened children" (*MBF*, 126). Like Amalia's, Melina's laughter accompanied by indecent self-exposure is the victim's incongruous laughter—a coping mechanism and a form of emancipation. It brings her momentary relief through participation in a nonverbal system of signification outside the patriarchal laws of the symbolic order, through a temporal existence outside established margins. We find this irreverent gesture repeated in the Neapolitan Novels by Lila, the tetralogy's most rebellious character who refuses to be contained by any law, order, or system and whose lacerating emotional eruptions terrorize the neighborhood. Lila and Melina are not just distant relatives and sexual victims of the Sarratore men, they are both susceptible to madness and excursions outside the boundaries of sociocultural, corporeal, and psychical reality. Lila empathizes and identifies with the crazy widow who embodies the destructive, disorienting effects on women of love and loss (de Rogatis 2018, 84).

More importantly, Lila and Melina share the carnivalesque legacy of women laughing and showing their bodies. Like Amalia and Melina, Lila adopts the grotesque act of self-exposure. In *Those Who Leave and Those Who Stay*, as Lila ages she uncensors her mouth: "She laughed nervously, almost a shriek, and spoke too loudly" (*TLTS*, 23). And in *The Story of the Lost Child*, Ferrante repeats verbatim the formula used to describe Amalia fanning herself with her skirt, but this time it is Lila who is "fanning herself with the edge of the skirt" (*SLC*, 167). The last time Elena and Lila meet in Naples before Elena moves to Turin, Lila appears as a 51-year-old madwoman "who grabbed the edge of her dress with her hands and fanned herself, showing Imma and me her underwear" (*SLC*, 451). The recurring scenes of women lifting their skirts can be read in the context of the Greek myth of Iambe/Baubo (Correll 2019) and what Larissa Bonfante calls "the Baubo gesture" (2008). In *The Homeric Hymn to Demeter*, the original text of the Demeter and Persephone myth, obscenities and laughter acquire a ritual significance. To cheer her mistress Demeter, who is mourning the loss of her daughter Persephone, Baubo speaks obscenities and lifts her skirt, exposing her sexual organs. Demeter laughs in response. Baubo's gesture amuses the mourning mother and manifests the apotropaic power of both female genitals and laughter.[36] Likewise, Ferrante uses laughter and self-exposure as a ritual expression of maternal loss.

Troubling Love enacts a reversal of the Demeter and Persephone myth—the daughter mourning the lost mother and searching for her in the underworld of Naples (Buonanno 2008; Elwell 2013; de Rogatis 2016a). In this inverted scenario, Delia's recollections of her mother's obscene language, self-exposure, and incongruous giggling serve as agents of relief from the bonds of loss. Amalia is the Baubo figure to Delia's Demeter. Amalia's laughter, expressive of her uncontainable sexuality and feminine corporeality, gradually restores to Delia her own vitality which she recognizes at the end of the novel. In *The Story of the Lost Child*, Ferrante revisits the Demeter myth. Lila is both the mourning mother who has lost her daughter Tina and the Baubo figure who shouts obscenities and lifts her skirt to expose her genitals. In a variant of the myth, what Demeter sees when Baubo exposes herself is a human face in lieu of her groin, a body with two mouths (Carson 1995; Bonfante 2008). In the grotesque figure of Baubo women's verbal leakages and their corporeal seepages intersect. Amalia's and Melina's laughter and their grotesque bodies re-appropriate all forms of feminine flow—verbal incontinence, nonverbal projections or eruptions, corporeal fluids—and resignify them as regenerative, life-giving and life-affirming. Lila's irreverent gesture, performed in the context of loss and mourning, provides a grotesque image or visual equivalent for her harrowing episodes of dissolving boundaries—*smarginatura*. During those episodes, the inner or underside of things is revealed, borders break and bodies collapse into disgusting, oozing mass. Lifting her skirt and revealing what's under, Lila enacts *smarginatura* as related to gender violence. By exposing her underpants, she lays bare the abused female bodies inhabiting her reality, the women deprived of their own language within the symbolic.

In Ferrante's novels the mothers lift their skirts to unmask the hidden reality of their beaten or mutilated bodies, the prison of their shapeless garments. But they also re-appropriate their corporeality and transform it into a vital affirmation of *superabilità*— of surmounting and superhuman ability. This is precisely why in *The Story of the Lost Child*, Elena's disabled mother performs a similar gesture: "she pulled up her dress and showed me her injured leg like the relic of an old battle" (*SLC*, 151) before she becomes a storyteller. In *The Days of Abandonment*, Olga too engages in a similar revelation. On the morning of the day when she remains locked in her apartment, she goes out to walk the dog wearing only her nightgown. She perceives the nightgown as a mantle painted on her body and depicting her surroundings (*DA*, 98). Then Olga performs the Baubo gesture and takes it to its logical carnivalesque completion: "Smiling scornfully—with scorn for myself—I pulled up my nightgown, I peed and shit behind a trunk. I was tired, tired, tired." (*DA*, 98). Olga's scornful smile followed by her grotesque act entails both mouths. She is the laughing and leaking mother, the ultimate threat to male *sophrosyne* and patriarchal norms of civilized propriety. In this scene Olga literally and metaphorically relieves herself of the weight of the male city inscribed onto her body and thereby she abjects both her body and the urban landscape that oppresses it.[37] She is partaking in a mechanism of degradation structured by Bakhtinian carnivalesque laughter and grotesque enjoyment of corporeal functions, embracing the body's prodigious abilities.

In Ferrante's novels to expose the maternal body and degrade it is tantamount to recuperating and celebrating its uncontainable vitality. To expose the maternal body is to acknowledge its instability and porousness, its corruptible borders and oozing, excessive fluids. And the most porous, most grotesque body is the corpse. By lifting their dresses and showing their flesh, Ferrante's protagonists gesture toward their own mortality. The blood dripping from their genitals—the menstruating Delia, Elena's dying mother—signals both a life-generating force and imminent death. The dead or dying mother is a crucial presence in Ferrante's maternal imaginary. At the end of *The Lost Daughter* Leda's two daughters call from Canada and ask her, jokingly, whether she is dead or alive. Leda responds, in what is the novel's enigmatic last sentence, "I am dead but I am fine" (*LD*, 125). Her response bridges the line between life and death, announcing her own demise but asserting her well-being because of it. Ferrante seems to propose the dead mother—or at least the death of traditional, normative motherhood—as the end point of her narrative. But Leda's statement also closes the novel's narrative frame, bringing us back to the opening and explaining the origins of the mysterious wound in her side which ushers the reader into the text and initiates the conflations-inversions of mothers, daughters, and dolls.

Dead Mothers and Corporeal Flows

Ferrante's texts elaborate a complexly focalized poetics of motherhood narrated from a double perspective—the mother's and the daughter's. But they are also inflected through the daughter's compulsive desire both to possess the mother and to detach herself definitively from the mother's body. As Leslie Elwell (2013, 71–80) and Tiziana de Rogatis (2018, 97–100) argue, Ferrante's daughters are always on the verge of matricide. They reject the maternal ethos resting on archaic models of submissive and violated or else furious and vengeful mothers. To rebel against the maternal inheritance, they commit implicit or symbolic violence against their mothers. Yet, matricide in Ferrante's novels works to undo the matrophobia entrenched in Western cultural traditions as it calls attention to the lacking maternal discourse (Elwell 2013). Symbolic matricide is the necessary, albeit difficult, path to repairing the relationship with the mother (de Rogatis 2018, 100).

If different forms of matricide are crucial to the daughter's acceptance of the mother's legacy, then different forms of maternal death are also negotiated on the pages of Ferrante's novels. The encounter with the mother's corpse—a representational taboo in Western art—assumes a creative, generative role despite its associations with mortality, decay, and disgust. The dead mothers populating Ferrante's texts constitute the mother and her daughter, herself a mother, as thinking, speaking, and writing subjects. *Troubling Love* opens with Delia calmly recounting her mother's death on the day of Delia's birthday. *The Days of Abandonment* conjures the dead body of an abandoned mother from Olga's childhood—the *poverella* who drowned in the gulf of Naples and who incites Olga to write and speak "from the depths of the maternal womb" (*DA*, 127). *The Lost Daughter* traces Leda's figurations of motherhood as she becomes involved with a mother-daughter pair and with the daughter's doll, to finally announce on the novel's last page that she is a dead mother herself. *The Beach at Night* revisits the mother-daughter plot but from the perspective of an abandoned doll who almost drowns. In the Neapolitan Novels, shortly before Elena's mother dies, she picks up her infant granddaughter and blood gushes from under her dress (*SLC*, 199). This image from the last novel in the tetralogy asserts the cyclical, generational connection between a daughter's birth and a mother's death, announced on the first page of *Troubling Love*.

In *The Lost Daughter* Leda recalls her mother's last words: "The last thing she said to me, some time before she died, in a fractured dialect, I feel a little cold, Leda, and I'm shitting my pants" (*LD*, 79).[38] As its final legacy, the maternal word enunciates the unspeakable and reifies the repugnant—the bodily dissolution that follows death, the erasure of corporeal boundaries. This scene links maternal discourse to death and to bodily fluids. It also anticipates the bleeding, dissolving body of Elena's moribund mother in the Neapolitan Novels. In her review of Alice Sebold's novel *The Almost Moon* (2007), Ferrante dwells at length on matricide and the daughter's "furious" love for the mother (2007, "Se l'amore è furioso"). In her review Ferrante analyzes one of the novel's most disturbing moments, the daughter (who is herself a mother) washing her mother's body: "In killing her mother, Helen transforms her into a doll-daughter, and she cleans off the defecation, washes her, dresses her, as in the game of a child who pretends she's the mother of an infant" (Ferrante 2007, "Se l'amore è furioso"). In Ferrante's analysis, Sebold's dead doll-mother leaking bodily waste recalls the deathbed words of Leda's mother in *The Lost Daughter*. More importantly, nurturing the maternal corpse becomes a generative gesture, a manifestation of the daughter's love, a simultaneous attachment and detachment (Ferrante 2007, "Se l'amore è furioso"). Like Delia who feels Amalia's corpse slide inside her, Sebold's Helen "feels the weight [si sente addosso] of the corpse of the woman who gave her life" (Ferrante 2007). Ferrante underscores the inversion-conflation of roles which undergirds her own poetics of the double maternal: the dead mother-daughter-doll is mothered by the daughter.

In analyzing Sebold, Ferrante of course draws on her own poetics of the maternal body. The maternal corpse and its variations function as the grotesque sight that generates and propels Ferrante's narratives. The maternal corpse, in other words, brims with textual life, situated as it is within a natural cycle of birth and death and within a generational relationship between mothers and daughters. It resembles the two prominent objects in *The Lost Daughter* that set the novel's plot into motion—the *still life* arrangement and the cicada Leda encounters upon arrival in her rented apartment. The tray of appetizing fruit turns out to be rotting and the cicada—female and dead. The maternal corpse is the liminal, permeable image that defies all borders and lingers on the verge of solid form and liquidity, between inside and outside (Grosz 1994). As the ultimate emblem of the leaking and abject body, the maternal corpse resides within the same semantic and ontological realm as *frantumaglia* and *smarginatura*, the psychosomatic reactions triggered by normative constructions of femininity and motherhood.

Ferrante stages the maternal body through the imagery of seepage and revulsion, showing the origins of the "leaky jar" metaphor: the inscriptions of patriarchal structures of power onto women's corporeality and identity, and onto their speech and gestures. Female physiological incontinence and verbal excess are correlated in a culture of masculine self-control and verbal discipline. Uncontainable body fluids and uncontainable words disrupt or breach boundaries. Ferrante's maternal subjects are guilty of uncontrollable verbal discharge. They laugh with unbridled enjoyment, they utter obscenities with delight, and they take pleasure in *language*—they write. By representing the maternal body and speech as unstable and abject, Ferrante reveals the mother's profound ambivalence toward disciplining constructions of "proper" or "clean" femininity. In doing so, Ferrante deconstructs the cultural myth of transparent and gratifying maternity, endorsing instead its problematic aspects: "I remain convinced that it's also essential to describe the dark side of the pregnant body, which is omitted in order to bring out the luminous side, the Mother of God" (*Fr*, 221). This statement is made in reference to *The Lost Daughter* whose Italian title, *La figlia oscura*, already gestures toward the *obscure*—hidden, unrepresentable, irrational—nature of the mother-daughter figure. To describe the dark side of motherhood is to unleash the maternal word, to indulge in proscribed verbal excesses, and to restore to the mother both her corporeal fluids and her voice.

As this chapter has shown, Ferrante employs the dual perspective of daughters who are in turn mothers to daughters to amplify the range of maternal discourse in her texts and disallow the objectification or simplification of the mother figure. In narrating from a doubly layered point of view, Ferrante's mothers-daughters elide the double trap of normative constructions of femininity and entrenched clichés of the mother/daughter plot. Ferrante's maternal imaginary embraces the deviant, transgressive mother, the dead mother wearing seductive lingerie. It mutilates her literally and metaphorically to expose the signs of violence hiding underneath her shapeless garments. Ferrante's mothers are compelled to utter obscenities, to laugh uncontrollably, and to make indecent gestures. Their bodies spill out unabashedly, desecrating cultural taboos and embracing their own corporeal flows. Ferrante's mothers urinate, defecate, and menstruate. And they die, their corpses furnishing a site/sight of disgust and fascination. But they also generate the impetus for the narrative and the momentum of storytelling. The inanimate mother, in other words, animates Ferrante's plots. It is not surprising then that the Neapolitan Novels conclude with the return of two abject mothers-daughters—the dolls Tina and Nu. In an interview with the Italian writer Nicola Lagioia, Ferrante confirms the generative function of the inanimate mothers as the creative engines behind *frantumaglia* and its literary expression:

> Our entire body, like it or not, enacts a stunning resurrection of the dead just as we advance toward our own death. We are, as you say, interconnected. And we should teach ourselves to look deeply at this interconnection—I call it a tangle, or, rather, *frantumaglia*—to give ourselves adequate tools to describe it. [. . .] we are a crowd of others. And this crowd is certainly a blessing for literature. (*Fr*, 366)

This "crowd of others" includes Ferrante's matrilineal literary heritage—the women writers with whom she engages implicitly or explicitly, and whose legacy she continues and expands. And, as the next chapter argues, by recuperating the maternal body and voice for literature, Ferrante also dislodges a patriarchal and patrilineal artistic tradition which marginalizes female creativity, a system which valorizes male genius and authorship.

4

Outside the Frame

The Aesthetics of Female Creativity and Authorship

> *I and Lila, we two with that capacity that together—only together—we had to seize the mass of colors, sounds, things, and people, and express it and give it power.*
> (*MBF*, 138)
>
> *The sale of female bodies has not declined on the art and industrial markets.*
> (Irigaray 1993a, 101)

The history of Western artistic production is overwhelmingly male, or more accurately, patriarchal, and constructed on a patrilineal basis. The woman artist must struggle against a tradition which not only excludes her but also defines and represents her as lacking autonomy and authority. More, she must combat an "anxiety of authorship" (Gilbert and Gubar 1979, 51) in the face of her artistic forefathers and in the absence of creative foremothers. In *Frantumaglia*, Elena Ferrante calls for a female artistic genealogy that reclaims the representation of women's experience and liberates it from the restrictive frame of androcentric traditions:

> We, all of us women, need to build a genealogy of our own, one that will embolden us, define us, allow us to see ourselves outside the tradition through which men have viewed, represented, evaluated, and catalogued us—for millennia. Theirs is a potent tradition, rich with splendid works, but one that has excluded much, too much, of what is ours. (*Fr*, 361)[1]

This programmatic statement resonates throughout her collection of essays in *Incidental Inventions* (2019) as well. In an essay titled "Creative Freedom" Ferrante insists on the necessity for women to step outside the "great warehouse of the arts, set up mainly by men" and break out of the "male cage" (*II*, 86 *Lio*, 82).[2] Women must countermand the frame of patriarchal representation and construct their own literary tradition. But to do that, Ferrante insists, they must fully inhabit the frame to then subvert and dismantle it: "The would-be writer must know the tradition thoroughly and learn to reuse it, bending it as needed" (*Fr*, 343). In an editorial for *The New York*

Times, Ferrante admits the challenge of this project: "To construct instead a potent genealogy of our own, a female genealogy, would be a delicate and arduous task" (Ferrante, May 17, 2019).³

Ferrante's own works are doubly involved in such a construction. First, in her non-fictional writing, she advocates for a female creative legacy that sidesteps the patriarchal tradition and she outlines the theory of such an aesthetic practice. She references her own literary progenitors, helping to generate a female genealogy by naming and participating in it. Implicit or explicit references to some of her literary "mothers"—Sibilla Aleramo, Elsa Morante, Anna Maria Ortese, Anna Banti, Alba de Cespedes, Natalia Ginzburg, among others—are interspersed in both *Frantumaglia* and in her fiction.⁴ Second, her literary works depict the struggles of creative women who define themselves outside "the male cage" by establishing a female artistic lineage based on shared artistic skill, collaborative creation, and mutual representation. Ferrante's female protagonists are all artists of sorts who experience the destabilizing effects of a violent and oppressive androcentric tradition, and work to upend it through sewing, painting, writing, and other acts of imaginative creation. Art making for Ferrante's female subjects is tantamount to identity formation and self-actualization outside male constructs and artistic forms. In short, Ferrante formulates and then puts into practice the tenets of her theory of gendered artistic production. This chapter outlines Ferrante's theory of feminine creativity and authorship and explores its manifestations in her literary iconography, mapping its germane figures and tropes. It also touches on Ferrante's construction of a female creative legacy that hails women writers and visual artists by subtly incorporating intertextual references to their work.

In an interview in the leading international art magazine *Frieze*, Ferrante presents aspects of what can be construed as her theory of art (*Fr*, 318–20). The interview opens with a question about the images that keep her company in her working space. In her response Ferrante sketches a visual tableau familiar to us from her novels and other interviews, making an analogy between a writer's (artist's) creative space and her poetics. In listing the objects that surround her, she creates a still life of sorts whose ekphrastic details evoke her novels' recurring images and narrative aesthetics.⁵ Ferrante's description assembles a collection of objects: a print by Mara Cerri, the illustrator of *The Beach at Night*, and a red metal cap which too belongs to the nocturnal beach landscape of Ferrante's children's book (*BN*, 11, 19, 20). Cerri's illustrations of Ferrante's children's book were discussed in Chapter 2, but it is worth reiterating the creative collaboration between the illustrator and the writer who in *The Beach at Night* together give visual form to Ferrante's verbal explorations of female identity and subjectivity. In the interview, Ferrante also mentions a reproduction of a Matisse painting of a woman and child reading by an open window—an image which parallels the representations of femininity, motherhood, and language that run as a thematic thread through all of her narratives. Finally, she describes an antique fan enclosed in a case. Figures of metaphorical or physical enclosure recur throughout her writing, beginning with Amalia's corpse in its coffin and the painting exhibited in the Vossi shop window in *Troubling Love*. Ferrante's working space, like her textual spaces, brims with visual images and aesthetic objects that offer a good starting point for exploring her theory of artistic production and its literary practice.

When asked about the first artwork that really mattered to her, she names Caravaggio's famous *The Seven Works of Mercy* in the Neapolitan church Pio Monte della Misericordia, a work she again mentions in *Incidental Inventions* (*II*, 35). But then Ferrante immediately retracts it, as she also does in *Incidental Inventions,* and discusses an entirely different work of art. In the interview she pays tribute to this prominent male painter only to veer away from her androcentric statement and focus on a woman artist and her peculiar form of creative expression:

> But the first piece of art that really mattered to me—I say this only half in jest—was the shape of a watch a childhood friend would make on my wrist by biting it. It was a game. Her teeth left a circle on my skin that I would look at, pretending [fingevo] to tell the time, until the circle faded away. Except I didn't pretend [non fingevo]: I really thought [mi sembrava davvero] it was a beautiful watch" (*Fr*, 318; *La fr*, 308).

The first important artwork for Ferrante is the imprint of her female friend's teeth on her wrist. The wrist becomes an inscriptive surface marred by perforations and wounds. These markings identify the body as a map of creative impulses which both enact a phallic penetration and elude violence by imbuing it with feminine intent. Moreover, Ferrante employs the logic of fetishistic substitution and disavowal to portray the infliction and aestheticization of this wound-artwork.

In Freud's theory of the fetish, the male subject renounces the knowledge of woman's lacking phallus, and hence the possibility of castration, by substituting the castrated female genitals with an object, such as a foot or a shoe that stands in for the missing phallus (1927, 154–5). The fetishized object signals both the male subject's awareness of woman's "wound" and the concomitant disavowal of that awareness. Ferrante's passage exemplifies precisely this suspension between believing ("non fingevo") and not believing ("fingevo"): "It was a game [...] Except I didn't pretend: I really thought it was a beautiful watch." She retains the belief that it was "really" a beautiful watch while also indicating that "it was a game." But Ferrante attributes this fetishistic procedure to a female subject who confronts a female-inflicted wound. This image of fetishized female penetration, the wound as fetish, can be found in Ferrante's novels as well. The narrated acts of incision, piercing, and fragmentation, as Chapter 2 argued, constitute creative gestures countermanding the violent inscriptions of the female body by patriarchal discourses and practices.[6] In co-opting Freud for a female fetishistic scenario, Ferrante not only radically revises his phallocentric theory but also discards the male subject altogether. Here, as well as in her novels, she performs what Naomi Schor (1995) terms "female fetishism"—the representation of fetishized wounds on the female body as the female author's refusal to anchor another woman on the axis of castration.

By creating a desirable, "beautiful" wound, Ferrante and her friend appropriate the penetrating, generative authority reserved for men. In becoming the agents of such creative violence, they short-circuit the power structures within the symbolic and reconfigure the artistic act as a shared feminine process. They hijack the fetishized object by stripping it of its androcentric significance and elevate it to a symbol of feminine creativity, collaboration, and authorship. And in a brilliant twist on Freud's emblematic fetishized shoe, Ferrante constructs a shoe-centered narrative by way of Lila's genius at crafting men's shoes. As Cynthia Gralla observes, Lila channels her prodigious creative gifts into designing men's shoes in the back of her father's store (2019). Not only do the Neapolitan Novels literalize Freud's theory by making the shoes designed by Lila the pivotal dramatic event in the first volume, they also portray Lila sabotaging men's—her father and brother's—ability to create and innovate.[7] Ferrante's intertwinement of female corporeality and artistic autonomy at the site of the punctured female body comprises a crucial element of her narrative aesthetics. The phallic thrust of the mouth inscribes an artwork generated by the shared feminine desire to create and leave a mark.[8] Ferrante's theory of art as developed in her novels can be located in this originary moment of double feminine creation.

Ferrante concludes her interview in *Frieze* with a statement that provides this chapter's rationale and organization: "I [. . .] feel attracted to anything that is enclosed within a frame, partly because it helps me to imagine what has remained outside it" (*Fr*, 320). A polysemous concept-object, the picture frame at once opens and closes the field of representation. It connects and separates art and reality. It is a figure of containment and transgression. Occupying a liminal position, it signals presence and absence, entrance and exclusion.[9] Frames and framed objects belong to Ferrante's visual poetics as figures of entrapment and violation. In depicting women enclosed within the literal and symbolic frame of patriarchy as objectified and commodified, penetrated and mutilated, she also imagines what exists outside that frame and gives it narrative presence. Her novels recuperate and represent what has been left out, erased, or fragmented—the possibility of female creativity and authorship.

Ferrante's female protagonists dismantle the cage of patriarchal aesthetics by exposing the operations of its frame and inaugurating their own artistic legacy.[10] This legacy originates in the arts of writing, sewing, painting or drawing, and in the fetishistic deployment of framed objects such as paintings, photographs, and mirrors. In establishing a female artistic genealogy, Ferrante's characters bypass a patrilineal creative practice, sidestepping its optics. Her novels depict a female gaze not contingent on male-centered hierarchies but rather on a shared female creative ethos. To accomplish this, Ferrante's characters must first inhabit the male tradition, and then, to use a phrase from Mary Beard's feminist manifesto, "turn the symbols that usually disempower them to their own advantage" (2018, 81). This chapter then is concerned with framed objects, gestures of framing, and acts of art making as sites/sights where female identity and forms of expression are negotiated. The chapter reads these pivotal sites/sights of artistic creation through the lens of visual theory and feminist art criticism, and through radical juxtapositions with the works of women artists such as Louise Bourgeois, Cindy Sherman, Marina Abramovic, and Ferrante's illustrator Mara Cerri. Along the way, the chapter also notes Ferrante's intertextual tribute to a genealogy of Italian women writers who place at the center of their narratives the question of motherhood and female creativity.

Inside the Frame: The (Nude) Female Body-as-Parts

The first painting evoked in the Neapolitan Novels conveys the objectifying power of the male gaze. When Lila and her friends from the *rione* are sitting at a café, an older man with a "professorial" look stares at Lila and then tells the young men in the group: "You are fortunate: you have here a girl who will become more beautiful than a Botticelli Venus" (*MBF*, 146). Botticelli's famous painting *The Birth of Venus* depicts the nude goddess stepping out of a seashell. This comparison stated by a male speaker to a male audience not only eliminates Lila's agency by excluding her from the conversation but also reduces her to a work of art to be appreciated by men. This scene's male gaze, shared by the "professorial" man and his male addressees, avers the role of women as the visual, ontological, and epistemological property of men. The speaker's authoritative appraisal of Lila's beauty in effect extols the male artist as the creator of beautiful and valuable objects. This idea of male artistic supremacy is founded on what Nochlin calls "a discourse of gender difference as power" (1988). The framing of Lila as a Botticelli Venus traps her within a patriarchal optics where she lacks both voice and agency.

As the "professorial" viewer predicts, Lila transforms into the femme fatale of the *rione*. Beautiful, daring, and dangerous, she exerts an indomitable, centripetal effect on the men around her. Marcello Solara lays siege to her and her family, hoping that Lila will accept his marriage proposal. Pasquale declares his feelings openly, while Stefano courts her despite Marcello's intentions. The collective male gaze not only frames Lila as a seductive object of desire but also downgrades her to what she calls "merchandize to barter" (*SNN*, 112) and cages her within a gendered economy of consumption. Marcello exchanges a coveted television set for the opportunity to spend time with Lila in her family's presence. And Stefano capitalizes on Lila's genius by investing in her father's and brother's shoemaking business. He buys and frames Lila's shoe drawings in a proprietary gesture intended not to showcase her talent but to declare his right to both her person and her creative work: "He didn't bat an eye and put down another twenty thousand in exchange for Lila's drawings, which he said he liked, he wanted to frame them" (*MBF*, 244). Stefano brings back Lila's framed drawings: "They were Lila's notebook pages, under glass, like precious relics" (*MBF*, 250). Right after the drawings are hung on the wall, Stefano announces to Lila's father that he wants to marry his daughter. The framing of Lila's drawings not only exemplifies women's status as objects traded between men but also emblematizes Lila's imprisonment within her marriage with Stefano and within the corrupt, abusive world he belongs to—the world of the Solara. The framing of her drawings does not posit her as an artist but rather corroborates her status as a commodity—an object to be acquired, framed, and enjoyed. Stefano's gesture, even if moved by affection for Lila, reveals the place of women within his society. And as Lila becomes Stefano's wife, he puts his proprietary stamp on her (*MBF*, 264) and turns her into his creation, expropriating both her and the product of her creativity—the shoes.

After their marriage, Ferrante's metaphor of framing as entrapment is confirmed: "the condition of wife has enclosed her in a sort of glass container" (*SNN*, 57). This enclosure does not ensure her physical wholeness, however. Stefano rapes her on their wedding night, beating her and humiliating her in what Tiziana de Rogatis defines as "a ritual of subjugation and conditioning" (2018, 217). After the wedding, Stefano agrees to the request of his business partner, Michele Solara, to exhibit the photograph of Lila in her wedding dress as an advertisement in their new, fashionable shoe store selling Lila's designs. Lila tells Elena, "They are going to display me in the shop" (*SNN*, 112), equating herself with her visual representation and internalizing a cultural discourse of women's commodification. The photograph testifying to her status as a married woman functions as the visual document of her containment within the male cage, a process implied also by the change of her last name, Cerullo, erased by her husband's last name, Carracci: "*Cerullo goes toward Carracci, falls into it, is sucked up by it, is dissolved in it*" (*SNN*, 124, italics in the original). Lila's marriage signifies a fall into anonymity, and it cancels out her identity. The male name *is* the cage.

These modes of visual and cultural appropriations of female identity underlie Ferrante's earlier novels as well by placing women and their creativity, their right to autonomy and authorship, within the hands of men. In Ferrante's novels men's words and works regulate and mediate any form of feminine artistic or intellectual activity. This visual and discursive entrapment is literalized in *Troubling Love* where paintings enclose Delia and Amalia within the prison of pictorial representation. The (nude) female body-as-parts, literally or symbolically mutilated, comprises a key image in this novel about artists and artistic legacies. Delia is a comic artist in Rome; her father is a Neapolitan painter of gaudy commercial canvases; and Amalia is an artist who works with fabric—as a seamstress, she invents and reinvents feminine clothes, bodies, and stories. Accordingly, the novel is framed by two artworks: the father's crude paintings of a seminude gypsy which doubles as a portrait of Amalia, and the canvas displayed in the window of the Vossi lingerie shop.

From the outset of the novel Amalia is introduced as the seductive body portrayed in the father's vulgar painting that transforms her into an object literally sold on the market. During Amalia's funeral procession, Delia carries the coffin containing her mother's body "butchered by the autopsy" (*TL*, 16). She then encounters another version of her mother's "butchered" body: a street vendor is carrying on his back a framed painting of a half-naked gypsy. Delia recognizes the artist:

> The maker of those paintings was my father. Maybe he was working on one of his trashy canvases at that very moment. He had made, for decades, and continued to make innumerable copies of that hateful Gypsy, sold on the streets and at country fairs, supplying for a few lire the constant demand of petit-bourgeois living rooms for ugly pictures. (*TL*, 16)

This literal framing of Amalia as a seminude gypsy evokes the pictorial genre of the female nude. The nude projects male fantasies of access, sexual availability, and possession, while securing the man's status as artist, spectator, and owner.[11] The picturesque subject of the gypsy woman reflects a fascination with exotic or wild sexual difference, as well as an attempt to harness, visually at least, the potentially subversive energy of the gypsy as an internal other (Lee 2000). Further, to represent Amalia as a woman from a marginalized, liminal community doubly excluded as neither Italian nor foreign (Trevisan 2017) is also to denote her status as similarly excluded. The painting constructs the father's position as central and superior, projecting a vision of both women and gypsies as others. The father's painting brings into relief the power relations embedded within the processes of visual depiction and verbal description, as David Forgacs has argued with respect to the photographic and textual production of marginal places and groups of people (2014).[12] Amalia's marginality and subalternity are encoded both socially and visually.

In the context of androcentric European art production and art history, the father's work belongs to the tradition of depicting nudes for the pleasure of male artists and male viewers. Likewise, Amalia partakes in a visual economy which posits her as a sight, coerced to perceive herself through the male gaze, as both surveyor and surveyed (Berger 1972, 47). This is exactly the optics that Ferrante critiques in *Frantumaglia* as a form of repressive surveillance belonging to the mothers of the past. Even at the end of her life, Amalia cannot escape this mode of self-surveillance which she has internalized: "she imagined herself caught between two sets of pupils, expropriated by two gazes" (*TL*, 128). When toward the end of the novel Delia imagines her mother's drowning (*TL*, 134), she pictures it as an escape from the "male cage" and as a reclamation of her nude body: Amalia goes swimming at night, naked, and never returns.

The novel pays attention to the father's artistic process which is more like mechanical reproduction than inspired creation. The father first copies the gypsy's poses from pornographic magazines leaving their faces blank: "He would leave those women without features but above the empty oval of the face he would skillfully draw a majestic construction, unmistakably similar to the beautiful creation that Amalia knew how to make with her long hair" (*TL*, 112). In turning Amalia into a reproducible commodity, her husband-painter defaces her, depleting her of personality. The gypsy painting reflects a social order which, as Luce Irigaray puts it, "requires that women lend themselves to alienation in consumption, and to exchanges in which they do not participate" (1985, 72). The father's art effaces Amalia's identity twice: first by visual representation, and then again within patriarchal discourse. Delia describes him as the man "who would cover [Amalia] with his name, who would annihilate her with his alphabet" *(TL, 110)*. Like Stefano's last name which dissolves Lila's identity in the Neapolitan Novels, here the name-of-the-father literally and symbolically erases Amalia, reduces her to her body parts. When Amalia objects to the circulation of her painted body, her husband asserts his right as artist, spectator, and owner in a scene of brutal violence which Delia recollects as a series of gory details (*TL*, 112–3). At the same time, the husband-artist who sells paintings of his nude wife, has violent bouts of jealousy triggered even by Amalia's most innocuous gesture which result in more brutal beatings. Delia recalls her mother as bleeding body parts—a nose, an elbow, an arm (*TL*, 100).

The painting Delia remembers being exhibited in the window of the Vossi lingerie shop supplies the second image in Ferrante's pictorial vocabulary of women's violation and mutilation. When Delia visits the shop to investigate the expensive underwear that had come into her mother's possession shortly before her death, she reminisces:

> I had often stopped outside because I especially liked the corner window, where women's garments were carelessly placed beneath a painting that I wasn't able to date, but that was certainly by a skilled artist. Two women, so close and so identical in movement that their profiles were almost superimposed, were running openmouthed, from the right side of the canvas to the left. You couldn't tell if they were following or being followed. The image seemed to have been cut away from a much larger scene, and so only the left legs of the women were visible and their extended arms were severed at the wrists. (*TL*, 55)

This passage thematizes the fragmentation and male domination already prefigured by the father's painting of the seminude gypsy. The scattered intimate garments work as a visual synecdoche for the eroticized female corporeality stripped of its identity and framed as fetishized body parts. The Vossi canvas itself perpetuates the image of the chopped-up female body on offer for the male gaze. The two painted women caught in the act of fleeing, their legs missing and their hands truncated at the wrists, are disfigured by the severed canvas.

This image recalls the intentional cropping of female figures we find in the work of European male artists depicting women as objects or fetishizing their body parts for their erotic potential (Nochlin 1994, 7–59). In Ferrante's text, the canvas embodies the representational violence in an androcentric artistic tradition. It also works as a visual metaphor for the literal violence that the father inflicts on Amalia. Like the two bodies in the painting, she is trapped, denied wholeness, and reduced to battered and bleeding body parts. Likewise, Delia is fleeing from a violent past she refuses to remember but which invades her present through the picture. Thus, the painting operates as a visual narrative mirroring the novel's plot while also exposing women's symbolic castration and their exclusion from participating in their own representation.[13]

The truncated canvas can be read as a visual metaphor for sexual difference, for the threat of castration that woman represents and that necessitates her subjugation, demystification, and fetishization. Freud's theory of the fetish as a substitute for the woman's lacking a phallus and Laura Mulvey's theory that woman-as-icon always threatens to evoke castration anxiety, provide a lens for interpreting Ferrante's techniques of cropping or cutting off.[14] The Vossi canvas makes visible the idea of "woman as lack" that organizes the symbolic order according to the law of the father. Perhaps that is why the "castrated" painting remains safely enclosed within the shop window, subordinate to the androcentric regimes of display, consumption, and visual/sexual pleasure. At the same time Ferrante subverts Freudian fetishism by portraying a mutilated male body missing a limb—Uncle Filippo, Amalia's violent brother, whose right arm was severed in an accident.

The sawed-off canvas not only reifies castration but also acquires fetishistic power rerouted through a female subjectivity. Delia endows the painting, and especially the women's truncated—or better, wounded—limbs, with special meaning. The picture comes to signify her violent childhood, her mother's injured body, and Delia's own abuse at the hands of the old Caserta. When toward the end of the novel Delia visits her father in his studio, she finds the Vossi painting there. Her second ekphrastic depiction differs from the first:

> The two shouting women whose profiles almost coincided—hurled from right to left in a mutilated movement of hands, feet, part of the head, as if the table [sic] had been unable to contain them or had been bluntly sawed off—had ended up there, in that room, among the stormy seas, the Gypsies, and the pastoral scenes. (TL, 117–18)

The father's studio—the spatial emblem of the male artist at work—now contains both the gypsy paintings and the Vossi canvas. The two figures in the Vossi painting are now depicted unequivocally as mutilated body parts. But in this second appearance, the mutilated bodies have acquired a voice ("shouting") and exceed the boundaries of the frame. As Delia herself negotiates her own emancipation from the traumas of the past and her father's violent legacy, she perceives the women in the painting as fleeing from the frame of (patriarchal) representation. Delia imagines, via the painting, an escape route for herself and Amalia.

Ferrante's literary appropriation of the iconography of cropping, fragmentation, and dismemberment invites comparison with the work of female artists depicting the female body. I propose an intermedial collage—or a radical juxtaposition—between Ferrante's literary representation of art and French-American artist Louise Bourgeois's print *Ste. Sebastienne* (1992), an artwork contemporaneous with *Troubling Love*.[15] In *Ste. Sebastienne* Bourgeois portrays a voluptuous, tree-like female form with its arms and head cut off. Arrows threaten to puncture her body parts intimately linked to child-bearing—breasts, hips and thighs, stomach. The artist evokes the European tradition of painting the early Christian martyr St. Sebastian as an idealized male nude pierced by arrows. But she inverts this tradition not only by depicting a female saint but also by highlighting her reproductive capacity. The arrows, instruments of St. Sebastian's torture, link the maternal body to martyrdom. More importantly the truncated head and arms deprive the female figure of identity—as if motherhood has erased her agency or subjectivity. In *Troubling Love*, the Vossi painting functions similarly to expose the literal and symbolic violation of women, their exploitation for sexual pleasure and procreation. Pregnant and working around the clock to support her family, Amalia is subjected to her husband's physical abuse and visual appropriation of her body for the gypsy paintings. The juxtaposition of Ferrante's literary cropping of the female body with Bourgeois's visual rhetoric suggests a reading of motherhood in *Troubling Love* as a form of martyrdom through suffering and self-sacrifice—Amalia's finger disfigured in a sewing needle accident emblematizes her tortured body. And hence the metaphorical fragmentation of Amalia-Delia's superimposed and mutilated bodies in the Vossi painting as well. The cover of *Troubling Love* portrays a headless woman in a red suit, whose decapitated body resonates with Bourgeois' print and hints at an emerging female literary-artistic genealogy. Likewise, the covers of the 2003 and 2007 Italian editions of *La frantumaglia* feature another headless female body—the 1915 "retouched and disfigured" portrait of Russian poet Anna Akhmatova by Nathan

Altman (Santovetti 2019, 281). That is, the trope of decapitation haunts the visual paratexts of Ferrante's novels.

As Chapter 3 argued, the Vossi painting exhibited in the window of the lingerie shop suggests feminine clothing as another kind of frame binding the female body. The seductive rust-colored and blue dresses and fine undergarments Amalia intends to give Delia for her birthday are in fact stolen by Caserta from the Vossi shop. When Delia enters the shop, she encounters a scenario of erotic availability that replicates the visual rhetoric of the gypsy painting: vulgar women parading their seminude bodies in front of a male salesperson. This male salesperson turns out to be Antonio, Caserta's son and Delia's childhood friend. The shop is then doubly entwined in the visual and sexual violence narrated in the novel: as the stage where women embrace their roles as objects of the male gaze, and as the space of the Caserta perpetrators in the novel. When at the end of *Troubling Love* Delia takes off the blue Vossi dress stained with Antonio's semen and puts on Amalia's indestructible blue suit, she renounces the ideology embodied by the gypsy paintings and the lingerie shop. By wearing Amalia's old suit, she accepts her mother's clothing as a frame made by another woman artist.

Inside the Frame: Mirrors, Collages, Still Lifes

In *The Days of Abandonment* Ferrante's techniques of cropping, cutting, superimposing, or fragmenting the image of the female body shape Olga's perception of herself and reality. Left by her husband, she loses the foundation of her existence—the need to cater to the male gaze and to perform the role of perfect mother and wife. She lets her body sink into abjection and her house fall into disorder. Her carefully constructed identity crumbles, and in the months that follow she struggles to reconstitute it. Beyond her lexical collapse into obscenities, she resorts to the vocabulary of painting to relate to her surroundings and then she uses the mirror as a tool for self-analysis and self-portraiture. On August 4, the most harrowing day of her ordeal, Olga, wearing only a nightgown, takes the dog for a walk in the Valentino park. The park appears to her "more like a watercolor than like reality" (*DA*, 98), and a few moments later, she experiences reality painted onto her body:

> I was wearing not my nightgown [camicia da notte] but a long mantle [un lungo manto] on which was painted the vegetation of the Valentino, the paths, the Princess Isabella bridge, the river, the building where I lived, even the dog. (*DA*, 98; *Iga*, 108)

Olga imagines her body bearing the weight of the city and of her own domestic obligations. Public and private space are gendered in Ferrante's novels. In *The Days of Abandonment*, the male-centered urban cityscape is aligned with Mario, while Olga embodies the docile feminine "angel of the house."[16] The heavy mantle expands to contain both urban and domestic space in a gesture of appropriation and subjugation.[17]

Olga's body, in other words, carries the painted traces, scars or wounds, of her domestication and objectification.

The figure of Olga in the park, despondent and disoriented, wearing a nightgown, calls forth the opening image of Anna Banti's 1947 novel *Artemisia* about the life of the seventeenth-century Italian painter Artemisia Gentileschi. Laura Benedetti sums up Artemisia's appeal as a feminist icon, the embodiment of survival and triumph in a male-dominated creative practice: she was a "victim of rape, protagonist—and again, victim—of what is probably the first documented rape trial in western history, single mother, great artist" (1999). Banti's narrative imagines Artemisia's life as an artist who has renounced motherhood as the price for her exceptional art—she entrusts her daughter to nuns and is subsequently alienated from her. On the novel's first page the narrator, a woman writer, who has fled her destroyed house, is sitting in the Boboli gardens in Florence, grieving a devastating loss: she has lost both her home and the completed manuscript of her book about Artemisia's life. Like Olga in the park, it is early morning in August and the narrator is wearing only a nightgown, "camicia da notte" (1988, 3–4; 2015, 5–6). Olga's comment about reality painted on and around her perhaps can be read in the context of Banti's opening. She, like the fictional Artemisia, faces the dilemma of choosing between motherhood and creativity.

As an intertext to Ferrante's novel, *Artemisia* offers another possible way out for Olga—to devote herself to her ambition, to become, as Banti's narrator puts it, "a woman who has renounced all tenderness, all claim to feminine virtues, in order to dedicate herself solely to painting" (1988, 94). Artemisia emerges as an alternative to the *poverella*, yet is anchored in a binary vision of woman as either mother or artist. Artemisia rejects motherhood after she gives birth to a daughter in Naples where she also founds a drawing school, therefore exchanging motherhood for painting. In evoking Banti's famous character (and novel), Ferrante places herself in relation to a woman writer whose works, as Ursula Fanning states (2007, 161), unquestionably posit the mother as the female artist's other. 1Ferrante also positions Olga as a modern successor to Artemisia—a role already perhaps played by the childless Delia in *Troubling Love*.

But it is the mirror as a tool for reflection and self-representation that supplies Olga with the most revealing picture of her body—an image of her destabilized subjectivity.[18] When she looks at herself in the bathroom mirror, she sees a fragmented self: "Thanks to the side panels of the mirror I saw the two halves of my face separately, far apart, and I was drawn first by my right profile, then by the left. They were both completely unfamiliar to me" (*DA*, 123). She experiences her body as the disjointed composition of two superimposed profiles, as her disaggregated self. This image recalls the iconography of the Vossi painting with its two women in profile, their arms and legs cut off by the frame. But Olga identifies the maker of this artwork, Mario, who has shaped her identity: "He had assembled me on the basis of those two shifting, disjointed, ephemeral sides, and I don't know what physiognomy he had attributed to me, what montage had made him fall in love" (*DA*, 124). Mario is the artist-owner-viewer who creates Olga as a montage of disparate fragments and thereby animates her, attributing to her a fake wholeness. This creative act positions him as the master puppeteer who directs Olga-Olympia's performance as wife and mother of his children.

By facing her split body in the mirror, Olga comes to recognize her own imprisonment within the visual-patriarchal frame imposed by Mario, her alienation from herself and her fragmented subjectivity. She realizes that she is a product of Mario's fantasy, that her life, words, and body have been subjected to his will and desire—exactly what in the Neapolitan Novels Elena Greco formulates as "female automatons created by men" (*TLTS*, 254). Or as Olga concludes, "The mirror was summing up my situation [stava facendo il punto della mia situazione]" (*DA*, 123; *Iga*, 137). The mirror which takes stock of Olga's situation can be read as a metafictional—and literally self-reflexive—moment in which the novel reflects on its own status as the narrative of Olga's situation. That is why perhaps in the Neapolitan tetralogy Ferrante revisits the figure of a writer contemplating her own image in the mirror. In *The Story of the Lost Child*, Elena, now the author of a new book, is photographed in her apartment posing in front of the bathroom mirror (*SLC*, 263). The mirror as a surface which inverts the image—or symbolically speaking, the status quo—captures Olga's nascent autonomy and Elena's emerging authorial agency.

The book covers of both the Italian and English editions of *The Days of Abandonment* feature a nude woman in front of a mirror in an oval frame. She stands with her back to the viewer (reader), but her face is reflected in the mirror. The book cover itself echoes the mirror as a polysemous trope and its variations depicting women gazing in mirrors. The mirror has often been used as a moralizing symbol of woman's vanity to conceal its distinctly erotic intent in displaying a nude female body for man's visual pleasure. Or, as John Berger elaborates, "The real function of the mirror [. . .] was to make the woman connive in treating herself as, first and foremost, a sight" (1972, 51). Looking at herself in the mirror after she has lost Mario's orienting, confining patriarchal gaze, Olga can no longer perceive herself as a mere sight. Her fragmented reflection parallels her destabilized identity. In Freudian psychoanalysis, the mirror is associated with Medusa's terrifying head with its implications of castration and emasculation (Freud 2003 [1922]). By placing Olga in front of the mirror, Ferrante narrates a "woman as icon" scenario whereby she recognizes her own sexual difference as a male construct, the product of Mario's montage. Thus, starting with its cover *The Days of Abandonment* proposes a framework for reading the text as a novel about women constructed either as sights of visual pleasure or as castrating sites of horror. The mirror for Olga becomes a tool for recognition, introspection, and self-representation.

The mirror as an object which brings self-understanding revisits an image in Elsa Morante's last novel, *Aracoeli* (1982). In *Aracoeli*, the son and first-person narrator Manuele tells the story of his return to his mother's native Spanish village many years after her death, a return which is also his allegorical journey back to mythical, pre-symbiotic symbiosis with her (Giorgio 1994, 94–5; Wehling-Giorgi 2013, 197). At the novel's outset he recalls his mother who has remained "enclosed in a heavy tortile frame painted with gold" (Morante 1989, 122) and this image gives way to reminiscences about her. The mirror opens a view into Manuele's psyche as he relives the bond with his mother in early childhood and dwells on her body, voice, and clothes. He perceives his reflection in the same framed mirror ("inquadrata nella nota cornice"; Morante 1982, 11) so that both he and his mother appear trapped in its frame, Manuele's preconceptual self merged with the maternal figure (Wehling-Giorgi 2013, 198). The connection between Ferrante and Morante has already been noted by a number of scholars of Italian studies, but what interests me here is how Ferrante's employment of the mirror in *The Days of Abandonment* as a maternal tool for reconstructing her identity echoes and modifies Morante's image of the mother-son symbiosis.[19] If in *Aracoeli* Manuele's eventual abjection of his mother as a site of horror and revulsion enables his new, autonomous self and his entrance into the paternal/symbolic realm (Wehling-Giorgi 2013), in Ferrante's novel the mirror enables the mother's path to self-knowledge and emancipation from the symbolic. By implicitly citing Morante, Ferrante inhabits a literary genealogy of Italian women writers who place at the center of their narratives the mother's complex identity, but she does so by privileging the mother's point of view.

Olga's confrontation with the patriarchal frame she has internalized continues with an artistic collage. She looks at family albums examining the faces and bodies of her children and seeking physical traces of Mario in them. Then in a gesture which anticipates Lila's modernist collage of her wedding photo in *The Story of a New Name* and Lila cutting her image from family photographs in the "Prologue" to *My Brilliant Friend*, Olga wields the scissors as a tool for creation and destruction:

> I took a pair of scissors and, for a long silent evening, cut out eyes, ears, legs, noses, hands of mind, of the children, of Mario. I pasted them onto a piece of drawing paper. The result was a single body of monstrous futurist indecipherability, which I immediately threw in the garbage. (*DA*, 163)

Olga's art making becomes an epistemological mode of seeing as knowing. Only by cutting up body parts and then piecing them together can she interrogate the illusory wholeness of her family, her seemingly perfect motherhood, and her own shattered identity. Bodily fragmentation, framing, and images of cutting, cropping, and mutilation are already familiar to us from *Troubling Love* as figures of physical or symbolic violence. Ferrante's use of such visual strategies warrants another intermedial juxtaposition with a woman artist. In her photographic collage *Portrait of Mother, Son, and Daughter* (1989), the American artist Cindy Sherman captures the mother as a monstrous assemblage of her own and her children's body parts. A kneeling woman, with her eyes closed and a rapturous expression on her face, is embracing her two children. The children's figures eerily blend into hers and their heads disappear behind her head so that the mother appears to be a one-headed creature with three bodies and four visible legs. The mother's body loses its discrete boundaries in a vision of motherhood as loss of agency and corporeal autonomy, and as self-sacrifice. Juxtaposing Sherman's and Ferrante's portrayals of motherhood sheds light on Olga's artistic endeavor to both represent and comprehend her own role as mother and wife.

Terrified by the monstrous image, Olga quickly throws out her artwork (*DA*, 163; "mi affrettai a gettare nella spazzatura," *Iga*, 184). A similar gesture occurs in *The Lost Daughter* when Leda arrives in the seaside town where she has rented a small apartment for the summer. On the table she finds a beautiful arrangement of glossy fruit in a tray, and she compares it to a still life painting (*LD*, 12). Still life or *natura morta* depicts realistically objects such as fruit, food, and flowers, often overripe or on the verge of decay as symbols of the vanity of human existence in the face of imminent death and corporeal decomposition. Ferrante's novel literalizes this allegorical meaning of the still life. The beautifully displayed fruits turn out to be black and rotting under their appealing surface. Disgusted, Leda throws them in the garbage (*LD*, 13; "buttai quasi tutto nella spazzatura," *Lfo* 10). But this incident unleashes Leda's repressed memories and feelings of guilt, so that the disgust associated with the rotting fruit becomes symptomatic of her identity as a mother, scholar, and woman. Both Olga and Leda dispose of a disturbing object—the photographic collage and the *still life* fruit—only to initiate a process of self-analysis. The correlation between trash and female identity noted by Cristina Mazzoni (2012) and revealed by the illustrations of *The Beach at Night*, as Chapter 3 showed, is at work here as well.

Leda's disgust, triggered by the rotting fruit, works on several levels. It signals her aversion to the prescribed feminine roles into which she was forced by an ambitious husband, two children, and a lineage of uneducated, dialect-speaking fecund mothers. Her emancipation through education does not suffice to liberate her from the fetters of domesticity and child rearing. Rent by resentment and fatigue, imprisoned within the daily struggles of raising children, maintaining a household, and continuing her graduate studies, Leda suffers from the fracturing or psychic fragmentation that Ferrante names *frantumaglia*. Stuck in a professional dead-end, she abandons her husband and two daughters to live with an established English academic who praises her scholarship. Eventually she returns to her daughters and devotes herself to them. Disgust then also relates to Leda's feelings of guilt as a failed—or what she calls "de-natured" (*snaturata*, *Lfo*, 149) mother who left her daughters for three years. But disgust also works to condemn the social mechanisms that have conditioned Leda's failure in a system where motherhood is incompatible with creative or intellectual work. Like Leda who excavates her past to admit her problematic choices as a mother, Ferrante removes the pleasant, glossy veneer of reality and exposes its dark, rotting, side. Ferrante uses the still life as a narrative tool as well: Leda's self-analysis which propels the plot of the novel arises precisely from her unpleasant encounter with the rotting fruit. The still life image supplies a visual-interpretative frame for reading the text while also reflecting in its shiny surface Leda's shattered female identity. *The Beach at Night*, Ferrante's children's book which reimagines the plot of *The Lost Daughter*, employs the heterotopic, liminal space of the beach to create a still life of sorts. Mara Cerri's darkly colored illustrations, as Chapter 3 proposed, depict the doll amid a jumble of discarded objects, thereby visualizing the landscape of *frantumaglia* as a still life.

Both Olga and Leda discard the visual object that disturbs them—the monstrous photographic collage of cut-out body parts and the repugnant fruit—in a kind of purification ritual preceding a rite of passage from one state into another.[20] The abandoned Olga must transition into her new role as a single parent while Leda, whose grown-up daughters have joined their father in Toronto, has been liberated from the bonds of motherhood. Subsequently, Olga gets rid of her idealized vision of marriage, motherhood, and domestic life, and thus sheds the identity of an abandoned woman. Leda begins to acknowledge and work through the traumatic experience of abandoning her daughters—her maternal failure. Leda takes a knife and cuts off (*tagliai via*, *Lfo*, 10) the fruit's rotten parts (*LD*, 13), an action that links her to Olga who cuts out (*ritagliai*, *Iga*, 184) body parts from photos. And the same verb, "to cut," links Olga to her seamstress-mother and to Delia's mother who is also a seamstress. In the Neapolitan Novels, Lila cuts up photographs in her quest to eliminate her bodily traces, cutting herself entirely out of the picture, literally and metaphorically.

These gestures of wielding a kitchen knife or scissors become modes of feminine creativity, self-assertion, and resistance to the frame of patriarchal optics and representation. In other words, Delia, Olga, Leda, and Lila use the tools inherited from their mothers for cutting, sewing, or drawing to annul the patrilineal bequest of artistic power. Employing pictorial genres and tropes drawn from the visual arts, Ferrante outlines a feminine artistic practice founded on the daughters' creative connection to their mothers—symbolic or biological—a connection based on creative affinity and mutual recognition. This shared artistic genealogy recalls Muraro's definition of feminism discussed in Chapter 1: "I am not referring to the feminism of rights and equality, but to the movement that has led us to choose to stay among women, to choose to act in accordance with the judgment of our fellow women, to accept the authority of women, and to seek the nourishment of female thought for our minds" (1994, 331). Accordingly, Ferrante revisits and elaborates the legacy of creative women artists and writers.

Outside the Frame: Creating a Female Artistic Legacy

In her novels Ferrante depicts the objectification, fragmentation, and commodification of women within a patriarchal culture and an androcentric artistic tradition where men—fathers and husbands—are painters, owners, and viewers. But her female protagonists carve out their own artistic practice outside this restrictive patriarchal cage, inhabiting and undoing the very visual symbols and artistic methods that have disempowered them. In *Troubling Love*, Delia resists the objectifying gaze of her painter-father by refusing to perceive herself as an object of visual pleasure:

> I saw myself in a large tall mirror in a gilded frame. The light dress was pasted to my body. I seemed thinner and at the same time more muscular. My hair was stuck to my skull, so that it seemed painted on. My face was as if disfigured by an ugly skin disease, dark with mascara around the eyes and flaking or in patches on my cheekbones and cheeks. (*TL*, 82)

Her as-if disfigured face foreshadows the splitting of Olga's profile by the mirror's two side panels. Both Delia and Olga train a defamiliarizing gaze at their own reflections thereby frustrating the visual scenario of "woman as image and man as bearer of the look" (Mulvey 1988, 62). In fact, when Delia visits her painter-father and finds the Vossi canvas in his studio, she occupies the position of artist-owner-viewer dispossessing her father of his privileged status. In an authoritative and dismissive gesture, Delia accuses him of lacking artistic vision. Observing him while he is painting, she tells him: "The sea can't be blue if the sky is that red" (*TL*, 114). The father does not recognize her and asks, "Who are you?". He fails to recognize his daughter precisely because she addresses him from the subject position of the (male) artist. The question undoes the familial ties between father and daughter, disrupts the patrilineal artistic legacy, and severs the social and visual bonds that link women to male artists. Delia asserts herself as a woman artist, claims for herself a female gaze, and gains power over the modes and means of visual representation in the novel which tie her to her mother.

The acts of cutting and sewing, erasing and disfiguring form the creative ties between mother and daughter. Delia's narrative in *Troubling Love* is choppy, oscillating between the past and the present, with scenes often blurring the boundaries between memory and reality, fact and fantasy. The daughter narrates in a fragmentary fashion gradually sewing together disparate episodes and sudden memory flashes into a coherent, if not entirely reliable, account. Each recollected fragment in Delia's story metaphorically clothes Amalia's body until it is dressed and the narrative complete (Pesca 2017). As Chapter 3 proposed, the ample vocabulary of sewing that permeates Delia's storytelling establishes a direct link to her seamstress-mother. But the memory fragments Delia sews together to recreate the traumas of the past acquire the characteristics of pictures or drawings. Her memories emerge first as rough sketches, mere outlines of events or figures of the past; then they are gradually filled until the past becomes a distinct visual tableau. This narrative procedure becomes apparent when Delia remembers Amalia and Caserta standing in the funicular station forty years earlier: "I chose details at random to color and clothe them" (*TL*, 73).This suturing of the narrative from pictorial fragments positions Delia as an artist-seamstress-narrator in her own right.

That is why she adopts the visual techniques of erasing and disfiguring that belong to the representation of women within a male-centered artistic tradition and to the novel's own iconography. Delia appropriates the visual rhetoric of her father's gypsy painting and of the Vossi canvas and reinvents it to tell another story. This process transpires through the manipulation of Amalia and Delia's photographs on their identity cards. But unlike the paintings which are entangled in the male gaze, the photographs visualize and then materialize a new, female gaze and a new artistic practice shared between women. An ekphrasis of Amalia's photographic portrait follows Delia's visit to the Vossi shop. A photograph of Amalia has been modified into a portrait of Delia:

> I looked at the photograph of my mother. The long, baroquely sculpted hair on her forehead and around her face had been carefully scraped away. The white that emerged around her head had been changed with a pencil to a nebulous gray. With the same pencil someone had slightly hardened the features of her face. The woman in the photograph wasn't Amalia: it was me. (*TL*, 61)

The alteration of Amalia's photograph recalls the father's artistic process of sketching empty faces and blank expressions: "someone [. . .] had disfigured her face to fit my body" (*TL*, 64). Here, however, the technique results in a new face—Amalia's face has been manipulated so that Delia's can be inscribed onto its white space. This image begins to resemble the superimposed, coinciding profiles of the two women in the Vossi canvas, but this time it is the work of a female artist. Amalia's official identity card in fact documents Delia's image, resulting in a double photographic portrait of Amalia-Delia.

This portrait becomes Delia's self-portrait, asserting her creativity as an inheritance from her mother and not from her father, and disrupting the androcentric tradition of male self-portraiture. *Troubling Love* concludes with this act of establishing a shared female artistic legacy. Delia revisits the place where her mother had drowned and takes out her own photo id card. Then, in the novel's final paragraph, she uses a pen to transform her own photo id into a portrait of Amalia and takes pleasure in the process:

> It was a recent photo, taken when I renewed the document. With a pen, as the sun burned my neck, I drew around my own features my mother's hair. I lengthened the short hair, moving from the ears and making two broad bands that met in a black wave, over the forehead. I sketched a rebel curl over the right eye, barely contained between the hairline and the eyebrow. I looked at myself, smiled at myself. That old-fashioned hairstyle, popular in the forties but already rare at the end of the fifties, suited me. Amalia had been. I was Amalia. (*TL*, 139)

This linkage through photography enacts a shared gaze between mother and daughter in which women are both object and subject at once. In this way, they bypass the male gaze entirely and create a new reciprocal gaze (Elwell 2013, 97–9). What is more, however, this act of artistic creation positions Delia as a woman artist so that she supplants both the father's gaze and his art, overriding the visual rhetoric of the gypsy painting and the Vossi canvas and creating an image that is not only whole but also double. Delia revokes the male gaze and gains autonomy over her own and her mother's visual representation. Manipulating official photographs is tantamount to invalidating official patriarchal discourse.

The same can be said of Olga in *The Days of Abandonment* who appropriates the photo collage with its techniques of fragmentation and assemblage to create a portrait of her family. She adopts the mirror as an allegory and tool for the self-representation that has long been associated with the male artist's self-portrait (Goscilo 2010). In occupying the subject position of the painter-artist, she rejects the visions of femininity and motherhood that have shaped her identity. After a long contemplation of her two "welded" profiles in the mirror (*DA*, 123), Olga perceives the *poverella*, the abandoned woman from her childhood: "looking hard into my half face on the left, at the changing physiognomy of the secret sides, I recognized the features of the *poverella* [. . .] her profile had been huddling in me for years" (*DA*, 124). The two women reflected in the mirror form an image akin to the superimposed female figures in the Vossi canvas; the *poverella*'s profile is "an artisan's soldering of my two profiles" (*DA*, 126). The *poverella* returns Olga's gaze and speaks from the mirror initiating a dialogue that continues when the *poverella* keeps cropping up around the house. Like Delia-Amalia's double self-portrait in *Troubling Love*, Olga's reflection in the mirror is a double self-portrait based on a shared female gaze. To take stock of her situation as an abandoned wife, Olga must encounter her female predecessors—the mothers of the past—and transform that encounter into a productive course of action in the present.

Seeing the framed reflection of the self or cutting up photographic images of the body are moments of epiphany and catharsis in *The Days of Abandonment*. Music in the novel also acts as an agent of revelation and emotional release. When she attends a concert in which her neighbor Carrano plays the cello, Olga is transported by the music and by the visible form of the musician's inner life:

> When he began playing the cello, he lost every remaining trace of the man who lived in my building. He became an exalting hallucination of the mind, a body full of seductive anomalies that seemed to extract from him impossible sounds, for the instrument was a part of him, alive, born from his chest, his legs, his arms, his hands, from the ecstasy of his eyes, his mouth [. . .] This was Carrano's true life. (*DA*, 174–5)

She perceives Carrano's body and psyche as simultaneously whole and fragmented, as parts that are extensions of his musical instrument and therefore the material, physical manifestations of his interiority, his "true life" (*DA*, 175). This blurring of corporeal, aural, and psychical boundaries as the self's interior landscape helps Olga accept her own psychical fragmentation by realizing that stable, seamless, and transparent identity is an illusion, that she, like Carrano, is at once whole and fragmented. Carrano provides the thread which sutures her life back: "I thought with gratitude that in those months, discreetly, he had worked to sew up around me [ricucirmi intorno] a world that could be trusted." (*DA*, 187; *Iga*, 210). The image of sewing (or rather, re-sewing, in Italian) evokes the mother-seamstress in *Troubling Love*, Delia as an artist-narrator-seamstress, and Ferrante's own mother whose "true beauty" is revealed when "she sew[s] together again and again the pieces of her fabrics" (*Fr*, 168). In *The Days of Abandonment*, Carrano becomes the mother-seamstress who re-sews Olga's fragmented self and reminds her that "every movement was narratable" (my translation, *Iga*, 210), restoring her authority over the narrative of her story.

In *The Lost Daughter*, Leda's professional success as a scholar originates not in her relationship with the esteemed professor Hardy, but in her desire to relate to another woman. When Leda and her husband give a ride to a hitchhiking foreign couple and then put them up for the night, Leda finds herself attracted by what the woman represents—freedom: "I was captivated by her, her name was Brenda. I talked to her all evening, imagined myself in her place, free, traveling with an unknown man whom I desired at every moment and by whom at every moment I was desired" (*LD*, 74). Brenda shows enthusiasm for Leda's work and asks for something of hers to read. Leda gives her a short article she has written. This brief encounter between the two women, inflected through mutual interest and desire, and through Leda's imaginary occupation of Brenda's position, establishes a bond between them, a momentary entrustment or *affidamento*, that enables Leda's academic success. Thanks to the "female mediation" (Elwell 2016) of Brenda, this short article ends up in the hands of professor Hardy who cites and lauds Leda's intellectual work at a conference that Leda is attending. Brenda supplies another model for Leda to inhabit and, this time, act upon—Brenda has left her husband to follow her travel companion who has left his wife and young children. Leda inherits from Brenda not only the fantasy of physical and sexual freedom but also the prospect of abandoning her family. Leda indeed leaves her husband and two daughters to follow professor Hardy. The bond with Brenda unleashes her suppressed intellectual and erotic potential and permits her to pursue self-actualization.

But the ultimate usurpation of male creative power and means of representation occurs in the Neapolitan Novels where Lila, like Delia and Olga, disfigures her own portrait to regain creative autonomy through self-effacement and self-fragmentation. Lila's appropriation by way of her shoe designs of the generative function of the male artist begins to unsettle the patriarchal frame. Her first name, Raffaella, evokes the renowned Renaissance artist Raffaello Sanzio or Raphael, and thus she obliquely inhabits the artist's position. That is, Ferrante portrays Lila not as a Botticelli Venus as the "professorial" intruder points out to Lila's male friends, but as the artist capable of creating such a masterpiece. Indeed, Lila creates not so much a *Venus* as a *Head of Medusa* overriding a misogynist literary, visual, and psychoanalytic tradition of treating Medusa as a sight/site of horror. Lila eliminates her body from her official wedding photograph, manipulating the image to produce a photographic collage not unlike Olga's. Lila refuses to become an object exhibited on a wall and negotiates the right to modify the image to her liking. She covers the white of her wedding dress with funereal black: "She spied a roll of black paper, and she took a pair of big scissors [. . .] she cut strips of black paper, with the manual precision she had always possessed, and pinned them here and there to the photograph" (*SNN*, 119). The resulting artwork reconfigures the pictorial rhetoric of the Vossi painting with its cut off body parts:

> The body of the bride Lila appeared cruelly shredded. Much of the head had disappeared, as had the stomach. There remained an eye, the hand on which the chin rested, the brilliant stain of her mouth, the diagonal stripe of the bust, the line of the crossed legs, the shoes. (*SNN*, 119)

Lila's body, truncated and mutilated, fragmented and concealed by the black paper, begins to defy the objectifying male gaze and reinvent the narrative of the Vossi painting as one of feminine authorial intent. Lila repossesses her own body and controls its representation and display. In cutting and concealing her body, she invalidates her own self-objectification. In this way, she also destroys the wedding dress and what it represents: marital abuse and enclosure within the patriarchal frame of representation. Ferrante has reached a visual solution to the problem posed by the Vossi painting. In another subversion of Freud's fetishized shoe, Ferrante exhibits the shoes, framed by Lila's own hand, as a symbol of Lila's irreducible creative force.

The process of self-erasure becomes one of creative euphoria, artistic freedom, and female bonding. It takes Lila and Elena outside the patriarchal order and into the whirlwind of shared female *jouissance*:

> They were magnificent hours of play, of invention [invenzione], of freedom, such as we hadn't experienced together perhaps since childhood. [. . .] With extreme precision (she was demanding) we attached the black paper cutouts. We traced red or blue borders between the remains of the photograph and the dark clouds that were devouring it. Lila had always been good with lines and colors, but here she did something more, though I wouldn't have been able to say what it was, hour after hour it engulfed me. [. . .] We forgot about Antonio, Nino, Stefano, the Solaras [. . .] We suspended time, we isolated space, there remained only the play of glue, scissors, paper, paint: the play of shared creation [invenzione]. (*SNN*, 122; *Snc*, 121)

As seen through Elena's eyes, covering the photograph with paper and erasing the traces of Lila's body become a liberating experience outside of conventional time and space. Men do not exist in this place of collaborative feminine creation; women wield the tools—paper and paint—of visual representation. The wedding photograph, a sign of Lila's confinement within her marriage and the patriarchal order, is converted into an abstract, modernist collage. Elena uses the noun *invenzione* (invention) twice to describe their shared creation underscoring the nontraditional nature of their artistic endeavor. And throughout the Neapolitan Novels Lila invents and reinvents herself and those around her, molding their behavior or appearance.[21] When Lila turns to computer programming, she establishes the first Italian center for informatics. The company's name, "Basic Sight," and the logo designed by Lila endorse both her artistic vision *and* her technological foresight.

Lila's self-erasing creative technique enacts her defiance of male-dominated structures and her need to control her own life. Her modernist collage resists male control and objectification, returning the viewer's gaze (Milkova 2016c).[22] Lila, as Elena recounts, has replaced her seductive body with an all-seeing eye, the locus of subjectivity: "I on the other hand was so enthralled by the upper part of the panel, where Lila's head no longer was, that I couldn't take in the whole. All you could see, at the top, was a very vivid eye, encircled by midnight blue and red" (*SNN*, 124). When contextualized in the Western literary and visual tradition, Lila's eye becomes a Medusa stare, a castrating site of horror, a monstrous female other.[23] When Lila narrates the scene of her rape on her wedding night, she depicts Stefano's penis about to tear into her flesh as a kind of stump, "like a puppet without arms or legs" (*SNN*, 42, "un pupattolo senza braccia e senza gambe," *Snc*, 42). This image of mutilation evokes both the Vossi canvas and the language Ferrante uses to describe beaten, abused, or suffering female bodies.[24] Lila uses the rhetoric of cutting to castrate symbolically the organ about to violate her. In other words, Lila's creative act of mutilating her photograph reflects the trauma of the rape and seeks to transform that trauma into artistic power: Medusa was, after all, raped and impregnated by Poseidon. And Lila is herself pregnant when she manipulates her photographic portrait.

The scene of Lila's and Elena's collaborative erasure of Lila's body in her wedding photograph marks the beginning of Lila's attempts to erase her existence as a form of resistance to the patriarchal frame: "With the black paper, with the green and purple circles that Lila drew around certain parts of her body, with the blood-red lines with which she sliced and said she was slicing it, she completed her own self-destruction *in an image*" (*SNN*, 123, italics in the original). To destroy her image is to delete—and hence liberate—herself from the system which contains and controls her. Photography gives her the creative license to annul herself figuratively, through the manipulation of visual representation. Simultaneously, she gains the creative power to represent—or erase—herself visually. Lila succeeds in completing the process of "erasing all traces" only in old age, at the opening of the tetralogy when Elena learns of Lila's disappearance. But Lila's final gesture generates the narrative itself—it prompts Elena to recount her friend's story. Elena creates the narrative out of Lila's self-erasure and produces her best literary work. This work can be read as the culmination and completion of Lila's and Elena's joyous feminine collaboration set into motion by the wedding photograph.

The Neapolitan Novels and Female Friendship, Writing, Authorship

When read together, Ferrante's novels establish a literary genealogy of creative women— Delia and Amalia, Olga, Leda, Lila and Elena. Leslie Elwell has proposed that Ferrante's novels belong to a new, subversive canon of women writing about motherhood (2016, 246), exemplifying her claim by discussing the "filial" relationship between *The Lost Daughter* and Sibilla Aleramo's novel *A Woman*. But it is only with the Neapolitan Novels that Ferrante consolidates women's artistic autonomy by framing the tetralogy as the product of female authorship. Writing—already implicit in Delia's narration and in Olga's renewed ambitions as a writer—provides a model for initiating a feminine creative legacy which excludes men and is founded instead on a specular relationship with another woman. This relationship, sketched in Ferrante's earlier novels, informs the plot and structure of the Neapolitan Novels. It generates the creation of the tetralogy as the product of Lila and Elena's fruitful albeit complex friendship, as their shared feminine creative practice. Scholars have duly noted the ways Lila's and Elena's lives are entwined in mutual emulation and competition. Their relationship evolves from what Ghezzo and Teardo argue is their reciprocal brilliance: "No longer the attribute of a vertical, non-inclusive relation that signals one person's superiority over another, brilliance instead becomes a fluid quality, one that emerges in the horizontal, reciprocal relation between the two girls, in their mutual incitement" (2019, 183). It is worth noting that this fluid brilliance is in fact a double female "genius," as the literal translation of the Italian title *L'amica geniale* or *The Genius Girlfriend* implies. The entire tetralogy operates as a "dual and specular narrative machine" (Gambaro 2014, 170, my translation) where Lila's voice is inserted into Elena's narration which is in turn shaped by Lila's writing.

In other words, both Lila and Elena's friendship *and* the Neapolitan Novels arise from mutual self-reflections, doublings, and relating to the other woman as a mirror of the self. Elena's narration too springs from the need to tell her own story by recounting Lila's, to validate her own existence by validating her friend's. Feminine creativity, Ferrante implies, is double and specular. The failure of each is the other's failure as well, and conversely, the success of each is the other's success. To develop further Ghezzo and Teardo's argument, Lila and Elena's horizontal relationship of specular brilliance dislodges the vertical power structure of the patriarchal literary and artistic tradition and dismantles the "male cage" that contains Ferrante's female subjects. If Ferrante's previous models of double female relationships were asymmetrical—the female subject acted in relation to an absent or dead woman (Amalia, the *poverella*, Brenda)—here the two friends act in tandem, symmetrically and symbiotically, over the course of their lives. Adalgisa Giorgio (2019a, 2019b) has already noted the "double acts of female creativity" as an agonistic collaboration whose female dialectic can be read as a subversive feminist act. Elena is empowered by Lila's thoughts, words, and actions, and Lila is in turn empowered by Elena, who does not let her intuitions go to waste (Giorgio 2019b). Their female collaboration provides a model outside traditional patriarchal structures that dismantles, or at least threatens, those very structures (Giorgio 2019b).

This agonistic collaboration begins with the narrative frame of the Neapolitan Novels, as the generative competition or productive rivalry between the two friends. In the prologue when Elena, now sixty-six and a successful writer living in Turin, finds out that her friend has disappeared without a trace, erasing all signs of her existence, she calls for a competition of sorts: "We'll see who wins this time, I said to myself. I turned on the computer and began to write—all the details of our story, everything that still remained in my memory" (*MBF*, 23). This competition is between Lila's desire "to eliminate the entire life she had left behind" (*MBF*, 23) and Elena's desire to reconstitute that life by narrating it. When she announces the competition, Elena insinuates the repetitive nature of their ongoing competition: "We'll see who wins this time." At stake for Elena as a writer is summoning, through the ekphrastic power of her narrative art, Lila's presence and bringing to life her voice, words, and even image. In fact, Lila has cut herself out of all photographs, not leaving a single trace of her corporeal existence. This gesture of unframing herself through self-erasure, of taking herself out of the frame of photographic representation is the culmination of Lila's project of self-destruction initiated with her wedding photo collage. But the triumphant culmination of this project is contingent on Elena's desire to narrate it. Both friends then are the co-authors and protagonists of the text as they are the co-creators of Lila's collage.

In this way Lila's self-erasure depends on Elena's writing, which is prompted by Lila's disappearance. This circular and specular nature of their friendship is reflected in pivotal scenes and images in the tetralogy. The foundational gesture of their friendship—Lila throwing Elena's doll in the basement and Elena reciprocating by throwing Lila's doll—sets into motion their specular and competitive relationship. The long-lost dolls, sent by Lila, reappear only at the end of the Neapolitan Novels, in the epilogue that closes the narrative frame. Lila's invisible hand opens and concludes the tetralogy despite her being absent throughout. Her discursive presence, her textual authority, permeates the four volumes as Elena realizes in the epilogue: "All our lives she had told a story of redemption that was hers, using my living body and my existence" (*SLC*, 473). Their bond suggests that Elena is the material and intellectual frame for Lila's existence and, conversely, Lila gives body and voice to Elena's storytelling which then confers to Lila lasting textual, if not material, form. In *Frantumaglia*, Ferrante confirms the idea of Lila's and Elena's mutual (self)-creation: "I love Lila a lot; that is, I love the way in which Elena tells her story and the way in which Lila tells her own story through her friend" (*Fr*, 360). Stephanie McCarter, in arguing that Ferrante is rewriting the *Aeneid* with two female characters at its center, makes a provocative statement which summarizes the logic of creative influence in the Neapolitan Novels: "Elena in fact finds it so impossible to create without Lila's influence that she sees *herself* as Lila's invention. Elena's panic over Lila's disappearance is that of an artist deprived of inspiration" (2016, italics in the original).

Framed objects and gestures of framing scaffold Ferrante's literary iconography of the creative couple Lila-Elena. The figure of the two friends, each nestled inside the other, evokes the image of the *poverella* who huddles inside Olga's mirror reflection and the two superimposed profiles of the women in the Vossi canvas. But Ferrante pursues further the image of nestled female bodies as a trope for feminine creative-competitive collaboration and a form of psychic and corporeal co-habitation. In *My Brilliant Friend*, Elena watches herself and her friends reflected ad infinitum in two facing mirrors: "Behind Lila and behind Carmela and me were the identical, dark wood sideboards with the mirrors in spiral frames. I looked at the three of us reflected to infinity and I couldn't concentrate" (*MBF*, 85). Elena describes a perfect instance of mise en abyme that encloses both her and Lila within the ornate mirror frames. This image captures the mirroring relationship between the two friends. Only a few pages later Elena, when propositioned by a male classmate, acts as if she were Lila: "in her absence, after a slight hesitation I put myself in her place. Or, rather, I had made a place for her in me" (*MBF* 97). This is what I mean by psychic and corporeal co-habitation—Elena conjures up Lila and accommodates her inside her mind and words. As Ferrante writes in *Frantumaglia*, "we are a crowd of others. And this crowd is certainly a blessing for literature" (*Fr*, 366).

This procedure applies to the writing of the Neapolitan Novels as the collaborative co-habitation of their two bodies and minds. Their identities are formed in the act of relating to the other by representing and narrating her. Here the tetralogy espouses a theory of representing the self as refracted in the other that resonates with Italian feminist philosopher Adriana Cavarero's notion of the narrative relationality of the self. The self is constituted through the narration of another, that is, through the storytelling implicit in human relations (2000).[25] Ferrante too hints at the relationality of Lila's and Elena's narrated selves: "Lila can only be Elena's tale: outside that tale she would probably be unable to define herself. It's the people who love us or hate us or both—who hold together the thousands of fragments we are made of" (*Fr*, 360). Mutual narration and storytelling frame the self and grant it wholeness and visibility. By positing this dual and mutual mirroring, Ferrante articulates a new form of female subjectivity and creative imagination which works to contain and give productive shape to the "jumble of fragments"—a psychic collage of sorts—that constitutes the feminine psyche and that Ferrante calls *frantumaglia*. Dual and specular creativity keeps at bay *frantumaglia* and *smarginatura* alike, transforming them into the more malleable material of narrative.

The mise en abyme observed by Elena functions as a visual metaphor and metafictional comment on the tetralogy's own mise en abyme structure. Ferrante literalizes a self-reflexive moment through the use of two mirrors, but the book brims with other scenes of mirroring or framing. When Lila criticizes her new book, Elena thinks, "Certainly Lila reinforced her role as a mirror of my inabilities" (*TLTS*, 249). Elena places herself in a position of inferiority which implies inequality or a vertical distribution of power where, despite appearances, Lila has the upper hand. And yet, Lila's ambitions are mobilized by Elena's potential greatness. As Lila tells her friend, "I want you to do better, it's what I want most, because who am I if you aren't great, who am I?" (*TLTS*, 273). The unevenness in their relations can be detected in the cruelty, envy, and jealousy characterizing their competitive-generative friendship. The more Elena flaunts her scholastic and intellectual victories, the more Lila is tortured by them and tortures Elena in return. Mutual torture is an indispensable element of Ferrante's theory of feminine creativity, its dark side.

If we revisit Ferrante's story about the first artwork that was important to her—the clock-wound made by her friend's teeth on her wrist—then joint feminine creation begins as a concrete, corporeal process as well as a disembodied narrative practice. Produced jointly by the two friends—one who performs the creative act and the other who narrates and aestheticizes it—the wound-artwork supplies a visual-corporeal parallel to Lila and Elena's relationship. This parallel also encompasses the various incision instruments Ferrante's female characters use as tools for (self-)creation and (self-)representation—burins, scissors, and needles in *Troubling Love*, paper cutters, safety pins, scissors, and knives in *The Days of Abandonment*, *The Lost Daughter* and the Neapolitan Novels. As Chapter 2 contended, incision imagery in Ferrante's novels furnishes material, corporeal evidence of women's violated bodies while also pointing toward a creative repurposing of their penetrating force. The creative process in Ferrante's novels, as implied by the wound-artwork, entails pain and suffering.

Elena and Lila's friendship in the Neapolitan Novels is a case in point: their creative rivalry-alliance is structured through a complex repulsion-attraction verging on mutual torture. Neither of them, however, removes herself from this torture. In fact, it becomes a necessary mechanism for the success of their psychic co-habitation. When Lila, already married to Stefano, steals the boy Elena has loved since elementary school and has a passionate love affair with Nino in Ischia, Elena does not confront her friend or leave the island to spare herself the suffering. Instead, she endures tacitly, perhaps even masochistically, the perfidious forms of torture Lila inflicts on her and agrees to cover up for Lila spending the night with Nino. That same night she allows herself to be seduced by Nino's father, Donato Sarratore, and sublimates her own and Lila's passion into writing her first novel. Ferrante's subtle specularity emerges here as well. Elena's first novel adopts the style and literary imaginary of *The Blue Fairy*, the book Lila wrote when they were children, itself "a classic Pygmalion-themed story about art's power to invent identity" (McCarter 2016). Wounds and suffering in Ferrante's novels turn out to be productive experiences and a source of inspiration.[26]

Elena's other writing projects too stem from her at once painful and productive competition with Lila. When she sets out to write a book about men who fabricate women, she notes "I discovered everywhere female automatons created by men. There was nothing of ourselves, and the little there was that rose up in protest immediately became material for their manufacturing" (*TLTS*, 254). What Elena denounces is women's derivative and therefore subordinate position within a patriarchal Judeo-Christian tradition, their lack of autonomy and agency in telling their own story, and their utter subjection within the male symbolic. The ironic twist in Elena's new project is that she has modelled her entire professional identity, her oral and written language, on the language and logic of men even while elevating Lila to a role model and seeking to emulate her expressive style. Nonetheless, when she is writing this new book, she resists consulting her erudite husband Pietro and substitutes Lila as her imagined interlocutor and collaborator. Elena evokes Lila and the fantasy of female collaboration and authorship as an antidote to the male creative tradition: "We would have written together, we would have been authors together, we would have drawn power from each other, we would have fought shoulder to shoulder because what was ours was inimitably ours" (*TLTS*, 354). The writing of the Neapolitan Novels *is* the fulfillment of that fantasy, the joint creation of a narrative that not only expresses feminine experience but also models a "feminine alliance" (Todesco 2019a), a collaborative feminine authorship outside the patriarchal frame.

In her interview in *Frieze*, Ferrante shares her favorite title of an artwork and names a female artist: "I also love *The Artist Is Present*. I admire the reversal that Marina Abramovic imposed on a formula that I once detested. The artist is present, but as body/work" (*Fr*, 319). Ferrante references Marina Abramovic's 2010 performance at the Museum of Modern Art in New York. The artist sat at a table in silence, waiting for visitors to sit at a chair across from her and engage in a silent dialogue by looking. This performance blurred the boundaries between artist and public challenging the notions of authorship and locating the creation—and experience of art—in the shared, embodied gaze between the artist and the spectator. What resonates for Ferrante is also the interplay of presence and absence, an overarching thematic and structural concern in her own novels. Abramovic is absent as an author but present as her embodied artwork. When Elena sees the Bay of Naples for the first time, Lila is absent but Elena envisions a double feminine creative prowess that can capture its beauty: "I and Lila, we two with that capacity that together—only together—we had to seize the mass of colors, sounds, things, and people, and express it and give it power" (*MBF*, 138). And they do so by co-authoring the Neapolitan Novels. Ferrante's own authorial effacement enacts a resistance (Santovetti 2019) to the male tradition Elena critiques while also investing the phenomenon of her own presence/absence (de Rogatis 2018) with productive tension and meaning. The tetralogy then can be read as Ferrante's theory *and* practice of feminine friendship, creativity, and authorship. And approached together, all of Ferrante's published works engage in the perpetuation of a female genealogy of women writers and artists paving the way out of the frame of patriarchal and patrilineal artistic production.

5

Mapping Urban Feminine Topographies

The transition to a new age requires a change in our perception and conception of space-time, the inhabiting of places, and of containers, or envelopes of identity.

(Irigaray 1993b, 9)

In *The Days of Abandonment*, Elena Ferrante specifies the location of the narrator's apartment in the northern Italian city of Turin: Olga lives on the fifth floor of a building overlooking the Valentino Park and the Princess Isabella bridge on the river Po. Olga's narrative springs from that location, her experiences and movements situated within a concrete urban area easily pinpointed on a map of Turin. In the Neapolitan tetralogy, Elena narrates from exactly the same location: from her Turin apartment overlooking the park and the Princess Isabella bridge. And lest the reader miss the significance of this setting, Ferrante brings up the location of Elena's apartment three times. Turin serves as the narrative frame for the tetralogy, it is the place *from where* Elena remembers and writes the novels we are reading. It is the origin and endpoint of the story—it opens and closes the quartet whose prologue and epilogue take place in Turin. And yet both *The Days of Abandonment* and the tetralogy are texts about Naples as well. Ferrante describes Naples as constituting the spatial, psychical, and corporeal existence of its inhabitants, spanning their interiority and exteriority: "that city is not an ordinary place, it's an extension of the body, a matrix of perception, the term of comparison of every experience" (*Fr*, 65). Naples is the urban matrix of embodied subjectivity, the framework that contains the female body and conditions its spatiality. Ferrante anchors her narratives in a topographic realism with her characters navigating concrete urban topographies that constitute their identities and shape their embodied subjectivities. Although the psychogeography of Ferrante's novels maps local realities, it expands to encompass a more universal environment emblematized by the contradictions and complexities of Naples as a global and contemporary metropolis.

Lived or narrated space is the intersection of ideologically constructed topographies where gender and power hierarchies are at once embedded and enacted.[1] Ferrante's novels unfold within Turin's and Naples's intensely mapped, identifiable, and traceable urban topography. Her characters encounter hostile cityscapes and negotiate streets and neighborhoods that assail them physically or psychologically. The city in Ferrante's imaginary is an aggressive, violent, male-dominated space poorly suited for women's bodies, ambitions, and desires. And yet, Delia, Olga, Elena, and Lila traverse the novels' precisely mapped reality, narrating their itineraries through each Italian city and naming sights, streets, intersections, parks, bridges, and neighborhoods, thereby delineating and producing an *ethnoscape*, "the landscape of persons who constitute the shifting world in which we live" (Appadurai 1996, 33). They create an urban landscape contingent on mobile bodies and narrated by female subjects whose identities are constituted, dismantled, and reconstituted precisely through their mobility. Ferrante's female narrators rechart and reinvent the city to fit their physical needs and their stories. As urban narrators, as storytellers of their own manipulations of city spaces, they insert themselves within a landscape that has traditionally excluded them. If the city shapes the body and provides the setting for the circulation of power (Grosz 1999), then Delia, Olga, Elena, and Lila begin to reshape the city and rechannel its power relations. Ferrante's narrated itineraries span the topography of Naples in *Troubling Love* and in the Neapolitan quartet, and that of Turin, the setting of *The Days of Abandonment* and the frame of the quartet.

This ostensibly linear and emancipatory trajectory from south to north, from the archaic backwardness of Naples to the civilized modernity of Turin, belies the role that the past plays in the present.[2] Ferrante's topography never abandons Naples as the foundation, the primary and primordial, generative and destructive spatial origins of her narrators' subjectivities. The present is always indebted to the past and to Naples, the city that has formed and marked Delia's, Olga's, Lila's and Elena's notions and expressions of selfhood. And their inner lives, their subjectivities, are often ambulatory, constituted through the act of walking. In Ferrante's novels, as women negotiate city streets, not only do they endure the weight of the "male city," as Ferrante herself describes Naples (*Fr*, 220), but also, as they walk, the streets themselves evoke memories of violence and oppression at the hands of men. As feminist geographers argue, gender relations and gender identities are constructed in and through space, and conversely, space constructs gender (Bondi and Davidson 2004, 20; McDowell 1999). Ferrante's poetics of topography links urban architectural structures—many of them liminal spaces such as courtyards, squares, staircases, cellars, balconies, and tunnels—to symbolic structures of patriarchal violence and oppression. The Neapolitan neighborhood contains Ferrante's female protagonists within a violent, male-dominated, crime-ridden urban frame. They are at once prisoners and exiles, trapped and excluded, as feminist geographer Gillian Rose contends about women often caught in dominant, oppressive geographies (1993, 149–50).

The Neapolitan streets function as memory zones or as a "warehouse of memories," to borrow Catriona Mortimer Sandilands's expression (2008, 274), where the history of the landscape and the psychical-corporeal history of the walking subject converge through the act of remembering. Ferrante's novels embody literally and figuratively this connection between urban landscape and memory. We see Delia in *Troubling Love* recall a history of molestation and domestic abuse as she traverses Naples. Olga, the protagonist of Ferrante's second novel, wanders compulsively through the city of Turin only to find in it traces of her Neapolitan past, of betrayed and abandoned Neapolitan women. Ferrante's plots emerge from the act of remembering the past

Mapping Urban Feminine Topographies 133

and remembering transpires as her characters walk through the city and experience its sights. Streets and memory, urban space and text, cityscape and storytelling are intertwined in Ferrante's novels. It is this convergence that Ferrante describes as "the streets of topographic memory" (*TL*, 17) and explores in her novels.

The two geographic coordinates of Ferrante's narratives, Naples and Turin are key forces in the production of female subjectivity and feminine locality, conditioning the protagonists' identities and movements. The two cities subjugate woman's body and psyche in distinct but related ways. If Naples wields the power of traditional gender inequality, Turin deploys political and military (male) power to perpetuate the narrative of its own (male) superiority. Naples is figured as a chthonic labyrinth (*Fr*, 66), Turin as an iron fortress (*DA*, 32). Delia and Olga, Lila and Elena are imprisoned within these larger architectural structures and then again within the boundaries of their respective neighborhoods and violent relationships. Ferrante constructs the Neapolitan neighborhood, the sub-proletarian *rione*, as the keystone of these women's identities. It structures and holds together their everyday lives through tacit rules, regulations, and institutions of power. A neighborhood, as Appadurai conceptualizes it, is the setting of a locality which produces, recognizes, and organizes reliably local subjects (1996, 181–4). The Neapolitan *rione* produces docile, mute female subjects and forms their identities through their roles in the home, as mothers and housewives, or as helpers in the husband's or father's business. The neighborhood in Ferrante's novels incarnates all the domestic conflicts and public fights—it is not only the architectural stage where violence unfolds daily but also the system that perpetuates violence and instills fear and compliance in all residents. Urban space, in other words, embodies, enacts, and enforces the forms, practices, and rituals of patriarchal control.[3]

Ferrante's architectural imagination is undergirded by a mythological foundation. Naples is imagined as a symbolic and literal labyrinth, an archaic architectural structure designed, as in the Greek myth of Theseus and Ariadne, to curb and punish feminine desire. In the myth, Theseus kills the Minotaur with the help of Ariadne who gives him a thread to lead him through the labyrinth. Delia, like a modern Ariadne, walks through the labyrinth-city, gets lost and disoriented, but then she finds the thread that leads her out (*Fr*, 144). Turin, the northern versant of Ferrante's narrative topography, acts similarly as a structure of containment, but through the inscription of male political, cultural, and military dominance onto the city map. Turin displays its hegemony through monuments, street names, and commemorative plaques, trapping the walking female subject within a recursive web of symbols and discourses of male power. To counter this architectural model of patriarchal control, Ferrante elaborates a theory of urban space as the topography of female identity:

> The problem [. . .] is that one has trouble imagining what sort of polis women could construct, if they sought to do so in their image and likeness. Where is the image-model, what female traits would it resemble? As far as I know the city, for women, always belongs to others, even when it's their native city. [. . .] Evidently the female city will be a long time coming and doesn't yet have true words. To look for them we have to descend beyond the squiggles of our blotting paper, into the

labyrinth of our childhood, into the unredeemed chaos of fragments of our past and our remote past. (*Fr*, 146–7)

Ferrante's vision of a feminine city relies on words that stem from the depths of feminine experience, from the dark labyrinth of childhood when women learn to orient themselves in the male city. She uses the verb "descend" (*discendere, La fr*, 156), a verb that belongs to literary Italian, especially to refer to a symbolic or mythological journey into the netherworld. Ferrante then uses this verb to figure memory's path as a descent underground, into the underworld. Naples *is* that underworld, with its underground caves and hollows where building material was mined to construct the city above, with its Greco-Roman association with the entrance to Hades, and with its dark and threatening underbelly where misery and violence are the norm.[4] Only from within this labyrinthine underworld, Ferrante declares, can women learn to write about—and create—a city "in their image and likeness."

And this is what Ferrante's protagonists do: they learn to circumnavigate and eschew its constrictive order through walking the aggressively male spaces, reshaping them to suit the exigencies of their personal narratives and identities. Walking manipulates spatial organization, it appropriates and redesigns the totalizing, colonizing space of the urban map (de Certeau 1988, 98–101, 121). Ferrante's walking women descend into the topographic and symbolic depths of the city, they plunge precipitously into their own psychic depths, reaching states of bodily abjection, experiencing *frantumaglia* and *smarginatura*. Since *frantumaglia* and *smarginatura* express compromised inner landscapes and bodily boundaries as the symptoms and consequences of an oppressive culture that dissolves women's identities, Ferrante's women walking in the city enact peripatetically their suffering and impose their own order on the spaces they traverse. Walking constitutes a practice of resistance, a reappropriation of female embodied subjectivity inasmuch as the body is always experienced spatially. Urban spaces are remapped to chart a specifically feminine topography, a woman's way of being in the city, a female polis. Ferrante proposes a concrete narrative model for mapping a female polis—the story of Dido who maps the territory of her city with a thread made from thinly cut strips of a bull's skin. This, the author reminds us, is the only time in Western culture a woman has created a polis of her own (*Fr*, 147–8). Ferrante expounds further on the image of Dido sewing together the strips of skin to create a rope, a long thread, that encloses the boundaries of a new city (*Fr*, 148). Dido, in Ferrante's retelling of Virgil, creates an Ariadne's thread to liberate herself from the labyrinth of male cities and to map her own. The image of Ariadne-Dido informs the narrative topography of Ferrante's novels.

This chapter examines the recurring *topoi* of Ferrante's urban imagination that shape female subjectivity in her novels. It reads the spaces of Ferrante's texts as "practiced places" (de Certeau 1988, 117) and porous realities constituted by and transformed through individual walking itineraries. It adopts the methodological routes outlined by Iain Chambers (2008, 71–129) and Silvio Perrella (2015) who study Naples by walking through it, combining their own kinetic perspectives with the layered sights and sounds of its urban space, allowing their texts to be permeated by the city's own narratives. The chapter follows the movements of Ferrante's heroines, reading their walking trajectories as texts, as acts of appropriation of gendered urban spaces. It moves from Delia's Naples in *Troubling Love* to Lila's and Elena's Neapolitan *rione* in the tetralogy to Olga's Turin in *The Days of Abandonment* to argue that Ferrante's female narrators rechart and reinvent the male city to fit their corporeal and narrative needs, to create a female polis not contingent on urban structures of male power.

Walking the Streets of Topographic Memory in *Troubling Love*

Delia, the protagonist of *Troubling Love*, maps her movements through the city as she searches for the truth of her mother's death. Along the way, she experiences the city as violent and oppressive. It overwhelms her senses, attacks her body, and triggers memories and repressed traumas. Naples becomes the topographic narrative of Delia's past, her childhood inscribed onto the very urban fabric. As she walks through the city, she begins to remember and to tell herself the story of her past so that streets become memories and memories evoke streets. Delia's itineraries through Naples compose a spatial and kinetic testimony to the violence of the past which seeps into the present. The city affects the body leaving traces on the subject's corporeality, but the body produces and transforms the city as well (Grosz 1999). As Delia walks, her body is directed, shaped, and transformed by the city and its male inhabitants, but in taking possession of her memories and coming to terms with the past and accepting her affinity with her mother, she re-appropriates the city and shapes its topography in turn.

This mutual production and transformation of bodies and cities is facilitated by the nature of Naples itself. Walter Benjamin defines the city as "porous"—a city which blurs the boundaries between inside and outside, private and public, past and present, up and down (Benjamin and Lacis 1986, 163–73). In Naples "building and action interpenetrate in the courtyards, arcades, and stairways. In everything they preserve the scope to become a theatre of new, unforeseen constellations" (Benjamin and Lacis 1986, 165–6). Time and space are commingled: "There is interpenetration of day and night, noise and peace, outer and inner lightness, street and home" (Benjamin and Lacis 1986, 172). Naples moreover exists in a time of festivities and festivals, "the festival penetrates each and every working day" (Benjamin 1986, 168) and its carnivalesque ontology facilitates the reversals—or rather, the conflations, of private and public, inside and outside. In other words, Naples is a liminal city of a double temporality encapsulating the archaic and the ultramodern. This is what Iain Chambers (2008) calls the "porous modernity" of Naples and what Serenella Iovino means when she characterizes Naples as "spatiotemporally porous" (2014, 100) with its layers of archaeological and architectural strata occupying a contiguous territory. Neapolitan architecture uses as building material the spongy, sandy, pale-yellow stone called "toof" (in Italian *tufo*), or as Serenella Iovino explains, a sedimentary formation resulting from lava flows (2014, 98).[5] The city is built directly on top of the caves where the construction material, the *tufo*, was mined so that the foundation of Naples is a network of caves and tunnels, a "subterranean anti-(or pre-) Naples," an invisible city lying under the visible one (Iovino 2016, 17).

The physical porousness of the city, combined with its ancient stratigraphy and its blurred boundary between inside and outside, public and private, and past and present, authorize Delia's peripatetic narrative in its conflation of spatiotemporal and physical, bodily boundaries. That is why many of the places Delia visits or relishes are liminal spaces, spaces on the threshold between inside and outside, darkness and light, life and death. Ferrante deploys threshold spaces such as the elevator, the dark storeroom, the basement, the tunnel, hallways and corridors, courtyards and stairways as the settings of critical encounters and the memories of those encounters. Ferrante complicates Bakhtin's *chronotope of the threshold* (1984, 172–6; 1981, 248) by making the threshold itself a map of memories and past traumas, a topography of hidden truths and untold narratives.

Naples is a "vertical city" (Chambers 2008, 84); its geography with its hilly relief is integrated into Delia's mode of remembering so that her movements up and down correspond to symbolic elevation or descent. As Ferrante explains to Mario Martone in relation to his film adaptation of *Troubling Love*, movement is intended as both literal and symbolic: "I was attached to Delia's moving from the high toward the low. [. . .] Delia is forced to go downward, a slide that is faintly present in the whole plan of the story" (*Fr*, 33). Delia moves up and down, traversing the city by bus, by funicular, by subway, and on foot, descending further and further into her past as well as into the violent periphery of her old neighborhood, sliding down into underground cellars and forgotten sentiments. These "climactic crossings" (Alsop 2014, 478) bear the directionality of a precipitous plunge into the risky but epistemologically crucial procedure of knowledge and self-knowledge (Alsop 2014, 482). But it is Delia's kinetic experience of the city that maps "an atlas of emotions," to borrow Giuliana Bruno's phrase (Bruno 2002, 2), or better, a symbolic geography of power, gender, and sociospatial hierarchies.

The city's topography relates to another idea inaugurated in *Troubling Love* and developed throughout Ferrante's novels—the city-as-labyrinth.[6] Ferrante describes the city as a labyrinth in which Delia-Ariadne must get oriented and then find her way out (*Fr*, 144). Delia's walking through the city is traversing the mythological labyrinth described in Robert Graves' *Greek Myths* (*Fr*, 145), following a magic thread to save herself from the Minotaur. *Troubling Love* is the narrative the adult Delia weaves together walking through the labyrinth of Naples and following the thread of her mother's life along with her own childhood memories. It is the story she tells herself about the child Delia, a five-year-old girl who witnessed domestic violence and was subjected to sexual abuse. Her childhood is a labyrinth where "the Beast is lying in ambush" (*Fr*, 146), an emotional-spatial landscape that she must traverse in order to conquer the Minotaur. In *Troubling Love*, the Minotaur, the monstrous man-bull, is a composite, hybrid conglomerate of all the abusive, violent male bodies Delia recalls or is subjected to during the course of her journey through Naples.

And as she ascends and descends the hilly terrain of the city, as she takes the subway to reach her old neighborhood, she literally crosses into the underworld figured also as an urban tunnel and a dark basement. Naples is not only the ancient Greek city Neapolis but also where the Greco-Roman imagination situated the entrance to Hades, the underworld.[7] And notably, at the entrance to the underworld, in the Temple of Apollo, Virgil's Aeneas sees and "reads" the story of Theseus and the Minotaur carved there by the labyrinth's own architect Daedalus. In short, Naples is a space "in-between" (Ponzi 2012, de Rogatis 2018), suspended between above and below, past and present. Ferrante's figuration of Naples as the underworld is indebted to Anna Maria Ortese's exploration of an urban hellscape. Ortese's reportage "The Involuntary City" (1953) exposes the appalling living conditions and the ghastly human misery of the inhabitants of a former granary turned into a residential complex for the displaced and the homeless. Ortese walks through the building's poorly lit corridors and tunnels to document the horrors of this infernal city within the city, but she remains very much a visitor who leaves when night approaches.

Ferrante's heroines, on the other hand, are psychologically and corporeally entangled with their surroundings. They move within and against the porous, multilayered, liminal landscape of a city-labyrinth. In traversing Naples, Delia also retraces her mother's steps—from Amalia's apartment to her old house in the *rione* to the site of her death at the beach—and in that journey she relives her own past. Naples provides not only the physical, topographic setting of *Troubling Love* but also its temporal dimension, the chronology of Delia and Amalia's lives mapped onto streets, squares, and tunnels, as well as onto bus, tram, and funicular routes. The city map operates as a complex, polysemous text, a narrative at once embedded into the landscape and generated in turn by it. Or as the literary critic and avid Neapolitan *flâneur* Silvio Perrella quips, Naples "transforms topography into typography" (2015, 316, my translation).

During her mother's funeral Delia carries Amalia's casket with three men and maps the procession from Piazza Carlo III to the "yellowish façade" of the Reclusorio and the Incis neighborhood (*TL*, 17). This itinerary evokes the past:

> The streets of topographic memory seemed to me unstable [...] I felt the city coming apart in the heat, in the dusty gray light, and I went over in my mind the story of childhood and adolescence that impelled me to wander along the Veterinaria to the Botanic Gardens, or over the cobbles of the market of Sant'Antonio Abate [...]
> I had the impression that my mother was carrying off the places, too, and the names of the streets. (*TL*, 17)

Walking in the city becomes synonymous with remembering and storytelling. Naming streets and buildings for Delia becomes a way of holding on to her mother's life story. To unravel the truth about her mother's death, Delia must cross her mother's city and name the streets and places of the past. In doing so, she also disentangles the traumas of her childhood, the truths she was never able to admit to herself. In *Frantumaglia*, Ferrante explains Delia's peripatetic narrative in topographic terms: "Delia must manage to tell herself a story, which she knows well from the beginning to the end—which she has never repressed. The story has remained entangled in certain spaces of the city [. . .] This woman comes into the labyrinth of Naples to capture it, put it in order, arrange space and time, finally tell her own story out loud" (*Fr*, 66).

This story is first and foremost one about violence which is inscribed onto the streets and inside buildings, beginning with the appearance of Caserta, the man-city of Delia's past who crops up during the funeral procession and unleashes more memories. Caserta is the name of a city near Naples, the seat of a grand eighteenth-century royal palace and gardens. Caserta is also the nickname of a man from Delia's past. Three generations of Casertas are implicated in Delia's memory: the bar-pastry shop owner Caserta; his son Caserta who was Delia's father's business partner; and the youngest one, the boy Antonio, Delia's childhood friend. And all of them are associated with domestic violence or sexual abuse. The old Caserta molested the child Delia physically and verbally. The younger Caserta tortured Amalia by sending her gifts which provoked her husband to beat her up and hurt her repeatedly—a sadistic game which Caserta had continued until Amalia's death. The youngest Caserta, Antonio, also took advantage of Delia as a child, touching her and forcing her to touch him. This vicious cycle of Caserta-inflicted violence resurfaces in the present when Antonio attempts to seduce Delia.

Seeing the man-city of her past engenders a strong psychosomatic response in Delia:

> But what my less easily verbalized emotions recorded under the word Caserta was a spinning nausea, vertigo, and a lack of air. Sometimes that place, which belonged to a less reliable memory, consisted of a dimly lighted staircase and a wrought-iron banister [. . .] Caserta was a place where I wasn't supposed to go, a bar with a sign [. . .] If little girls went in they never came out again. (*TL*, 34)

Delia's panic attack is similar to Eugenia's disorientation and physical collapse in Ortese's story "A Pair of Eyeglasses." In Ortese's story, the myopic Eugenia is overwhelmed and nauseated by her Neapolitan neighborhood's landscape of trash and human misery fully visible to her for the first time. In Ferrante's novel, Caserta triggers Delia's inner sight. The images she sees are visions-recollections of sites/sights of abuse: the claustrophobic cellar of the bar-pastry shop where the old Caserta and the little Antonio had molested her; the staircase where her father and his brother had attacked and almost killed Caserta and Antonio. But above all Caserta is figured as a dark, threatening space, a labyrinth of sorts where little girls get lost and never come out. Caserta is both the monster-Minotaur of Delia's childhood and the city-labyrinth—an image that Ferrante revisits in the first volume of the Neapolitan Novels.

Caserta follows Delia after the funeral procession. Not recognizing him, she asks him where she can find a drugstore. He points her to a drugstore on Corso Garibaldi and then yells obscenities at her in dialect, "a soft river of sound that involved me, my sisters, my mother in a concoction of semen, saliva, feces, urine, in every possible orifice" (*TL*, 19). This verbal abuse of the women in Delia's family comes from the mouth of a man who is himself "as if pasted" to the long and large façade of the Albergo dei Poveri, imagined as part of urban architecture. The city with its built environment covers metaphorically Delia with a deluge of bodily fluids doubly gendered male (through both speaker and "semen"). Dialect and verbal abuse are spatialized.

Delia's trip to the Vossi lingerie shop in Piazza Vanvitelli is another "warehouse of memory" (Mortimer-Sandilands 2008) which stores another topos defined by the masculine imaginary. As the bus climbs the hill toward the upscale Vomero neighborhood, Delia observes "women suffocated between male bodies," men ogling women and trying to touch them (*TL*, 52) in the excessive corporeality of the city (Iovino 2014). Her observation triggers another memory—Delia and Amalia taking the tram up the same hill to go to the Vomero and deliver the garments Amalia sewed for her clients. Delia relives Amalia's being subjected not only to the gazes and touches of other men on the tram but also to her husband's savage and perpetual punitive mechanisms. Bus and tram, past and present violence merge as Delia travels uphill toward Piazza Vanvitelli and the shop of the three sisters Vossi.

What she imagined as a dark, elegant shop ruled by the three genteel Vossi sisters, a feminine city of sorts, turns out to be a vulgar, bright and loud display of women "forced into a city-prison, corrupted first by poverty and now by money, with no interruption" (58).[8] In one of her editorials in *The Guardian,* Ferrante writes that "the male gaze has continuously invented [women] as a function of the man's sexual needs" (*Lio*, 33, my translation) and then she suggests that even today women have not escaped their role of conforming to the sexual and social norms established by men (*Lio*, 34). The vulgar women parading seminude in the Vossi shop exemplify precisely this logic of women internalizing and normalizing their subservience to patriarchal modes of domination. What Delia had pictured as the Vossi sisters' autonomous realm of autonomous female bodies, turns out to be populated by women-automatons, or as Elena Greco's second book posits, "female automatons created by men" (*TLTS*, 354).

To control the sense of disorientation, the destabilized and destabilizing cityscape of her memories, Delia continues to map her journey, uncovering its unchanged mechanisms of violence, subjugation, and objectification. After her visit to the Vossi shop where she meets the manager Antonio Polledro, who will turn out to be her childhood friend Antonio, the youngest Caserta, Delia sees the older Caserta and is drawn into a chase through the streets of the Vomero in the rain. Wearing a short dress, Delia seems to comply with the paradigm of femininity displayed for the male gaze she witnessed in the lingerie shop. In a few pages of intensely mapped, topographically specific movements, Delia experiences yet again the city as a male-dominated, violent space. After spotting Caserta, she begins following him, again naming meticulously streets, corners, intersections (*TL*, 67). Lest Delia be thought to assume the male role of the pursuer (rather than the pursued), she is almost immediately disciplined for her transgression.

She is assaulted by a young man who literalizes the city's abstract violence: "a young man came suddenly out from the shelter of a doorway, grabbed me by one arm, laughing, and said to me in dialect 'What's the rush? Let me dry you off'! The tug was so strong that I felt the pain in my collarbone and slipped on my left leg" (*TL*, 67).

Within an urban space codified as male, Delia cannot simultaneously be feminine (in a short dress) and exercise the power of the pursuer. Thus, she is relegated to her proper place as the object of male desire and abuse, as many of the women are in Ferrante's Naples. And this operation transpires by way of male physical contact and by way of the Neapolitan dialect—just like Caserta's "concoction" of bodily fluids shouted in dialect. But Ferrante does not end the chase there. After another intense plotting of movements and the appearance of Antonio Polledro, Caserta's son (*TL*, 67–8), all the characters converge in the funicular station. Delia and Antonio follow the old Caserta inside and the chase resumes as the funicular goes downhill.

Inside the funicular car, Delia watches Caserta persistently seek bodily contact with a young girl, leaning against her buttocks, then pursuing her when she tries to escape his touch (*TL*, 70–1). The male body, facilitated by the swaying movement of the funicular, weighs upon the female body, subjugating it in a display of domineering virility. Delia gets out at the station of Chiaia and conjures up the figures of her mother and her presumed lover Caserta, standing in a corner of the station as if they were figures she is drawing—she colors them, dresses them, adds details and final touches to the sketch. Chapter 4 discussed in detail Delia's mode of reconstructing the past as visual tableaux, but here her imaginative remembering spans several pages so that the past is superimposed onto the urban space of the funicular station and closely related to Delia's traversing of Naples' cityscape, above and below ground. Railway stations are heterotopic spaces that undermine the polarities of space and time, ancient and modern (Fusillo 2011, 45–6). The funicular station positions Delia in a topographic limbo enabling her to paint carefully in her imagination the ghosts of her mother and Caserta.

Delia continues her journey through Naples, now in a taxi with Antonio. The smell of the taxi, Antonio's voice, his account of his father's and Amalia's meetings, of his father stealing lingerie from the Vossi shop, unleash another set of memories. Delia recalls her childhood in a poor Neapolitan neighborhood, the underground interior of the bar-pastry shop owned by the old Caserta, and the shop's cellar as the place of illicit and mysterious events. When Antonio takes her to a faded hotel, she recognizes it from her childhood fantasies as the kind of place she imagined her mother escaped to every time she left the house. The hotel, another site of transience and mobility, is coopted into Delia's recreation of the past: with its sleazy appeal it reminds her of the storeroom of her childhood where she hid to await her mother's return. As the boundary between past and present blurs, the storeroom turns into the cellar of the bar-pastry shop and Delia sees her mother and Caserta descending in it, lying on the floor on their stomachs and crawling, laughing: "The cellar extended as a long, low space. One could advance only on all fours [. . .] Caserta and my mother crept along" (*TL*, 84–5). The storeroom and the cellar-tunnel at once hide and reveal the secret of Delia's traumatic experiences. The cellar-tunnel becomes a secret passage underneath the building, a labyrinthine underworld. It also evokes the presence of a literal tunnel, an architectural structure crucial to Ferrante's spatial poetics.

Delia's final expedition within Naples is a descent into the underworld, but also a reappropriation of urban space. She decides to visit her old neighborhood where her father still lives: "As I descended into the underground at Piazza Cavour, a warm wind blew in, making the metallic walls sway and mixing the red and blue of the escalator, and I imagined I was a figure from Neapolitan cards: the eight of spades, the woman who, calm and armed, advances on foot ready to jump into the game of *briscola*" (*TL*, 107). Her imagination molds the walls and colors of the underground and Delia becomes a foot soldier, a woman determined to win her battles, to conquer the city's hostile streets and men, as Chapter 2 has pointed out. This image attests to Delia's internal transformation from a passive victim to an active force in reconstructing her mother's story (Parisi 2017, 188; Pesca 2017, 11). She rides to the end of the line, exits at Piazza Garibaldi, and approaches her old neighborhood on foot. First, she must cross the tunnel she recalls from her childhood and negotiate its dark, ominous interior:

> I recalled a single endless passage, deserted and constantly shaken by the trains on the siding overhead. Instead I took no more than a hundred steps, slowly, in a shadowy light stinking of urine, squeezed between a wall that sweated large drops of water and a dusty guardrail that protected me from the crowded automobile lane. (*TL*, 108)

The tunnel as urban reality and as visual metaphor recurs throughout Ferrante's texts. It appears in *The Days of Abandonment*, a passage covered with obscene graffiti and it constitutes a key spatial symbol in *My Brilliant Friend*, the first volume of the Neapolitan Novels. *Troubling Love* describes the originary image of the tunnel already anticipated by Delia's fantasy of the cellar as tunnel. Here it is less terrifying than Delia remembers it yet equally oppressive. Delia now recalls Amalia in the tunnel, pursued and touched by aggressive men:

> Amalia had been followed in the tunnel by peddlers, railway workers, idlers, stonemasons [. . .] they stayed close, at her side, often breathing in her ear. They tried to touch her hair, her shoulder, her arm. Some tried to take her hand while making obscene remarks. (*TL*, 108)

The tunnel, like the tram, the bus, and the funicular, enables and incarnates the relationship between women's bodies and urban space.

The porosity and liminality of Naples, its metaphorical and ontological instability in Ferrante's novel, its oscillation between destabilizing and destabilized notions of space and time, at first serve to reinforce the physical and ideological subjugation of women within the symbolic (patriarchal) order. As we have seen, the poetics of topography in *Troubling Love* relies on a network of urban sites and practices—walking, riding the bus/tram/funicular, being attacked physically or verbally. To counter this network of public porous spaces, Ferrante constructs a series of equally porous and liminal interiors—the sarcophagus-elevator in Amalia's building which Delia uses as a place for introspection and remembering, the storeroom of her childhood where she anxiously awaited her mother's return, and finally, the basement of the bar-pastry shop. These are spaces where Delia can resist the city's onslaught on her body and her psyche, where she can transform the map of the past by narrating in the present the truth about what happened. Delia begins this reclaiming of spaces and narratives when she crosses the tunnel to reach her old neighborhood.

Walking through the tunnel conjures Amalia's body and the two women merge into one: "Was it possible that I, passing through there, carried her in my aging, unsuitably dressed body? Was it possible that her sixteen-year-old body, in a homemade flowered dress, was passing through the shadowy light by means of mine?" (*TL*, 109). It is precisely the crossing of this boundary between the present and the past, between the rest of Naples and her old neighborhood that generates Delia's acceptance of her mother inside her. As Katrin Wehling-Giorgi notes, the gradual recuperation of the mother's silenced and abused self is negotiated through the recurring trope of the tunnel (2016a, 2021). After crossing the tunnel, Delia acquires a new perception of the *rione*. She notices its ugliness and decaying banality, and then she maps it out in her head as a way of conquering its hostile urban space: "As I went up I tried to redraw the map of it in such a way that the impact with that space wouldn't be too disturbing" (*TL*, 110). Delia goes over the layout of her old building in minute detail—gate, entrance, doorway, staircase. Then she describes her parents' apartment, meticulously outlining each room with its furniture. Each space evokes memories and she delves into scenes and images from the past: her father painting in the bedroom, his process of creating the gypsy painting, Amalia working on her sewing machine. After Delia confronts her father, he too attacks her physically and verbally, closing the circle of men-inflicted abuse within male-dominated public and private space. When she leaves, she no longer feels rooted or indebted to the past—in fact, she feels free of its weight which is also the weight of the house.[9] Exiting the house is dissolving her father's control of the narrative of her own past.

To gain control of her own story, Delia must venture inside the most terrifying, most traumatic and hence, most hidden, space of her memories—the pastry shop where she was abused by the old Caserta and where she played with the little Antonio. It is also the place where she imagined she saw Amalia engaging in sexual behavior with her friend Caserta and reported to her father what she had seen and heard. Before she descends into the shop located in the basement of the building, Delia also walks around the courtyard, peeks inside the stairs that led to Caserta's apartment and recalls how her father and uncle had gone up those stairs to murder Caserta. This memory takes a distinctly spatial shape, as if embedded inside the stairs and the banisters, encrusted upon the building's surfaces: "The story, shattered into a thousand incoherent images, struggled to correspond to stone and iron. But the violence came to an end now, wrapped around the railing of the stairway, and it seemed to me that it had been here—here and not there—for forty years, screaming" (*TL*, 130). These are precisely the stairs and banisters Delia associates with the name Caserta, the brutal revenge her father and uncle had taken on Caserta and his son. In facing the building which contains the traumas of the past, Delia begins to exorcise them.

Inside the cellar-shop, Delia finds Caserta's lair where he has laid out all of Amalia's belongings, as well as tickets and receipts mapping Amalia's last movements from Naples to Formia to the beach at Minturno. This dark space becomes a stage or screen on which Delia sees, as if unfolding before her, her mother's final days, reconstructing her actions and imagining her motivations (*TL*, 124). Delia descends further into the underworld-underground of the shop which can also be read as a spatial metaphor for the unconscious (Bachelard 1994, 19), into the lower level of the cellar, where she finally faces the scenes from the past and is able to narrate them once and for all: "I slid down three slippery steps. I agreed, on the way, to tell myself everything: whatever truth the lies preserved" (*TL*, 131). She manages to tell the truth to herself only within the lower space of the cellar which is also the tunnel of her fantasies of Amalia and Caserta crawling and laughing. This lower level is also the "subterranean space" (*TL*, 130) where Antonio spoke obscenities to Delia, where he touched her and forced her to touch him. And it is the stage of the novel's most traumatic revelation—that Delia had been abused by the old Caserta.

Delia finally manages to articulate and come to terms with the truth that her mother never had an affair with Caserta and that Delia, in her love-hatred-jealousy for Amalia, had attributed the abuse inflicted on her by the old Caserta to her mother and her father's friend.[10] This displacement, this screen memory, occurred within the space of the bar-pastry shop and thus the place carries for Delia the markers and the experiences of the displacement. To admit to herself the truth, to reconstruct the events of the past as they occurred within the cellar and inside the building, on the stairway and the banisters, is to arrange the past in its sequential order, to give spaces their meaning and their chronology It is to sew everything together, to connect it by means of a thread, which is Ariadne's thread and the thread of the narrative that links the past to the present, the imagined spaces to the real places. As Chapter 3 argued, it is the mother's art—the art of the seamstress, Dido's art of charting the territory of a new city—that Delia borrows. "To speak is to link together lost times and spaces" (*TL*, 133), she concludes when the narrative is complete and ready to occupy its proper spatiotemporal coordinates.

Troubling Love narrates the traversal of the labyrinth of Naples imagined also as the container of stories Delia had been unable to admit to herself. As a modern Ariadne she follows the thread of her memories, a thread that traces the literal and symbolic map of Naples with its ascending and descending paths, uncovering narratives of violence but also weaving a new narrative. The novel concludes when Delia revisits the site of her mother's death, the beach at Minturno, and taking a pen out, transforms her photograph into a portrait of Amalia, accepting both her mother and her mother's city as parts of herself. Conquering her memories, Delia also conquers their spatial dimensions and therefore the topography that had imprisoned her within a past she was unable to narrate. In doing so, Delia-Amalia can resist both the city and its violence, for she becomes the city herself:

> It's possible that in the end the most elusive, hardest to grasp, most densely ambiguous person, this Amalia who absorbs difficulties and beatings but doesn't give in, was charged with the least definable Neapolitanness, and so is a sort of woman-city who is tugged, trapped, shaken, pursued, humiliated, desired, and yet endowed with an extraordinary capacity to endure. (*Fr*, 67)

In this excerpt from *Frantumaglia* Ferrante begins to elaborate her idea of the woman-city—the female polis or the feminine labyrinth—which she develops further in the Neapolitan Novels.

Symbolic and Literal Labyrinth in the Neapolitan Novels

The labyrinth as a spatial-architectonic and social-symbolic structure underlies the four Neapolitan Novels. Like in *Troubling Love*, buildings, courtyards, squares, staircases, cellars, and tunnels are linked to symbolic structures of oppression. This architectonic foundation of her texts functions as both an urban architectural setting *and* a symbolic foundation—the underworld, the underlying framework—of the novels' mythological and sociocultural imaginary. As such, the city in the tetralogy shapes the bodies and the psyches of the two protagonists, Elena and Lila, and it frames and contains them within their violent, male-dominated Neapolitan neighborhood. This same "gang-riddled, lawless" (Purvis 2018) Neapolitan neighborhood serves as the foundation of Elena's literary creativity whereas Lila continues to be for Elena her source of inspiration, her imagined and real interlocutor, collaborator, and her desired audience. As the novels progress, Elena leaves Naples and the *rione* for Pisa and Florence, then returns and lives in Naples for many years in an attempt to master and control its ungovernable space, to finally leave again and settle in Turin, in an apartment overlooking the Princess Isabella bridge.

Elena's most productive, most fertile periods of writing coincide with her return to Naples. When she moves back to Naples, she first takes residence in an apartment in the upscale and uphill Via Tasso, therefore realizing her ambition to move up the Neapolitan socio-spatial hierarchy. Elena's balcony now overlooks the gulf of Naples with the neighborhood of her humble origins obscured in the flatlands of the periphery down below (*SLC*, 115–16) and her new elevated social position clearly inscribed as a topography of identity. But she finds her rarefied life among the intellectual elite less productive. She moves back to the neighborhood and rents an apartment above Lila's. The friends' architectonic bond—Elena's floor is Lila's ceiling—dissolves the boundary between them, their lives become spatially porous and architecturally connected. The new arrangement turns out to be fertile ground for Elena's writing—living in the neighborhood she completes her third book, a narrative about the life of the *rione*.

Unlike her friend, Lila never leaves her city.[11] After her daughter disappears in *The Story of the Lost Child*, she dedicates herself to daily wandering, exploring its sites and studying its topographic history, its buildings, monuments, streets, and squares. Lila's explorations unearth strata of violence embedded in the map of Naples as well as the urban myths and legends attached to places so that every monument, every stone acquires "a density of meaning, a fantastic importance" (*SLC*, 445). Lila compiles and becomes a walking atlas of Naples, an ambulatory encyclopedia of the city, an oral history that she imparts to Elena's youngest daughter, Imma, but never writes down. Lila gradually comes to embody Naples, irrational and metamorphic, porous and permeable like it, to eventually dissolve into its interstices.[12] Elena too walks in the city but her approach is significantly different: she adopts the outsider's gaze, preferring the more picturesque, "postcard locations" (degli Esposti 2019) of the city that inscribe her own acquired superiority onto the cityscape.

Nonetheless, Elena is the one who can transform the *rione* into narrative, who can recount and dramatize the events of their childhood, adolescence, and adulthood. She does so in several of her novels and in her masterpiece, the novella *A Friendship*, which she writes in 2006, during a visit in Naples, and which is a mise en abyme of the Neapolitan Novels we are reading (Santovetti 2016, 2018; Wehling-Giorgi 2016a). Elena transforms topographic space into words (topography into typography), whereas Lila's perambulations remain unwritten, mediated only through Imma's oral accounts of her urban explorations with Lila. Lila's great Neapolitan novel that Elena imagines her friend to be writing never materializes. Instead, as Chapter 4 argued, Elena as the author of the four volumes chronicling her and her friend's lives, functions as their composite feminine voice charting a double feminine topography, mapping the movements, exiles and returns, of two women.[13] Transmitting her knowledge to Imma, Lila seeks to establish a feminine city, but ultimately fails (degli Esposti 2019). I propose that Lila and Elena together succeed not only in building a feminine city-labyrinth by expropriating the *rione*'s literal and symbolic labyrinth but also in narrating it. And as Ferrante declares, the origins of this labyrinth must be traced back to childhood where words can be found to dismantle it (*Fr*, 144).

If in *Troubling Love* Naples is the city-labyrinth Delia must traverse, in the Neapolitan tetralogy the labyrinth is mirrored in the power structures of the neighborhood itself. The topography and architectural spaces of the first volume, *My Brilliant Friend*, trace the literal labyrinth of the place where Lila and Elena live, trapped in the periphery, their neighborhood confined by a tunnel and train tracks. This labyrinth is also the underworld of domestic violence and organized crime, of a patriarchal culture that subjugates and disciplines women. It is an underworld where women are punished for any transgression or desire. The labyrinth is also the archaic locus of the Minotaur, the man-beast of Greek mythology, the monster who terrifies Lila and Elena in *My Brilliant Friend*. And if Elena Greco is writing the story of her friend Lila who never left Naples, to reconstruct Lila's life is also to reconstruct the place where they grew up, to rebuild "space as storyteller" (Chiesa 2016, 1). The four novels then chart not only the history of Elena and Lila's friendship but also the history of their unnamed Neapolitan neighborhood, mapping the two girls' lives onto the topography of the *rione* and of the city. *My Brilliant Friend* tracks Elena and Lila's movements through the labyrinth of their childhood—city streets, squares, and gateways; inside courtyards, buildings, and cellars; and within tunnels, corridors, and staircases.

From the opening pages of *My Brilliant Friend*, Elena recounts her childhood as dominated by the spatial and social hierarchies of the *rione*. At the center of this universe is the former loan shark and black-market dealer Don Achille who instills fear in the community: "we didn't know the origin of that fear-rancor-hatred-meekness that our parents displayed [toward Don Achille] [...] and transmitted to us, but it was there, it was a fact, like the neighborhood, its dirty-white houses, the fetid odor of the landings, the dust of the streets" (*MBF*, 51). Elena depicts Don Achille as an inextricable element of the architectonic and social fabric of the neighborhood, a node of power and terror regulating children's and parents' behavior. The built environment, urban architecture and topography, provide the physical context in which we internalize and then enact proper social, sexual, and political behavior: the city, that is, produces and circulates power (Grosz 1999). Don Achille's power, in Elena's words, pervades the physical dimensions of the *rione*, its streets and houses, dictating obedience and silence. What is more, the *rione* maps a topography of violence and suffering. The neighborhood's architectural spaces become the sites for scandals and aggressions, the stage where the fragility of the human body and the insignificance of human life are made visible. Lila and her classmate Enzo fight with rocks in the street until they're both bleeding. Lila's father throws her out of the window. Melina Cappuccio and Lidia Sarratore attack each other viciously on the stairs. And Don Achille throws his enemy Alfredo Peluso against a tree in the public gardens. Don Achille thus lives up to the implication of his name as raw masculine power that inflicts pain and suffering.[14]

As the central embodiment of power, Don Achille organizes Lila and Elena's conception of both space and time. It is not by chance that part one of the first volume is entitled "Childhood. The Story of Don Achille." Don Achille and his dark menacing building structure the spatial configuration and plot development of the girls' childhood and the origins of their lifelong friendship. Don Achille's building acquires the physical and symbolic dimensions of a labyrinth with the terrifying man-eating monster at its center. And this labyrinth, recalling the Greek myth of Theseus and the Minotaur, creates the myth of origins of Lila and Elena's friendship. And as Grace Russo Bullaro has suggested, Don Achille is also the fulcrum of Elena and Lila's understanding of time, of their notions of before and after he had revealed his monstrous nature (Bullaro 19–20; *MBF* 36–7).

Greek mythology belongs to Elena Ferrante's poetics and her female protagonists enact archaic rituals and rites of passage.[15] In *Frantumaglia*, Ferrante herself admits, time and again, the formative influence of Greek myth on her creative process:

> I returned to Naples for several months; I had my own problems. I retraced many of the routes of my childhood, including the one I had taken with my sister in the rain. [...] I recalled the image of the labyrinth as an ordinary space, a known place that, with oneself, is suddenly disrupted by a strong emotion. I got some books (including that vast captivating hodgepodge that is Graves's *The Greek Myths*), I wanted to see if the myth would help me describe, by giving me distance, a story of intolerance, love, flight, and abandonment. (*Fr*, 145)

This passage articulates the idea of Naples itself as a labyrinth, a recurring idea in Ferrante's imaginary (*Fr*, 66, 142–3). But it also names the nexus between retracing the routes of childhood, Greek mythology, and narrative. This passage anticipates Elena and Lila's own walking through the labyrinth of the *rione* and Don Achille's building.

Following the prologue, the narrative proper of *My Brilliant Friend* opens with Lila and Elena walking up the dark stairs to Don Achille's top-floor apartment: "My friendship with Lila began the day we decided to go up the dark stairs that led, step after step, flight after flight, to the door of Don Achille's apartment" (*MBF* 27). The arduous process of advancing toward a terrifying goal, emphasized by the insistence on its spatiotemporal duration "step by step, flight by flight," transpires within the liminal spaces of the dark entryway, the staircase, the landings. Their ascent is a descent into the underworld where a monstrous beast awaits the two girls, as Elena narrates:

> I was frozen with fear. Don Achille was the ogre of fairy tales, I was absolutely forbidden to go near him [. . .] He was a being created out of some unidentified material [. . .] I was trembling. Every footfall, every voice was Don Achille creeping up behind us or coming down toward us with a long knife [. . .] Maria, Don Achille's wife, would put me in the pan of boiling oil, the children would eat me, he would suck my head the way my father did with mullets. We stopped often, and each time I hoped that Lila would decide to turn back. I was all sweaty. (*MBF*, 27–8)

Thus, from the very beginning Don Achille becomes a fairy-tale monster, a child-devouring Minotaur at the center of a dark and dreadful space. Robert Graves's *Greek Myths* (1957) recounts the myth of Theseus and the Minotaur. The queen of Crete, Pasiphae, falls in love with a white bull. This illicit passion is King Minos's punishment for his own transgressions. The Minotaur, half-bull and half-human, is born out of the union of Pasiphae and the white bull. To conceal the shame of such monstrous offspring, the king of Crete closes him in the labyrinth, a prison constructed by the architect Daedalus. King Minos feeds this anthropophagous beast with seven young women and seven young men sent every nine years by Athens. Until Theseus, the son of the Athenian king, kills the Minotaur with the help of Ariadne, the daughter of Minos. Ariadne falls in love with Theseus and to save him from certain death in the labyrinth, she gives him a thread. The thread, tied to the labyrinth's entrance, guides him through the labyrinth and helps him find the exit.

In the myth, the labyrinth is the architectonic symbol of feminine desire and transgression—Pasiphae's forbidden lust for the white bull that must be punished and contained. Classics scholar Paul Allen Miller has shown that in fact, in the *Aeneid*, another important influence on Ferrante's poetics, Virgil's image of the labyrinth serves as a warning against women's uncontainable desire (1995, 225–40). Miller argues that the labyrinth embodies the male symbolic order whose role is to suppress, control, and guard against the monstrous:

> From this point of view, the labyrinth would be analogous to the symbolic itself, the social realm of language and ideology whose role is to subsume and contain the monsters of the imaginary. The labyrinth as the symbolic functions as a mechanism of repression, which makes a controlled, socially sanctioned desire possible. At the beginning of Book 6 of the *Aeneid*, the labyrinth is depicted as a

rational structure built to contain the Minotaur, a monstrous offspring "created from the blending of female and animal passion." It simultaneously holds within itself that which is dangerous to let out, and keeps out those who would try to probe too deeply within and fall prey to monsters better left undisturbed. (1995, 234)

The labyrinth then is an architectonic mechanism for control, an architectural warning against feminine excess and transgression. It is synonymous with the male-dominated space and patriarchal order of the *rione*. It is a symbol of the city which produces and circulates power as it produces and circulates acceptable and appropriate forms of the body.

To connect further the labyrinth described by both Robert Graves and Virgil to the Neapolitan setting of *My Brilliant Friend*, it must be noted that the *Aeneid* is an important intertext in the Neapolitan Novels. Virgil describes the myth of the Minotaur in the sixth book of the *Aeneid*—Aeneas who has just arrived in Italy, is at Cuma, the ancient Greek colony that founded Neapolis or Naples. In Apollo's temple, built by none other than Daedalus, Aeneas sees depicted the story of the Minotaur: Pasiphae's lust for the bull, the labyrinth designed to contain their offspring, and Daedalus himself who guides Ariadne's steps with a thread (VI: 14–33). The image of the Minotaur and the labyrinth is then located, textually, mythologically, within the territory of Naples, as a literary and topographic link between the labyrinth and the city. Moreover, still in Book VI, after proper sacrifices, Aeneas enters Hades, the underworld, near lake Averna and near Naples. We can understand the opening of *My Brilliant Friend* in which two girls walk, step by step and flight by flight, through a dark terrifying space as an evocation of the labyrinth as both the patriarchal order of their neighborhood and the central power that organizes it—the monster Don Achille. But theirs is also a journey into the underworld just as Delia must enter the underworld of the *rione*—the tunnel and the cellar—before she can master her narrative and her city.

The ancient myth, the archaic world of women punished for their desires, erupts from within the mundane reality of the *rione* and the Minotaur's first victims are Elena and Lila's dolls, Nu and Tina. The two girls play with their dolls, placing them deliberately next to the windows of a building's cellar. When Lila pushes Elena's doll through the grating and Elena reciprocates by throwing Lila's doll, they must descend to the basement to retrieve them. The cellar-underworld recalls Caserta's realm in *Troubling Love*, the bar-pastry shop as the site of male-inflicted abuse and violence where Delia finally confronts her past, connecting stories, times, and places. Elena and Lila too must go down to the basement to confront their own fears: "Once inside, we descended, Lila in the lead, five stone steps into a damp space, dimly lit by the narrow openings at street levels" (*MBF*, 55). Lila leads Elena down the stairs to the basement in the same way she leads her up the stairs to Don Achille's apartment.

Lila and Elena's ordeal inside the labyrinth constitutes the entire first part of the volume, "Childhood. The Story of Don Achille," and thus defines the story of their childhood and their friendship. The narrative does not progress in a linear manner—it shifts back and forth, as Lila and Elena proceed up the stairs and pause at the landings, plummeting down to the basement where they go first, then culminating in their ascent to the top floor and the encounter with Don Achille. Ferrante's mode of narrating follows the pace of Lila and Elena's journey up and down the stairs, the plot emerging from spatial coordinates and bodily movements. The figure of the Minotaur Don Achille appears first in the underworld of the building's basement where Lila and Elena search in vain for their dolls. There, among the dark objects, Lila finds an antigas mask and puts it on in a defiant gesture: "She had put the face with the glass eyes over hers and now her face was enormous, with round, empty eye sockets and no mouth, only that protruding black chin swinging over her chest" (*MBF*, 56). This image renders Lila less human and more beast-like, evoking the bull-headed, human-bodied Minotaur.[16]

On the next page Elena confirms Don Achille's presence underneath the buildings when she imagines what has happened to Tina and Nu, the Minotaur's victims, "The shapeless mass of Don Achille running through the underground tunnels, arms dangling, large fingers grasping Nu's head in one hand, in the other Tina's" (*MBF*, 57). Don Achille is simultaneously beneath and above, inside and outside—a spatial metaphor for the pervasiveness of male power and control. Beginning with the descent in the basement and the search for the dolls, Elena feels physically oppressed by the *rione* with its spatial and symbolic constraints, she becomes painfully aware of her neighborhood as an architectonic trap:

> When I returned to the streets and to school, I felt that the space, too, had changed. It seemed to be chained between two dark poles: on one side was the underground air bubble that pressed on the roots of the houses, the threatening cavern the dolls had fallen into; on the other, the upper sphere, on the fourth floor of the building where Don Achille, who had stolen them, lived. The two balls were as if screwed to the end of an iron bar, which in my imagination obliquely crossed the apartments, the streets, the countryside, the tunnel, the railroad tracks, and compressed them. I felt squeezed in that vise. (*MBF*, 57)

This passage outlines the parameters of the labyrinth of Elena and Lila's childhood, the *rione* as the imposition of patriarchal logic, physical violence, and pervasive fear. Ferrante describes Naples as a male-governed space where men "crush and torture" women, where women feel the weight of the male city on their existence, "silent victims" to it (*Fr*, 54; 219–20). Don Achille seems only the symptom of a larger condition, one that manifests spatially for Elena who feels "squeezed" by the weight of the neighborhood, the weight of the male city, and for Lila as *smarginatura*, the disorienting and terrifying dissolution of physical boundaries. The underground space reaches out and above, to the top floor, and spreads out to enclose the whole neighborhood, abolishing the boundary between up and down, inside and outside, vertical and horizontal, myth and modernity. Elena's experience of the *rione* reflects and exposes the spatiotemporal porosity of Naples. Elena and Lila's movement from the basement to the top floor can also be read as a movement from the cellar to the attic via the staircase, in Gaston Bachelard's conceptualization of the verticality of the home as shelter (1994, 17–19, 24–6). But Don Achille's building collapses the distinction between cellar and attic, dismantling the very structure of the house and denying Lila and Elena the safety and intimacy of the home.

The two girls' walk through the labyrinth initiates their friendship as the moment that binds them forever and thus generates the narrative itself, the story of Elena and Lila that spans the four volumes of the Neapolitan Novels. We know from the first chapter of *My Brilliant Friend* that their friendship begins the moment Lila takes Elena's hand on the stairs to Don Achille's apartment:

> We climbed slowly toward the greatest of our terrors of that time, we went to expose ourselves to fear and interrogate it. At the fourth flight Lila did something unexpected. She stopped to wait for me, and when I reached her she gave me her hand. This gesture changed everything between us forever. (*MBF*, 29)

And inasmuch as the four volumes that Elena Greco is writing originate in this gesture, this is the tetralogy's self-reflexive moment of genesis, creation reconfigured as feminine. This gesture is made possible only through the girls' journey through the labyrinth, their joining hands against the Minotaur. Almost forty pages later, Elena returns to the climactic scene of their childhood, to finally narrate its resolution:

> So we climbed the stairs: at every step I was on the point of turning around and going back to the courtyard. I still feel Lila's hand grasping mine [. . .] So, one beside the other, I on the wall side and she on the banister side, sweaty palms clasped, we climbed the last flights. At Don Achille's door my heart was pounding, I could hear it in my ears, but I was consoled by thinking that it was also the sound of Lila's heart. (*MBF*, 65)

The image of their sweaty hands clasped together reiterates the gesture that initiated the narrative. The more they climb the stairs and the farther they reach into the labyrinth, the closer they become, not only their hands but also their bodies becoming one. The merging of sweaty hands and pounding hearts lies at the beginning of the long journey of Lila and Elena's lives, it forms the narrative thread that weaves the fabric of the story, the plot of the Neapolitan quartet. The sweat literally seals the pact of friendship between the two girls as the exchange or blending of their bodily fluids.

Don Achille gives Elena and Lila money to buy new dolls. With the money they buy Louisa Alcott's book *Little Women* and read it obsessively for months, side by side in the courtyard. And their pact of friendship is transformed into a pact of readers and writers, creators and collaborators who plot to write a book. When Lila does write a book, *The Blue Fairy*, Elena discovers her friend's talent for storytelling. And from that point on, Elena models her own writing on Lila's, competing with her friend but also drawing on her literary genius for her own creative work. Even the very tetralogy, Elena's long narrative about her friend, exists in competition with—or thanks to—the novel Elena imagines Lila could have written. As Rebecca Falkoff writes, "The Neapolitan Novels (according to their fiction) are only a shadowy approximation of the work of [Lila's] genius" (2015). The genesis of Lila and Elena's creative collaboration can be read architectonically as situated at the moment their sweaty palms touch and they climb together the dark staircase.

The mythological layer underlying this scene and the creation of a feminine polis with which I began this section can now be revisited. In *My Brilliant Friend* Ferrante reconfigures the myth of Theseus and the Minotaur as a modern, female-centered narrative. The two clasped and sweaty hands establish a bond, a magic thread which allows Elena and Lila to find their way in the labyrinth and then out of it. The thread that connects and metaphorically stitches together the lives of the two friends is Ariadne's thread, the narrative thread that runs throughout the tetralogy and holds it together as the story of Lila and Elena's friendship. From the image of Lila and Elena walking together, unified by clasping hands and pounding hearts, emerges a double Ariadne. Theseus—the powerful Athenian hero—has been replaced by a feminine couple. This new configuration subverts the symbolic order of the labyrinth and the *rione* and enacts a new system, a new movement through space produced by two women. The metaphorical thread which connects Elena and Lila from the moment in which they join hands runs throughout their lives transformed into a long creative collaboration between women whose literary voices and narrative styles become intertwined in Elena's writing and ultimately produce the text of the Neapolitan Novels. In other words, the physical and metaphorical bond between Lila and Elena, the two brilliant friends, constitutes Ariadne's thread.

The image of Ariadne plays an important role in Ferrante's literary imagination and creative process. In an essay titled "Cities" she discusses her literary sources and influences, linking them to the representation of Naples in her own works and mapping the relationship between feminine bodies and cities. She recounts her fascination with the myth of Theseus and Ariadne, and particularly with a variant of the myth in which Theseus abandons the pregnant Ariadne on an island. To console her the local women write to her love letters, pretending they are from Theseus (*Fr*, 145). While in Naples, Ferrante works on an Ariadne story of her own, set on the Amalfi coast, about "a city of female friendship and solidarity but free in its thoughts and in its conflicts. I imagined a community of modern women writing consoling love letters to a modern Ariadne" collaborating in a "true, harmonious" project (*Fr*, 146). But Ferrante's creative process stalls as she comes to the realization that "even in the case of cities dominated by women one can and must write only of city-labyrinths, the repositories of our complex and contradictory emotions, where the Beast is lying in ambush and it's dangerous to get lost without having first learned to do so" (*Fr*, 146). Elena and Lila become lost in the labyrinth of the *rione* precisely in order to learn how to find their way in a male-dominated urban space and social order, and how to unfurl the magic thread which unites them.

The connection between women and cities is crucial to Ferrante's poetics of topography. She reflects on the figure of Dido, depicted in the *Aeneid* whose ingenuity helps her found a new city, subverting male power through feminine creativity and skill (*Fr*, 147–8). Dido, fleeing from Tyre, seeks refuge in Northern Africa. The king of the Gaetuli tells her that she can have as much land as the hide of a bull. Dido cuts and sews the hide all night, reducing it to almost invisible strips, which were then sewed together in such a way that the seams couldn't even be guessed at, a very long Ariadne's thread, a ball of animal skin which would unroll to enclose a vast piece of African land and, at the same time, the boundaries of a new city. (*Fr*, 148)

Ferrante combines the image of the bull (the Minotaur), Ariadne's thread, and Dido's city. In her telling, Ariadne's thread, the product of skilled feminine hands, unrolls to enfold the land of a feminine city. In the same way Lila and Elena create their own Ariadne's thread to mark and circumscribe their own space within the male-dominated *rione*, to find their way out of the male city-prison.

The narrative of Elena and Lila's childhood concludes with the murder of Don Achille, the text thus tying together the two stories—that of Lila and Elena's early friendship and that of Don Achille. Although Alfredo Peluso is arrested for the murder, the novel never confirms that he was the perpetrator. Lila, fascinated with the gory details, keeps imagining the scene of the murder, insisting that it was a woman who killed Don Achille: "with great seriousness, always adding new details, she compelled us to hear the story as if she had been present [. . .] Surely she imagined that the murderer was female only because it was easier for her to identify with her" (*MBF*, 84). In having Lila narrate the murder of Don Achille at the hands of a woman, Ferrante in effect rewrites the myth of Theseus and the Minotaur while also underscoring Lila's superb storytelling skills. In Ferrante's own version of the myth, a double Ariadne enters the labyrinth and defeats the monster. This victorious Ariadne inaugurates Lila and Elena's friendship and thus inaugurates the story of that friendship.

This double Ariadne, two women lost in a city-labyrinth, too belongs to Ferrante's urban imaginary. She recalls a scene from her own childhood: she and her sister getting lost in Naples and running to find their way home: "I had to stop, tug on my sister so that she wouldn't run away, grasp the thread of orientation, which is a magic thread, to tie one street to the next, making tight knots, so that the streets would calmly settle down and I could find the way home" (*Fr*, 142). In this passage Ferrante brings together Ariadne's and Dido's threads into a single thread which conquers disorientation and in doing so molds and marks the territory of a feminine city. And the outcome of getting lost is crucial: "I mean the resorting to a thread that reconnects the places shattered by emotions and allows us not only to get lost but to govern our getting lost" (*Fr*, 142). Likewise, Elena and Lila govern their fear and thus govern the space of Don Achille's building to find their way in the Minotaur's labyrinth, unfurling the magic thread woven by the sweat of their hands. It is not by chance that in the second part of *My Brilliant Friend*, "Adolescence," Lila becomes a passionate reader of Virgil's *Aeneid* while Elena writes an essay on Dido's feminine city, developing the ideas of her friend, producing a doubly authored text.

The first volume of the Neapolitan tetralogy posits a female couple at the center of the labyrinth. Lila and Elena cross the labyrinth, defeat the Minotaur, and find their way out by making their own Ariadne's thread and delineating the territory of their own feminine labyrinth at the heart of patriarchal urban topography. But, above all, the journey through the labyrinth initiates their new feminine identity, not entirely contingent on the symbolic order, but on the bond between the them that determines and guides their lives in the Neapolitan Novels. Ferrante also revisits and combines two ancient, pre-Minotaur conceptions of the labyrinth—as a line dance with labyrinthine, tortuous movements (Kern 2000) and as a building or a city with a complex urban plan (Sarullo 2017). Lila and Elena's tortuous negotiation of Don Achille's building can be read as the construction of their own labyrinth. As Richard Carvalho remarks, Lila does not enter the maze and she does not get out, "she *is* the maze" (2018, 106, italics in the original).

The two dolls, Tina and Nu, appear again in Turin, at the closing of the narrative frame in the fourth volume as Elena completes the tetralogy. She reads the dolls' arrival as a last sign from Lila who has sent her Tina and Nu sixty years after their disappearance in the basement. Perhaps, Ferrante suggests, it was Lila who had the two dolls all along. And perhaps it was Lila who architected the walk in the labyrinth and the encounter with the Minotaur. In Virgil's *Aeneid* Daedalus, the labyrinth's architect, guides Ariadne's steps with a magic thread (VI: 14–33), just like Lila has led Elena both down the stairs to the basement and then up to Don Achille's top-floor apartment. Lila, then, has taken the architect's role and redesigned the labyrinth from inside. Within Ferrante's logic of urban space where orientation is contingent on disorientation, where finding one's way in the city is also mapping a feminine polis, the walk in the labyrinth is intended to appropriate the literal and symbolic architecture of the neighborhood and to reconfigure it from within; to change its dynamics from an androcentric locus of power to a feminine city-labyrinth of women's creative power—the city of Ariadne and Dido, Lila and Elena.[17]

From Naples to Turin: Urban Itineraries of Abandonment

Turin serves literally and figuratively as the narrative frame of the Neapolitan tetralogy. The fourth and last volume, *The Story of the Lost Child*, concludes with an epilogue set in Turin, just like the prologue which opens the tetralogy. Elena, who lives in an apartment overlooking the Princess Isabella bridge, takes her dog out for a walk in the nearby Valentino park, and when she comes back she finds a package on top of her mailbox. In the package are the two dolls, Tina and Nu, who have crossed space and time, arriving from Naples to Turin sixty years after being thrown into the basement (*SLC*, 473). Elena's writing has succeeded in conjuring up Lila through the appearance of the two dolls, it has bridged the spatiotemporal distance between the past (Naples) and the present (Turin). Naples, in other words, has arrived in Turin. This is one of the key topographic developments in Ferrante's second published novel, *The Days of Abandonment*, in which a Neapolitan woman, Olga, is abandoned by her husband and left alone with her two children in their large apartment overlooking the Valentino Park and the Princess Isabella bridge in Turin. Naples and Turin are opposed culturally and geographically: the southern, poor, and backward Naples stands in contrast to the northern, modern, industrialized Turin. And yet, they have something in common.

A significant thematic thread that runs through all of Ferrante's works is the idea of a city without love. In Ferrante's poetics of urban topography, the city is associated with both the psyche and the body so that memories, emotions, and traumas are mapped onto the Neapolitan cityscape and conversely, the cityscape evokes memories, emotions, and traumas. The loss of love thus reorients and remaps the experience of the city, transforming the urban landscape into a labyrinth. In Virgil's *Aeneid*, Dido is abandoned by Aeneas, and Carthage, the city she has founded and built as the topographic embodiment of their love, collapses as well. Ferrante revisits this story before she begins writing *The Days of Abandonment*, her novel about a city without love:

> Only when I reread Virgil, to help me write the story of Olga, did I suddenly like Dido in every aspect. But what made the strongest impression was Virgil's use of the city. Carthage isn't a background, isn't an urban landscape for people and events. Carthage is what it has not yet become but is about to be, material that is being worked, stone exploded at times by the internal movements of the two characters. [...] If the love between Aeneas and her is happily fulfilled, becoming a joyful long-lasting connection, Carthage will gain power from it, the work will start up again, the stones will welcome the positive feeling of the human beings who are shaping it. Instead, Aeneas abandons her. Dido, the happy woman, becomes furious, raging. The past is joined to the future, Tyre virtually reaches Carthage, every street becomes a labyrinth, a place to get lost without art, and the blood that Dido has left behind returns to stain the new city. [...] This is the result of getting lost in the urban labyrinth without art, without a thread: *No love, no accords*. (*Fr*, 150, italics in the original)

Cities without love become labyrinths without an Ariadne's thread, mere traps or prisons, leading to disorientation, and in Dido's case, to suicide. *The Days of Abandonment* is the literary enactment of Ferrante's urban theory: Turin becomes a city without love, a modern Carthage, and Olga, the furious narrator, gets lost in its labyrinth, enclosed within its iron fortress. In her rage, she joins Ferrante's genealogy of abandoned women in myth and literature that inhabit her texts and haunt her characters—from Ariadne, Medea, and Dido to Tolstoy's *Anna Karenina* and Simone de Beauvoir's *Woman Destroyed*. Ferrante, however, situates her abandoned and raging women within a contemporary metropolis to explore their modern experience of a city without love. This topography spans the two key poles of her narrative geography—Naples and Turin.

In *Troubling Love*, Delia wanders through the city to piece together places and stories and thus map and reconstruct her mother's life story. Naples functions as the landscape of Delia's memories and in traversing it, the daughter accepts her mother and restores love to the city itself. She accordingly regains control over streets and spaces, refusing to be frightened by the past inscribed onto the built environment. In *The Days of Abandonment*, the narrative returns to the topos of a city without love, but in a different key: abandoned and deprived of her husband's love, Olga must learn to negotiate an aggressive, domineering urban landscape that manifests centuries of male political, military, and scientific power. And she must do that while also negotiating her own childhood memories of another abandoned Neapolitan wife—the *poverella* from Piazza Mazzini. Abandonment is thus mapped twice: onto the streets of Turin in the present and onto the Neapolitan cityscape in the past. It is also narrated by a woman who in writing her story attempts to put spatial and temporal order to her inner and outer life, to organize her thoughts, feelings, and movements.

Olga is a 38-year-old woman who speaks three foreign languages and has lived in several different countries with her engineer husband Mario. They have settled in Turin with their two children, Gianni and Ilaria. Both Olga and Mario are from Naples, but Mario has adapted to his new city and lost his Neapolitan accent while Olga struggles to find her place. She is a former writer whose only publication, "a long story set in Naples" (*DA*, 30), was written during her first pregnancy. She has now become resigned to her role as mother and housewife, at the service of her husband's successful career. She has renounced agency and authority, thereby constructing an identity for herself exclusively within the patriarchal order and within the domestic sphere. She has become what Elena Greco has refused to be: a pretty, dutiful, and subservient wife whose intellectual and emotional needs are always secondary to her husband's. When they embark on their narratives both Elena and Olga live in Turin, in apartments overlooking the same bridge and the same park, where they both sit on a bench and read. This shared urban and intellectual space creates a nexus between them, situates them within Ferrante's overarching literary topography, and asserts the intra-textual genealogy of women writers emerging from Ferrante's texts.

A wealthy, international city with burgeoning cultural life and industries, Turin fits perfectly the ambitions of a literary woman. Elena who moves to Turin to direct a small publishing house exemplifies that position. Olga, also a writer, is stifled by both her husband and his adoptive city. Like Medea, she is a foreigner and an exile. Like Ariadne, she has fled her home to follow the man she loves. And like Dido, she tries to construct a city, a home, and an identity contingent on her husband's love. When Mario leaves her without an explanation, she unravels physically and psychologically. And since she cannot take revenge on Mario, she takes her rage out on the city's streets and squares, on its monuments and buildings. In the days and weeks after the abandonment, Olga walks through Turin, mapping her movements and identifying her locations. Like Naples in *Troubling Love* and the Neapolitan tetralogy, Turin is conceived and experienced as a city dominated by the male imaginary (Sambuco 2013). If Delia's and Lila's itineraries through Naples chart a porous city of cyclical, symbolic, and literal violence, Olga's perambulations map an objective, topographical reality with actual, identifiable markers.

The Days of Abandonment traces Olga's itineraries through an urban topography conceived, imagined, and experienced as a masculinist space. The city shapes both her physical and psychical landscape producing a spatial and corporeal subjectivity that is negotiated on the streets of Turin. The novel maps with cartographic precision Olga's movements in the city so that Turin becomes the topographic and psychic ground upon which her trauma is enacted and ultimately resolved. When five years earlier Olga arrives in Turin with her family, she dislikes the city—it seems metallic and cold (*DA*, 10). But Mario's colleague Gina and her daughter Carla help Olga find a beautiful, comfortable apartment overlooking the Valentino park and the river Po. Olga's familiarity with the city occurs through the mediation of the apartment, and in particular its balcony—a liminal space bridging inside and outside, public and private: "But I soon discovered how pleasant it was to watch the seasons from the balcony of our house [. . .] I had quickly adapted since mother and daughter immediately did whatever they could to alleviate any discomfort, helping me to get to know the streets" (*DA*, 10). Olga's formative experience of Turin's territory transpires, on the one hand, through her position as a spectator of time passing (as the novel's title announces), and on the other, as a transaction between women, as a feminine initiation into the male-gendered nature of Turin's and of modern urban space at large. Here Ferrante embeds a topographic pun perhaps to be decoded only by those familiar with the city's landmarks. Olga helps the reader identify her apartment's location—from the balcony she can see the arches of the Isabella bridge as well as the passing of the seasons. In fact, next to the Isabella bridge, in the Valentino park, is the *Fountain of the 12 Months*, also known as the *Fountain of the Seasons*, Turin's most important fountain-monument (Rossotti 2015, 23). Olga watching from her balcony the passing of the seasons is also seeing the *Fountain of the Seasons*, comprised of twelve nude or seminude statues of women representing the twelve months. This topographic pun implies the codification of the female body on display for the male gaze. It also ties Olga's spectatorship to the city's sights.

After Mario leaves, Olga drives and walks aimlessly around the city, experiencing the city's effects directly on her body and projecting her disorientation onto her surroundings: "I rushed from one end of the city to the other on errands [. . .] I wanted my movements to seem purposeful, and instead I scarcely had control over my body" (*DA*, 32). She perceives Turin as an iron fortress, the site of her imprisonment within the home and within the parameters of her husband's career in this hostile city: "Turin seemed to me a great fortress with iron walls, walls of a frozen gray that the spring could not warm" (*DA*, 32). Olga perhaps references an actual fortress, the medieval citadel now part of Palazzo Madama in the city's historic center, and thereby initiates her cataloging of urban sites and spaces. She traverses the map of Turin from south to north and from west to east, tracing the city's grid-like rectilinear layout with straight streets intersecting at straight angles. Since Turin's urban plan follows that of the ancient Roman military camp *Augusta Taurinorum*, Olga's perambulations repeat the grid-like pattern of Turin's map, charting the sights of Turin's past and present military, political, and industrial power. As the "cradle of the house of Savoy," the city has named numerous streets, squares, and boulevards after the key figures of the Savoy dynasty (Rossotti 2015, 39) and erected numerous monuments to celebrate their victories. In 1861, Turin became the capital of unified Italy, the seat of the Parliament and King Vittorio Emanuele II. Although the capital was moved to Florence and then to Rome, Turin's industrial power flourished—the 1884 and 1898 international industrial expositions established the city as the center of rapidly developing modern technologies—from automobiles to cinema to electrical engineering to aerospace industries. Olga and Mario settle in Turin because Mario teaches engineering at the Polytechnic University.

When she drives on her errands designed to keep her sense of purpose, she often forgets she is in the car and loses herself in topographic memories: "The street was replaced by the most vivid memories of the past or by bitter fantasies" (*DA*, 33). To keep herself grounded in a physical, objective reality she names streets and landmarks: "I was driving on Corso Massimo D'Azeglio, and had reached Galileo Ferraris" (*DA*, 33). In this scene, helpfully mapped for the reader, she breaks suddenly so as not to run over a pedestrian, and as a result her daughter Ilaria bangs her forehead against the windshield. Olga grabs her, leaving the car at the traffic light, and begins walking in search of water: "I abandoned the car, took Ilaria in my arms, went in search of some water. I crossed the tram tracks, walked in a daze toward a gray urinal [...] Then I changed my mind, what was I doing. I sat on the bench at the tram stop with Ilaria screaming in my arms" (*DA*, 34).

Olga identifies the place of the accident and locates it at a particular intersection. The names she specifies evoke Turin's nineteenth-century male political-historical power—the politician and prime minister Massimo D'Azeglio (1798–1866), and scientific-industrial power—the Institute Galileo Ferraris named after the Turinese physicist and electrical engineer Galileo Ferraris (1847–1897). It is not by chance that Ferrante sets the car accident right in front of Istituto Galileo Ferraris, located at Corso Massimo D'Azeglio number 42. There is a traffic light exactly there, as well as a tram stop nearby. This scene is grounded in an identifiable topographic reality, framed by the names of two important male figures, thus making a broader claim for the gendering of urban space. At the same time, this objective topography helps Olga hold on to concrete, tangible coordinates to situate her firmly within reality.

Mapping the car accident has further implications. When she sets out in search of water, she is looking for a public water fountain—a *fontanella*, but instead she finds a street urinal—a *vespasiano* (*Iga*, 35). The mother and daughter set out to look for water, but the city offers them a public urinal constructed to satisfy men's bodily needs and to collect men's bodily fluids. If the city participates in the production of sexed corporeality (Grosz 1999), then the street urinal produces Olga's body as secondary and subordinate, mapping the subjugation of her corporeal needs and identity. Not very far from where Olga has her car accident, on Corso Massimo D'Azeglio, by the Institute Galileo Ferraris, there is such a gray *vespasiano* (urinal)—one of a few public urinals to be found in Turin. The novel charts an objective, identifiable topographic reality.

From the novel's very beginning then the city is defined for Olga by the gendered spatial hierarchy of *fontanella* (water fountain) and *vespasiano* (urinal). The city displays its masculinity in other ways which Olga begins to experience as she loses the grounding coordinates of Mario's male presence. She continues to walk obsessively through the city streets, visiting in particular its monuments to soldiers, generals, and rulers. During the summer, she drags her children through squares and parks, meticulously listing her itineraries and naming her destinations. Thus, she maps Turin's city center with its main streets and sights—from Via Cernaia to Via Pietro Micca to the Artillery Gardens to Via Meucci to Piazza Solferino (*DA*, 64–6). She enumerates all the monuments along the way—to Pietro Micca, to Ferdinand of Savoy, to Vittorio Emanuele II, to Emanuele Filiberto—monuments erected to memorialize military and political power. On one occasion, she leaves her children next to the monument to the eighteenth-century patriotic soldier Pietro Micca situated at a busy traffic intersection, and defiantly walks away fantasizing she would never return to collect her children (*DA*, 66).

Olga's fantasy of abandoning her children in the midst of the city is a fantasy about escaping male-dominated narratives and reclaiming her own identity, regaining the authority and agency to abandon rather than be abandoned.[18] What she flees from is also the perpetuation of both physical and discursive genealogy of male mastery over the city. On the one hand, a city whose numerous public monuments fall into four categories—rulers from the Savoy dynasty, generals and military figures, politicians and patriotic heroes, and men of science or letters (Lanzardo and Poli 2012, 6–7), and whose presence Olga notes and lists during her wanderings—has male power embedded into its urban fabric. In fact, in the long list of Turin's public monuments, there is not even one to an identifiable, historical woman (Lanzardo and Poli 2012, 8). On the other hand, Olga's husband and son tell and retell the stories of those monuments which inscribe the city in terms of male voice, word, and power, excluding Olga from the possibility of telling her own version:

> [Gianni] wanted to see, yet again, the monument to Pietro Micca, whose story Mario had told him in every detail. [. . .] Once we quarrelled right there, in the gardens in front of the Artillery Museum, under the dirty-green statue of Pietro Micca, with the big sword and the fuse. I knew almost nothing about these murdered heroes, fire, and blood. (*DA*, 64)

This scene exemplifies Olga's powerlessness as an outsider but also as a failed storyteller. She cannot inscribe herself within an urban landscape and an urban history coded through the symbols of male military and political power, especially when those are associated, literally and metaphorically, with her absent/unfaithful husband. Just across the street, in piazza Solferino, in front of the monument to Ferdinand of Savoy, Olga start yelling at her children after Gianni tells her "You don't know how to tell a story" (*DA*, 64). Her son's accusation triggers her own condemnation of a city which enables and perpetuates stories between men about other men:

> that city of kings and princesses, of haughty people, cold people, metal automatons. I screamed and screamed, out of control. Gianni and Ilaria loved the city, the boy knew its streets and its legends, his father often let him play near the monument at the end of Via Meucci, there was a statue they both liked: what nonsense, memorials of kings and generals on the streets, Gianni dreamed of being like Ferdinand of Savoy at the battle of Novara, when he jumps down from the dying horse, saber in hand, ready to fight. Ah yes, I wished to wound them, my children, I wished to

wound above all the boy, who already had a Piedmontese accent, Mario, too, spoke like a Turinese now, he had eliminated the Neapolitan cadences utterly. (*DA*, 65)

This passage illustrates the intensely gendered meaning of Turin's map, especially in the center which concentrates the visual manifestations of women's multilayered exclusion from the city, from history, and from the narration of history. The "metal automatons" are perhaps also the countless bronze monuments occupying the city's strategic locations. This intersection of gender and place reveals the underlying patriarchal structure of the organization and codification of Turin's urban space despite its status as one of Italy's most modern and civilized cities. Just like in Naples, gender oppressions and aggressions are embedded in, and produced through, material and symbolic places and spaces. The city partakes in a patrilineal, androcentric, and circular transmission of history, power, and their discourses: from male heroes and generals (Pietro Micca, Ferdinand of Savoy) to father (Mario) to son (Gianni) who dreams of being like the male heroes and generals. Turin thus becomes literally an embodiment of the father(s) and their stories.

At stake in Olga's outburst is also the question of Neapolitan identity. She protests against Mario's and Gianni's cultural and linguistic assimilation, their seamless and eager adoption of a new city. She imagines punishing the boy who repeats the father's language and therefore hurting the father and what he stands for. Olga's own Neapolitan origins—her unbridled anger, her screaming in public—emerge as ever more in contrast with this cold and reserved city of bronze statues and "metal automatons." What Olga displays is, in a way, a performance of Neapolitan-ness, of the permeable boundary between public and private actions: violent passions, fights, and feuds enacted in the street as they are in *Troubling Love* and the Neapolitan quartet. This carnivalesque porosity (Benjamin and Lacis 1986) is most evident in the Naples of Ferrante's tetralogy but here it begins to infiltrate Turin. Olga loses her own personal boundaries, her language becomes obscene, inflected through dialect, and she abandons self-discipline. She releases the tight grip on her surroundings, discards the veneer of elegant refinement she had imposed on her body and speech, and regresses to her past—that is, Naples comes to haunt her in Turin. Turin's perfectly rational, rectilinear map begins to yield to Neapolitan "irrationality" (Carvalho 2018) and spatiotemporal porosity.

Naples erupts into Olga's present through her memories of another abandoned woman—the *poverella* from her childhood who lived in Olga's building behind Piazza Mazzini (*DA*, 15). The *poverella* is associated not only with the past but also specifically with Naples' topography. Consumed by grief when her husband leaves her for another woman, she tries to commit suicide with poison, but fails, so she drowns herself in the gulf of Naples. For Olga, the *poverella* at first functions as a negative model, of what she must *not* become—a "woman destroyed," drained of her vitality, femininity, and literally, of all her bodily fluids: "she's as dry now as a salted anchovy," Olga remembers thinking of the *poverella* (*DA*, 16). Yet the more Olga is consumed by her own grief, the closer she resembles the *poverella*: "the life had been drained out of me like blood and saliva and mucus from a patient during an operation" (*DA*, 38). She even begins to see the Neapolitan woman from her childhood in her Turin apartment. When Olga is leaning out of the balcony shouting obscenities after Mario who is leaving the building, she notices the horrified look of her children and imagines that the *poverella* is standing next to her: "Maybe I had beside me, stiff as a sepulchral statue, the abandoned woman of my childhood, the *poverella*. She had come from Naples to Turin to grab me by the hem of my skirt before I flew down from the fifth floor" (*DA*, 44).

Obsessed by the idea to find where her husband lives with his lover, Olga continues to wander around Turin, both on foot and by car. In the middle of the night she arrives in Largo Brescia, a working-class neighborhood, and begins surveying its streets (*DA*, 46). She wanders for a long time around this run-down area, with dilapidated buildings and balconies with hanging laundry. She again compulsively maps her path—Corso Brescia, Largo Brescia, Corso Palermo, Via Teramo, Via Lodi—within an urban area where all streets are named after cities and thus reinforce the idea of the city's cartographic domination. In Via Alessandria she leans on a wall and reads the sign on the building across: "Prince of Naples Nursery. Thirty years ago the *poverella* of Piazza Mazzini had been leaning against a wall, a house wall, as I was now, when her breath failed, out of desperation" (*DA*, 47). Olga can finally orient herself in the city: "That's where I was, accents of the south cried in my head, cities that were far apart became a single voice, the blue surface of the sea and the white of the Alps" (*DA*, 47). This is a key moment in Olga's psychic and physical meanderings. Turin and Naples converge: the rectilinear, modern grid-like northern city converges with the porous, archaic, labyrinth-like Neapolitan geography. Her journey is not only through Turin's streets but also through the streets of her Neapolitan past, her childhood in Piazza Mazzini. The Prince of Naples Nursery Olga encounters during her nocturnal walk is in fact on Via Alessandria in Turin, at number 12, with the sign "Asilo Principe di Napoli" still visible today. Ferrante again situates Olga in a real, identifiable place.

This mapping of objective reality informs Ferrante's deployment of topography in *The Days of Abandonment*. Olga's daily walks name landmarks and places that still exist and thus allow an inquisitive reader or researcher to locate and tour her itineraries. When she walks the dog, Otto, she passes by "the green stump of a submarine that Gianni liked" and then "through the tunnel full of obscene graffiti" (51). Both the submarine and the graffiti are located exactly where Olga describes them: the gray-green military submarine "Provana" abuts the Valentino park and commemorates the sailors who perished at sea, as the plaque on it explains. Moreover, the submarine is on Viale dei Marinai, the street where Olga finds her neighbor Carrano's driver's license (*DA*, 75). The tunnel, still colored with graffiti, though not all of them obscene, passes under the Princess Isabella bridge, at the end of Viale dei Marinai. The tunnel recalls another crucial element of Ferrante's urban architecture: the tunnel in *Troubling Love* and in *My Brilliant Friend*. Neapolitan spaces infiltrate Olga's daily life while the novel's plot continues to unfold on Turin's streets.

Another such cartographic plotting occurs when Olga goes to Via Meucci to file a complaint with the telephone company that has disconnected her landline. She describes the company's headquarters as a building with a "grand façade of streaked marble blocks" (*DA*, 68). This building, with its black-and-white streaked marble façade, in fact stands at Via Meucci 4, and today it houses the City of Turin Department of Urban Planning (perhaps another obscure pun on Ferrante's part). In the novel, the telephone company sends Olga to an office on Via Confienza where she is turned away so that her complaint remains unfiled. About to collapse, she again resorts to reading names or signs to get a grip on reality: "I felt as if I were about to lose my breath and sink to the ground. As if it were prehensile my eye grasped the letters of a plaque on the building opposite. Words so I wouldn't fall" (*DA*, 69).[19] Olga reads the plaque commemorating the house where the Turinese poet Guido Gozzano (1883–1916) was born. This house is located on Via Confienza 13A, with the memorial plaque clearly visible (though perhaps barely legible from a distance). Gozzano was famous not only for his poetry but also for his love affair with another Turinese poet, Amalia Guglielminetti (1881–1941), whom he abandoned claiming he did not love her, insisting on a chaste friendship (Saccà 2002; de Toma 1986). Although Olga does not comment on Gozzano, she does read to herself the text on the memorial plaque. Ferrante encodes another mapping of abandonment onto the city's streets and buildings.

The turning point in the narrative occurs shortly after that, when Olga literally takes a turn into a street nicknamed "la diagonale" (the diagonal) because it breaks the perfect rectilinear geometry of Turin's urban plan (Coppo and Spallone 1995). Olga swerves into Via Pietro Micca, named after the eighteenth-century hero her son admires. And there she runs into Mario and his lover: city map and narrative coincide. Ferrante makes a bold cartographic and textual move, exposing the interdependence of mapping and plotting: "I wandered at random, past the Alfieri theater, ending up in Via Pietro Micca. I looked around disoriented, certainly the car wasn't there. But in front of a shop window, the window of a jewelry store, I saw Mario and his new woman" (*DA*, 69). Mario's lover turns out to be twenty-year-old Carla, the daughter of Mario's colleague Gina, who together with her mother had initiated Olga into Turin's topography. Mario's adultery, along with his lover's identity, are narrated in cartographic terms.

That this striking discovery occurs on Via Pietro Micca is consistent with the poetics of mapping in the novel—Via Pietro Micca cuts across diagonally the otherwise perfectly rectilinear city grid thereby performing a cartographic shortcut, a narrative move to the side. The architect of this urban development as well as of several buildings on Via Pietro Micca was Carlo Ceppi (1829–1921), the architect of the *Fountain of the Seasons* across from Olga's apartment. In this way, Via Pietro Micca takes us back to Olga's home—the house that Carla and Gina had found for her. Ferrante inscribes Mario's adultery onto the city's plan and onto its architecture. But instead of asserting the topography of male power, the encounter on Via Pietro Micca performs a cartographic and narrative shift by revealing the identity of Mario's lover and inciting Olga to violence. She appropriates the aggression she attributes to the male heroes her husband and son admire. She attacks Mario in the street and beats him until he is bleeding: "I grabbed him by the shirt and yanked him so violently that I tore it off the right shoulder [. . .] blood dripped amid the grizzled hairs of his chest. I hit him again and again, he fell down on the sidewalk" (*DA*, 71).

Olga inflicts on her adulterous husband what the jealous Neapolitan men typically do to women in Ferrante's novels. This description recalls the violent outbursts of Amalia's husband in *Troubling Love* or the recurring domestic violence in the Neapolitan tetralogy. Ferrante's topographic imaginary structured around Turin's urban plan and enacted upon Turin's map here provides a release from the grip of rectilinear correctness, from Turin's iron fortress as perceived and lived by Olga. In usurping the male role, she manages to reverse the map's oppressive effect and becomes an active agent in reclaiming her identity, in reclaiming women as agents and not victims of violence in the streets: "A woman can easily kill on the street, in the middle of a crowd, she can do it more easily than a man" (*DA*, 72). It is not the Neapolitan men who have come to Turin, it is the Neapolitan women—Olga herself and the *poverella* from Piazza Mazzini.

Olga's ultimate emancipation from the city's grip occurs at the novel's climactic moment, the morning of her most excruciating day when she manages to relieve herself—quite literally—from the weight of the male city, and with it to rid herself of Mario's presence in her life. While she is taking the dog out for a walk in the park, she experiences a collapse of self, language, and social order. She feels the weight of the entire city mapped onto her body:

> But I felt everything right on top of me, breath against breath. And then it seemed to me that I was wearing not my nightgown but a long mantle on which was painted the vegetation of the Valentino, the paths, the Princess Isabella bridge, the river, the building where I lived, even the dog. That was why I was so heavy and swollen. I got up groaning with embarrassment and stomachache, my bladder full, I couldn't hold it any longer. [. . .] I pulled up my nightgown, I peed and shit behind a trunk. (*DA*, 98)

This scene illustrates the two main functions of the city map in the novel. Turin's specific topography—its concrete sites, the Valentino park, the Princess Isabella bridge, even Olga's apartment building and her dog—are inscribed onto her body, claiming possession of it. Her body has been appropriated by an urban space imagined and lived as masculine and characterized by the literal and metaphoric street urinal. On the other hand, Olga feels the weight of the city inside her, as a burden hurting her body, so she relieves herself of the city map. She urinates and defecates in the park. This is a moment of double abjection: in abjecting her own body, she abjects the city mapped on her nightgown. The city map along with the actual park become her own public urinals. She appropriates the urban space which had kept her prisoner, she turns the tables on it by breaking the rules of proper feminine behavior. In doing so, she expels from her body both Naples and Turin and gets rid of both her distant and more recent past. This climactic scatological gesture can be understood as cleansing or purging, but also as Olga's marking of urban territory as hers, for her body and for her bodily fluids—for what Grosz calls "women's corporeal flow" (1994, 202), as her feminine appropriation of an aggressively male topography. We can read Ferrante's other leaking or dissolving female bodies, along with the psychical landscape of *frantumaglia* and *smarginatura*, as feminine appropriations of an aggressively male urban topography.

This is also when Olga begins to distance herself from the ghost of the *poverella* and from her Neapolitan past as well. If the *poverella* can be read as the resurrection of an archaic, patriarchal model of femininity,[20] then her mapped identity (Piazza Mazzini) also suggests an oppressive, violent urban topography. Olga realizes that to give in to the *poverella* inside her, to open herself to the inimical visions and influences of an archaic order is to imprison herself in "a labyrinth so dense that I would never get out of it" (*DA*, 113). If Naples is the labyrinth of the past, then she must recover Turin for herself. At the end of the novel, she revisits the sites of her earlier wanderings and restores their neutrality. She goes back to the Valentino park and spends autumn mornings sitting in the rocky garden, writing (*DA*, 162), literally writing over a landscape previously experienced as a burdensome weight. Olga goes back to the "iron fortress" of her first Turin impressions, the medieval citadel in Piazza Castello. She sits by the enormous bronze monument to Emanuele Filiberto, Duke of D'Aosta, a general from the First World War, and watches calmly her son wield a fake gun—a gift from his father (*DA*, 173). Olga observes Turin's monuments to male heroes, acknowledging that they hurt her but did not break her (*DA*, 173). She is no longer affected by the disorienting and subjugating effects of urban space and the male imaginary. And the *poverella* herself has become a monument, a statue: "The *poverella* had become again an old photograph, the petrified past, without blood" (*DA*, 184).

The three walking itineraries outlined in this chapter—Delia's descent into the Neapolitan underworld, Lila and Elena's journey through the labyrinth, and Olga's mapping of Turin's streets and monuments—construct topography as the literal and symbolic space where identities are negotiated and articulated. Against the restrictive and punitive function of the city Ferrante positions another vision of Naples and Turin. The city-as-labyrinth (Naples) and the city-as-fortress (Turin) are traversed by a modern Ariadne-Dido and by a "modern Medea in downtown Turin" (Lucamante 2008, 81) who narrate and thus reconfigure the city through their female subjectivities. Women stand as metaphorical city builders, the creators of their own identities and the storytellers of their own narratives. They begin to find the "true words" to tell the story of a female polis (*Fr*, 147) and in this way reconfigure and re-write urban space into a new feminine topography. Ariadne's thread, as J. Hillis Miller argues, is not only the line that traces the labyrinth but also the rope, or the rope-walk, that in tracing the labyrinth becomes another labyrinth itself (1992, 16). It is this feminine labyrinth-polis that Ferrante maps and investigates in her novels by giving women the power of the needle and the pen, neutralizing or subverting the position of men as the traditional masters of the creative act. Thus, walking through the city becomes conducive to writing and storytelling, which in Ferrante's poetics is imagined as the feminine art of sewing: "what counts is to try and keep trying to sew for ourselves with needle and thread the perimeter of the city" (*Fr*, 152).

In remapping the city through their moving bodies and through their writing, Delia, Olga, Lila, and Elena co-opt patriarchal localities into the charting of a universal feminine urban landscape, subverting male-governed space and articulating a female subjectivity constructed through the mobility of bodies, ideas, and discourses. Delia appropriates the streets and *topoi* of Amalia's city to create a new feminine space, one that, like her feminine artistic legacy, bypasses the patriarchal labyrinth. Olga undoes the social and cultural codes that govern urban topography and abjects Turin in a scatological gesture of defiance and liberation. Lila and Elena traverse the liminal space of the urban labyrinth to found, like Dido, a new feminine polis, embodied and realized through their friendship and lifelong creative collaboration.

Epilogue

Reverse Maps, Familial Objects, and Open Frames in *The Lying Life of Adults*

Elena Ferrante's latest novel *The Lying Life of Adults* (*La vita bugiarda degli adulti*, 2019) revisits the motifs, images, and narrative strategies already developed in her earlier novels but from a new perspective—that of Giovanna, an adolescent girl whose sentimental and intellectual education we follow from age twelve to sixteen. Giovanna's narration unfolds against a double background—the immediate surroundings of her family and its milieu, and the city of Naples with its hierarchical topography of sociocultural and linguistic difference. Unlike Ferrante's earlier novels whose thematic preoccupations lie with women's emancipation from an illiterate, sub-proletarian, and violent *rione* in the periphery of Naples, *The Lying Life of Adults* locates its central concerns in a different class setting—Giovanna's cultured middle-class family residing in the upscale Rione Alto neighborhood whose name indicates both its topographic elevation and its status. Unlike Ferrante's preceding novels whose female protagonists negotiate a hybrid cultural and linguistic identity oscillating between dialect and standard Italian (de Rogatis 2019b), Giovanna initially operates entirely within the strict linguistic boundaries imposed by her teacher parents—speaking in Neapolitan dialect is forbidden in her house.

The novel begins with a paragraph-long chapter that introduces Giovanna as the first-person narrator narrating from an indeterminate point in the future, looking back at her adolescence. In a typical semantically rich opening, Ferrante packs the entire book within three sentences while also evoking her earlier novels:

> Two years before leaving home my father said to my mother that I was very ugly. The sentence was uttered under his breath, in the apartment that my parents, newly married, had bought in Rione Alto, at the top of Via San Giacomo dei Capri. Everything—the spaces of Naples, the blue light of a very cold February, those words—remained fixed. But I slipped away, and am still slipping away, within these lines that are intended to give me a story, while in fact I am nothing, nothing of my own, nothing that has really begun or really been brought to completion: only a tangled knot, and nobody, not even the one who at this moment is writing, knows if it contains the right thread for a story or is merely a snarled confusion of suffering, without redemption.[1]

Like *The Days of Abandonment*, Ferrante's novel opens with the dissolution of a family but reoriented through the daughter's perspective and in relation to Giovanna's physical appearance. Like *Troubling Love* that identifies the date and place of Amalia's death, Giovanna identifies the exact location of the overheard conversation, establishing the spatial and symbolic hierarchy of Neapolitan topography. And then in a metanarrative gesture she references the lines she is writing which fail to give her a definite form, a fixed identity. She is a tangle of words, stories, and identities, "a crowd of others," to cite Ferrante in *Frantumaglia* (*Fr*, 366). Like all of Ferrante's narrators, Giovanna writes to conjure up her past self, using narration as a tool for introspection. And if Lila in the Neapolitan Novels describes herself as a scribble or squiggle, *scarabocchio* (*SBP*, 17), Giovanna is a tangle, *garbuglio* (*Lvb*, 9), another twisted form that necessitates unfurling. In three sentences, the first chapter outlines the recurring trajectories of Ferrante's poetics I have discussed in my book: Naples as the topography of identity; the struggle to capture in words a complex, unstable female subjectivity; and the corporeal traces of a family genealogy.

Mapping in Reverse

Coming to terms with the corporeal traces of a family genealogy comprises the novel's key plot line, which explores questions of identity and language. Giovanna's face is identical to that of her paternal aunt, Vittoria, a crude, semiliterate woman who lives in a distant, peripheral neighborhood and speaks in dialect. The novel's central query is one about identity as determined by family heritage. Will *zia* Vittoria erupt from inside the adolescent girl, like Don Achille from Stefano Carracci's body in the Neapolitan Novels, warping her face and body? Will she, like Delia, accept the face of the other woman inscribed onto hers? Or will she find another way of articulating and asserting her own identity? The novel dwells on Giovanna's paternal lineage, exploring its ramifications and manifestations through the daughter's changing appearance and Vittoria's potential as her symbolic mother.

The figure of Aunt Vittoria is the formative presence in Giovanna's adolescence and the exact opposite of the girl's educated family. Giovanna's mother, Nella, is a high school teacher of Greek and Latin who works on the side as a copyeditor of romance novels, often rewriting them herself. Her father, Andrea, a well-respected progressive intellectual, teaches history and philosophy at the most prestigious high school in Naples. Giovanna's best friends, Ida and Angela, are the daughters of her parents' best friends, Costanza and Mariano, a refined and wealthy couple. Unlike Elena Greco in the Neapolitan Novels, Ferrante's protagonist no longer needs to pretend to be middle class because she *is* middle class (de Rogatis 2019b). And yet, as Giovanna fixates on meeting her aunt and getting to know her father's relatives, the novel veers into familiar territory: the literal and symbolic erasure of identity through education, language, and upward social mobility. Giovanna learns that Andrea grew up in Vittoria's peripheral, low-class, dialect-speaking neighborhood Pascone, a perfect antithesis to the Rione Alto. Through education, discipline, and ambition Andrea has moved up in the class hierarchy, embracing a new milieu and eliminating the traces of his family and origins. Ferrante maps identity onto the city's internal spatial-social stratigraphy.

The narrative is suspended vertically between the Pascone which lies down below in the industrial zone and Giovanna's apartment up in the Neapolitan hills. Likewise, Giovanna's identity occupies these two different poles with their sociocultural and linguistic characteristics. Her maternal parents, whom she calls "the grandparents of the Museum" (*Lvb*, 15) because they live behind the museum, belong to a concrete and reputable topography, while in her imagination her father's family comes from an indefinite, nameless place. At first, the only thing she knows about her father's place of origin is that to get there you have to go farther and farther down (*Lvb*, 15). This mysterious underworld attracts her especially after she overhears her father's remark that her face resembles Aunt Vittoria's. Giovanna misinterprets that remark because the only memory she has of her aunt is of a monstrous creature that stains and infects everything it touches (*Lvb*, 12), a figure lying in wait in the corners of the house when darkness falls (*Lvb*, 13). She assumes that her aunt must be ugly and that she herself is becoming like Vittoria. We enter Ferrante's world of ugly monsters hiding in the storeroom (the beast in *Frantumaglia*) or at the top of the dark stairs (Don Achille in *My Brilliant Friend*). Giovanna descends into the world of the Pascone to track down her roots and come to terms with her paternal lineage.

She sets out on a journey of self-discovery through bonding with her uncouth but seductively vital Aunt Vittoria who still lives in her father's old neighborhood. The question of Giovanna's identity thus becomes one of spatial and topographic mobility: to reach her aunt, she must learn to navigate the map of Naples, memorizing routes, streets, and neighborhoods. Her mother gives her a street map (*stradario*, *Lvb*, 36) and tells her that she should familiarize herself with the routes that would take her to the Pascone. Giovanna defines her newly acquired knowledge of Neapolitan topography as the end of her childhood and the beginning of her adolescence (*Lvb*, 36). As she does with Turin's landmarks in *The Days of Abandonment*, Ferrante encodes a topographic pun in Vittoria's and Giovanna's last name, Trada. When Giovanna is examining the street map of Naples, the *stradario*, and reading the unfamiliar street names ("nomi sconosciuti di strade"), she dwells on the literal and metaphorical path to her aunt's neighborhood, "una strada di tormenti" (*Lvb*, 37). And then she realizes her aunt's last name is the same as hers, Trada. The word *strada* is repeated three times in the paragraph preceding the first mention of Vittoria's last name, Trada, reinforcing the topographic reading of Giovanna's, Vittoria's, and Andrea's identities through their shared last name.

And as she forms a friendship with Vittoria, her aunt takes her on a tour of Naples to visit her many paternal relatives so that map and family "blood" overlap (*Lvb*, 77). In *The Lying Life of Adults*, then, Ferrante traces a journey exactly the opposite of what we have seen in her previous novels—the regressive movement from sociocultural and topographic heights to ground-level plebeian origins. This reverse mapping introduces a new direction in Ferrante's writing that explores the paternal legacy as it invades Giovanna's life through Vittoria's possessive claim on her niece. We follow Giovanna's education unfold in reverse as well: she fails her school year, learns some dialect, and cultivates new friendships in the Pascone. But as in Ferrante's earlier novels, the daughter must descend into the underworld of the past and begin to articulate from there the psychical and corporeal coordinates of her identity. The formation of Giovanna's identity is negotiated spatially, through the streets and neighborhoods of Naples. The *psychical-corporeal-spatial* paradigm of feminine experience undergirds this novel, situating the text firmly within Ferrante's imaginary.

Giovanna's reverse itinerary from the Rione Alto to the Pascone and from standard Italian to dialect gives her a new point of view. Vittoria urges her to observe carefully her parents, so Giovanna begins to spy on them. Ferrante uses the verb "sorvegliare" to describe Giovanna's scrutiny (*Lvb*, 99), so that the visual practice of (self)-surveillance associated with women's ontology in Ferrante's novels emerges here as well, and as prompted by another woman. Vittoria's imperative equips her niece with a new lens through which to observe reality. Giovanna gradually perceives the lies that hold her family together, uncovering a web of deceit, selfishness, and oppression. Her father turns out to be an ambitious but mediocre social climber and an unfaithful husband. Her mother who too cheats on her husband remains subservient to him even after the two separate and he moves in with his lover's family. Giovanna in turn adopts the adults' practice of lying and looks for truth and authenticity among her low-class relatives in Naples' underbelly. This downward trajectory opens space for Giovanna's exploration of her roots as a way of constructing her present and cobbling together her identity. She forms an alliance with Vittoria and becomes part of Vittoria's own nontraditional familial structure. By dramatizing the aunt-niece bond Ferrante continues to explore the familiar terrain of superimposed feminine faces, identities, and legacies.

Familial Objects

At the heart of this terrain are three intertwined images also drawn from Ferrante's visual repertoire: a bracelet, several photographs, and a mirror. The bracelet which Vittoria had given her brother as a gift for Giovanna for her baptism serves as both the narrative device that structures the novel and a fetishized object invested with symbolic power by the characters. The centrality accorded to the bracelet situates it in relation to Elsa Morante's first novel, *House of Liars* (*Menzogna e sortilegio*, 1948), where an engagement ring plays an important part.[2] *The Lying Life of Adults* alludes to the title of Morante's novel which likewise shows how identities are constituted through a continuous reversal of truths and lies (de Rogatis 2019b). Giovanna's bracelet changes hands many times, its movements between the Rione Alto and the Pascone mapping a series of expropriations and cultural crimes. As Vittoria's gift to Giovanna, at first it betokens a material connection to the paternal family, a sign of belonging and acceptance. This function recalls Olga's earrings in *The Days Abandonment* received as a gift from Mario's mother and symbolizing her identity as Mario's wife, a rightful heir to, and wearer of, the family's jewelry. When Mario gives the earrings to his lover, Olga's identity collapses as well. She has been expropriated of both her status as his wife and of what she considers hers and her daughter's property. In the Neapolitan Novels, Elena wears her mother's bracelet as a sign of her acceptance of the maternal legacy.

In Ferrante's feminine imaginary jewelry forges an intergenerational link between women.

In *The Lying Life of Adults* the bracelet links not only generations of women but also women from different classes and social milieus. Giovanna's adolescence and formative experiences coincide with the bracelet's narrative wanderings so that the narrative of Giovanna's identity is also the story of the bracelet. Or to put it differently, the bracelet drives the narrative and the girl's coming of age. And it enters the text as an absence. The gift that Vittoria had given Andrea for his daughter's baptism has disappeared. Neither Giovanna nor her mother knows about its existence. The daughter's quest for the missing bracelet exposes the characters' machinations, egotism, and dishonesty beginning with the discovery that her father had given it to his lover instead of his daughter. The lover's identity is another of Ferrante's plot twists whose revelation, as in *The Days of Abandonment*, transpires in public, in the street. When one day Vittoria picks up Giovanna and her friends Angela and Ida, she recognizes the bracelet on the wrist of their mother, Costanza. As the novel progresses, the bracelet's story becomes more tangled. Giovanna eventually reconstructs it and finds a productive solution to the problem posed by this object. But its history is also entangled in her family history and Vittoria's role in her father's past.

Andrea has deleted his past by erasing Vittoria's face from family photographs. When Giovanna rummages through old photo albums to find a picture of Vittoria and compare her face to her own, she finds family photographs in which her father has traced a black rectangle around Vittoria's face and covered it with a black marker (*Lvb*, 19). Ferrante revisits the image and lexicon of erasure (*cancellature, cancellare, Lvb*, 19, 20) associated with Lila's disappearance as an assertion of her autonomy in the Neapolitan Novels. Giovanna's father has enclosed both Vittoria and the figure of another person within a black frame reminiscent of obituaries. Giovanna is threatened by this abstract violence, terrified of resembling her father's deleted sister ("la sorella cancellata di mio padre," *Lvb*, 20). The photographic representation of the female face and body bespeaks an insidious form of erasure as domination that we have seen in Ferrante's earlier novels. In *Troubling Love*, it is the pictorial technique of Delia's painter-father who draws blank faces on his voluptuous seminude gypsies. It is also the symbolic erasure of Amalia's agency whose painted body circulates on the market. Amalia's photograph is disfigured, her face altered to resemble Delia's. But in the novel's final scene Delia appropriates the father's painting tools, undoes their symbolic erasure, and paints Amalia's face over her own photograph. Likewise, Lila cuts herself out of family photographs as an act of resistance to the regime of patriarchal optics. In *The Lying Life of Adults*, Giovanna tries to scrape off (*raschiare, Lvb*, 20) the black rectangle with a knife, using the verb with which Delia describes Amalia's defaced photo in *Troubling Love* (*Am*, 73, 78), but in vain—the white paper underneath shows through. Giovanna cannot undo the damage before she understands its origins.

The mystery of the blacked-out photo is resolved soon enough. On her first visit to Vittoria, Giovanna learns that seventeen years earlier her aunt had had an affair with a married man, Andrea's friend Enzo, now dead. It's his figure standing next to Vittoria that Andrea has also erased in the family photographs. Vittoria invites Giovanna to visit Enzo's grave on the anniversary of their first meeting, May 23. Ferrante repeats this date four times in less than ten pages (*Lvb*, 54, 56, 61, 62), clearly calling attention to its significance, recounting in detail Vittoria and Giovanna's trip to the cemetery. May 23 is the date when Amalia drowns in *Troubling Love* as well as Delia's birthday. The opening words of *Troubling Love*, "My mother drowned on the night of May 23, my birthday" (*TL*, 11) link mothers and daughters through the life cycle of birth and death. The novel concludes this cycle with a metaphorical rebirth when Delia announces on the last page "Amalia had been. I was Amalia" (*TL*, 139). The same date specified in *The Lying Life of Adults* establishes a nexus between life, death, and rebirth, connecting the erased Vittoria to the dead Enzo to Giovanna who looks like Vittoria. The physical resemblance between aunt and niece posits Vittoria as Giovanna's symbolic mother and an alternative model of femininity—crude and vulgar, but vital and irrepressible. Their friendship is the first superimposition of faces and identities in the novel—*siamo identiche*, Giovanna tells her friends Angela and Ida, claiming that she and her aunt are identical (*Lvb*, 86).

With this novel Ferrante expands her exploration of forms of female friendship. Besides Vittoria and Giovanna's intergenerational bond, she introduces Vittoria's relationship with Enzo's widow, Margherita, and her three children. Vittoria and Margherita have become friends and Vittoria all but lives with Enzo's family. She has taken charge of Enzo's three children—Giuliana, Tonino, and Corrado—and of the house, occupying the empty space left by the dead husband-lover. This unusual arrangement of a home with "two mothers" (*Lvb*, 87) provides Giovanna with another model for a familial structure. She befriends the three children who are all older than her and each of them plays an important role in her life.[3] But like all the family structures and appearances in the novel, Vittoria's and Margherita's nontraditional household turns out to be deceptive. The framed photograph of the dead husband-lover dressed in his police uniform and carrying his gun occupies a central space in the apartment, placed in a panoptic position of power. Vittoria and Margherita often look at the photo, seeking the man's approval and venerating his authority.[4] Giovanna notes that his policing gaze keeps under surveillance the two women, bringing the wife and the lover together through the cult of his image (*Lvb*, 275). The two women's ostensibly feminine household is only another form of their subalternity. Enzo's framed picture and Andrea's disfigured family photographs belong to Ferrante's visual poetics of surveillance, erasure, and defacement as strategies for symbolic violence and domination. Giovanna discovers that the paternal legacy embodies a patriarchal order. Despite their class difference, Vittoria and Nella, Giovanna's mother, are alike: they both occupy subservient positions within the symbolic. Vittoria remains in thrall to Enzo's panoptic gaze while Nella rewrites romance novels, unable to free herself from her husband's tyranny.

This second overlapping of seemingly different feminine identities enacts the blurring of topographic difference—the order that reigns up in the Neapolitan hills is identical to the order that reigns down in the industrial zone. Giovanna, whose identity is yet not fully fixed, operates as a bridge between families and social classes, oscillating between her maternal legacy and her paternal roots.[5] The bracelet which makes its way from the Pascone to the Rione Alto and then back to the Pascone embodies Giovanna's mobility. Costanza, her father's lover, returns Vittoria's bracelet to Giovanna who eventually gives it back to Vittoria who gives it to Enzo's daughter Giuliana who forgets it in Milan when she visits her fiancé and Giovanna goes to Milan to retrieve it. The reasons behind the bracelet's precipitous "comings and goings," to use Elisa Gambaro's apt phrasing (2020), can be found in the faces in the old family photos Andrea has disfigured with a black marker. Photography in Ferrante's poetics has the potential to visualize invisible mechanisms and repressed stories.

Giovanna's mother shows her daughter the family photos she has kept in her old Italian dictionary (*Lvb*, 147). The narrative literally conjoins words (the dictionary) and images (the photos) to enable the daughter's gaze. One of the photos is an undamaged copy of the picture Andrea has defaced with a black marker. This undamaged photograph restores to Vittoria and Enzo their faces, undoing Andrea's act of disfigurement and revealing the history of the bracelet. Giovanna notices that in the photo her paternal grandmother is wearing the bracelet. As Giovanna delves into the family history, she finds out from Enzo's daughter Giuliana that the bracelet belonged to Enzo's dying mother. Enzo had stolen it from her to give it to Vittoria's mother who was fonder of him than of her own eldest son Andrea. The bracelet—like the tangled knot in Giovanna's opening paragraph—is entwined in a web of expropriations, lies, jealousy, and resentment. Unlike the earrings in *The Days of Abandonment* which are handed down to Olga by her mother-in-law as an official symbol of her status as Mario's wife, the bracelet in *The Lying Life of Adults* is stolen by the son from his mother to give to his lover's mother in exchange, perhaps, for Vittoria's availability. The bracelet then stands for the processes of women's objectification and commodification in a patriarchal economy of exchange and substitution.

This economy is corroborated by another familiar topos in Ferrante's visual poetics—the female body reflected in a mirror. At the end of the novel Giovanna must face the metamorphosis of her body and articulate an identity that fits her new image. When she visits Vittoria, her aunt attempts to teach her niece how to use her seductive body to her advantage. Vittoria positions Giovanna in front of a large mirror and orders her to look at her body. The aunt examines and praises the niece's feminine charms—legs, buttocks, and breasts, lifting her skirt and reaching inside her shirt. Lifting one's skirt is another image emblematic of Ferrante's poetics. As Chapter 3 proposed, Ferrante's laughing women lift their skirts as acts of defiance and self-expression. Here, however, it is not Giovanna who lifts her skirt as an act of defiance and resistance. The aunt pulls up Giovanna's skirt to display her niece's attractive body and therefore inscribe it within the frame of the male gaze.

Vittoria displays her niece's attractive body as a way of co-opting Giovanna into the frame of the objectifying male gaze, into a patriarchal system where sex and seduction are women's only means for happiness and emancipation. This scene in which Vittoria appraises Giovanna's body as a commodity to be traded carefully and profitably opens a rift between the two. Giovanna does not see her own reflection in the mirror but that of Vittoria standing behind her (*Lvb*, 316–17). But the mirror does not display a double portrait of Giovanna-Vittoria, as in the Vossi painting or in Amalia-Delia's double portrait in *Troubling Love*. This divergence of gazes—Giovanna's inability to recognize her body as a tool for seduction and Vittoria's privileging of Giovanna's corporeality as her only asset—ruptures their superimposed identities. Giovanna is not a reflection of Vittoria, she is extraneous to her aunt's limited, oppressed, and oppressive world of female subalternity. That is why in the novel's last chapter Giovanna rejects both her mother's and her aunt's legacies cobbling together her own identity and getting rid of the bracelet which chains her to a lineage of submissive women.

Open Frames

The Lying Life of Adults concludes with Giovanna's first sexual intercourse as an act of liberation and empowerment. She dictates the terms of this rite of passage and enters the world of adulthood unencumbered by the past. In the novel's last lines Giovanna leaves Naples for Venice accompanied by her friend Ida, embarking on a new journey of self-discovery. Ferrante thus ends the novel with the image of a female friendship which supplants the heteronormative model of relationships underwriting her parents' world. The narrative frame introduced in the opening chapter does not close, leaving the reader stranded inside Giovanna's narration. This structural choice could be explained by Ferrante's initial conception of *The Lying Life of Adults* as the first installment in a multivolume project (Ferrante 2019, "Devo mentire per dire la verità"). But by not closing the narrative frame, the text leaves room for other voices and forms of feminine writing, occluding any finalized or totalizing formation of female identity. In fact, Giovanna's friend and travel companion Ida is a writer herself whose stories mirror the plot events in the novel and who emerges as its possible coauthor.

The presence of multiple women writers in the text—Giovanna who narrates, Ida who chronicles Giovanna's life, and Nella who rewrites romance novels—amplifies and complicates the polyphony of Ferrante's other novels. The polyphony in *The Lying Life of Adults* is comprised of the words of different writing and speaking women whose voices capture from different perspectives a composite and unstable female subjectivity. The novel uses an adolescent girl as the focalizer precisely because Giovanna's yet unformed identity allows her to channel and reconcile a variety of worldviews, languages, and utterances. Ferrante expands the scope of her universal feminine imaginary, showing its breadth and reach while mapping its coordinates in reverse and exploring different forms of patriarchal violence and power. At the same time, *The Lying Life of Adults* revives many of her signature tropes and *topoi*, creating a network of references internal to her poetics but equally recognizable and relatable when viewed from outside.

Notes

Chapter 1

1 For definitions of, and debates on, world literature, I rely on Moretti (1998, 2000), Damrosch (2003), Casanova (2004), and Apter (2013).
2 Elena Ferrante's vision of literary translators as border-crossing agents who partake in the refraction of a national culture into a global, translocal cultural landscape aligns with Damrosch's concept of world literature as dealing with the local and the universal, the ethnic and the essential. World literature is a refraction of national literatures—that is, "works continue to bear the marks of their national origin even after they circulate into world literature" (Damrosch 2003, 283). At the same time, translation plays a key part in constituting and setting apart works of world literature "when they gain on balance in translation, stylistic losses offset by an expansion in depth as they increase their range" (ibid., 289). Emily Apter, on the other hand, warns against the dangerous tendencies of world literature toward the "reflexive endorsement of cultural equivalence" or the "celebration of nationally and ethnically branded 'differences'" which market commercialized identities (2013, 2). Ferrante's own awareness of the correlation between economic power and literature echoes Pascale Casanova's concept of the "World Republic of Letters," a world literary domain governed by power relations that dictate the form and circulation of texts (2004). This highly politicized terrain is split into a dominant European center (Paris) and periphery whose literary frontiers and territories are ruled by rivalry and inequality. Within the domain of letters forms, ideas, and structures migrate "downstream" from hegemonic powers and metropolitan centers to peripheral or colonized regions from the center to the periphery (Moretti 1998, 2000; Damrosch 2014). Within this system, Italy occupies a semi-peripheral position (Moretti 1998, 173).
3 Ferrante's first two novels, *Troubling Love* (*L'amore molesto*, 1992) and *The Days of Abandonment* (*I giorni dell'abbandono*, 2002) were adapted for the cinema by Italian directors Mario Martone (*L'amore molesto*, 1995) and Roberto Faenza (*I giorni dell'abbandono*, 2005). Her third novel, *The Lost Daughter* (*La figlia oscura*, 2006), is being adapted for the cinema by Maggie Gyllenhaal. And Ferrante's new novel, *The Lying Life of Adults* (*La vita bugiarda degli adulti*, 2019), will be adapted as a TV series by Netflix. Intermediality—or the adaptation to different artistic mediums—is a key feature of the global novel (de Rogatis 2019a, 2021).
4 De Rogatis (2018, 2019a) considers Ferrante's works as global novels, arguing for their urgent uncanny underground realism and feminist storytelling. On the new global novel, see Ganguly's (2016) discussion of the contemporary world novel as a global form produced at the intersection, post-1989, of the geopolitics of war and violence, hyperconnectivity through informational technologies, and a new sensibility in the context of visible suffering. Adam Kirsch (2017) likewise contributes to this dialogue in his slim volume. For a narratological study of the global novel, see Pennacchio (2018).

5 Falotico (2015) proposes that the four novels constitute a single book which combines autobiography, history, and metafiction and which comprises a large-scale historical "fresco" of postwar Europe. De Rogatis argues that "the map of time is more complex than it appears: the compelling game of the quartet is that of defending the relevance of minor lived events while endowing this existential sumptuousness with historic, if indirect, intensity" (2019a, 254).

6 Elisa Segnini (2017), drawing on Appadurai (1996) and Robertson (1994), attributes the success of Elena Ferrante's novels to their capitalizing on their glocal appeal, exporting a vision of "Neapolitan-ness" to the Anglophone reader/consumer. Silvia Caserta (2019) stresses the liminal position of Ferrante's Neapolitan Novels between the local and the global, their "familiar unfamiliarity" (9).

7 Tim Parks, a renowned translator and writer, identifies "the dull global novel" (2010) as a contemporary phenomenon. His objections concern the quality of the literary prose produced as a result of globalization and the demands of the international literary market. Contemporary writers, Parks argues, remove obstacles to international comprehension, employ simple vocabulary, and engage highly visible literary tropes to create easily translatable—and digestible—texts (2010).

8 Generally, I adopt the term "female" with respect to the identity and subjectivity of women, whereas "feminine" is employed as an adjective to describe an ethos or a set of corporeal, sociocultural, or artistic practices performed by or intended for women.

9 For example, in 1992, she did not attend the ceremony for the prestigious prize "Premio Procida, Isola di Arturo—Elsa Morante" awarded to *Troubling Love*.

10 An English translation of the 2003 edition of *Frantumaglia* was produced as part of Elda Buonanno's doctoral dissertation, *La Frantumaglia: Elena Ferrante's "Fragmented Self"* (2008). Buonanno (2008) also engages in an insightful scholarly analysis of the text in which she reads *La frantumaglia*, along with Ferrante's first three novels, as a narrative about fragmented identity, recovery, and reshaping of the self.

11 For more on the Russian modernist project of "life creation" (tvorchestvo zhizni), see Paperno and Grossman (1994).

12 See, for example, Paolo di Paolo (2014, 2018). Laura Benedetti (2016) suggests that the most scathing criticism of the Neapolitan Novels was generated by their extraordinary success in America. Schwartz (2020) provides a thorough and persuasive account of the reception of Ferrante's novels in the Italian mainstream press and in online journals and collective blogs.

13 Ferrante's critics in the Italian press include di Paolo (2014, 2018), Randall (2015), Gatti (2016b), and Jossa (2017), among others.

14 Tiziana de Rogatis (2018, 19) defines the Italian critics' adverse reviews of Ferrante's works as phobic and poorly argued. Lucamante (2008, 18–19) asserts that female writers in Italy often face misogynistic criticism and suggests that Italian "militant critics" lack updated analytical tools to approach the new forms of the Italian novel.

15 Chapters in English on Ferrante in edited volumes or in scholarly monographs on Italian women's writing appeared as early as 2002 (see Giorgio 2002; Benedetti 2007; Lucamante 2008; Sambuco 2012). They were followed by James Wood's essay (2013) in *The New Yorker*, my own article on disgust in Elena Ferrante (Milkova 2013), Sambuco's (2013) on gendered space, and Alsop's original reading of *Troubling Love* and *The Days of Abandonment* through the lens of *La frantumaglia* (2014). Some of

the trail-blazing Italian scholars of Elena Ferrante include Giancarlo Lombardi (1999), Laura Benedetti (2007, 2012), Stefania Lucamante (2007, 2008), Elisa Gambaro (2014) and Tiziana de Rogatis (2014). Post-2014, scholarship on Elena Ferrante and especially on the Neapolitan quartet has expanded enormously to include many academics from different fields and disciplines both in Italy and abroad. Multiple significant contributions by Katrin Wehling-Giorgi, Olivia Santovetti, and Enrica Ferrara have defined and advanced the field of Ferrante Studies.

16 De Rogatis (2018, 17-18) proposes that Lila's and Elena's survival is precisely one of the reasons for the success of the Neapolitan Novels—the heroines' refusal to submit to the plots and narratives of victimization.

17 Alsop (2014) defines Ferrante's representation of psychic disequilibrium as mimetic realism—that is, she contends that the plot elements of disintegration, disorientation, and fragmentation are reproduced in the formal structures of her first two novels. De Rogatis (2018) defines Ferrante's realism as "underground," as digging under the surface of the ordinary and excavating the intimate and private realities of her characters.

18 There are a number of male Italian scholars such as Gianni Turchetta, Massimo Fusillo, Raffaele Donnarumma, Luciano Parisi, and Rocco Coronato who have published in Italian serious investigations of her writing.

19 Several scholars have noted the mythological inflections of Ferrante's plots: Buonanno (2008), Elwell (2013), de Rogatis (2014, 2016a, 2017, 2018), Wehling-Giorgi (2016a, 2017), Pinto (2019b).

20 For an extended argument about patriarchal urban space as a literal and symbolic labyrinth in *My Brilliant Friend*, see Milkova (2017). De Rogatis (2018) builds on my argument, borrowing the concept of the patriarchal labyrinth and applying it more broadly to Ferrante's portrayal of symbolic violence.

21 The mythological realism of Madeline Miller's acclaimed novel *Circe* (2018), an instant *New York Times* bestseller like Ferrante's novels, and other recent literary reworkings and translations of classical texts speak to a revival of the classics in an effort to recuperate liminal women from the grip of masculinist texts and literary translations by men. It is not surprising then that we are witnessing the first translations in English by women of foundational classical texts—Emily Wilson's translation of *The Odyssey* (2018) and Stephanie McCarter's forthcoming translation of Ovid's *Metamorphoses*.

22 It is worth noting that classics scholars such as McCarter (2016), Graziosi (2016), and Geue (2016) have turned their attention to Ferrante's writing and the ways it incorporates classical texts.

23 "Literary truth is the truth released exclusively by words used well, and it is realized entirely in the words that formulate it" (*Fr*, 261). In her interviews, she revisits the question of literary truth a number of times (*Fr*, 315, 351, 342, 360).

24 The latter half of this statement has been omitted from the English translation. It reads "sommo insieme anche posizioni distanti" (*La fr*, 323).

25 Ferrante's novels have generated a significant corpus of scholarly analysis employing the feminist philosophers that Ferrante herself singles out. See, for example, De Rogatis (2018); Van Ness (2016); Wehling-Giorgi (2016b, 2017); Elwell (2013, 2016); Mandolini (2016); Sotgiu (2018, 2017); Sciubba (2019); Caffè (2019); and Pinto (2019a, 2019b) who refers to Ferrante's "cyber feminism," among others.

26 Ferrante cites Fielding and Defoe, Flaubert and Tolstoy, Dostoevsky and Hugo (*Fr*, 265).

27 Comparative readings have focused on Elena Ferrante and women writers such as Louisa May Alcott, Virginia Woolf, Simone de Beauvoir, Christa Wolf, Margaret Atwood, Toni Morrison, Alice Sebold, Elsa Morante, Anna Maria Ortese, Matilde Serao, Cristina Comencini, and Milena Agus.
28 Muraro interviewed Ferrante in 2007 (*Fr*, 218–26), while Cavarero (2016, 2020) reads Ferrante's Neapolitan Novels as confirming her theory of the narratable self. Rachel Cusk (2015) reviewed *The Story of the Lost Child*, while Elizabeth Strout features prominently in Durzi's film *Ferrante Fever* (2017). Jhumpa Lahiri discussed Ferrante's writing at an event presenting the last volume of the tetralogy, *Story of the Lost Child* at the Center for Fiction on January 27, 2016. Lahiri says she corresponded with Ferrante who sent her "a personal manifesto" (https://www.youtube.com/watch?v=ZlnNyqqyYh4&t=437s).
29 Caserta (2019) notes that in fact Ferrante has been criticized for some of her odd lexical choices in Italian—peculiarities that make her texts more difficult to translate.
30 Pinto (2020) interprets the absence of dialect in the Neapolitan Novels as a form of cultural and class appropriation, as embodying Elena's social mobility at the cost of erasing her identity: her standard, upper-class Italian absorbs and dominates Lila's voice.
31 This glossing occurs a few more times (*Fr*, 101, 124, 224).
32 Lahiri's story "Lo scambio" was originally published in Italy in 2015 as part of her language memoir *In altre parole*, translated subsequently by Ann Goldstein and published in the bilingual volume *In Other Words* (2016). *In altre parole* details the writer's experience learning Italian, moving to Italy, and negotiating her identity in the new language. I cite from the bilingual 2016 edition, referencing the page numbers of both Italian and English versions.
33 In June 2014, Jhumpa Lahiri published an open letter to Elena Ferrante in the Italian newspaper *Corriere Della Sera* in which she not only calls her one of the best writers in the world but also states that she shares Ferrante's need for invisibility.
34 "The body of the bride Lila appeared cruelly shredded. Much of the head had disappeared, as had the stomach. There remained an eye, the hand on which the chin rested, the brilliant stain of her mouth, the diagonal stripe of the bust, the line of the crossed legs, the shoes" (*SNN*, 119).
35 At the time of writing this chapter, *The Lying Life of Adults* has not yet been released in English translation.
36 Since this book addresses Ferrante's textual production, it does not analyze the cinematic or television adaptations of Ferrante's novels although they have contributed to her popularity as well.

Chapter 2

1 Rocco Coronato notes that sexual penetration in the Neapolitan Novels either eliminates a woman's identity or blurs it (2016, 119–20).
2 Pierre Bourdieu (2002) proposes the term "symbolic violence" to describe different forms of insidious yet invisible masculine domination underpinning everyday social practices and power dynamics.

3 For a feminist reading of the image of the woman artist as a weaver and the silencing of female language in the plot of male dominance, see Patricia Klindienst (1991).
4 Wehling-Giorgi suggests that the self-mutilation enacted metaphorically onto the photograph works to reclaim conventional male constructs of the female body as formless flow (2017, 11).
5 For Freud's theories of infantile sexuality, see *Three Essays on the Theory of Sexuality* (1975). On fetishism, see Freud's essay "Fetishism" (1927) and Fusillo (2017).
6 For more on Freud's phallocratic scheme, see Rosemary Balsam (2018).
7 Tiziana de Rogatis reads this as Ferrante's revision of the archetype of the Mother (2018, 91–6).
8 Alsop's extensive theory of Ferrante's "falling women" posits that Delia and Olga are "modern women haunted by ancient mores" who "must work through existing systems to cobble their own" (2014, 469–70).
9 Richard Carvalho reads *frantumaglia* as the manifestations of "the metaphorical lava beneath everyone's surface," while the logic of the irrational explains Ferrante's mother's mysterious actions "not traceable to a single cause" (2018, 105).
10 Katrin Wehling-Giorgi contends that *smarginatura* and the focus on the deformed and dislocated body in the Neapolitan Novels is Ferrante's way of expressing her female protagonists' resistance to a deep sense of subalternity and liminality (2016a, 210). And Tiziana de Rogatis elaborates: the battle between the sexes is what activates or fuels *smarginatura*—men who exercise their power through colonizing women's physical forms, women whose bodies are devoured, cannibalized, broken down in the violent, brutal reality of the *rione* (2016b, 135).
11 David Kurnick reads this scene as an example of pathetic fallacy or the correlation of psychic states and natural phenomena, an aesthetically obsolete trope that Ferrante "casually redeems" (2015).
12 To quote Carvalho, "*Smarginatura*—'falling apart,' 'fragmenting,' 'shattering,' 'falling forever,' 'dissolving'—is something that any of us can experience given a powerful enough emotional experience—witness panic. [. . .] Emotion is the metaphorical lava beneath everyone's surface, which, given sufficient intensity, can become a literal experience" (2018, 104–5).
13 My reading of *smarginatura* in relation to agoraphobia is intended to suggest that *smarginatura* arises from Lila's and Elena's internalization of, and reaction against, a male-dominated, violent patriarchal urban space which reinforces the social and cultural restrictions imposed on women. In other words, *smarginatura* arises from sociological causes rather than medical-biological. I follow the methodology and argument of Emanuela Caffè (2021) who shows that Ferrante shifts the perception of trauma from rare to common events such as domestic violence, explores various reactions to traumatic circumstances, and gives particular prominence to the complex sociopolitical contexts underlying traumatic experiences.
14 I am thankful to Serena Todesco for pointing this out.
15 Leda's wound is "lesione" in Italian (*Lfo*, 6), from the Italian verb "ledere," to offend, to hurt. Perhaps Leda's name can be read in relation to "ledere." I am indebted to Chiara Belluzzi for pointing this out.
16 I would propose that this "dissolvimento" or dissolving provides a textual ground for Ann Goldstein's translation of *smarginatura* as "dissolving margins"—that is, the translator's lexical choice draws on Ferrante's own vocabulary.

17 Goldstein translates Ferrante's word "sfaldamento" (*Lfo*, 33) as a "sensation of flaking layers" (*LD*, 32). Lucamante (2018, 10) uses the term "sfaldamento" instead of the more widely noted *frantumaglia* and *smarginatura* to describe Lila's psychical and corporeal undoing.
18 For an extended analysis of Ferrante's invocation of Aleramo in *The Lost Daughter*, see Elwell (2016). Benedetti (2007, 28–32) discusses Aleramo's novel and its revolutionary questioning of the institutions of motherhood.
19 In the Neapolitan Novels, Elena invokes the chain that links mothers to daughters when she contemplates the prospect of becoming a published author as precisely a breaking of the chain: "Elena Greco, me, breaking the long chain [punto di rottura] of illiterates, semi-literates, an obscure name that would be charged with light for eternity" (*SNN*, 450; *Snc*, 448–9).
20 Elizabeth Alsop has in fact proposed that *Troubling Love* and *The Days of Abandonment* can be read as "revisionary histories: as Ferrante's reimagining of certain plights, and plots, that have long plagued Western literary heroines" (2014).
21 De Rogatis persuasively argues that this "regressive power of chronology" produces "the metamorphosis of time" (2018, 108–9), that is, the conflation and confluence of archaic and modern, of the caves of the mothers and the computer on which Elena is writing the tetralogy we are reading.

Chapter 3

1 For example, this is the case in Deborah Levy's *Hot Milk* (2016), Elizabeth Strout's *My Name Is Lucy Barton* (2016), and Alice Sebold's *The Almost Moon* (2007).
2 Shafak compiles a long list of childless women writers (Virginia Woolf, Simone de Beauvoir, Louisa May Alcott, George Eliot, Ayn Rand, Sandra Cisneros), of women writers who were absent mothers or couldn't cope with motherhood (Muriel Spark, Doris Lessing, Sylvia Plath, Alice Walker), and of women who could have been great writers but were stifled by multiple pregnancies and despotic husbands (Sophia Behrs, Tolstoy's wife).
3 They can be situated within the relatively new interest in the mother-daughter relationship in wide-ranging fields such as psychoanalysis, philosophy, sociology, and comparative literature. Following Anglo-American feminist writing in the 1970s and French and Italian feminist theories of the 1970s and 1980s, the genealogies established between mothers and daughters, and their corporeal and cultural bonds, have taken center stage in literary narratives of the past four decades. For further discussions of the mother-daughter relationship in Italian literature, see Sambuco (2012), Benedetti (2007), Karagoz (2001), Giorgio (2002), and Lucamante (2008).
4 Ferrante's literary debt to Elsa Morante has been noted by many scholars. In addition, Benedetti (2007, 106) points out the intriguing similarities between Ferrante's *Troubling Love* and Fabrizia Ramondino's *Althénopis*, while Lucamante (2018) maintains that Ferrante disavows Ramondino's influence.
5 For a mainstream perspective, see James Wood who acknowledges Ferrante's "less familiar" narrative of "despair and revulsion around motherhood" (2013).
6 For an insightful reading of this scene, see Elwell (2013).

7   I am grateful to Malvina Rousseva for pointing out that many pages of the essay "La frantumaglia" in fact read like unpublished excerpts from *Troubling Love*. This mixing of narrative and metanarrative confirms the project of *Frantumaglia* as Ferrante's metafictional commentary on both "Elena Ferrante" and her novels.
8   Serena Todesco's unpublished paper "Il corpo molesto della madre: elementi ferrantiani in Slavenka Drakulic" explores the mother's body as "molesto" or troublesome (2019b). See also Todesco (2021).
9   For an illuminating discussion of Neapolitan dialect as the mother tongue in Ferrante's novels, see Wehling-Giorgi (2017, 2016b).
10 For more on abjection and Elena's mother tongue, see Van Ness (2016), Wehling-Giorgi (2017).
11 Ghezzo and Teardo read Elena's attachment to Lila's healthy body as replacing the vertical, genealogical bond with her mother with a "horizontal, sisterly yet competing relationship between peers" (2019, 180).
12 De Rogatis analyzes this scene in which the dialectal magma underlying Ferrante's—and Elena's—controlled, neutral linguistic register erupts and takes over (2018, 187).
13 I wish to thank the anonymous reviewer of *Elena Ferrante as World Literature* who pointed me to Cristina Mazzoni's (2012) article and to Lindsay Myers's (2011) chapter on doll's autobiography.
14 Emma Van Ness reads this scene as the girls' foundational anti-maternal act—a rejection of the traditional motherhood embodied by their own mothers (2016, 297–8).
15 On dolls, automata, and puppets, see Stewart (1993), Kuznets (1994), and Gross (2012). Mazzoni (2012) and Myers (2011) argue that dolls in nineteenth-century children's books played a crucial role in the formation of the protagonist's identity, providing complex representations of the processes through which we become who we are. Myers (2011) argues further that narratives about dolls and other inanimate objects in post-Unification Italy were particularly suited to the sociopolitical and cultural ideologies of the new Italian state.
16 For an extended reading of the emergence of the maternal voice from a Western tradition of mute and suffering mothers, see Van Ness (2016).
17 Pinto (2019b) reads the doll as personified through her archaic, abject, and post-human motherhood, arguing for Ferrante's cyberfeminism.
18 Interestingly, Jean Nathan's biography of Dare Wright was recently published in Italian translation as *Vita segreta della bambola solitaria* (2019) by edizioni e/o, Elena Ferrante's publisher.
19 Alessia Ricciardi (2017) has argued that Elena and Lila's relationship is structured as a practice of *affidamento* or entrustment between a mentor (Lila) and a mentee (Elena). But this model is too limited as each in turn assumes the role of mentor and mentee. Moreover, the tetralogy leaves open the question of whose "genius" the title refers to, allowing the reader to assign that adjective according to his or her preference (Petrova 2019).
20 Tina's disappearance foreshadows Lila's, but it also realizes Lila's life goal to erase all traces of her existence.
21 The noun "obscurity" (*oscurità*) perhaps references the title of *The Lost Daughter*, *La figlia oscura* or "The Obscure Daughter," therefore establishing another textual link between lost and found dolls and daughters.

22 For example, "Ho continuato a strisciare allo stesso modo, ma l'ho guardato al di sopra della mia spalla" (Perkins Gilman 2011, 62); "Così ogni volta ho dovuto strisciare sopra di lui" (Perkins Gilman 2011, 62).

23 There are further parallels between Ferrante's literary imagination and "The Yellow Wallpaper." The color "yellow" occurs twenty-four times in *Troubling Love* in various lexical forms and eleven times in *The Days of Abandonment*—such as "giallo, "giallastro," and "ingiallito." The yellow paper in which the old Caserta wraps pastries is "la carta gialla" in what might be an explicit reference to "La carta da parati gialla" or "The Yellow Wallpaper." Since the old Caserta abused Delia as a child precisely in the shop's cellar, yellow assumes implications of fear, molestation, and trauma. Likewise, in *Frantumaglia*, the monster in the storeroom is "ugly as the yellowish [giallastra] larva of a cicada" (*Fr*, 110). And in *The Days of Abandonment*, yellow is the color of bodily fluids—for example, the "viscid yellow stripe" [*striscia viscida, giallastra*] of Carrano's semen (*DA*, 87; *Iga*, 96). Yellow accrues semantic associations with (sexual) violence, trauma, and with oozing discharge—the inside coming out.

24 Carmela Pesca (2017) argues that dressing, clothing, and narration are related in *Troubling Love* so that fragments of Delia's memories shape the narrative's fabric. Eleonora Conti (2015) examines the symbolic power of feminine clothing and the mother-seamstress in *Troubling Love*.

25 The visual metaphor of cutting off limbs or truncating bodies appears time and again in Ferrante's poetics. In *Troubling Love*, the Vossi painting, described twice, depicts women's hands cut off at the wrists. In *The Days of Abandonment*, Olga cuts up photographs of her family reducing the figures to body parts. In *The Lost Daughter* and *The Beach at Night* the doll is literally eviscerated. And in *The Story of a New Name* Lila fragments and mutilates her own photographed portrait. For a discussion of the violated and mutilated female body, see Chapter 2. For a discussion of visual representations of women's suffering, see Chapter 4.

26 Trips on the crowded tram or funicular are particularly excruciating for the child Delia: "It was wasted effort, Amalia's body couldn't be contained. Her hips spread across the aisle towards the hips of the men on either side of her legs, her stomach swelled toward the knee or shoulder of whoever was sitting in front of her" (*TL*, 53). Delia's proprietary spectatorship of Amalia's seductive body aligns her with the subjectivity of the jealous and possessive father who beats his wife for attracting attention on the tram.

27 Conti (2015) proposes that the theme of feminine clothing in *Troubling Love* reflects the mirroring of mother and daughter. Sambuco (2012, 144–51) also pays attention to the symbolic function of dresses in Ferrante's novel.

28 Gilman's anonymous narrator likewise creates a double—the woman behind the yellow wallpaper. By liberating her from her prison, the narrator liberates herself vicariously while remaining trapped in both her room and her text.

29 Ferrante readily admits the influences of classical mythology and Greek and Latin texts on her poetics (*Fr*, 145, 252, 347). As far as biblical references are concerned, in the Neapolitan Novels Elena Greco writes a book discussing Genesis as the assertion of linguistic dominion of men over women (*TLTS*, 364).

30 Cixous elaborates: "laughs exude from all our mouths; our blood flows and we extend ourselves without ever reaching an end; we never hold back our thoughts, our signs, our writing; and we're not afraid of lacking" (1976, 878).

31 The dialect Delia hears on the streets of Naples "was the language of my mother, which I had vainly tried to forget, along with many other things about her" (*TL*, 21). And when she resorts to dialect, her words carry "an echo of the violent quarrels between Amalia and my father" (*TL*, 21). On the role of dialect and the mother tongue in Ferrante, see Wehling-Giorgi (2016b, 2017).

32 Torunn Haaland (2018) analyzes Ferrante's *The Lost Daughter* as trauma fiction. Likewise, *Troubling Love* can be read as trauma fiction in which Delia must work through the traumatic experiences—sexual abuse, domestic violence, obscene language—that haunt her. By repeating and narrating her mother's obscene language, Delia acknowledges the past and is able to transform it into narrative memory. For more on trauma and narrative, see Caruth (1996). For an analysis of gender violence and repressed memory, see Mandolini (2016) and Parisi (2017).

33 The first to note the role of laughter in Ferrante's novels, Elizabeth Correll (2019) argues that laughter is a "destabilizing force in Ferrante, able to distend social order and normative power dynamics—a conceptualization that echoes historical, mythological, and biblical precedents" (1). Correll then examines these precedents through the lens of Bakhtinian carnival and Anne Carson's gendered sound to propose links between Ferrante's texts and the biblical story of Sarah and the mythological figure of Iambe/Baubo.

34 The father's possessive and controlling discourse echoes the Duke's dramatic monologue in Robert Browning's "My Last Duchess." The Duke, unable to control his wife's joyful disposition, silences her forever, attempting to control instead the display of her portrait and its life-like "spot of joy" (Loucks and Stauffer 2007, 58–9). Likewise, Amalia's husband flaunts his possession of her body by painting her, throughout his life, as a seminude gypsy.

35 Zarour Zarzar (2020) argues that Olga overcomes the crisis of abandonment and recomposes her life through linguistic reconstruction.

36 Larissa Bonfante discusses the apotropaic function of laughter in the Greek myth of Baubo and Freud's reading of it (2008). Anne Carson too discusses the significance of Iambe/Baubo (1995). For the original myth of Demeter and Iambe/Baubo, see *The Homeric Hymn to Demeter* (Foley 1994). I am grateful to Sophia Zandi for pointing out the ritual significance of laughter and profanities in *Troubling Love*.

37 On the inscription of the urban landscape onto Olga's body, see Chapter 5.

38 Elisa Segnini (2017) notes that this is the only expression in dialect in Ferrante's first three novels. The mother's last word is then even more tightly imbricated in the body and its functions.

Chapter 4

1 In the same interview, she insists: "This will be possible only if we build a grand female tradition that men are forced to measure themselves against. It's going to be a long battle, centered on women's industry in every field, on the excellence of female thought and action. Only when a man publicly recognizes his debt to a woman's work, without the condescending kindness typical of those who feel themselves superior, will things really start to change" (*Fr*, 363).

2. "Being co-opted into the long, authoritative tradition created by men should not be the cost of making art. The stakes are higher: women have to contribute to an artistic genealogy of our own that stands up—in terms of intelligence, refinement, skill, richness of invention, emotional density—to the male tradition" (*II*, 86; *Lio*, 82).
3. Elsewhere in *Frantumaglia*, Ferrante claims that "we have to fight against submissiveness, and boldly, in fact proudly, seek a literary genealogy of our own" (*Fr*, 343).
4. Chapters 2 and 3 explore in more detail the intertextual network of Ferrante's literary mothers that undergirds both *Frantumaglia* and Ferrante's novels. Stefania Lucamante (2018) has proposed that Ferrante avoids mentioning what Lucamante considers a key figure in the formation of Ferrante's literary imaginary—the Neapolitan writer Fabrizia Ramondino. Lucamante suggests that this omission is effectively anti-feminist and undoes the work of building a feminine literary genealogy.
5. For example, Delia's portrayal of the past in *Troubling Love* adopts the iconography of still life painting to depict traumatic scenes of domestic violence (Milkova 2016a). In *The Lost Daughter*, Leda discovers a tray laden with glossy fruit like in a still life painting, while toward the end of the novel she views various objects for sale at the market stalls. See Chapter 2, which relates Leda and the market scene in *The Lost Daughter* to the landscape of *frantumaglia* and to the symptoms of agoraphobia characteristic of *smarginatura*.
6. For example, Delia fetishizes Amalia's finger pierced by the needle of the sewing machine transforming it into an object of desire. See Chapter 2 for a discussion of needles, scissors, burins, and safety pins in Ferrante's novels as tools for inscribing feminine corporeality, creative agency, and artistic/authorial production.
7. The beautiful shoes Lila creates do not emancipate her, however, from the *rione*'s patriarchal cage. They become consumer goods that allow her future husband Stefano to buy Lila's freedom by investing in the large-scale production of her shoe designs. Even if Ferrante supplants Freudian fetishism with a system where fetishes have larger cultural meaning as objects invested with symbolic, affective, and emotional value (Fusillo 2017), the deployment of the shoes in the Neapolitan quartet remains within the boundaries of a patriarchal frame.
8. An image of a mouth-shaped wound appears in *The Lost Daughter* when a pinecone hits Leda in the back and the bruise resembles a mouth: "a livid spot that looked like a mouth, dark at the edges, reddish at the center" (*LD*, 28). At the same time, pinecones remind Leda of her mother's mouth crushing the shells of pine nuts (*LD*, 14) and imply a connection between the wounded body and the mother's teeth.
9. On frames and the borders of representation, see Marin (2001), Duro (1996), Phelan (2006), as well as Wolf and Bernhart's edited volume (2006). For the way the frame operates within a literary text and in relation to ekphrasis, see Milkova (2016d). Psychoanalyst Richard Carvalho associates liminality—the rite of passage between critical states or stages—with creativity and creation (2010). The frame belongs to this ritual-liminal position by marking the passage between art and non-art, representation and reality.
10. This frame also functions on the literal level as a prison-labyrinth which contains and punishes female desire. Chapter 5 explores the image of the labyrinth as a literal and symbolic structure in Ferrante's works.

11 For a discussion of the female nude and its ideological implications, see Berger (1972, 47, 63) and Nochlin (1988, 1–19; 1991, 42–4).
12 Forgacs discusses Roma camps (*campi nomadi*) in Italy and their production and depiction as social and spatial margins particularly through photographic documentation (2014, 263–89). One of the photographs Forgacs briefly mentions bears a striking similarity to the description of the father's gypsy painting in *Troubling Love*—Marco Delogu's 2000 photograph *Senada and Jonathan* depicts a young gypsy mother breastfeeding her son, her breast exposed. She stares "confidently" at the camera, the background completely out of focus (2014, 268–9). Forgacs does not analyze this photograph beyond mentioning its interesting approach to representing Romani people, but I see it as an image confirming the exotic and erotic allure of the seminude gypsy in *Troubling Love*. The blurred background abstracts the young mother from her social and ethnic situation, concentrating on her erotic and maternal identity. The Italian edition of Forgacs's book, *Margini d'Italia* (2015), features precisely this image on its cover therefore relying on its visual appeal as well.
13 Giancarlo Lombardi suggests that the Vossi canvas stands for the narrative itself (1999). Tiziana de Rogatis contends that the two women's superimposed profiles provide a metaphor for the doubling of Amalia-Delia within the narrative (2016c, 303). De Rogatis further notes that the Vossi canvas is the price Caserta has paid to obtain the father's permission to court Amalia (2016). The painting thus becomes embroiled in the objectification of women, confirming their status as exchangeable objects.
14 Mulvey writes: "[U]ltimaltely, the meaning of woman is sexual difference, the absence of penis as visually ascertainable, the material evidence on which is based the castration complex essential for the organization of entrance to the symbolic order and the law of the father. Thus the woman as icon, displayed for the gaze and enjoyment of men, the active controllers of the look, always threatens to evoke the anxiety it originally signified" (1988, 64).
15 What I have in mind is Susan Stanford Friedman's (2011) comparative methodology which posits collage as a radical juxtaposition of texts from different geohistorical and cultural locations that can produce new insights and new theories.
16 Chapter 5 analyzes in detail the gendering of Turin's urban topography and Olga's domestic domain in the novel, along with modes of subverting the gendered construction of space.
17 This image of the female body wearing a voluminous mantle (*manto*) recalls the iconography of *The Virgin of the Sheltering Cloak* or *The Madonna del Manto* in which the Virgin Mary spreads a protective cloak over a congregation of Christians as an allegory of Mercy or Charity. I am grateful to Tiziana de Rogatis who suggested this analogy. For more on the iconography of the *Madonna of the Sheltering Cloak*, see Van Asperen (2013).
18 Maria Reyes Ferrer (2016) argues that there are three forms of specularity in the novel: Olga in front of the mirror, Olga and her daughter, and Olga and the *poverella*. Reyes Ferrer proposes that these types of specularity are crucial to Olga's reconstructing her female identity in relation to herself and to other women. Zarour Zarzar (2020, 335) mentions in a footnote that the mirror scene echoes a very similar scene in Clarice Lispector's story "Daydream and Drunkenness of a Young Lady."

19 Scholars who have discussed Ferrante's connection to Elsa Morante include Gambaro (2014), Falotico (2015), de Rogatis (2014, 2016c, 2018), Santovetti (2018), and Wehling-Giorgi (2017, 2021). Morante's *Aracoeli* elaborates a complex and ambivalent image of motherhood: the elemental and innocent peasant girl Aracoeli is colonized and subjugated by the "gilded cage" of her husband's upper-class patriarchal culture. After the death of her second child, Aracoeli comes undone, succumbing to self-degradation and nymphomania, trapped in her body and sexuality. Giorgio (1994) reads the mother's trajectory in Morante's novel as one from nature to culture to nature. As in Morante's "Lo scialle andaluso," here the narrative privileges the son's perspective.

20 De Rogatis in fact argues that Ferrante's three novels, *Troubling Love*, *The Days of Abandonment*, and *The Lost Daughter* are all based on a ritual structure, formalizing a ritual/rite, a "transformative performance" that articulates the protagonists' female subjectivity in relation to the ghost of the mother and a lineage of archaic female ancestors (2017).

21 The most striking and tragic examples of Lila's inventive power are Alfonso's metamorphosis into Lila, a metamorphosis she encourages and even assists, and Michele Solara who lives his erotic passion for Lila through the "hermaphrodite" Alfonso-Lila (de Rogatis 2018, 281–3).

22 Olivia Santovetti has recently re-proposed Lila's act of self-erasure as a "strategy of empowerment and resistance" (2019).

23 On Medusa as the "myth in which the dominance of the male is violently reasserted against the illegitimate power of the woman" and its recurrence throughout Western literature, culture and art, see Mary Beard (2018, 70–9). On Medusa as a site of horror, see Adriana Cavarero (2009). On the iconography of Medusa's head in *fin de siècle* culture, see Dijsktra (1986, 309–11). Wehling-Giorgi (2017) reads Medusa in relation to Ferrante's portrayals of the violated, crippled maternal female body to suggest that in this way Ferrante unsettles conventional patriarchal constructions of femininity and motherhood. Santovetti (2019) argues for the symbolic value of Lila's self-inflicted beheading as overthrowing the classical misogynist implications of Medusa's head.

24 In *Frantumaglia* Ferrante uses the same phrase to describe an empty dress as an emblem of women's violation and suffering: "the body of a woman worn out by her troubles, without a head, without legs, without arms and hands" (*Fr*, 156).

25 Elwell (2016) and Ghezzo and Teardo (2019) discuss Cavarero's theory of relationality and narrating the self as underpinning Ferrante's novels.

26 In analyzing Titian's painting *Marsyas* and its portrayal of torture, the psychoanalyst Richard Carvalho links torture, pain, and suffering to affectivity and the unconscious. The affective experience of creativity, of artistic endeavor, he argues, can feel like torture (2010).

Chapter 5

1 On ideological constructions of space, see Iovino (2016, 2), Nelson and Seager (2004, 7), McDowell (1999), Grosz (1999), and Rose (1996).

2 Iain Chambers describes Naples' dual nature as spanning both the archaic and the ultramodern: "With its violent mixture of antiquated street rites and global-design capitalism, Naples confronts us with a riddle" (2008, 73).

3   See McDowell (1999); Rose (1993); Sambuco (2013); Bondi and Davidson (2004); Smarr (2003, 9–11).
4   Italian scholar Andrea Baldi calls Naples as figured in twentieth-century literary representations "a labyrinthine, sepulchral Naples," a "necropolis" (2003, 230). Ferrante acknowledges the formative influence of Anna Maria Ortese's account of the Granili buildings housing Naples' outcasts in her reportage "The Involuntary City" (*Fr*, 64).
5   Iovino extends Benjamin's notion of the city's porosity when she defines Naples as "a porous, volcanic city built up with porous volcanic rock" (2014, 98).
6   Elda Buonanno (2008) proposes that the mother's body is the labyrinth in *Troubling Love* and at the same time the very map to the labyrinth—the answers and clues lie on that body for Delia to read and exit the labyrinth.
7   See Virgil, *Aeneid*, Book VI.
8   It is worth noting that the three Vossi sisters are echoed in the image of Delia and her two sisters. In *Frantumaglia*, Ferrante recounts having two sisters as well (*Fr*, 110–11). Childhood in her literary imagination is then also linked with the image of three sisters. Chekhov's play "Three Sisters" comes to mind and its thematization of women trapped in the provinces. Ferrante is clearly familiar with "the great Chekhov" and his works (*Fr*, 22, 225).
9   It is Delia's weight now that dictates the integrity of the house: "I was afraid that my weight would cause [the house] to collapse. I hurried out to the landing and shut the door carefully" (*TL*, 120).
10 For an extended analysis of the psychical dynamics of this substitution, see Chapter 3.
11 Franco Gallippi (2016) reads Lila as Parthenope, the siren who in Greek myth drowned near the place where the city of Naples was founded. Thus, for Gallippi, Lila attempts to found a new city based on love, to transform the *rione* through her mediation, and she succeeds partially, through Elena's emancipation.
12 On this point, see Carvalho (2018); de Rogatis (2018); and degli Esposti (2019).
13 As if to credit her coauthor, she reveals compulsively that her writing, her very literary language, is indebted to Lila's various texts: the story *The Blue Fairy* Lila wrote as a child, Lila's ideas on Dido and the city of love, Lila's rewriting of Elena's article on religion, Lila's letters, and Lila's eight notebooks-diaries which she entrusts to Elena in 1966.
14 The reference is to the Homeric hero Achilles and the etymology of his name, the Greek word "ἄχος" (*achos*) which means "grief, pain, distress" (Liddell and Scott 1999).
15 For insightful analyses of the rites and rituals underpinning Ferrante's imaginary and her construction of female identity, see Elwell (2013), Wehling-Giorgi (2016a), Milkova (2017), de Rogatis (2016a, 2017, 2018).
16 I borrow this idea—the gas mask as the image of a bull's head—from Georgi Gospodinov's novel *The Physics of Sorrow* (2015, 126) where a photograph makes the comparison explicit.
17 Tiziana de Rogatis extends my argument (Milkova 2017) to propose that the tetralogy itself becomes the labyrinth of the two girls' intertwined lives in which they constantly lose and find each other (de Rogatis 2018, 153).
18 Unlike Leda in *The Lost Daughter* who abandons her children and husband to live abroad with her lover, Olga never fulfils her fantasy.

19 Words for Olga constitute a safety net, a "stop-gap between self and nothingness" (Alsop 2014, 474). Written language lends her an epistemological grid to harness chaos and the drifting of subject identity (Ferrara 2016, 130). Or to put it differently, words help her control her *frantumaglia* and give it verbal expression, imposing on it the order of narrative.
20 As has been done by Sambuco (2013, 125), Alsop (2014, 270), and de Rogatis (2017, 83).

Epilogue

1 Since *The Lying Life of Adults* has not been released in English translation at the time of writing this epilogue, this citation is from the egalleys provided by Europa Editions.
2 Ferrante herself has indicated that *House of Liars* was fundamental for her (*Fr*, 330).
3 The names of Enzo's sons—Tonino and Corrado—appear in Ferrante's third novel *The Lost Daughter* where Nina's husband is Tonino and the pregnant Rosaria's husband is Corrado. Rosario is another name that appears in *The Lying Life of Adults*. This recycling of names is in line with the network of references from within Ferrante's works that the novel constructs.
4 Vittoria, however, has the upper hand in this nontraditional family configuration. She commands and directs the lives of Margherita and her children, attempting to control them as a way of compensating for her own failures. Giovanna ultimately rebels against her aunt's regime of power.
5 In fact, Giovanna's mediation effects Vittoria and Andrea's reconciliation.

Works Cited

Alcott, Louisa. 2007. *Piccole donne*. Translated by Rossana Guerrieri and illustrated by Mara Cerri. Fabbri editori.
Aleramo, Sibilla. 2011 [1906]. *Una Donna*. Milan: Feltrinelli.
Alfano, Barbara. 2015. "The Fact of the Matter: Ethics and Materiality in Elena Ferrante's Neapolitan Novels." *Italian Quarterly* 203-6 (Winter-Fall): 24-41.
Alsop, Elizabeth. 2014. "Femmes Fatales: 'La Fascinazione di Morte' in Elena Ferrante's *L'amore molesto* and *I giorni dell'abbandono*." *Italica* 91(3): 466-85.
Appadurai, Arjun. 1996. *Modernity at Large: Cultural Dimensions of Globalization*. Minneapolis: University of Minnesota Press.
Appolodorus. 2008. *The Library of Greek Mythology*. Translated by Robin Hard. New York and Oxford: Oxford University Press.
Apter, Emily. 2013. *Against World Literature: On the Politics of Untranslatability*. London and New York: Verso.
Bachelard, Gaston. 1994. *The Poetics of Space*. Translated by Maria Jolas. Boston: Beacon Press.
Bakhtin, Mikhail. 1965. *Rabelais and His World*. Translated by Helene Iswolsky. Cambridge, MA: MIT Press.
Bakhtin, Mikhail. 1984. *Problems of Dostoevsky's Poetics*. Translated by Caryl Emerson. Minneapolis: University of Minnesota Press.
Bakhtin, Mikhail. 1981. *The Dialogic Imagination: Four Essays*. Translated by Caryl Emerson and Michael Holquist. Austin: University of Texas Press.
Baldi, Andrea. 2003. "Ortese's Naples: Urban Malaise through a Visionary Gaze." In *Italian Women and the City*, edited by Janet Levarie Smarr and Daria Valentini, 215-38. Madison: Farleigh Dickinson University Press.
Balsam, Rosemary H. 2018. "Castration Anxiety Revisited: Especially Female 'Castration Anxiety.'" *Psychoanalytic Inquiry* 38(1): 11-22.
Banti, Anna. 1988. *Artemisia*. Translated by Shirley D'Ardia Caracciolo. Lincoln and London: University of Nebraska Press.
Banti, Anna. 2015 [1947]. *Artemisia*. Milan: SE.
Beard, Mary. 2018. *Women & Power: A Manifesto*. London: Profile Books.
Benedetti, Laura. 1999. "Reconstructing Artemisia: Twentieth-Century Images of a Woman Artist." *Comparative Literature* 51(1): 42-61.
Benedetti, Laura. 2007. *The Tigress in the Snow: Motherhood and Literature in Twentieth-Century Italy*. Toronto: University of Toronto Press.
Benedetti, Laura. 2012. "Il linguaggio dell'amicizia e della città. *L'amica geniale* di Elena Ferrante tra continuità e cambiamento." *Quaderni d'italianistica* XXXIII(2): 171-87.
Benedetti, Laura. 2016. "Elena Ferrante in America." *Allegoria* 73: 111-17.
Benjamin, Walter and Asja Lacis. 1986. "Naples." In Walter Benjamin, *Reflections. Essays, Aphorisms, Autobiographical Writings*, translated by Edmund Jephcott, 163-73. New York: Schocken.
Berger, John. 1972. *Ways of Seeing*. London: Penguin Books.

Berman, Antoine. 2012. "Translation and the Trials of the Foreign." In *The Translation Studies Reader*, edited by Lawrence Venuti, 240–53. London and New York: Routledge.

Bondi, Liz and Joyce Davidson. 2004. "Situating Gender." In *A Companion to Feminist Geography*, edited by Lise Nelson and Joni Seager, 15–31. Wiley & Sons.

Bonfante, Larissa. 2008. "Freud and the Psychoanalytical Meaning of the Baubo Gesture in Ancient Art." *Notes in the History of Art*. Special Issue on *Art and Psychoanalysis* 27(2/3): 2–9.

Bourdieu, Pierre. 2002. *Masculine Domination*. Translated by Richard Nice. Stanford: Stanford University Press.

Bruno, Giuliana. 2002. *Atlas of Emotions. Journeys in Art, Architecture, and Film*. New York: Verso.

Bullaro, Grace Russo. 2016. "The Era of the 'Economic Miracle' and the Force of Context in Ferrante's *My Brilliant Friend*." In *The Works of Elena Ferrante. Reconfiguring the Margins*, edited by Grace Russo Bullaro and Stephanie Love, 15–44. New York: Palgrave Macmillan.

Bullaro, Grace Russo and Stephanie Love. 2016. *The Works of Elena Ferrante. Reconfiguring the Margins*. New York: Palgrave Macmillan.

Buonanno, Elda. 2008. *La Frantumaglia: Elena Ferrante's "Fragmented Self."* PhD dissertation. City University of New York.

Caesar, Ann Hallamore. 2014. "Confinement and Shifting Boundaries in Post-Unification Writing by Women." In *Italian Women Writers 1800–2000: Boundaries, Borders, and Transgression*, edited by Patrizia Sambuco, 3–15. Madison: Farleigh Dickinson University Press.

Caffè, Emanuela. 2019. "Staging a Word: Overcoming and Recovering Familial Bonds in Elena Ferrante's Neapolitan Novels." *Carte Italiane* 12(1): 105–24.

Caffè, Emanuela. 2021. "Global Feminism and Trauma in Elena Ferrante's *My Brilliant Friend*." Forthcoming in *MLN* 136(1).

Carson, Anne. 1995. "The Gender of Sound." In *Glass, Irony, and God*, 119–41. New York: New Directions.

Caruth, Cathy. 1996. *Unclaimed Experience: Trauma, Narrative, and History*. Johns Hopkins University Press.

Carvalho, Richard. 2010. "Titian's *Marsyas* as an Image of the Creative Process." *Journal of Romance Studies* 10(3): 27–37.

Carvalho, Richard. 2018. "Smarginatura e spiragli: Uses of Infinity in Ferrante's Neapolitan Quartet." *Allegoria* 77: 94–111.

Casanova, Pascale. 2004. *The World Republic of Letters*. Translated by Malcolm Debevoise. Cambridge, MA: Harvard University Press.

Caserta, Silvia. 2019. "World Literature and the Italian Literary Canon: From Elena Ferrante to Natalia Ginzburg." *Modern Languages Open* 1: 1–18.

Cavanaugh, Jillian. 2016. "Indexicalities of Language in Ferrante's Neapolitan Novels: Dialect and Italian as Markers of Social Value and Difference." In *The Works of Elena Ferrante. Reconfiguring the Margins*, edited by Grace Russo Bullaro and Stephanie Love, 45–70. New York: Palgrave Macmillan.

Cavarero, Adriana. 2000. *Relating Narratives: Storytelling and Selfhood*. Translated by Paul Kottman. London and New York: Routledge.

Cavarero, Adriana. 2009. *Horrorism: Naming Contemporary Violence*. Translated by William McCuaig. New York: Columbia University Press.

Cavarero, Adriana. 2020. "Storytelling Philosophy and Self Writing: Preliminary Notes on Elena Ferrante. Interview with Adriana Cavarero." Translated by Stiliana Milkova and Isabella Pinto. *Narrative* 28(2): 236–49.

Cavarero, Adriana and Isabella Pinto. 2016. "Intervista ad Adriana Cavarero. Filosofia della narrazione e scrittura di sé: primi appunti sulla scrittura di Elena Ferrante." *Testo e Senso* (17):1–14.

Chamberlain, Lori. 1988. "Gender and the Metaphorics of Translation." *Signs* 13(3): 454–72.

Chambers, Iain. 2008. *Mediterranean Crossings. The Politics of an Interrupted Modernity*. Durham, NC: Duke University Press.

Chiesa, Laura. 2016. *Space as Storyteller. Spatial Jumps in Architecture, Critical Theory, and Literature*. Evanston: Northwestern University Press.

Chihaya, Sarah, Merve Emre, Katherine Hill and Jill Richards. 2020. *The Ferrante Letters: An Experiment in Collective Criticism*. New York: Columbia University Press.

Cixous, Hélène. 1976. "The Laugh of the Medusa." *Signs* 1(4): 875–93.

Cohn, Dorrit. 1978. *Transparent Minds: Narrative Modes for Presenting Consciousness in Fiction*. Princeton: Princeton University Press.

Conti, Eleonora. 2015. "Abiti, madri e figlie ne L'amore molesto di Elena Ferrante." *Lettera Zero* 1: 103–13.

Conti, Eleonora. 2017. "Smarginature: lo scarto tra vita e scrittura ne L'amica geniale di Elena Ferrante." *Lettera Zero* 4: 69–78.

Conybeare, Catherine. 2013. *The Laughter of Sarah: Biblical Exegesis, Feminist Theory, and the Concept of Delight*. New York: Palgrave Macmillan.

Coppo, Secondino and Roberta Spallone. 1995. "Rilievo di Via Pietro Micca." In *Torino nell'ottocento e nel novecento. Ampliamenti e trasformazioni entro la cerchia dei corsi napoleonici*, 534–8. Turin: Politecnico di Torino.

Coronato, Rocco. 2016. "L'amica poco congeniale. Elena Ferrante contro l'immedesimazione." *Allegoria* 73: 118–22.

Correll, Elizabeth. 2019. "'Laughter is a Short, Very Short, Sigh of Relief': On the Subversive Laughter of Elena Ferrante." Unpublished research paper. Oberlin College, USA.

Cusk, Rachel. 2001. *A Life's Work: On Becoming a Mother*. New York: Picador.

Cusk, Rachel. 2015. "The Story of the Lost Child by Elena Ferrante." *The New York Times*, August 30. https://www.nytimes.com/2015/08/30/books/review/the-story-of-the-lost-child-by-elena-ferrante.html.

Damrosch, David. 2003. *What Is World Literature?* Princeton: Princeton University Press.

Damrosch, David. 2014. "Translation and National Literature." In *A Companion to Translation Studies*, edited by Sandra Bermann and Catherine Porter, 349–60. Chichester, UK: John Wiley & Sons.

Davidson, Joyce. 2003. *Phobic Geographies: The Phenomenology and Spatiality of Identity*. Aldershot: Ashgate.

Davis, Diane. 2000. *Breaking Up [at] Totality: A Rhetoric of Laughter*. Carbondale and Edwardsville: Southern Illinois University Press.

de Certeau, Michel. 1988. *The Practice of Everyday Life*. Translated by Steven Rendall. Berkeley, Los Angeles, and London: University of California Press.

degli Esposti, Chiara. 2019. "Wandering Women: Feminist Urban Experiences in Simone de Beauvoir and Elena Ferrante." *Annali d'Italianistica* 37(Fall): 153–75.

de Rogatis, Tiziana. 2014. "L'amore molesto di Elena Ferrante. Mito classico, riti di iniziazione e identità femminile." *Allegoria* 69–70: 273–308.
de Rogatis, Tiziana. 2016a. "Metamorphosis and Rebirth: Greek Initiation Rites in Elena Ferrante's *Troubling Love*." In *The Works of Elena Ferrante. Reconfiguring the Margins*, edited by Grace Russo Bullaro and Stephanie Love, 185–206. New York: Palgrave Macmillan.
de Rogatis, Tiziana. 2016b. "Metamorfosi del tempo. Il ciclo de *L'amica geniale*." *Allegoria* 73: 123–37.
de Rogatis, Tiziana. 2016c. "Elena Ferrante e il Made in Italy. La costruzione di un immaginario femminile e napoletano." In *Made in Italy e cultura*, edited by Daniele Balicco, 288–317. Palermo: Palumbo.
de Rogatis, Tiziana. 2016d. "Uncovering Elena Ferrante and the Importance of a Woman's Voice." *The Conversation*, October 5. http://theconversation.com/uncovering-elena-ferrante-and-the-importance-of-a-womans-voice-66456
de Rogatis, Tiziana. 2017. "Ripensare l'eredità delle madri. Cerimoniale iniziatico e strutture rituali ne *L'amore molesto*, *I giorni dell'abbandono*, e *La figlia oscura* di Elena Ferrante." In *Nel nome della madre. Ripensare le figure della maternità*, edited by Daniela Brogi, Tiziana de Rogatis, Cristiana Franco, and Lucinda Spera, 71–91. Bracciano: Del Vecchio Editore.
de Rogatis, Tiziana. 2018. *Elena Ferrante. Parole chiave*. Rome: Edizioni e/o.
de Rogatis, Tiziana. 2019a. *Elena Ferrante's Key Words*. Translated by Will Schutt. New York: Europa Editions.
de Rogatis, Tiziana. 2019b. "La vita bugiarda degli adulti." *La Repubblica*, November 29.
de Rogatis, Tiziana. 2021. "Global Perspectives: Trauma and the Global Novel." Forthcoming in *MLN* 136(1).
de Toma, Aldo. 1986. "Lo sconosciuto unico incontro d'amore di Guido Gozzano e Amalia Guglielminetti." *Lettere Italiane* 38(4): 527–41.
Didi-Huberman, Georges. 2004. *Invention of Hysteria: Charcot and the Photographic Iconography of the Salpêtrière*. Translated by Alisa Hartz. Cambridge, MA: MIT Press.
Dijkstra, Bram. 1986. *Idols of Perversity: Fantasies of Feminine Evil in Fin-de-Siècle Culture*. Oxford: Oxford University Press.
di Paolo, Paolo. 2014. "Il caso Ferrante, il romanzo italiano secondo il New Yorker." *La Stampa*, October 13. https://www.lastampa.it/cultura/2014/10/13/news/il-caso-ferrante-il-romanzo-italiano-secondo-il-new-yorker-1.35601618
di Paolo, Paolo. 2018. "Perché ha successo la Ferrante? Boh." *La Repubblica*, February 12. https://espresso.repubblica.it/visioni/2018/02/08/news/paolo-di-paolo-perche-ha-successo-la-ferrante-boh-1.318125
Duro, Paul. 1996. *The Rhetoric of the Frame: Essays on the Boundaries of the Artwork*. Cambridge: Cambridge University Press.
Elias, Norbert. 2000. *The Civilizing Process: Sociogenetic and Psychogenetic Investigations*. Translated by Edmund Jephcott. Oxford: Blackwell.
Elwell, Leslie. 2013. *Italian Female Epistemologies Beyond 'The Scene of the Crime.'* PhD dissertation. University of California, Berkeley.
Elwell, Leslie. 2016. "Breaking Bonds: Refiguring Maternity in Elena Ferrante's *The Lost Daughter*." In *The Works of Elena Ferrante: Reconfiguring the Margins*, edited by Grace Russo Bullaro and Stephanie Love, 237–69. New York: Palgrave Macmillan.
Falkoff, Rebecca. 2015. "To Translate Is to Betray." *Public Books*. https://www.publicbooks.org/to-translate-is-to-betray-on-the-elena-ferrante-phenomenon-in-italy-and-the-us/
Falotico, Caterina. 2015. "Elena Ferrante: Il ciclo dell'*Amica geniale* tra autobiografia, storia e metaletteratura." *Forum Italicum* 49(1): 92–118.

Fanning, Ursula. 2007. "Feminist Fictions? Representations of Self and (M)Other in the Works of Anna Banti." *Women in Italy 1945–1960: An Interdisciplinary Study*, edited by P. Morris, 159–76. New York: Palgrave Macmillan.
Ferrante, Elena. 1992. *L'amore molesto*. Rome: edizioni e/o.
Ferrante, Elena. 2002. *I giorni dell'abbandono*. Rome: edizioni e/o.
Ferrante, Elena. 2003. *La frantumaglia*. Rome: edizioni e/o.
Ferrante, Elena. 2005. *The Days of Abandonment*. Translated by Ann Goldstein. New York: Europa Editions.
Ferrante, Elena. 2006. *La figlia oscura*. Rome: edizioni e/o.
Ferrante, Elena. 2006. *Troubling Love*. Translated by Ann Goldstein. New York: Europa Editions.
Ferrante, Elena. 2007. *La spiaggia di notte*. Rome: edizioni e/o.
Ferrante, Elena. 2007. "Se l'amore è furioso." *La Repubblica*, November 30. https://ricerca.repubblica.it/repubblica/archivio/repubblica/2007/11/30/se-amore-furioso.html
Ferrante, Elena. 2007. *The Lost Daughter*. New York: Europa Editions.
Ferrante, Elena. 2008. "Elena Ferrante on Alice Sebold's New Novel, *The Almost Moon*." Translated by Ann Goldstein. https://www.europaeditions.com/news/340/elena-ferrante-on-alice-sebold-s-new-novel-the-almost-moon
Ferrante, Elena. 2011. *L'amica geniale*. Rome: edizioni e/o.
Ferrante, Elena. 2012. *My Brilliant Friend*. Translated by Ann Goldstein. Rome: edizioni e/o.
Ferrante, Elena. 2012. *Storia del nuovo cognome*. Rome: edizioni e/o.
Ferrante, Elena. 2013. *Storia di chi fugge e di chi resta*. Rome: edizioni e/o.
Ferrante, Elena. 2013. *The Story of a New Name*. Translated by Ann Goldstein. Rome: edizioni e/o.
Ferrante, Elena. 2014. *Storia della bambina perduta*. Rome: edizioni e/o.
Ferrante, Elena. 2014. *Those Who Leave and Those Who Stay*. Translated by Ann Goldstein. Rome: edizioni e/o.
Ferrante, Elena. 2015. *The Story of the Lost Child*. Translated by Ann Goldstein. New York: Europa Editions.
Ferrante, Elena. 2015. *La frantumaglia. Edizione ampliata*. Rome: edizioni e/o.
Ferrante, Elena. 2016. *Frantumaglia. A Writer's Journey*. Translated by Ann Goldstein. New York: Europa Editions.
Ferrante, Elena. 2016. *The Beach at Night*. Translated by Ann Goldstein. New York: Europa Editions.
Ferrante, Elena. 2019. "A Power of Our Own." Translated by Ann Goldstein. *New York Times*, May 17. https://www.nytimes.com/2019/05/17/opinion/elena-ferrante-on-women-power.html
Ferrante, Elena. 2019. "Devo mentire per dire la verità." *La Repubblica*, November 30.
Ferrante, Elena. 2019. *L'invenzione occasionale*. Rome: edizioni e/o.
Ferrante, Elena. 2019. *Incidental Inventions*. Translated by Ann Goldstein. New York: Europa Editions.
Ferrante, Elena. 2019. *La vita bugiarda degli adulti*. Rome: edizioni e/o.
Ferrante Fever. 2017. Directed by Giacomo Durzi. Malia & RAI Cinema. Film.
Ferrara, Enrica Maria. 2016. "Performative Realism and Post-Humanism in *The Days of Abandonment*." In *The Works of Elena Ferrante: Reconfiguring the Margins*, edited by Grace Russo Bullaro and Stephanie Love, 129–57. New York: Palgrave Macmillan.
Ferrara, Enrica Maria. 2017. "Elena Ferrante e la questione dell'identità." *Oblio* VII (26–27): 47–55.

Foley, Helene P. 1994. *The Homeric Hymn to Demeter: Translation, Commentary, and Interpretive Essays*. Princeton: Princeton University Press.
Forgacs, David. 2014. *Italy's Margins: Social Exclusion and Nation Formation since 1861*. Cambridge: Cambridge University Press.
Forgacs, David. 2015. *Margini d'Italia. L'esclusione sociale dall'Unità a oggi*. Rome: Laterza.
Foucault, Michel. 1997. "Of Other Spaces. Utopias and Heterotopias." In *Rethinking Architecture*, edited by Neil Leach, 350–6. New York: Routledge.
Freud, Sigmund. 1927. "Fetishism." In *The Complete Psychological Works of Sigmund Freud*, translated by James Strachey, 149–57, Vol. XXI. London: Hogarth Press.
Freud, Sigmund. 1971 [1919]. "The Uncanny." Collected Papers. Vol. IV. Translated by Joane Riviere, 368–407. London: Hogarth Press.
Freud, Sigmund. 1975. *Three Essays on the Theory of Sexuality*. Translated by James Strachey. New York: Basic Books.
Freud, Sigmund. 1995. "Infantile Sexuality." Translated by James Strachey. *Psychological Writings and Letters*, 80–113. New York: Continuum.
Freud, Sigmund. 1997 [1905]. "Fragment of an Analysis of a Case of Hysteria." *Dora: An Analysis of a Case of Hysteria*. Translated by Philip Rieff. New York: Touchstone.
Freud, Sigmund. 2000 [1931]. "Female Sexuality." In *Psychoanalysis and Woman: A Reader*, edited by Shelley Saguaro, 21–34. New York: New York University Press.
Freud, Sigmund. 2003 [1922]. "Medusa's Head." In *The Medusa Reader*, edited by Marjorie Garber and Nancy J. Vickers, 84–5. New York and London: Routledge.
Friedman, Susan Stanford. 2011. "Why Not Compare?" *PMLA* 126(3): 753–62.
Fusillo, Massimo. 2011. "The Railway Station as Heterotopia: Between Sacredness and Sexuality." In *Spaces of Desire—Spaces of Transition: Space and Emotions in Modern Literature*, edited by Gertrud Lehnert and Stephanie Siewert, 45–73. Frankfurt am Main: Peter Lang.
Fusillo, Massimo. 2017. *The Fetish: Literature, Cinema, Art*. Translated by Thomas Simpson. New York: Bloomsbury Academic.
Gallippi, Franco. 2016. "Elena Ferrante's *My Brilliant Friend*. In Search of Parthenope and the 'Founding' of a New City." In *The Works of Elena Ferrante: Reconfiguring the Margins*, edited by Grace Russo Bullaro and Stephanie Love, 101–27. New York: Palgrave Macmillan.
Gambaro, Elisa. 2014. "Il fascino del regresso. Note su *L'amica geniale* di Elena Ferrante." *Enthymema* XI: 168–77.
Gambaro, Elisa. 2020. "L'andirivieni di un braccialetto." *L'Indice dei libri del mese* N.1, January 14, 2.
Ganguly, Debjani. 2016. *This Thing Called the World: The Contemporary Novel as Global Form*. Durham, NC: Duke University Press.
Gatti, Claudio. 2016a. "Elena Ferrante: An Answer?" *The New York Review of Books*, October 2. https://www.nybooks.com/daily/2016/10/02/elena-ferrante-an-answer/
Gatti, Claudio. 2016b. "Ecco la vera identità di Elena Ferrante." *Il Sole 24 Ore*, October 2. https://st.ilsole24ore.com/art/cultura/2016-10-02/elena-ferrante-tracce-dell-autrice-ritrovata-105611.shtml
Geue, Tom. 2016. "Elena Ferrante as the Classics." *Melbourne Historical Journal* 44(2): 1–31.
Ghezzo, Flora and Sara Teardo. 2019. "On Lila's Traces: *Bildung*, Narration, and Ethics in *L'amica geniale*." *MLN* 134: 172–92.
Gilbert, Sandra M. and Susan Gubar. 1979. *The Madwoman in the Attic: The Woman Writer and the Nineteenth-Century Literary Imagination*. New Haven and London: Yale University Press.

Ginzburg, Natalia. 1993. *Cinque romanzi brevi e altri racconti*. Turin: Einaudi.
Ginzburg, Natalia. 2014 [1963]. *Lessico famigliare*. Turin: Einaudi.
Ginzburg, Natalia. 2017. *Family Lexicon*. Translated by Jenny McPhee. New York: New York Review Books.
Giorgio, Adalgisa. 1994. "Nature vs. Culture: Repression, Rebellion and Madness in Elsa Morante's *Aracoeli*." *MLN* 109(1): 93–116.
Giorgio, Adalgisa. 2002. "The Passion for the Mother: Conflicts and Idealizations in Contemporary Italian Narrative." In *Writing Mothers and Daughters: Renegotiating the Mother in Western European Narratives by Women*, edited by Adalgisa Giorgio, 119–54. New York and Oxford: Berghan Books.
Giorgio, Adalgisa. 2019a. "Double Acts of Female Creativity in Elena Ferrante's *My Brilliant Friend*." Unpublished conference talk. *Elena Ferrante in a Global Context*, Durham University, 7–8 June.
Giorgio, Adalgisa. 2019b. "The Power of Female Alliance According to Elena Ferrante's Neapolitan Novels." Unpublished symposium presentation. *Contemporary Women's Writing: Writing / Reading for Change. A Celebration of the Work of Gill Rye*. Centre for the Study of Contemporary Women's Writing. Institute of Modern Languages Research. The School of Advanced Study. University of London, November 8.
Goscilo, Helena. 2010. "The Mirror in Art: Vanitas, Veritas, and Vision." *Studies in 20th & 21st Century Literature* 34(2): 282–319.
Gospodinov, Georgi. 2015. *The Physics of Sorrow*. Translated by Angela Rodel. Rochester, NY: Open Letter Books.
Gralla, Cynthia. 2019. "Nine Fashionable Books That Make Clothes a Main Character." *Electric Literature*, April 22. https://electricliterature.com/9-fashionable-books-that-make-clothes-a-main-character/
Graves, Robert. 1957. *The Greek Myths*. New York: G. Braziller.
Graziosi, Barbara. 2016. "Elena Ferrante Is My Mother." *Eidolon*, October 10. https://eidolon.pub/elena-ferrante-is-my-mother-3149471c7336
Gross, Kenneth. 2012. *On Dolls*. London: Notting Hill Editions.
Grosz, Elizabeth. 1994. *Volatile Bodies: Toward a Corporeal Feminism*. Bloomington and Indianapolis: Indiana University Press.
Grosz, Elizabeth. 1995. *Space, Time, and Perversion*. New York and London: Routledge.
Grosz, Elizabeth. 1999. "Bodies-Cities." In *Feminist Theory and the Body: A Reader*, edited by Janet Price and Margrit Shildrick, 381–7. New York: Routledge.
Haaland, Torunn. 2018. "Between Past and Present, Self and Other. Liminality and the Transmission of Traumatic Memory in Elena Ferrante's *La figlia oscura*." In *Transmissions of Memory: Echoes, Traumas, and Nostalgia in Post-War Italian Culture*, edited by Patrizia Sambuco, 143–60. Madison: Farleigh Dickinson University Press.
Hanson, Clare. 2015. "The Maternal Body." In *The Cambridge Companion to the Body in Literature*, edited by David Hillman and Ulrika Maude, 87–100. New York: Cambridge University Press.
Hillis Miller, J. 1992. *Ariadne's Thread. Story Lines*. New Haven and London: Yale University Press.
Hirsch, Marianne. 1989. *The Mother/Daughter Plot: Narrative, Psychoanalysis, Feminism*. Bloomington and Indianapolis: Indiana University Press.
Homer. 2018. *The Odyssey*. Translated by Emily Wilson. New York and London: Norton.
I giorni dell'abbandono. 2005. Directed by Roberto Faenza. Medusa Film. Film.

Iovino, Serenella. 2014. "Bodies of Naples: Stories, Matter, and the Landscapes of Porosity." In *Material Ecocriticism*, edited by Serenella Iovino and Serpil Oppermann, 97–113. Bloomington: Indiana University Press.
Iovino, Serenella. 2016. *Ecocriticism and Italy*. New York: Bloomsbury Academic.
Irigaray, Luce. 1981. "And the One Doesn't Stir Without the Other." Translated by Hélène Vivienne Wenzel. *Signs* 7(I): 60–7.
Irigaray, Luce. 1985. *This Sex Which Is Not One*. Translated by Catherine Porter and Carolyn Burke. Ithaca: Cornell University Press.
Irigaray, Luce. 1993. *Je, Tu, Nous: Toward a Culture of Difference*. Translated by Alison Martin. New York and London: Routledge.
Irigaray, Luce. 1993b. *An Ethics of Sexual Difference*. Translated by Carolyn Burke and Gillian C. Gill. London and New York: Continuum.
Jossa, Stefano. 2017. "Non si deve studiare la Ferrante all'Università." *Doppiozero*, May 20. https://www.doppiozero.com/materiali/non-si-deve-studiare-la-ferrante-alluniversita
Jung, Carl. 1981. *The Archetypes and the Collective Unconscious*. Translated by R. F. C. Hull. Princeton: Princeton University Press.
Karagoz, Claudia. 2001. *Amori molesti: The Mother-Daughter Relationship in Contemporary Italian Women's Writing*. Ph.D. dissertation. University of California, Berkeley.
Kern, Hermann. 2000. *Through the Labyrinth: Designs and Meanings over 5,000 Years*. Munich and London: Prestel.
Kirsch, Adam. 2017. *The Global Novel: Writing the World in the 21st Century*. New York: Columbia Global Reports.
Klein, Melanie. 1999 [1928]. "Early Stages in the Oedipus Conflict." In *Female Sexuality: The Early Psychoanalytic Controversies*, edited by Russell Grigg, Dominique Hecq and Craig Smith, 146–58. New York: Routledge.
Klindienst Joplin, Patricia. 1991. "The Voice of the Shuttle Is Ours." In *Rape and Representation*, edited by Lynn A. Higgins and Brenda R. Silver, 35–64. New York: Columbia University Press.
Kristeva, Julia. 1980. "Motherhood According to Giovanni Bellini." In *Desire in Language. A Semiotic Approach to Literature and Art*, edited by Leon S. Roudiez and translated by Thomas Gora, Alice Jardine, and Leon Roudiez, 237–70. New York: Columbia University Press.
Kristeva, Julia. 1982. *Powers of Horror: An Essay on Abjection*. Translated by Leon Roudiez. New York: Columbia University Press.
Kurnick, David. 2015. "Ferrante, in History." *Public Books*. https://www.publicbooks.org/ferrante-in-history/.
Kuznets, Lois R. 1994. *When Toys Come Alive: Narratives of Animation, Metamorphosis, and Development*. New Haven and London: Yale University Press.
Lahiri, Jhumpa. 2014. "Cara Elena Ferrante, hai ragione, l'invisibilità è un valore." *Corriere Della Sera*, June 9. https://www.corriere.it/cultura/14_giugno_09/jhumpa-lahiri-cara-elena-ferrante-hai-ragione-l-invisibilita-un-valore-56a1917a-f008-11e3-85b0-60cbb1cdb75e.shtml?refresh_ce-cp
Lahiri, Jhumpa. 2015. *In altre parole*. Milan: Guanda Editore.
Lahiri, Jhumpa. 2016. *In Other Words*. Translated by Ann Goldstein. New York: Vintage.
L'amore molesto. 1995. Directed by Mario Martone. Angelo Curti & Lucky Red. Film.
Lampl de Groot, Jeanne. 1999 [1928]. "The Evolution of the Oedipus Complex in Women." In *Female Sexuality: The Early Psychoanalytic Controversies*, edited by Russell Grigg, Dominique Hecq and Craig Smith, 159–71. New York: Routledge.

Lanzardo, Dario and Francesco Poli. 2012. *Torino: la città delle statue. Fantasmi di pietra sulla scena urbana*. Turin: Edizioni del Capricorno.
Lee, Ken. 2000. "Orientalism and Gypsylorism." *Social Analysis: The International Journal of Social and Cultural Practice* 44(2): 129–56.
Levy, Deborah. 2016. *Hot Milk*. New York: Bloomsbury USA.
Librandi, Rita. 2019. "Una lingua silenziosa. Immaginare il dialetto negli scritti di Elena Ferrante." In *Dal dialogo al polilogo: l'Italia nel mondo. Lingue, letterature e culture in contatto*, edited by Elzbieta Jamrozik e Anna Tylusinska-Kowalska, 385–98. Warsaw: Polish Academy of Science.
Liddell, Henry and Robert Scott. 1889, 1999. *An Intermediate Greek-English Lexicon*. Oxford: Oxford University Press.
Lombardi, Giancarlo. 1999. "Scambi d'identità: Il recupero del corpo materno ne *L'amore molesto*." *Romance Languages Annual* 10: 288–91.
Loucks, James and Andrew Stauffer. 2007. *Robert Browning's Poetry*. New York: Norton.
Lucamante, Stefania. 2007. "L'atroce smacco della madre." *Leggendaria* 60: 42–3. https://www.edizionieo.it/review/244
Lucamante, Stefania. 2008. *A Multitude of Women. The Challenges of the Contemporary Italian Novel*. Toronto: University of Toronto Press.
Lucamante, Stefania. 2018. "Undoing Feminism. The Neapolitan Novels of Elena Ferrante." *Italica* 95(1): 1–19.
Mandolini, Nicoletta. 2016. "Telling the Abuse: A Feminist-Psychoanalytic Reading of Gender Violence, Repressed Memory, and Female Subjectivity in Elena Ferrante's *Troubling Love*." In *The Works of Elena Ferrante: Reconfiguring the Margins*, edited by Grace Russo Bullaro and Stephanie Love, 271–92. New York: Palgrave Macmillan.
Marin, Louis. 2001. *On Representation*. Translated by Catherine Porter. Stanford: Stanford University Press.
Mazzoni, Cristina. 2012. "Treasure to Trash, Trash to Treasure: Dolls and Waste in Italian Children's Literature." *Children's Literature Association Quarterly* 37(3): 250–65.
McCarter, Stephanie. 2016. "Elena Ferrante's Virgil. Rewriting the *Aeneid* in the Neapolitan Novels." *Eidolon*, November 17. https://eidolon.pub/elena-ferrantes-vergil-2f6babd05f16
McDowell, Linda. 1999. *Gender, Identity & Place: Understanding Feminist Geographies*. Cambridge: Polity Press.
Mihai, Mihaela. 2018. "Epistemic Marginalisation and the Seductive Power of Art." *Contemporary Political Theory* 17(4): 395–416.
Milkova, Stiliana. 2013. "Mothers, Daughters, Dolls: On Disgust in Elena Ferrante's *La figlia oscura*." *Italian Culture* 31(2): 91–109.
Milkova, Stiliana. 2016a. "Artistic Tradition and Feminine Legacy in Elena Ferrante's *L'amore molesto*." *California Italian Studies* 6(1): 1–15.
Milkova, Stiliana. 2016b. "The Translator's Visibility or the Ferrante–Goldstein Phenomenon." *Allegoria* 73: 166–73.
Milkova, Stiliana. 2016c. "Elena Ferrante's Visual Poetics: Ekphrasis in *Troubling Love, My Brilliant Friend*, and *The Story of a New Name*." In *The Works of Elena Ferrante: Reconfiguring the Margins*, edited by Grace Russo Bullaro and Stephanie Love, 147–70. New York: Palgrave Macmillan.
Milkova, Stiliana. 2016d. "Ekphrasis and the Frame: On Paintings in Gogol, Tolstoy, and Dostoevsky." *Word & Image* 32(2): 153–62.

Milkova, Stiliana. 2017. "Il Minotauro e la doppia Arianna: Spazio liminale, labirinto urbano e città femminile ne *L'amica geniale* di Elena Ferrante." *Contemporanea* 15: 77–88.
Miller, Madeline. 2018. *Circe*. New York: Little, Brown and Company.
Miller, Nancy. 2019. *My Brilliant Friends: Our Lives in Feminism*. New York: Columbia University Press.
Miller, Paul Allen. 1995. "The Minotaur Within: Fire, the Labyrinth and Strategies of Containment in *Aeneid* 5 and 6." *Classical Philology* 90(3): 225–40.
Moebius, William. 1986. "Introduction to Picturebook Codes." *Word & Image* 2(2): 141–58.
Momigliano, Anna. 2019. "The Ferrante Effect: In Italy Women Writers Are Ascendant." *The New York Times*, December 9. https://www.nytimes.com/2019/12/09/books/elena-ferrante-italy-women-writers.html.
Morante, Elsa. 1982. *Aracoeli*. Turin: Einaudi.
Morante, Elsa. 1989. "The Mirrors." In *New Italian Women: A Collection of Short Fiction*, edited by Martha King, 122–9. New York: Italica Press.
Morante, Elsa. 2009. *Aracoeli*. Translated by William Weaver. Open Letter.
Morante, Elsa. 2014 [1948]. *Menzogna e sortilegio*. Turin: Einaudi.
Morante, Elsa. 2015 [1963]. *Lo scialle andaluso*. Turin: Einaudi.
Morante, Elsa. 2016 [1959]. *Le straordinarie avventure di Caterina*. Turin: Einaudi.
Moretti, Franco. 1998. *Atlas of the European Novel*. New York and London: Verso.
Moretti, Franco. 2000. "Conjectures on World Literature." *New Left Review* 1: 54–68.
Mortimer-Sandilands, Catriona. 2008. "Landscape, Memory, and Forgetting: Thinking Through (My Mother's) Body and Place." In *Material Feminisms*, edited by Stacy Alaimo and Susan Hekman, 265–85. Bloomington and Indianapolis: University of Indiana Press.
Mulvey, Laura. 1988. "Visual Pleasure and Narrative Cinema." In *Feminism and Film Theory*, edited by Constance Penley, 57–68. New York: Routledge.
Muraro, Luisa. 1994. "Female Genealogies." In *Engaging with Irigaray: Feminist Philosophy and Modern European Thought*, edited by Carolyn Burke, Naomi Schor, and Margaret Whitford, 317–34. New York: Columbia University Press.
Murgia, Michela. 2009. *Accabadora*. Turin: Einaudi.
Myers, Lindsay. 2011. "The Memoir Fantasy: 1870–1896." In *Making the Italians: Poetics and Politics of Italian Children's Fantasy*, 19–42. Frankfurt am Main: Peter Lang.
Nathan, Jean. 2004. *The Secret Life of the Lonely Doll: The Search for Dare Wright*. New York: Picador.
Nathan, Jean. 2019. *Vita segreta della bambola solitaria. Alla ricerca di Dare Wright*. Translated by Silvia Montis. Rome: edizioni e/o.
Nelson, Lise and Joni Seager. 2004. *A Companion to Feminist Geography*. Chichester, UK: Wiley & Sons.
Nochlin, Linda. 1988. *Women, Art, and Power, and Other Essays*. New York: Harper & Row.
Nochlin, Linda. 1991. *The Politics of Vision: Essays on Nineteenth-Century Art and Society*. New York: Harper & Low.
Nodelman, Perry. 2005. "Decoding the Images: How Picture Books Work." In *Understanding Children's Literature*, edited by Peter Hunt, 128–39. London: Routledge.
Nohclin, Linda. 1994. *The Body in Pieces: The Fragment as a Metaphor of Modernity*. London: Thames and Hudson.

Noson, Kate. 2014. "From superabilità to transabilità: Towards an Italian Disability Studies." *Modern Italy* 19(2): 135–45.
Noson, Katherine. 2015. *Mermaid Without a Tale: Disability, Sexuality, and the Limits of Discourse in Italian Narrative (1975–2009)*. PhD dissertation. University of California, Berkeley.
Ortese, Anna Maria. 1994 [1955]. *Il mare non bagna Napoli*. Milan: Adelphi.
Ortese, Anna Maria. 2018. *Neapolitan Chronicles*. Translated by Ann Goldstein and Jenny McPhee. New York: New Vessel Press.
Paperno, Irina and Joan Delaney Grossman. 1994. *Creating Life: The Aesthetic Utopia of Russian Modernism*. Stanford: Stanford University Press.
Parisi, Luciano. 2017. "Trauma e riparazione nell' *Amore molesto* di Elena Ferrante." *Studi novecenteschi* XLIV(93): 167–88.
Parks, Tim. February 9, 2010. "The Dull Global Novel." *The New York Review of Books*. https://www.nybooks.com/daily/2010/02/09/the-dull-new-global-novel/.
Paster, Gail Kern. 1993. *The Body Embarrassed. Drama and the Discipline of Shame in Early Modern England*. Ithaca: Cornell University Press.
Pennacchio, Filippo. 2018. *Il romanzo global. Uno studio narratologico*. Milano: Biblion Edizioni.
Perkins Gilman, Charlotte. 1980 [1892]. "The Yellow Wallpaper." In *The Charlotte Perkins Gilman Reader*, edited by Ann J. Lane, 3–20. New York: Pantheon Books.
Perkins Gilman, Charlotte. 2011. *La carta da parati gialla*. Translated by Cesare Ferrari. Milan: La vita felice.
Perrella, Silvio. 2015. *Doppio scatto. La città nascosta*. Milan: Bompiani.
Pesca, Carmela. 2017. "The Narrative Function of Clothing in Elena Ferrante's *Troubling Love*." *Altrelettere*, October 19. https://www.altrelettere.uzh.ch/article/view/al_uzh-35.
Petrova, Vera. 2019. Interview. December 28. Sofia, Bulgaria.
Phelan, Richard. 2006. "The Picture Frame in Question: American Art 1945–2000." In *Framing Borders in Literature and Other Media*, edited by Werner Wolf and Walter Bernhart, 159–75. Amsterdam and New York: Rodopi.
Pinto, Isabella. 2019. "*Storia della bambina perduta* di Elena Ferrate: Il desiderio di narrare oltre la dichotomia autore/lettore." *Diacritica*, June 25. https://diacritica.it/letture-critiche/storia-della-bambina-perduta-di-elena-ferrante-il-desiderio-di-narrare-oltre-la-dicotomia-autore-lettore.html
Pinto, Isabella. 2019b. "Elena Ferrante: Storie di affinità postumane." *DWF. Sister of the Revolution. Letture politiche di fantascienza* 1–2(121–2): 74–81.
Pinto, Isabella. 2020. "Discorso indiretto libero e soggettiva libera indiretta: leggere Elena Ferrante attraverso Pier Paolo Pasolini. Prime note sulla narratrice traduttrice." *L'Ospite Ingrato. Rivista online del Centro Interdipartimentale di Ricerca Franco Fortini*. http://www.ospiteingrato.unisi.it/
Ponzi, Mauro. 2012. "Napoli come topografia degli spazi intermedi. Walter Benjamin e la soglia tra vecchio e nuovo." In *Soglie. Per una nuova teoria dello spazio*, edited by Mauro Ponzi and Dario Gentili, 131–49. Milano: Mimesis.
Post, Chad. 2011. *The Three Percent Problem*. Rochester: Open Letter Books.
Purvis, Xenobe. 2018. "Elena Ferrante. *My Brilliant Friend*." In *Literary Landscapes. Charting the Worlds of Classic Literature*, edited by John Sutherland, 232–4. New York: Black Dog & Leventhal.

Raja, Anita. 2016. "Translation as a Practice of Acceptance." Translated by Rebecca Falkoff and Stiliana Milkova. *Asymptote*, October. https://www.asymptotejournal.com/criticism/anita-raja-translation-as-a-practice-of-acceptance/

Randall, Frederika. 2015. "Elena Ferrante è una geniale iniziativa commerciale." *Internazionale*, January 2. https://www.internazionale.it/opinione/frederika-randall/2015/01/02/un-paese-di-santi-poeti-e-complottisti

Reyes Ferrer, Maria. 2016. "La funzione dello specchio nel romanzo *I giorni dell'abbandono* di Elena Ferrante." *Quadernos de Filologia Italiana* 23: 221–36.

Ricciardi, Alessia. 2017. "Can the Subaltern Speak in Elena Ferrante's Neapolitan Novels?" *Estetica: studi e ricerche* 7(2): 293–312.

Robertson, Ronald. 1994. "Globalisation or Glocalization?" *The Journal of International Communication* 18(2): 191–208.

Rose, Gillian. 1993. *Feminism and Geography: The Limits of Geographical Knowledge*. Polity Press.

Rose, Gillian. 1996. "As If the Mirrors Had Bled. Masculine Dwelling, Masculinist Theory and Feminist Masquerade." In *Body Space*, edited by Nancy Duncan, 56–74. London and New York: Routledge.

Rossotti, Renzo. 2015. *Torino. I Monumenti Raccontano*. Genova: Ligurpress.

Saccà, Annalisa. 2002. "Amalia Guglielminetti." *Italian Prose Writers, 1900–1945*, edited by Luca Somigli and Rocco Capozzi. Detroit, MI: Gale. Dictionary of Literary Biography, Vol. 264.

Sambuco, Patrizia. 2012. *Corporeal Bonds: The Daughter-Mother Relationship in Twentieth-Century Italian Women's Writing*. Toronto: University of Toronto Press.

Sambuco, Patrizia. 2013. "Construction and Self-Construction in Elena Ferrante's Gendered Space." In *Beyond the Piazza: Public and Private Spaces in Modern Italian Culture*, edited by Simona Storchi, 115–27. Brussels: Peter Lang Publishing.

Santovetti, Olivia. 2016. "Lettura, scrittura e autoriflessione nel ciclo de *L'amica geniale* di Elena Ferrante." *Allegoria* 73: 179–92.

Santovetti, Olivia. 2018. "Melodrama or Metafiction? Elena Ferrante's Neapolitan Novels." *The Modern Language Review* 113.3(July): 527–45.

Santovetti, Olivia. 2019. "'Io non ci sto': Elena Ferrante, the Theme of Erasure, and the *Smarginatura* as Poetics of Resistance." In *Resistance in Italian Culture from Dante to the 21st Century*, edited by Ambra Moroncini, Darrow Schecter, and Fabio Vighi, 281–94. Florence: Franco Cesati Editore.

Sarullo, Giulia. 2017. "Iconografia del labirinto. Origine e diffusione di un simbolo tra passato e futuro." *Tra Passato e Futuro* (1): 81–136.

Schor, Naomi. 1995. "Female Fetishism: The Case of George Sand." In *Bad Objects: Essays Popular and Unpopular*, 93–100. Durham and London: Duke University Press.

Schwartz, Cecilia. 2020. "Ferrante Feud: The Italian Reception of the *Neapolitan Novels* Before and After Their International Success." *The Italianist*. Published online on May 5. https://www.tandfonline.com/doi/full/10.1080/02614340.2020.1738122.

Sciubba, Jessica. 2019. "Blurring Bodily Boundaries: On the *rione*'s Abjective Agency in Ferrante's Cycle of *L'amica geniale*." *Annali d'Italianistica* 37: 503–25.

Sebold, Alice. 2007. *The Almost Moon*. New York: Little Brown and Company.

Seger, Monica. 2015. *Landscapes in Between: Environmental Change in Modern Italian Literature and Film*. Toronto: University of Toronto Press.

Segnini, Elisa. 2017. "Local Flavour vs. Global Readerships: The Elena Ferrante Project and Translatability." *The Italianist* 37(1): 100–18.

Shafak, Elif. 2011. *Black Milk: On the Conflicting Demands of Writing, Creativity and Motherhood*. New York and London: Penguin Books.
Smarr, Janet Levarie and Daria Valentini, eds. 2003. *Italian Women and the City*. Madison: Farleigh Dickinson University Press.
Sotgiu, Elisa. 2017. "Elena Ferrante e il femminismo della differenza. Una lettura dell'*Amica geniale*." *Allegoria* 76: 58–76.
Sotgiu, Elisa. 2018. "Il femminismo no-global di Elena Ferrante." *Flash Art*, December 18. https://flash---art.it/article/elena-ferrante/.
Spackman, Barbara. 2009. "Puntini, puntini, puntini: Motherliness as Masquerade in Sibilla Aleramo's *Una Donna*." *MLN* 124(5): S210–223.
Stewart, Susan. 1993. *On Longing: Narratives of the Miniature, the Gigantic, the Souvenir, the Collection*. Durham, NC: Duke University Press.
Strout, Elizabeth. 2016. *My Name Is Lucy Barton*. New York: Random House.
Todesco, Serena. 2019a. "Città come corpo, madre, mondo: soggettività e abiezione dello spazio urbano al femminile in Elena Ferrante e Anna Maria Ortese." In *Studi sull'immaginario italiano. Una prospettiva interdisciplinare*, edited by Eliana Moscarda Mirković, 75–87. Novate Milanese, Milan: Prospero Editore.
Todesco, Serena. 2019b. "Il corpo molesto della madre: elementi ferrantiani in Slavenka Drakulic." Unpublished conference talk. *Elena Ferrante in a Global Context*, Durham University, 7–8 June.
Todesco, Serena. 2021. "Maternal Troubling Bodies in Slavenka Drakulić and Elena Ferrante." Forthcoming in *MLN* 136(1).
Tolstoy, Leo. 2016. *Anna Karenina*. Translated by Rosamund Bartlett. Oxford University Press.
Trevisan, Paola. 2017. "Gypsies in Fascist Italy: From Expelled Foreigners to Dangerous Italians." *Social History* 42(3): 342–64.
Turchetta, Gianni. 2009. "Fuori e dentro il cuore di mamma Napoli." In *Tirature*, edited by Vittorio Spinazzola, 50–8. Milan: Mondadori.
Turchetta, Gianni. 2016. "Dal rione al mainstream. L'amica geniale di Elena Ferrante." In *Tirature. Un mondo da tradurre*, edited by Vittorio Spinazzola, 104–11. Milan: Mondadori.
Van Asperen, Hanneke. 2013. "The Sheltering Cloak. Images of Charity and Mercy in Fourteenth-Century Italy." *Textile: Cloth and Culture* 11(3): 262–81.
Van Ness, Emma. 2016. "Dixit Mater: The Significance of the Maternal Voice in Ferrante's Neapolitan Novels." In *The Works of Elena Ferrante: Reconfiguring the Margins*, edited by Grace Russo Bullaro and Stephanie Love, 293–312. New York: Palgrave Macmillan.
Venuti, Lawrence. 1992. *Rethinking Translation: Discourse, Subjectivity, Ideology*. New York: Routledge.
Venuti, Lawrence. 2008 [1995]. *The Translator's Invisibility: A History of Translation*. New York: Routledge.
Virgil. *The Aeneid*. 1990. Translated by Robert Fitzgerald. New York: Vintage Books.
Von Flotow, Luise. 2009. "Contested Gender in Translation. Intersectionality and Metramorphics." *Palimpsestes. Revue de traduction* 22: 245–56.
Walkowitz, Rebecca. 2017. *Born Translated: The Contemporary Novel in the Age of World Literature*. New York: Columbia University Press.
Walton, Stuart. 2004. *A Natural History of Human Emotions*. New York: Grove Press.
Wehling-Giorgi, Katrin. 2013. "'Totetaco': The Mother-Child Dyad and the Preconceptual Self in Elsa Morante's *La storia* and *Aracoeli*." *Forum for Modern Language Studies* 49(2): 192–200.

Wehling-Giorgi, Katrin. 2016a. "Elena Ferrante's Novels: Writing Liminality." *Allegoria* 73: 204–10.
Wehling-Giorgi, Katrin. 2016b. "'Ero separata da me': Memory, Selfhood and Mother-Tongue in Goliarda Sapienza and Elena Ferrante." In *Goliarda Sapienza in Context: Intertextual Relationships with Italian and European Culture*, edited by Alberica Bazzoni, Emma Bond, and Katrin Wehling-Giorgi, 215–30. Madison: Fairleigh Dickinson University Press.
Wehling-Giorgi, Katrin. 2017. "Playing with the Maternal Body: Violence, Desire, and Mutilation in Ferrante's Novels." *California Italian Studies* 7(1): 1–15.
Wehling-Giorgi, Katrin. 2019. "Rethinking Constructs of Maternity in the Novels of Elena Ferrante and Alice Sebold." *Women: A Cultural Review* 30(1): 66–83.
Wehling-Giorgi, Katrin. 2019a. "Dressing the Female Body in Elena Ferrante's and Alice Sebold's Writings." Unpublished conference talk. *Elena Ferrante in a Global Context*. Durham University, June 7–8.
Wehling-Giorgi, Katrin. 2021. "Unclaimed Stories: Narrating Sexual Violence and the Traumatized Self in Alice Sebold's and Elena Ferrante's Works." Forthcoming in *MLN* 136(1).
Weinberger, Eliot. 2013. "Anonymous Sources (On Translators and Translation)." In *In Translation: Translators on Their Work and What It Means*, edited by Esther Allen and Susan Bernofsky. New York: Columbia University Press.
Wilson, Robert Rawdon. 2002. *The Hydra's Tale: Imagining Disgust*. Edmonton, Alberta: University of Alberta Press.
Wolf, Werner and Walter Bernhart. 2006. *Framing Borders in Literature and Other Media*. Amsterdam and New York: Rodopi.
Wood, James. 2013. "Women on the Verge. The Fiction of Elena Ferrante." *The New Yorker*, January 21. https://www.newyorker.com/magazine/2013/01/21/women-on-the-verge.
Wright, Dare. 1957. *The Lonely Doll*. New York: Houghton Mifflin.
Zarour Zarzar, Victor Xavier. 2020. "The Grammar of Abandonment in *I giorni dell'abbandono*." *MLN* 135(1): 327–44.

Index

abjection   14, 28, 52, 134, 164, 179 n.10
   Kristeva n   25, 66
   of maternal body   25, 69, 71, 72, 74,
      75, 77, 86, 87, 98, 100, 102, 103,
      114, 117, 162, 179 n.17
   maternal legacy renunciation   68
Abramovic, Marina   108, 129
Accabadora (Murgia)   94
agora, significance of   50, 53
agoraphobia and *smarginatura*   42–3,
      177 n.13, 182 n.5
Agus, Milena   176 n.27
Alcott, Louisa May   73, 78, 176 n.27
Aleramo, Sibilla   29, 51, 56, 58, 63, 69,
      76, 106, 125
Alfano, Barbara   29
Almost Moon, The (Sebold)   101–2
Alsop, Elizabeth   39, 55, 174 n.15,
      175 n.17, 177 n.8, 178 n.20,
      186 nn.19–20
Altman, Nathan   113–14
"Andalusian Shawl, The" ("Lo scialle
   andaluso") (Morante)   91
Anna Karenina (Tolstoy)   52, 154
Appadurai, Arjun   3, 133, 174 n.6
Apter, Emily   4, 173 nn.1–2
Aracoeli (Morante)   116–17, 184 n.19
Ariadne, significance of   11–12
   as abandoned woman   53, 81
   urban feminine topographies and
      133, 134, 136, 143, 147, 148,
      151–5, 163
Artemisia (Banti)   115
Arturo's Island (Morante)   91
Atwood, Margaret   176 n.27
authorial power   59, 90, 94, 182 n.6
   absence of   13
   agency and   116
   effacement and   129
   intent and   123
   world literature and   5, 6, 17, 24

Bachelard, Gaston   149–50
Bakhtin, Mikhail   63, 95, 97–8, 136
Baldi, Andrea   185 n.4
Balsam, Rosemary   177 n.6
Banti, Anna   106, 115
Baubo gesture   99, 100
Beach at Night, The (*La spiaggia di notte*)
   (*BN*)   5, 22, 49, 53, 77–83, 118
   bodily fluids in   81
   creativity in   106
   doll theme in   73, 75, 77–83, 86
   female body violation in   180 n.25
   feminine imaginary in   11–12
   motherhood in   83
   mother's death in   101
   picture book theory in   78
   still life theme in   118
Beard, Mary   108, 184 n.23
"Beast in the Storeroom, The" (essay)
      87, 88
Benedetti, Laura   16, 63, 115, 174 nn.12,
      15, 178 n.18 (Ch 2), 178 nn.3–4
      (Ch 3)
Benjamin, Walter   97, 135
Berger, John   55, 116, 183 n.11
Berman, Antoine   8, 18
Bernhart, Walter   182 n.9
Best of Husbands, The (*Dalla parte di
   lei*)   93
Biggs, Joanna   10
birth and death cycle   4, 70, 71, 98, 102, 170
Birth of Venus, The (painting)   109
Black Milk (Shafak)   62
bodily fluids   139
   dead mothers and   101–3
   excessive   66, 67
   female   57, 61, 62, 64, 66, 69–70, 100,
      150, 162
   as instruments of male aggression   81
   male   31, 157
   relinquishing of   48

shared experience of 64
uncontainable 102
yellow color and 180 n.23
Bondi, Liz 42
Bonfante, Larissa 99, 181 n.36
Bourdieu, Pierre 176 n.2
Bourgeois, Louise 108, 113
bracelet metaphor 168–72
Braidotti, Rosi 14
Browning, Robert 181 n.34
Buonanno, Elda 174 n.10, 175 n.19, 185 n.6
Butler, Judith 14

Caffè, Emanuela 43, 175 n.25, 177 n.13
Caravaggio 107
carnival
  Baubo gesture and 100
  Bakhtinian 97, 100, 181 n.33
  laughter 95, 98–100, 181 n.33
  mask 97
  Naples and 135
  Neapolitan world and 97–8, 159
  Renaissance 95, 97
  as subversion 97–8
Carson, Anne 95, 181 nn.33, 36
Caruth, Cathy 181 n.32
Carvalho, Richard 153, 177 nn.9, 12, 182 n.9, 184 n.26, 185 n.12
Casanova, Pascale 5, 19, 173 nn.1–2
Caserta (character) 65, 67, 81, 90, 94, 95, 96, 112, 114, 138–40, 142–3
Caserta, significance of 138
Caserta, Silvia 9, 174 n.6
castration, threat of 13, 34, 107, 112, 116, 183 n.14
Cavarero, Adriana 15, 72–3, 127, 176 n.28, 184 n.23
Cerri, Mara 78, 106, 108, 118
Chambers, Iain 134, 184 n.2
Chihaya, Sarah 15
Circe (Miller) 175 n.21
city without love, idea of 154
Cixous, Hélène 29, 57–8, 62, 63, 95–6, 180 n.30
collage, theme of 20, 32–3, 64, 183 n.15
  female creativity and authorship and 113, 117–18, 121, 123, 124, 128

Comencini, Cristina 176 n.27
Contessa Lara 78, 81
Conti, Eleonora 32, 180 nn.24, 27
Conybeare, Catherine 96–8
Coronato, Rocco 175 n.18, 176 n.1
corporeality 166, 168, 172, 174 n.8, 178 n.17 (Ch 2), 178 n.3 (Ch 3). *See also* feminine corporeality
  female creativity and authorship and 108, 112, 117–18, 122, 126–8
  universal feminine imaginary and 27–32, 34, 36, 41–3, 45, 47–8, 51, 57–8
  urban feminine topographies and 131, 132, 135, 137, 139, 155, 157, 162
  world literature and 1, 4, 10, 15, 20, 22–3
Correll, Elizabeth 99, 181 n.33
"Creative Freedom" (essay) 105
Cusk, Rachel 15, 62, 176 n.28

Damrosch, David 2, 4, 5, 9, 173 nn.1–2
dark cellar, significance of 86–7
dark well metaphor 84
Davidson, Joyce 42
Days of Abandonment, The (*I giorni dell'abbandono*) (*DA*) 5, 22, 37, 51, 86, 168, 171
  abjection in 25, 52, 75, 100, 114, 162
  apartment metaphor in 88
  collage theme in 117, 121
  conscious surveillance in 31
  doll theme in 73
  female body image fragmentation in 114
  and female body violation 180 n.25
  as "cannon fodder" in 64
  feminine imaginary in 11
  gendered public and private spaces in 114–15
  grotesque gestures in 97, 100
  incision instruments in 128
  locked door metaphor in 88–9
  maternal cannibalism in 77
  maternal voice in 74
  mirror theme in 115–17, 121
  motherhood in 46–7, 62, 74–7

mother's death in 101
music as agent of revelation and
 emotional release in 122
mythological model of women in 53
poverella and 47, 90, 121, 163
pregnancy portrayal in 44
as revisionary history 178 n.20
storeroom metaphor in 88
surveillance in 56, 57
transformative performance in
 184 n.20
tunnel metaphor in 141
urban feminine topographies in 131,
 132, 153–62
weaving and sewing metaphors in
 32, 122
writing women in 58
 correlation with sewing 90–1
yellow color in 180 n.23
de-animation, significance of 76, 83
de Beauvoir, Simone 52, 154,
 176 n.27
decapitation, trope of 113–14
de Cespedes, Alba 14, 63, 93, 94, 106
degli Esposti, Chiara 185 n.12
Delogu, Marco 183 n.12
de Rogatis, Tiziana 7, 21, 46, 101,
 110, 173 n.4, 174 nn.5, 14,
 175 nn.15–16, 19–20, 25,
 177 nn.7, 10, 178 n.21, 179 n.12,
 183 n.13, 184 nn.19–21,
 185 nn.12, 15, 17, 186 n.20
dialect 15, 139, 166–8, 179 n.12,
 181 n.38
 absence of 17, 176 n.30
 female 118, 126
 fracture of 48, 101
 mother tongue and 181 n.31
 Neapolitan 4, 17, 18, 35, 49, 66–8, 70,
  71, 96, 140, 165, 179 n.9
 obscenity in 95, 138, 159
 significance of 17
Dido 11, 185 n.13
 smarginatura and 52, 53
 urban feminine topographies and
  134, 143, 151–5, 163, 164
Dijkstra, Bram 184 n.23
di Paolo, Paolo 174 nn.12–13

disappearance 5, 12, 43, 54, 125, 169,
 176 n.34, 179 n.20
 female creativity and authorship and
  117, 125–7
 maternal body and voice and 69, 76,
  84–6, 88
 as revisionary history 178 n.20
 resistance as 5, 125, 169
 translator as seamstress and 19–21
 urban feminine topographies and
  144, 153
disgust 23, 118, 174 n.15
 affect of 44
 desire and 63–73
 maternal body and voice and 62,
  74–5, 77, 81, 86–8, 91, 95, 96,
  100, 101, 103
 significance of 44–5, 118
 universal feminine imaginary and 30,
  40, 48, 49
disintegration, of female body and
 psyche 28
dissolving boundaries 2, 15, 18, 83, 92,
 100. *See also smarginatura*
 disgusting male body and 40
 fear of 49
 significance of 40–1
 threat of 54
dissolving margins 2, 18–19, 29, 38, 59,
 177 n.16. *See also smarginatura*
 experience of 42
 internal surveillance for 41
 interstitial landscape and 43
doll, theme of 12, 118, 126, 148, 149,
 153, 179 n.17
 maternal body and voice and 64, 69,
  71–3, 75–86, 101–3
 significance of 179 n.15
 universal feminine imaginary and 31,
  41, 49, 51–4
domestic space 47, 61, 86, 89, 90, 114, 155
Donnarumma, Raffaele 175 n.18
*Dora: Fragment of an Analysis of a Case of
 Hysteria* (Freud) 35
Duro, Paul 182 n.9
Durzi, Giacomo 3, 176 n.28

earthquake metaphor, for *smarginatura* 41
écriture féminine, notion of 14

ekphrasis 50, 106, 113, 120, 126, 182 n.9
Elena Ferrante: Parole Chiave
  (de Rogatis) 21
Elias, Norbert 44
Elwell, Leslie 99, 101, 121, 123, 125,
  175 nn.19, 25, 178 n.18 (Ch 2),
  178 n.6 (Ch 3), 184 n.25, 185 n.14
Emre, Merve 15
ethnoscape 132
evisceration 39, 57, 74, 76, 77, 80,
  180 n.25
"Exchange, The" (Lahiri) 19-21
  sartorial importance in 20-1
  self-erasure imagery in 20

Faenza, Roberto 173 n.3
Falkoff, Rebecca 5, 150-1
Falotico, Caterina 174 n.5, 184 n.19
Family Lexicon (Ginzburg) 60, 67
Fanning, Ursula 115
female artistic legacy 119-25
female body 171, 177 n.4, 183 n.17,
  184 n.23. *See also* maternal body
  and voice
  -as-parts 109-14
  female creativity and authorship and
    107-8, 116, 124, 127
  fragmentation, mutilation, and
    disfigurement of 20, 30-3,
    180 n.25
  phallocratic and phallocentric system
    and 31
  as trapped and uncontainable 30
  universal feminine imaginary 28-9,
    34, 36, 38-9, 44-5, 58, 60
  urban feminine topographies and
    131, 139, 140, 156, 162
  world literature and 10, 14, 19-20,
    22, 23, 25
female creativity and authorship,
    aesthetics of 105-8
  collage theme and 117-18
  female artistic legacy and 119-25
  mirror theme and 114-17
  Neapolitan novels and 125-9
  nude female body-as-parts and 109-14
  still life theme and 118
female fetishism 107. *See also* fetish

female gaze, significance of 28, 47, 56,
  59-60, 96, 108, 116, 120-2, 171
female genealogies 13-16, 24, 105-6,
  113, 129
female genius, theme of 8-9, 22,
  108-9, 125
female identity 133, 152, 170, 172,
  183 n.18, 185 n.15
  female creativity and authorship and
    106, 108, 110, 118
  fragmented 6, 36, 108
  maternal body and voice and 70, 72, 74
  universal feminine imaginary and 28,
    43, 53
  world literature and 5-8, 13, 19, 22
"Female Sexuality" (Freud) 65
female subjectivity 15, 61, 127, 133, 163
  embodied 1, 10, 13, 22, 29, 55, 62, 63,
    131, 134
  feminine "I" and 58
  fetishism and 112
  laughter and 96
  transformative performance and
    184 n.20
female voice 3, 9, 145. *See also* maternal
  body and voice
feminine corporeality 15, 29, 45, 108,
  112, 182 n.6. *See also* bodily
  fluids; maternal body and voice
  maternal body and voice and 62, 95, 99
feminine experience 8-10, 13, 19, 22,
  33-4, 62, 129, 134, 168
  universal feminine imaginary and
    28-9, 33, 35, 36, 44, 60, 64
  world literature and 8, 13, 19, 22
feminine imaginary 10-13, 20, 25, 61,
  90. *See also individual entries*
  jewelry and 169
  maternal subjectivity and 62
  mutilated female body and 64
  universal 22, 27-8, 172
    Frantumaglia parameters 34-8
    incisions and inscriptions of body
      30-4
    significance of 29
    smarginatura in Neapolitan novels
      38-43
    smarginatura mothers 43-53

writing mothers   54–60
feminine watchfulness/surveillance   56–7
feminism, definition of   119
feminist philosophers   15, 27, 127, 175 n.25
feminist philosophy   13–14
Ferrante, Elena. *See also individual entries*
   creation of   6, 13
   female genealogies of   13–16
   feminine imaginary of   10–13
   identity of   7
   as pseudonym   5–9
   as translated author   4–5
"Ferrante Effect"   9
Ferrante Fever (documentary film)   3, 176 n.28
Ferrara, Enrica Maria   54, 59, 175 n.15
Ferri, Sandro   5
fetish, idea of   13, 14, 34, 66, 68–9, 107–8, 112, 168, 177 n.5, 182 nn.6–7
   female creativity and authorship and   107–8, 112, 123
Firestone, Shulamith   13
Foley, Helene P.   181 n.36
Forgacs, David   111, 183 n.12
Foucault, Michel   78
fracture   28, 37, 43. *See also frantumaglia*
   of body   28
   of dialect   48, 101
   of female identity   43, 48
   inner self as   37
   of narrative   37
   of subjectivity   28
   vortex-like   36
fragmentation, mutilation, and disfigurement, of body   20, 30–3, 64, 83, 92, 111–14, 123
frames and borders, of representation   182 n.9
framing as entrapment metaphor   108–9
Frankfurter Allgemeine Zeitung   8
frantumaglia   92, 102, 118, 128, 177 n.9. *See also* psycho-corporeal-spatial female subject
   as embodied subjectivity   29
   feminine "I" and   58
   feminine imaginary and   35–6
   as feminine unconscious   33–5, 86
   fragmentation of time and   46, 53
   inanimate mothers and   103
   as loss of boundaries   36
   motherhood and   45, 48–51
   mythological model of women as   52
   origin of   53
   significance of   2, 15, 18, 22–3, 28, 34–5
   as spatiotemporal prison   47
   specter of   48
   as still life   118
   symptoms of   35
   walking women and   134
   woman's suffering and   44, 53
   as women's psychic fragmentation   64
Frantumaglia (*La frantumaglia*) (*Fr*)   78, 80, 81, 182 n.4
   battered and fragmented body in   20
   creativity in   107, 108
   on dolls   83
   female genealogy in   14, 105
   on female tradition   181 n.1
   feminine imaginary in   12, 61
   feminine psyche in   10
   Ferrante as translator in   17
   foreignness in   18
   Greco-Roman mythology and   53
   grotesque gestures in   95
   guilt portrayal in   87–8
   incisive images in   33
   intertextual influences in   13
   on literary genealogy   182 n.3
   maternal body in   87–8, 92
   maternal clothing in   93
   maternal legacy in   70
   motherhood in   45–6, 62, 65, 74, 76
   parameters of   34–8
   poverella and   52
   pregnancy portrayal in   44, 45, 77, 102
   self-creation in   127
   significance of   6
   suffering and   36–8, 184 n.24
   surveillance in   55–7, 111
   translation as act of acceptance in   21
   urban feminine topographies in   132–4, 136–8, 143, 145, 146, 151–2, 154, 163
   Vossi sisters and   185 n.8
   weaving and sewing metaphors in   32, 91, 93

"Women Who Write" 54–8
world literature and 1, 3, 5, 7, 8, 22
yellow color in 180 n.23
"frantumaglia tears" 57
Freud, Sigmund 35, 63, 65, 107, 177 nn.5–6
Freudian psychoanalysis 13
Friedman, Susan Stanford 183 n.15
Frieze (magazine) 78, 93, 106, 108, 129
Fusillo, Massimo 175 n.18, 177 n.5, 182 n.7

Gagliasso, Elena 14
Gallippi, Franco 185 n.11
Gambaro, Elisa 171, 175 n.15, 184 n.19
Ganguly, Debjani 3, 173 n.4
Gatti, Claudio 8, 174 n.13
geography 133, 136, 153, 154, 160
 feminist 24, 25, 42, 132
 sexist 23, 24
 spatial 3
 urban 23
Geue, Tom 175 n.22
Ghezzo, Flora 179 n.11, 184 n.25
Gilbert, Sandra M. 74
Ginzburg, Natalia 9, 29, 60, 63, 67, 92, 106
Giorgio, Adalgisa 126, 174 n.15, 178 n.3, 184 n.19
Goldstein, Ann 2, 5, 16–19, 21, 176 n.32, 177 n.16, 178 n.17
Gospodinov, Georgi 185 n.16
Gralla, Cynthia 108
Graves, Robert 136, 147
Greek mythology 12, 24, 53, 84, 99, 133, 145–8, 180 n.29, 181 n.36, 185 nn.11, 14. *See also* Ariadne; Dido; Medea; Medusa; Minotaur
 Dido in 11, 185 n.13
  smarginatura and 52, 53
  urban feminine topographies and 134, 143, 151–5, 163, 164
 grotesque gestures in 99
 Medea in 11, 51, 53, 154, 155, 163
 Medusa in 96, 116, 123, 124, 184 n.23
 Minotaur in 11, 12, 133, 136–8, 145–53
 smarginatura and 50, 53
 Theseus in 133, 137, 146, 147, 151–2
 world literature and 12, 17, 24

Greek Myths (Graves) 136, 147
Gross, Kenneth 179 n.15
Grossman, Joan Delaney 174 n.11
Grosz, Elizabeth 25, 29, 57, 88, 162, 184 n.1
grotesque gestures 95–100
Guardian, The (newspaper) 1, 3
Gubar, Susan 74
guilt 8, 87–8, 102, 118
 innate 93
 natural 87
Gyllenhaal, Maggie 173 n.3
gypsy woman, portrayal of 110–14, 120, 181 n.34, 183 n.12

Haaland, Torunn 181 n.32
Haraway, Donna 14
Heilbrun, Carolyn 15
heterotopias 78, 79, 118, 140
Hill, Katherine 15
Hillis Miller, J. 163
Hoffmann, E. T. A. 73
House of Liars (*Menzogna e sortilegio*) (Morante) 168, 186 n.1
hysteria 35, 89, 91, 95

Il romanzo della bambola (*The Doll's Story*) (Contessa Lara) 78–9, 81
In altre parole (Lahiri) 176 n.32
Incidental Inventions (*L'invenzione occasionale*) (*II*) 2, 5, 6, 182 n.2
 creativity in 105, 107
 laughter in 98
 male cage and 22, 105, 106, 110, 111, 126
 on male gaze 139
 translation significance in 19
"interstitial landscape" 43
introspection, incision as 23, 33
"Involuntary City, The" (Ortese) 137
Iovino, Serenella 135–6, 184 n.1, 185 n.5
Irigaray, Luce 13, 14, 29, 60, 63, 77, 86, 88, 93, 111
itineraries, of abandonment 153–5. *See also* Turin

Joos, Ruth 61
Jossa, Stefano 174 n.13
Juggler, The (Rachilde) 35

Karagoz, Claudia   178 n.3
Kirsch, Adam   27, 173 n.4
Klein, Melanie   63
Klindienst Joplin, Patricia   177 n.3
Kristeva, Julia   25, 29, 63, 66, 77
Kurnick, David   177 n.11
Kuznets, Lois R.   179 n.15

labyrinth   7, 11, 185 n.6
  city as   50, 133, 136–8, 145, 151–4, 163
  as feminine   12, 144, 145, 150, 152–3, 163, 185 nn.6, 17
  frantumaglia and   47
  mythological   136, 147, 148, 151–3
  Naples as   7, 53, 133, 136, 138, 140, 143, 145, 146, 152, 163
  patriarchal   11, 75, 134, 148, 164, 175 n.20
  symbolic and literal   22, 42, 133, 144–53, 175 n.20, 182 n.10
"La frantumaglia" (essay)   34, 52, 86
Lagioia, Nicola   103
Lahiri, Jhumpa   15, 19–21, 176 nn.28, 32–3
Lampl de Groot, Jeanne   65, 66
landscape   18, 106
  achronic   46
  of city-labyrinth   137
  cultural   2, 3, 16, 78, 173 n.2
  of debris   80, 138
  emotional-spatial   136
  ethnoscape and   132
  of *frantumaglia*   38, 39, 50, 118, 181 n.37
  inner   122, 134
  interstitial   43
  literary   3
  of maternal turmoil   51
  psychic   23, 34, 55, 73, 78, 155, 162
  psychical-corporeal-spatial   4
  psychical-topographic   45, 58
  social   43, 78
  unstable   46, 50, 55, 80
  urban   19, 100, 132, 154–5, 158, 163, 181 n.37
  vertical   3
laughter   23, 171, 180 n.30, 181 n.36
  and language   95–100

maternal body and voice and   62, 63, 87, 90, 102, 103
  significance of   181 n.33
  urban feminine topographies and   139, 140, 143
leaky jar metaphor   102
Le straordinarie avventure di Caterina (Caterina's Extraordinary Adventures) (Morante)   72
Levy, Deborah   178 n.1
Library of Greek Mythology (Apollodorus)   53
Liddell, Henry   185 n.14
Life's Work: On Becoming a Mother, A (Cusk)   62
Lispector, Clarice   14
literary truth   13, 62
  significance of   175 n.23
Little Women (Alcott)   73, 78
locality, significance of   3
Lombardi, Giancarlo   175 n.15, 183 n.13
Lonely Doll, The (Wright)   79
Lonzi, Carla   13
"Lo scambio" (Lahiri)   19, 176 n.32
Lost Daughter, The (*La figlia oscura*) (*LD*)   5, 18, 22, 37, 60, 178 n.18
  beach in   78
  doll theme in   73, 75–8, 80, 83, 84, 86, 102
  and female body violation   180 n.25, 182 n.8
  as "cannon fodder"   64
  feminine imaginary in   11
  feminine insemination in   31
  frantumaglia in   48–50, 53, 55, 102, 182 n.5
  grotesque gestures in   100
  incision instruments in   128
  maternal cannibalism in   77
  maternal voice in   74
  motherhood in   48–52, 75–7, 118–19
  mother's death in   101
  pregnancy portrayal in   44, 80
  self-actualization theme in   122–3
  smarginatura in   49, 102
  still life theme in   117–18, 182 n.5
  transformative performance in   184 n.20

as trauma fiction   181 n.32
women's corporeal flow in   57
Loucks, James   181 n.34
Lucamante, Stefania   174 n.14, 175 n.15, 178 n.17 (Ch 2), 178 nn.3–4 (Ch 3), 182 n.4
Lying Life of Adults, The (*La vita bugiarda degli adulti*) (*LLA*)   3, 22, 25, 165–6, 172
   familial objects in   168–72
   female friendship   170–1
   frame   169–72
   mirror   171–2
   narration as introspection   166
   photographs   169–71
   policing gaze   170
   reverse mapping in   166–8
   topography of identity   166–8

McCarter, Stephanie   127, 175 nn.21–2
McDowell, Linda   184 n.1
male cage metaphor   22, 24, 105, 106, 108–10, 119, 126, 182 n.7.
   See also patriarchy
   frantumaglia and *smarginatura* triggered by   22
   resisting   24
male gaze   24, 42, 56, 139, 156, 183 n.14.
   See also patriarchy
   female creativity and authorship and   109, 111, 112, 114, 116
   maternal body and voice and   74, 82, 94
   resistance to objectification of   119–20
   revoking of   121
   significance of   42, 170
   women's internalization of   55–6, 110, 111, 117, 139, 171
Mandolini, Nicoletta   175 n.25, 181 n.32
mapping. *See* urban feminine topographies
Marin, Louis   182 n.9
Martone, Mario   60, 136, 173 n.3
maternal body   1, 22, 23, 35, 44–5, 53, 179 n.16
   abjection and   25, 69, 71, 72, 74, 75, 77, 86, 87, 98, 100, 102, 103, 114, 117, 162, 179 n.17

bleeding   64, 74
disappearance and   69, 76, 84–6, 88
disgust and   62, 74–5, 77, 81, 86–8, 91, 95, 96, 100, 101, 103
enclosing   86–94
labyrinth and   185 n.6
mirrors and   64, 79, 90
patriarchy and   75, 81, 83, 88, 92, 95, 96, 100, 102
poverella and   89–90, 98, 101
rione and   68, 72, 85
seamstress and   92–4
maternal cannibalism   77
maternal discourse   23, 61, 62, 71, 74, 80–1, 101, 103
maternal legacy   67–9, 71, 74, 82, 93, 101, 103, 168, 170
   acceptance of   71
   maternal clothing and   93
   renunciation of   68
   visual appropriation of   67–8
maternal loss and grotesque gestures   99–100
maternal subjectivity   62–3, 92, 94.
   See also female subjectivity
matricide   87, 101–3
Mazzoni, Cristina   72, 78, 118, 179 nn.13, 15
Medea   11, 51, 53, 154, 155, 163
Mediapart (website)   8
Medusa   96, 116, 123, 124, 184 n.23
memory   6, 15, 120, 126, 167, 180 n.24
   maternal body and voice and   64, 65, 68, 84, 90, 91, 93, 96, 98
   narrative   11, 181 n.32
   painful   45–6, 85
   repressed   12, 73, 76, 118, 181 n.32
   universal feminine imaginary and   31, 33, 45–9
   urban feminine topographies and   132–44, 154–5, 157–9
metramorphic paradigm   21
Middlebrook, Diane   15
Mihai, Mihaela   10–11
Milkova, Stiliana   16, 33, 42, 59, 75, 124, 175 n.20, 182 n.9, 185 nn.14, 17
Miller, Madeline   175 n.21
Miller, Nancy K.   15

Miller, Paul Allen   147–8
Minotaur   11, 12, 133, 136–8, 145–53
mirrors, theme of   20–1, 24, 183 n.18
   female creativity and authorship and   108, 112, 114–17, 122, 127–8
   in Freudian psychoanalysis   116
   maternal body and voice and   64, 79, 90
   as tool for reflection and self-representation   115, 116, 121, 171
   universal feminine imaginary and   36, 47–8, 55
mise-en-abyme   85, 127, 145
   as visual metaphor   128
misogyny   8, 9, 27, 74, 87, 123, 174 n.14, 184 n.23. *See also* patriarchy
Momigliano, Anna   9
Morante, Elsa   9, 14, 63, 72, 91, 106, 116, 117, 168, 176 n.27, 178 n.4, 184 n.19
Moretti, Franco   5, 9, 173 n.1
Morrison, Toni   176 n.27
Mortimer-Sandilands, Catriona   132, 139
"Mother, The" ("La madre") (Ginzburg)   92
mother-daughter relationship   170–1, 178 n.19 (Ch 2), 178 n.3 (Ch 3). *See also Lost Daughter, The* (*La figlia oscura*) (*LD*); maternal body and voice
   female creativity and authorship and   115, 118–21
   in Italian literature   178 n.3
   universal feminine imaginary and   28, 31, 45–6
   urban feminine topographies and   154, 156, 157, 161
   world literature and   1, 11, 14–15, 23
motherhood   61–2, 89, 91, 101, 118, 178 n.18, 184 n.23
   in *Aracoeli*   184 n.19
   dead, and corporeal flows   101–3
   definition of   62
   desire and disgust for   63–73
   dolls and   74–86
   laughter and   95–6
   as loss of agency and corporeal autonomy   117
   martyrdom and   113

   maternal failure and   118–19
   renouncement of   115
   representation, in Italian literary context   62–3
   smarginatura and   45–6, 48–52
   traditional, rejection of   179 n.14
   writing and   54–60, 74
"Mothers' Dressmakers" (essay)   91, 93
Mulvey, Laura   112, 183 n.14
Munro, Alice   14
Muraro, Luisa   14, 15, 27, 119, 176 n.28
Murgia, Michela   94
My Brilliant Friend (*L'amica geniale*) (*MBF*)   1, 8, 9, 17, 51
   bodily fluids in   69–70
   bonding through bodily insertion in   31
   collage theme in   117
   doll theme in   54, 71–2, 83, 84, 148
   female authorship and collaboration in   129
   feminine imaginary in   12
   feminine surveillance in   59
   fetish formation mechanism in   68–9
   grotesque gestures in   98–9
   labyrinth portrayal in   147–51
   male gaze in   109
   mirror theme in   127
   mother's body in   68
   patriarchy in   175 n.20
   self-erasure in   19, 126
   significance of   2
   smarginatura in   38–9, 41–2
   tunnel metaphor in   141
   urban feminine topographies in   145–52
My Brilliant Friends. Our Lives in Feminism (Miller)   15
Myers, Lindsay   78–9, 179 nn.13, 15

Naples
   Baldi on   185 n.4
   convergence with Turin   160
   Greek mythology and   136–7
   as labyrinth   7, 133, 136, 138, 140, 143, 145, 146, 152, 163
   as male-governed space   149
   nature of   135, 184 n.2
   as porous   135–6, 141, 144, 185 n.5

poverella and   159
significance of   132, 134, 154
as underworld   137, 140–1
as urban matrix of embodied
    subjectivity   131
as vertical city   136
narrative relationality, of self   127,
    184 n.25
Nathan, Jean   79, 179 n.18
Neapolitan Chronicles (*Il mare non bagna
    Napoli*) (Ortese)   60
Neapolitan Novels   1, 12, 124, 168,
    174 n.6, 178 n.19
  Aeneid and   12, 127, 148
  battered and fragmented body in   20
  beach in   78
  biblical reference in   180 n.29
  creativity in   108, 109
  Cusk on   62
  dialect absence in   17, 176 n.30
  doll theme in   72, 83, 84, 85,
      103, 126
  female friendship, writing, and
      authorship and   125–9
  grotesque gestures in   99
  incision instruments in   128
  labyrinth theme in   12
    symbolic and literal   144–53
  metalinguistic gloss in   4, 17
  mirror theme in   116
  mother's death in   101
  plot of   4
  porousness and   97–8
  relating narratives in   73
  self-effacement and self-fragmentation
      in   123
  sexual penetration in   176 n.1
  shared experience of motherhood
      in   71
  significance of   2–3
  smarginatura in   38–43, 56
  success of   3, 16, 22
  surveillance in   56, 59
  translator significance in   16–19
Nelson, Lise   184 n.1
Netflix   173 n.3
New York Review of Books   8
Nochlin, Linda   109, 112, 183 n.11

Noson, Kate   70
nude female body-as-parts   109–14

Oliviero, Maestra   68
Ortese, Anna Maria   9, 14, 29, 59–60,
    106, 137, 138, 176 n.27, 185 n.4
Ozzola, Sandra   5

"Pair of Eyeglasses, A" ("Un paio di
    occhiali") (Ortese)   59, 60, 138
Paperno, Irina   174 n.11
Parisi, Luciano   175 n.18, 181 n.32
Parks, Tim   4, 174 n.7
parturition   28, 44, 45, 74, 77
patriarchy   12, 20, 51, 170, 175 n.20,
    184 n.23. *See also* male cage;
    male gaze; misogyny
  Cusk on   62
  female body contained within cage
      of   89
  female creativity and authorship and
      105, 107, 108, 111, 116, 117, 119
  maternal body and   75, 81, 83, 88, 92,
      95, 96, 100, 102
  problems of   27, 42
  resistance to   8, 49, 119, 125, 129,
      169, 171
  urban feminine topographies and
      139, 145, 155
Pennacchio, Filippo   173 n.4
Perkins Gilman, Charlotte   35, 55, 89, 90,
    180 n.22
Perrella, Silvio   134, 137
Pesca, Carmela   120, 141, 180 n.24
Petrova, Vera   17, 179 n.19
Phelan, Richard   182 n.9
photography   32, 57, 108, 117, 168,
    177 n.4, 185 n.16
  authorial agency and   24, 116, 123–4
  children's books, in   79, 82
  disappearance and   69, 169
  double female portrait   46, 59, 67
  female creativity and   117–25
  female gaze and   120–1
  maternal legacy and   46, 59, 67–8, 71,
      121, 143
  patriarchal aesthetics   108, 110
  poverella and   163

of Roma camps 183 n.12
self-erasure and 19, 20, 32–3, 117, 124–6
staged 79, 82
symbolic erasure and 169–70
as visual document 110, 111, 125
as visual metaphor 180 n.25
Physics of Sorrow, The (Gospodinov) 185 n.16
picture book, theory of 78
Pinto, Isabella 17, 73, 175 nn.19, 25, 176 n.30, 179 n.17
porous modernity 135
porousness 97–8, 100, 135–6, 141, 159, 185 n.5
Portrait of Mother, Son, and Daughter (Sherman) 117
poverella 183 n.18
    female creativity and authorship and 115, 121–2, 126, 127
    maternal body and voice and 89–90, 98, 101
    smarginatura and 47, 48, 51–3
    universal feminine imaginary and 33, 47–9, 55, 57
    urban feminine topographies and 155, 159–60, 162, 163
pregnancy 44–5, 113, 124, 155
    maternal body and voice and 69–70, 76–7, 80, 84, 102
prosthetic knowledge, notion of 10–11
psychic disequilibrium, as mimetic realism 175 n.17
psycho-corporeal-spatial female subject 23, 27. *See also frantumaglia*
    significance of 28

Rachilde 35
Raja, Anita 8, 20, 21
Ramondino, Fabrizia 178 n.4, 182 n.4
Randall, Frederika 174 n.13
relating narratives 73
repressive surveillance 55, 56, 111
Reyes Ferrer, Maria 183 n.18
Ricciardi, Alessia 179 n.19
Richards, Jill 15
rione 109, 165, 177 n.10, 182 n.7, 185 n.11
    maternal body and voice and 68, 72, 85

significance of 42
universal feminine imaginary and 28, 29, 40, 42, 54, 60
urban feminine topographies and 133, 135, 137, 142, 144–6, 148–9, 151–2
world literature and translation and 3, 9, 17, 18, 24
Robertson, Ronald 174 n.6
Rose, Gillian 42, 132, 184 n.1

Sambuco, Patrizia 93, 155, 174 n.15, 178 n.3, 180 n.27, 186 n.20
Sandman, The (Hoffmann) 73
Santovetti, Olivia 33, 114, 129, 145, 175 n.15, 184 nn.19, 22–3
sartorial metaphor 19, 20, 90, 92
Schor, Naomi 15, 107
Schwartz, Cecilia 10, 174 n.12
Sciubba, Jessica 175 n.25
Scott, Robert 185 n.14
Seager, Joni 184 n.1
seamstress 7, 9, 11, 32, 33, 71, 143, 180 n.24
    complicity of 91
    female creativity and authorship and 110, 119, 120, 122
    maternal body and 90–4
    translator as 16–21
Sebold, Alice 101–2, 176 n.27, 178 n.1
Seger, Monica 43
Segnini, Elisa 174 n.6, 181 n.38
self-erasure 20, 69, 124, 125, 126, 184 n.22
    through translation 19
self-observation model 55–7
self-surveillance 111
    through writing 56, 85
Serao, Matilde 176 n.27
Seven Works of Mercy, The (artwork) (Caravaggio) 107
sewing metaphor 120, 122, 182 n.6
    correlation with writing women 90–1
    and translation, nexus between 20
    urban feminine topographies and 134, 139, 163
    and weaving 32, 91, 93
sexuality, blocked 66–7
Shafak, Elif 62, 178 n.2

Sherman, Cindy 108, 117
smarginatura 92, 102, 177 n.10
    affectivity and 41, 42
    agoraphobia and 42–3, 177 n.13, 182 n.5
    antidote to 59
    conflation-inversion and motherhood and 83–4
    grotesque gestures and 100
    "mothers" of 43–53
    in Neapolitan novels 38–43
    permeability and fragility of body and 34
    poverella and 47, 48, 51–3
    psychic and narrative mechanism of 40–1
    reversibility and 41, 42
    significance of 2, 15, 18, 22–3, 29, 30, 56, 177 nn.12, 16
    translation of 18–19
    as visual experiences 60
    walking women and 134
sophrosyne 95–7, 100
Sotgiu, Elisa 175 n.25
Spackman, Barbara 52
space of otherness 78, 79. *See also* heterotopias
Starnone, Domenico 8
Stauffer, Andrew 181 n.34
Ste. Sebastienne (painting) (Bourgeois) 113
Stewart, Susan 179 n.15
still life, theme of 102, 106, 118, 182 n.5
storeroom
    metaphor 87–8
    topos 90, 136, 140–1, 167, 180 n.23
Story of a New Name, The (*SNN*) 17, 32–3
    collage theme in 117, 123
    and female body violation 180 n.25
    as "cannon fodder" in 64
    feminine surveillance in 59
    male cage in 109–10
    male gaze in 109
    mutilation image in 124, 176 n.34
    pregnancy portrayal in 44
    self-disfigurement as visual metaphor in 33

    self-erasure in 124, 125
    smarginatura in 40
Story of the Lost Child, The (*SLC*) 127
    corporeal bond in 70
    dialect in 17
    doll theme in 72, 84–6, 153
    grotesque gestures in 99, 100
    mirror theme in 116
    mother-daughter role reversal in 70–1
    mother's death in 101
    pregnancy portrayal in 84
    smarginatura in 39–41, 43
    urban feminine topographies in 144, 153
    writing women in 59, 85
Strout, Elizabeth 15, 176 n.28, 178 n.1
subalternity 9, 22, 29, 97, 111, 172
    feminine household and 170
    smarginatura and 177 n.10
subversive laughter 96
suffering, significance of 70, 92, 113, 129, 134, 146, 173 n.4, 179 n.16
    universal feminine imaginary and 36–8, 44, 53
"superabilità" 70, 100
surveillance 35, 58, 170
    affirmative 56, 85
    conscious 31, 55
    expressive 55
    feminine 57, 59
    internal 41
    literary 59
    productive 74
    repressive 55, 56, 111
    self- 56, 111, 168
    shared 59
"surveyor and surveyed" model 55–7, 59, 111
symbolic violence, significance of 176 n.2

Teardo, Sara 125–6, 179 n.11, 184 n.25
tetralogy. *See* Neapolitan Novels
Theseus 133, 137, 146, 147, 151–2
Those Who Leave and Those Who Stay (*TLTS*) 9, 29, 39–40, 59, 116
    biblical reference in 180 n.29
    female authorship in 129
    grotesque gestures in 99

maternal inheritance in 69, 70
mirror theme in 128
threshold spaces, significance of 44, 77, 136
time, fragmentation of 46, 53
Todesco, Serena 129, 177 n.11, 179 n.8
Tolstoy, Leo 52, 154
topography 10, 22, 24, 34, 42, 45, 58, 88, 165–7, 170. *See also* urban feminine topographies
   urban 23, 43, 53, 131, 152, 154, 155, 162–4, 183 n.16
translation 2–4, 12. *See also* translator
   as acceptance 21
   of *frantumaglia* 58
   literary 2, 175 n.21
   metaphorics of 16, 19, 21
   as self-effacement 19, 21
   and sewing, nexus between 20
   significance of 2, 173 n.2
   of *smarginatura* 18–19
"Translation as a Practice of Acceptance" ("La traduzione come pratica dell'accoglienza") (Raja) 20
translator 8, 174 n.7, 177 n.16
   importance of 2
   literary 12, 173 n.2
   as seamstress 16–21
Troubling Love (*L'amore molesto*) (*TL*) 5, 22, 37, 86, 117, 170, 185 n.9
   beach in 78
   bodily fluids in 81, 180 n.23
   creativity in 106
   dialect in 181 n.31
   doll theme in 74
   enclosed space in 90
   female gaze in 120–1
   feminine imaginary in 11
   feminine insemination through penetration in 31
   fragmentation and male domination in 112–13
   grotesque gestures in 95, 98, 99
   incision instruments in 128
   laughter in 96–7
   male gaze in 119
   maternal body in 70–1, 87
      bleeding 64, 74

      disgust for 74
      labyrinth and 185 n.6
   maternal clothing in 92–4, 180 nn.24, 27
   motherhood in 45, 70, 75, 115, 183 n.12
      disgust and desire for 63–8
      as martyrdom 113
      slippage/seepage between mother's and daughter's bodies 71
   mother's death in 101
   nudity in 111, 169
   patriarchal violence in 20, 64, 81
   as revisionary history 178 n.20
   self-erasure in 69
   self-surveillance in 111
   sewing metaphors in 32, 33, 120, 122
   shared female artistic legacy in 121
   "sticky realism" of Neapolitan dialect in 66, 67
   still life theme in 182 n.5
   storeroom metaphor in 88
   surveillance in 56, 57
   tram trip significance in 180 n.26
   transformative performance in 184 n.20
   as trauma fiction 181 n.32
   urban feminine topographies in 132–3, 135–44, 154, 162
   violated and mutilated female body in 180 n.25
   violent incision in 30–1
   visual and discursive entrapment in 110
   walking trajectories in 135–44
   writing women in 58–9
   yellow color in 180 n.23
tunnel as metaphor and liminal space 132, 136, 140–5, 148–9, 160
Turchetta, Gianni 4, 75, 175 n.18
Turin 9, 11, 12, 24–5, 42, 53, 69, 85–6, 98, 126, 131–3, 153–64
   abandonment itineraries and 162–4
   as city without love 154, 156
   convergence with Naples 160
   as masculinist space 155, 157–9
   maternal body and voice and 69, 85–6, 88, 98, 99

significance of   131, 133, 153, 156–8, 161, 183 n.16
  topographic pun and   156, 167

Una donna (*A Woman*) (Aleramo)   51–2
unconscious, reversibility of   38, 41–2
urban feminine topographies   131–5
  itineraries of abandonment and   153–64
  symbolic and literal labyrinth in Neapolitan Novels and   144–53
  walking trajectories in *Troubling Love* and   135–44
urban space   24. *See also* urban feminine topographies
  hostile   42, 142
  oppressive   25
  patriarchal   12, 133, 140, 151, 175 n.20, 177 n.13
  significance of   133
  as topography of female identity   133–4
  violent   24, 42, 131–2, 135, 139, 163

Van Asperen, Hanneke   183 n.17
Van Ness, Emma   85, 175 n.25, 179 nn.10, 14, 16
Venuti, Lawrence   16, 20
visual art   106, 119. *See also* photography
von Flotow, Luise   21
Vossi painting   20, 30, 32, 64, 110–14, 120–4, 139–40, 171, 180 n.25, 183 n.13
  female creativity and authorship and   106, 110–15, 120–1, 123, 124, 127

walking women, as subjects   132–134, 151
Walkowitz, Rebecca   4
Wehling-Giorgi, Katrin   28, 33, 41, 116, 117, 142, 145, 175 nn.15, 19, 25, 177 nn.4, 10, 179 nn.9–10, 181 n.31, 184 nn.19, 23, 185 n.14
Western art, and artistic tradition   55, 61, 101, 105, 115, 124, 179 n.16, 184 n.23
white ink metaphor   57, 62, 65, 67
Wilson, Emily   175 n.21
Wolf, Christa   176 n.27
Wolf, Werner   182 n.9
Woman, A (Aleramo)   56, 125
"woman as icon" scenario   112, 116
Woman Destroyed (de Beauvoir)   52, 154
Wood, James   14, 174 n.15, 178 n.5
Woolf, Virginia   14, 176 n.27
world literature   1–25. *See also individual entries*
  Damrosch on   2, 173 n.2
  Ganguly on   3
  as locally inflected and translocally mobile   5
  translatability of   4
"World Republic of Letters"   19, 173 n.2
Wright, Dare   79, 82, 179 n.18

"Yellow Wallpaper, The" (Gilman)   35, 55, 89–91, 180 n.23

Zarour Zarzar   66–7, 181 n.35, 183 n.18

www.ingramcontent.com/pod-product-compliance
Lightning Source LLC
Chambersburg PA
CBHW072233290426
44111CB00012B/2078